Wanda Landowska

Landowska on Music

COLLECTED, EDITED, AND TRANSLATED BY
DENISE RESTOUT · ASSISTED BY ROBERT HAWKINS

STEIN AND DAY / Publishers / New York

Second Printing, 1965

Grateful acknowledgement is made
for permission to reprint excerpts from the following:

"Keyboard Aristocrat" from the *Encyclopedia Yearbook,* 1949,
published by Grolier Incorporated, New York

"Apropos of Couperin" from the March 31, 1951, *Saturday Review*

"Strings Plucked and Struck" from the February 28, 1943,
New York Herald Tribune

Stein and Day / Publishers
7 East 48 Street, New York, N.Y. 10017

CONTENTS

Part One

Foreword to Part One   29

1 Is Music a Progressive Art?   33

2 The Power of Sonority Is Not a Novelty   42

3 From Classicism to Romanticism   47

4 Innovations   56

5 Vocal and Instrumental Music   62

    The Eighteenth-Century Orchestra   66

6 French and Italian Music—
  Influence on the Germans   72

    French Influences on Bach's Keyboard Music   80

7 Style   85

8 Tradition in the Interpretation
of Music of the Past   93

9 Transcriptions   98

10 Of Movement and Measure   105

11 About Ornaments   112

12 Keyboard Instruments   123

     Confusion   123

     The Clavichord   125

     The Harpsichord   126

     Organ and Harpsichord   133

     The Advent of the Fortepiano   134

     Bach's Keyboard Instruments   139

13 Virtuosity, Now and Then   151

14 The Return to the Music of the Past   159

Part Two

Foreword to Part Two   163

1 On the Interpretation of
  Johann Sebastian Bach's Keyboard Works   165
    Cantable Art   165
    The Two-Part Inventions   170
    The Well-Tempered Clavier   172
    The Goldberg Variations   209
    The Fantasias   220
    The Keyboard Suites   221
    The Toccatas   222
    For the Lute-Harpsichord: Prelude,
      Fugue, and Allegro in E Flat Major   223
    A Descriptive Work: *Capriccio on the
      Departure of His Beloved Brother*   225
    A Transcription: The Sonata in A Minor   226
    Bach and the Italian Concerto Grosso   226
    The Keyboard Concertos   230
    The Sonatas for Harpsichord and Violin   233
    The Universality of Bach   234

2 George Frederic Handel   236
    The Harpsichord Suites   237
    The Concerto in B Flat Major   243

3 Domenico Scarlatti   245
    The Sonatas   247

4 A Glorious Trinity — 253

5 French Music of the Past — 256
Jacques Champion de Chambonnières — 257
François Couperin Le Grand — 259
Jean Philippe Rameau — 267
Chopin and French Music of the Past — 274
La Bourrée d'Auvergne — 279

6 Polish Music of the Past — 281
Polish Composers — 281
Influence of Polish Music on Foreign Composers — 287
Polish Folklore — 290

7 English Music of the Past — 292
At the Time of Shakespeare — 292
Purcell's Ground and the Portuguese Fado — 300

8 The Gallant Style — 302
Wilhelm Friedemann and
Karl Philipp Emanuel Bach — 302
Wolfgang Amadeus Mozart — 306
THE PIANO CONCERTOS — 311
ABOUT SOME OF MOZART'S KEYBOARD WORKS — 317
J. F. C. Lanner — 325
Joseph Haydn — 326

Part Three

Foreword to Part Three   333

1 Thoughts on Modern Music   335
   Why Does Modern Music Lack Melody?   336
   At Random from Saint-Saëns to Poulenc   340
      TCHAIKOVSKY AND COUPERIN   343
      TCHAIKOVSKY AND DVORAK   343
      ON PROKOFIEV AND SCRIABIN   344
      STRAVINSKY   344
      AFTER HEARING A SYMPHONY BY SHOSTAKOVICH   345
      GERSHWIN   345
      MANUEL DE FALLA   346
      FRANCIS POULENC   347

2 Is Music of the Past Understood Today?   349
   About Music of the Past and Us   349
   The Art of Listening   351
   Fluctuations in Taste   354
   Authenticity in the Interpretation
     of Music of the Past   355
   On Musicology   357
   Blessings and Failures of Recordings   358

3 The Making of an Interpreter   360
   About Genius and Gifts   360
   About Teaching   362
   How to Work   367

4 Reflections on Some Problems of Interpretation   372
    On Fingering   372
    On Touch   375
    About Phrasing   376
    On Registration   377
    About Rhythm   379
    On Tempo   381
    About Allargando   382
    About Rubato   383
    The Dance in Music of the Past   384
    Rhythmic Alterations   386
    Interpreting the Ornaments   387
    The Role of the Accompanying Harpsichordist   394
    About Climax and Monotony   396
    Encores   398

5 The Mysteries of Interpretation   399
    Criticism   399
    The Liberties I Take   400
    Being an Interpreter   403

Postlude   409
Landowska's Discography   411
Index   425

ILLUSTRATIONS

IN TEXT

Landowska's portrait by Serov.   *Frontispiece*

Title page from J. S. Bach's *Clavierübung*.   87

Excerpt from Scarlatti's Sonata in D Major (Longo 415)   101

Bach's Table of Ornaments from the *Clavier-Büchlein* of 1720.   115

Andante from *The Italian Concerto* as it would have appeared had Bach written the ornaments in signs instead of incorporating their realization among the main notes of the melodic line.   118

J. S. Bach's autograph title page for *The Well-Tempered Clavier*—1722.   146

J. S. Bach's autograph of Fugue 1 from Book I of *The Well-Tempered Clavier*.   178

Landowska's autograph of her Cadenza for the first movement of Mozart's Piano Concerto in D Minor (K. 466).   315

Mozart's autograph of the opening bars of the Sonata in D Major (K. 311).   318

PLATES *following page 242*

1   Landowska after her arrival in Paris in 1900.

2   Landowska and her husband, Henri Lew, at the time they wrote *Musique Ancienne* (1909).

3   Landowska playing the harpsichord in Auguste Rodin's studio in 1908.

4   Reception at the Pleyel Salon in 1907.

PLATES *following page 242*

5   Landowska playing in the Hall of Mirrors at Versailles, 1921.

6   The program of one of Landowska's first public appearances in Paris in 1901.

7   A typical Landowska recital program, Town Hall, April 4, 1950.

8   Plate designed by Edouardo Chavarri, Spanish musicologist and composer.

9   Seventeenth-century fretted clavichord from the Landowska Collection.

10   1737 Swiss organ from the Landowska Collection.

11   Sixteenth-century Italian harpsichord from the Landowska Collection.

12   Ruckers Spinet from the Landowska Collection.

13   Nordquist fortepiano from the Landowska Collection.

14a Landowska's Pleyel harpsichord.

14b Inscription on the bar of the Pleyel harpsichord.

15a-d A master class at Saint-Leu, August 5, 1934.

16   Landowska at the entrance of her concert hall at Saint-Leu.

17a-d Landowska's hands.

18   Landowska demonstrating one of her technique exercises.

19   Landowska at her desk, 1949.

20   Landowska autograph.

21   A page from Landowska's work-score of *The Well-Tempered Clavier*, Book I, Fugue XXIII.

22   Landowska in 1951.

23   Landowska's hands in repose.

24a-b Autograph of a few of Landowska's notes on music.

25   Landowska annotating a Bach Fugue.

LANDOWSKA ON MUSIC

Landowska the Writer

"READER,

Whether you are a dilettante or a professor, do not expect to find in these compositions any profound intention, but rather an ingenious jesting of the art to prepare you for bold playing on the harpsichord. . . . Show yourself more human than critical, and thus you will increase your own pleasure. . . . Live happily!"

In this direct, witty, and genial manner Scarlatti prefaced the publication of a number of his sonatas. It seemed to me particularly fitting to open the book of Wanda Landowska's writings on music with these very words and to complement them with Landowska's own response, " 'Ingenious jesting rather than profound intention,' a laconic warning indeed, the irony of which unveils its strength as we explore the work. Surprised at first, then falling more and more under its spell, we marvel at the richness of invention, at the flavor and boldness of Scarlatti's imagination. We are captivated by the unexpected diversity of the images it offers."

Nothing could describe better Landowska's writings and even Landowska herself. Whether she played for large audiences or for a few friends, whether she addressed the learned gathering of a musicological congress or stopped during her daily walk to talk to a gardener raking leaves, whether she wrote about the complexity of a five-part fugue or described a travel incident, Wanda Landowska's approach to other human beings was always

3

direct, witty, and friendly. Yet her genuine simplicity and charm were merely delightful attributes that allowed her to communicate the richness, depth, and originality of her cultivated mind, the compassion and kindness of her heart, as well as the glory of her musical genius.

Wanda Landowska became a legend in her own lifetime. Now she has entered history, the history of music. Her name generally evokes identifications such as "high priestess of the harpsichord" or "incomparable interpreter of Bach"; they were bestowed upon her in all sincerity by the best critics long before becoming publicity slogans. Thanks to the wealth of recordings Landowska has left us, her artistry will speak for itself as long as recordings will be played. Now that the harpsichord has become quite popular, many people know that Landowska was responsible for its revival at the beginning of our century, and she is recognized as an authority on the performance of seventeenth and eighteenth century music. Some music lovers know that she was also a great interpreter of Mozart on the piano and a revered teacher. Those people who read program notes and record jackets with more than a casual interest know that Landowska wrote about the music she played with vivacity, enthusiasm and in a way that was evocative and learned, though never pedantic. There are a few who may have consulted her long out-of-print book, *Music of the Past,* in public libraries.

Although Landowska's fame is widespread and although the controversies her pronouncements stirred up among the "specialists" are still quite lively, very few are they who are truly aware of the scope and real nature of her musicianship.

Virtuoso? Musicologist? Landowska was both, but first and foremost, she was an *interpreter* in the broadest sense of the word. Music, all of it, was her religion. Interpreting it was her mission and her life's dedication. If she limited herself mainly to the domain of keyboard music of the seventeenth and eighteenth centuries, it was because of an innate affinity with and love for this particular expression of music, and also because a lifetime was hardly enough to explore this realm with the thoroughness that Landowska brought to anything she undertook. It was the irrepressible urge to communicate and share with others the beauty of the music that inhabited her which prompted Landowska to use words as well as sounds; they enhanced the carrying power of her playing and set the proper atmosphere for the listeners.

Music came very early into Wanda Landowska's life. Reminiscing, she said, "I began to play the piano at the age of four.* My first teacher was a kind and indulgent man; he allowed me to browse freely in the music which pleased me; and what pleased and fascinated me particularly was the music of former times. At home, in Warsaw in the 1880's, life flowed quietly and modestly. But once daily monotony was broken by the announcement that a pianist, a pupil of Liszt, was coming for a visit. Imagine seeing at close range a pupil of Liszt and perhaps hearing her play! What excitement! The pianist arrived; and even before she was asked, she sat at the piano, my small upright with its carved inset profile of Mozart on the front panel. First, she played a movement from a Beethoven sonata, followed by a succession of bravura pieces—*La Campanella, Rakoczy March,* some transcriptions, interrupted now and then by a sentimental piece. After all these, and without announcing its title, she attacked a piece that I did not know. Its rhythm and melodic outline struck me. The purity of the motive reminded me of some popular dance, and its simplicity was all the more noticeable after the clangorous artifices of the transcriptions that had just been rattled off. The woman stood and said, 'Le Tambourin of Rameau.' Every time I have played this *Tambourin* since, I have recalled my delight when I first heard it so many years ago!

"My happiness, alas, was short-lived, for my mother made me change teachers. A stern, dry, and tiresome man took the place of my good and gentle master. My delightful roaming through the gavottes and the bourrées of Bach were at an end. Instead came the pitiless order to play twenty-five times, each hand separately, the studies of Kalkbrenner and Thalberg. I was very unhappy and full of longing for my old-time music which they had taken away from me. It was then that I vowed that some day I would do the thing I wanted to do, the thing that I loved; I would play a program devoted entirely to Bach, Mozart, Rameau, and Haydn. I wrote this neatly on a sheet of paper decorated

* To set the record straight, let me state here on the authority of her passport and other documents that Wanda Landowska was born in Warsaw, Poland, July 5, 1879.

with Christmas pictures and sealed it in an envelope, on which I inscribed, "To be opened when I am grown up."

And that, no doubt, was Landowska's very first writing on music as well as her profession of faith!

Another early musical experience was later recorded by Landowska in these words: "I was hardly eight years old when my mother took me to a piano exhibit. At one of the stands they showed the Kerntnopf instruments, and to extol them they had engaged an admirable pianist, Kownacka, 'the crazy one.' I stood there for hours, listening to her playing. She was crazy . . . with music!" And Landowska added, "I think of myself; sometimes I feel that music invades me to the point of that total oblivion when will and intention do not exist anymore. It is because music has penetrated so deeply into me that it alone directs my movements and my inflections."

Although young Wanda was in the hands of some insignificant piano teachers for short periods, she really had only two masters, both specialists of Chopin. Jan Kleczynski, author of *The Works of Chopin and Their Proper Interpretation*, loved his little pupil; and with tears in his eyes, he used to say, "This child is a genius!" That was probably the reason which prompted Wanda's mother to send her to a more demanding teacher. At the Warsaw Conservatory Wanda studied with Alexander Michalowski, a renowned interpreter of Chopin. Of him Landowska wrote, "He was a marvelous master. He played constantly for his pupils, thus adding great value to his teaching. I often had the feeling that he was playing especially for me because he felt my musicality. I understood him."

The repertoire Wanda studied with him was comprised mainly of romantic compositions. The only works of Bach she approached were transcriptions by Liszt, Bülow, or Tausig. For Wanda always insisted on playing Bach along with the rest of the imposed curriculum. At her first concert in public she played, among others, Bach's English Suite in E Minor. Later, when she was about fourteen, the celebrated conductor Nikisch heard her play a prelude and a fugue from *The Well-Tempered Clavier*. Half in amazement, half in jest, he nicknamed her "Bacchante."

Around 1895 the young Landowska was sent to Berlin to study counterpoint and composition with Urban, who also taught Paderewski, Rudolph Ganz, Josef Hofman, and others. Concerning this period of her adolescence, Landowska reflected, "What did I learn? Nothing, really nothing. I was refractory to rules and laws. As soon as they were imposed on me, I stiffened, terrified. My music was covered with exercises in which I had no interest at all. Counterpoint? Yes, but through the direct channel of Bach. I sang the voices separately with a limitless joy. I punctuated them, and they became lively; they sprang forth. Was my teacher inadequate? Or was I a bad pupil?"

During these formative years Wanda Landowska developed a great passion for vocal music. She knew by heart the part of Zerlina from *Don Giovanni*. Her compositions included many lieder. Also she heard for the first time Bach's *Christmas Oratorio* and was profoundly impressed.

In 1900 Wanda Landowska eloped to Paris with her compatriot Henry Lew, who was a journalist, an actor, and a remarkable ethnologist specializing in Hebrew folklore. This interest in folklore was shared by Landowska, who as a child in the country near Kielce, where she spent the summers, heard and sang with relish innumerable folk songs and danced with Polish peasants authentic mazurkas and polonaises.

Paris in the early twentieth century was a most interesting center of the arts and literature. New trends, new ideas were taking shape. A spirit of rebellion against nineteenth century romanticism was fomenting. In music a new language was being born, generally inspired by a return to the classical era. Debussy's *Pelléas et Mélisande* was first performed in 1902, exploding like a bombshell and igniting heated debates between reactionaries and the avant-garde. A few years hence the Russian ballets of Diaghilev performing the early works of Stravinsky also created a sensation in the French capital. Many musicians, however, and the public at large remained under the spell of Wagner, César Franck, and of all the manifestations of a romanticism that was verging on decadence.

As for the music of the past, not only was it relatively unknown, but even worse, it was misunderstood and despised. The attempts of the pianist Louis Diémer to revive the keyboard music of the seventeenth and eighteenth centuries on the harpsichord, around 1889, had been more disastrous than helpful to the cause.

The deficient instrument he used and the insignificance of the pieces he chose to play were probably responsible for the failure of his efforts.

All the while, musicology, a relatively new field, had been establishing a firm stronghold in the French capital during the last decade of the nineteenth century. This too was the reaction of a host of musicians against romanticism. Among its first momentous achievements one should mention the creation in 1892 of the Chanteurs de St-Gervais by the choirmaster Charles Bordes, "that admirable, witty, and indefatigable man, devoured by a passion for music that led him to unlimited audacities" (Louis Laloy, *La Musique Retrouvée*, 1928). With his choristers he revived the sacred music of the Renaissance. Two years later, associating himself with Alexandre Guilmant and Vincent d'Indy, he founded the Schola Cantorum. This school, dedicated at first to the study of plainsong, soon added to its curriculum vocal and instrumental repertoire extending to the end of the eighteenth century.

In 1894 Henry Expert published the first volume of the works of the French masters of the Renaissance. The following year, Saint-Saëns, Malherbe, and Maurice Emmanuel began the publication of the complete works of Rameau. In 1898 Alexandre Guilmant and Pirro started their *Archives des Maîtres de l'Orgue*. Researchers like Michel Brenet, La Laurencie, Quittard, Pirro, Ecorcheville, and others were exploring the wealth of documents buried in libraries, and accounts of their discoveries were given in musicological reviews. But, as Landowska wrote in 1951 in her article entitled "Apropos of Couperin," "Hardly anyone but musicologists read these remarkable works. Modestly, the authors went their way, preparing the ground."

Such was, briefly stated, the musical climate as Wanda Landowska found it upon her arrival in Paris. Wanda, the exceptionally gifted Polish girl who since childhood had been instinctively attracted to the music of the past, who had been steeped in the beauty of her native folklore, and who—brought up in the romantic tradition prevailing in Poland and Germany at the end of the nineteenth century—was emerging at twenty-one as a piano virtuoso of renown and as a composer of lieder and instrumental works of a decidedly romantic flavor. The program of a concert given November 23, 1901, at Enoch's, the publisher, is an almost unbelievable testimony to this melting pot. Among the fifteen participating artists, Diémer played first his own compositions and then *Le Coucou* of Daquin, sandwiched between Schumann and Liszt. Wanda Landowska played at the piano one of her own works, *Rhapsodie Orientale*. At another concert, on March 14, 1902, four melodies, three piano solos, and variations for two pianos by Wanda Landowska were performed.

But freed at last from all tutelage and beset as she was by her love for Bach, Wanda Landowska's first objective when she settled in Paris was to seek enlightenment about the music she loved best. Because of this keen interest of hers, she was soon introduced to the circle of musicians of the Schola Cantorum. She attended all concerts and rehearsals and was invited to play Bach concertos on the piano, of course, with the instrumental ensemble of the school. Meanwhile she was avidly reading treatises and manuscripts, and she visited museums, studying collections of ancient instruments. Lew, who loved music, although he was not a professional, helped her in her research. Charles Bordes became their good friend, as well as Ecorcheville, La Laurencie, Pirro, Quittard, Henri Expert, Maurice Emmanuel, and Albert Schweitzer. Landowska said, "I had the rare privilege of living in the midst of these eminent scholars and musicians who honored me with their friendship. I often had the opportunity to discuss musical matters with them. Progressing in my studies, I came to the realization that the keyboard works of the seventeenth and eighteenth centuries ought to be played on the instrument for which they had been composed, the harpsichord. This idea took complete possession of me, and I decided to carry it out. I started to look for an instrument. The modern reconstructions made around 1900 by Erard and Pleyel were not the ones I dreamed of. At the beginning, however, I had to use them as they were. The instruments constructed by Arnold Dolmetsch were unknown to me because from 1902 to 1909 he was in America.

"I told my friends at the Schola Cantorum of my intention to devote myself to music of the past and to playing the harpsichord. Most of them approved and encouraged me as far as the repertoire was concerned. But, surprise. . . very few of them were in favor of the harpsichord! Why? Probably Diémer's previous attempts were still alive in their memories; and since they liked me as a pianist, they were afraid to see me abandon the piano for this old 'tin-pan' instrument, as the harpsichord was then disdainfully called."

If this seems incredible, read the following letter, or rather the familiar Parisian *petit-bleu*, dated July 31, 1903, that Landowska received from her friend Charles Bordes, he who was the most enthusiastic defender of the revival of the music of the past: ". . . . I would like to see you . . . I want to put you to a big task, one which may become for you a splendid specialty. Play all the works of the harpsichordists, *but not on the harpsichord*; enough of this 'cage for flies' which reduces superb and often large-scale works to the size of its tiny, spindly legs. Therefore, harpsichord (works) on the piano, like those of Bach; but you will have to work hard on Couperin, Chambonnières, and Rameau. I would like to give a whole series of concerts with you this winter, at the Schola, to build up your name in this repertoire. And I am already organizing three concerts in Geneva. We must absolutely discuss this."

"Fortunately," continued Wanda Landowska, "there were a few who thought differently. I remember the interest of Gabriel Fauré, who once sat close to me to watch as I played on the harpsichord a suite of Bach. My friend Paul Dukas, for whom I had a limitless admiration, presented me with an original edition of Couperin's *Pièces de Clavecin*. As for Albert Schweitzer, I did not have to convince him of the importance of the revival of the harpsichord. He knew and understood Bach as he alone does. Moreover, he was eagerly interested in the reconstruction of baroque organs and supervised himself the repairs made on several Silberman instruments. In his book *Bach, Le Musicien-Poète* (1905), Schweitzer wrote this: '. . . anyone who has heard Wanda Landowska play *The Italian Concerto* on her wonderful Pleyel harpsichord finds it hard to understand how it could ever again be played on a modern piano.' " Wanda Landowska also treasured what he wrote her more than forty years later in one of his letters from Lambaréné dated November 19, 1949, "I recall being with you at the Schola Cantorum—it must have been in 1901 or 1902; you were playing Bach, still on the piano, and I marveled at the plasticity you knew how to bring out from a fugue of *The Well-Tempered Clavier*."

Undaunted by these mixed reactions and perhaps spurred

on by the tremendous challenge she was facing, Wanda Landowska threw herself into the battle with all the energy of her youth and the fiery temperament of a Pole of Jewish descent, sustained by the inner self-confidence of her God-given genius. Her husband espoused the cause with the ardor of his radical turn of mind. A voracious and discriminating reader, Lew collected a large amount of documentation from current literature as well as from that of the past. He also acted as what we call today "personal repre- sentative" for his wife. A campaign had started. Its first objective was, in Landowska's own words, "to reconstitute a harpsichord approaching as closely as possible those of the middle eighteenth century when they had reached the height of their glory for rich- ness of registers and beauty of sonority. The harpsichord . . . people knew it only as a museum piece. Adorned with rich carvings, decorated with faded colors and dim gold, they appeared like phantoms, formerly magnificent, now forever mute. What was the voice of these harpsichords of which the musicians of the period speak with such delight? To make it live again, to give it jubilant or pathetic accents, to evoke polyphonic purity, to make the coupled keyboards resound, to sing with lingering tones the amorous cantilenas, such was my dream, a multiple and vast dream."

But it was not enough to dream. Landowska discussed the matter with Gustave Lyon, the director of the piano firm of Pleyel. Accompanied by her husband and Pleyel's chief engineer, M. Lamy, she visited numerous museums, especially Wilhelm Heyer's *Musikhistorischen Museum* in Cologne, one of the richest in Europe. M. Lamy drew plan after plan until an instrument was built that corresponded to Landowska's dream. One of her specific demands for the new instrument was the adjunc- tion of a deep register, called 16-foot, sounding one octave below normal pitch, as a counterpart to the 4-foot register, which is tuned an octave above normal pitch. A two-keyboard instrument, it had also two 8-foot registers, a coupler, and a lute-stop. Similar well-balanced instruments were used by Bach and Handel. Its completion took several years, and Landowska had to wait until 1912 before she could introduce her first large Pleyel harpsi- chord at a Bach festival in Breslau.

While this was in progress, Landowska worked on the re- constitution of the proper touch and registration as well as on all the forgotten elements contributing to a truthful interpretation of the music of the past, such as ornamentation, rhythmical particularities, tempi, etc. She began to present the harpsichord in public as early as 1903, even though it was still the small and inadequate instrument that she had at her disposal. At first she played only one piece of the program on it, the rest on the piano. Gradually she augmented the harpsichord group until she could dare to play it for a whole evening. She undertook concert tours in Germany, Italy, Spain, Russia, etc. But despite the fact that her success as a performer was great, it was not sufficient to win complete acceptance of the harpsichord nor understanding of the music of the past. Wanda Landowska understood that she had to muster the help of another language, that of words. She had to write to carry her convictions across to musicians and laymen alike.

In 1905, the year that saw the publication of two of the most important works on Bach, those of Pirro and Schweitzer, Landowska and Lew began to gather and classify the numerous documents they had been collecting and to plan for a book. With an astonishingly all-encompassing grasp of what had caused the current status of the music of the past, they agreed that a powerful blow had to be struck at all the prejudices and false ideas under which innumerable musical masterpieces were crushed. This music had to be replaced in its proper perspective; its fluctuations over the span of two or three centuries and in different countries had to be studied anew. Landowska was well trained for this incursion into the past. Her mother had taught her history and geography, and Wanda recalled that "thanks to her prodigious and powerful memory, that of a visionary, her lessons became rhapsodic tales."

Of Lew, Wanda said, "He was an enlightened dogmatist, although he lacked psychological acumen where isolated human beings were concerned; he despised the magnifying glass and the subjective sense of observation of the biologist. But ebbs and flows of crowds, great movements of collective stupidity, 'inspired' impulses of the public, and their sheeplike reactions in following enthusiastically any order given by a dictator or by publicity—all these had in him an admirable observer and sarcastic critic."

As for Wanda's specific field—that is, music itself—she had

to prove the necessity of renovating the harpsichord and had to clarify certain mystifying problems of interpretation. To be convincing, all the assertions made in the book had to be backed by a great variety of quotations from the most authoritative sources of the particular times and places involved.

It was of prime importance that this book should reach far beyond the musicological circle. It had to be addressed to all musicians, to all lovers of music. Remember that Landowska was first and foremost an *interpreter*; efficacious communication with her audience was vital. Therefore, the tone had to be attractive, provocative, and understandable even to a lay reader. Questioned much later about the significance of this volume, Wanda Landowska answered, "It was an alarm signal, a war cry to awaken interest in the music of the past, to reveal the harpsichord and its literature. When one reads this book today, one cannot understand the reason for the belligerent, combative tone which dominates the entire work. It seems unbelievable that musicians and public alike could have been so unacquainted with the music of former times and that such a vehement defense was needed of Bach, Couperin, Scarlatti, their predecessors, and even their successors. For however incredible it may seem today, this defense was to extend beyond Mozart and Haydn. Yes, music of the past was scarcely known. . . ."

As a harbinger of the coming volume, Landowska's first essay, entitled "La Tradition," appeared November 15, 1905, in the newly formed *S.I.M.*, a French branch of the International Musicological Society, under the direction of Louis Laloy and Jules Ecorcheville. A month later, the *Mercure de France,* the most important French literary publication of that time, printed a second, more extensive essay by Landowska, "Bach et ses Interprètes, Sur l'Interprétation des Oeuvres de Clavecin de J. S. Bach." Both were received with praise and approbation by Landowska's colleagues and the press. Most of the content of these two articles was later incorporated in the book then in preparation, together with a third paper, "Les Oeuvres de Clavecin de Bach," published in 1907 in *Musica,* a music magazine.

The next writings of Wanda Landowska to appear in print made for an interesting interlude. After a triumphant concert tour in Russia and a memorable visit to Tolstoy, she voiced her impressions in "Tolstoy Musician" for *Musica* (June 1908), and

"Une Visite à la Comtesse Tolstoy" for *Fémina,* a women's magazine (July 15, 1908). Tolstoy's understanding and enthusiastic love for the old music Landowska had just revealed to him at the harpsichord was a great booster in her campaign.

Finally in 1909 the much awaited book, under the appropriate title of *Musique Ancienne,* was released by *Mercure de France* and created quite a sensation in the musical world.

Now that an overall defense of the music of the past had been forcefully pleaded and presented to the public, Wanda Landowska was free in her next writings to single out and develop specific problems of interpretation. The first subject she chose was one that had begun to stir considerable polemic, especially among German musicologists. It concerned the selection of the proper instrument on which Bach's keyboard works should be played—harpsichord, clavichord, or modern piano. Until today this has been probably one of the most controversial subjects among musicians. During her lifetime, Wanda Landowska stated again and again her convictions in the matter based, of course, on thorough research and documentation, but above all, on evidence found in the music itself, evidence clear as the light of day for those who have penetrated truly and completely the essence of Bach's music and who know intimately the resources of every one of the three instruments. Landowska's public performances and her harpsichord recording of *The Well-Tempered Clavier,* the work on which the controversy centered, will remain an eloquent *pièce à conviction* in favor of her thesis. Yet there are still a few die-hards who continue to agitate the old feud. Under the pretext of authenticity, some of them are eager to prove that "it can be done" on the clavichord. But in order to be heard, even in small halls, they have to resort to electronic amplification of sound. And there goes authenticity, since Bach, obviously, had no such device at his disposal, a device that distorts one of the very characteristics of the clavichord—namely, its softness and delicacy of sound.

The contenders for the modern piano may show more practical sense—Landowska herself has never been against its use—but they either adapt Bach's music to the possibilities of the piano or try to imitate on it what they think are the characteristic qualities of the harpsichord. In so doing, they reveal too often their superficial and misconstrued knowledge both of Bach's spirit and of the true resources of the harpsichord.

On this subject Landowska published "Le Clavecin chez Bach" in *S.I.M.* in 1910, and the following year in German "Für Welches Instrument Hat Bach Sein Wohltemperirtes Klavier Geschrieben?" in *Neue Zeitschrift für Musik*, May 20-22, 1911. The latter was reprinted in French in *La Revue Musicale* December 1, 1927, as well as in English in *Dominant*, November 1927. Parts of it were always included in program notes every time Landowska played a group of Preludes and Fugues, and they accompanied her complete recording of *The Well-Tempered Clavier* in 1954.

While studying manuscripts and autographs in the Berlin Library, Wanda Landowska made an important musicological discovery concerning the rhythmical pattern of the theme of the C Major Fugue from Book I of *The Well-Tempered Clavier*. Not satisfied with showing documentary evidence, she substantiated it with purely musical reasons. Her report was published in German in the *Bach Jahrbuch* of 1913.

Another subject attracted Landowska's attention—the influence of French music on the Germans in the eighteenth century and particularly on Bach. These influences, as she discovered, were the key to many interpretative problems. She wrote two essays on this theme: "Bach und die Französische Klavier Musik" for the *Bach Jahrbuch* of 1910, reprinted in French as "Les Influences Françaises chez Bach" by *Courrier Musical*, July 15, and August 10, 1912; and "Les Allemands et la Musique Française au 18e Siècle" for *Mercure de France*.

It was around that time that Landowska was asked her opinion on the interpretation of Chopin. She gave it in a paper entitled "L'Interprétation de Chopin," *Courrier Musical*, January 1, 1910. Translated into English, it appeared in America in 1926 in *The Etude*. With the same acute sense of the fluctuations of taste she had displayed in writing about the seventeenth and eighteenth centuries, Wanda Landowska exposed many of the distortions inflicted by various virtuosos upon Chopin's music. This was followed by a discussion of "La Nationalité de Chopin," *Mercure de France* and *Monde Musical*, 1911.

All the while Wanda Landowska and her harpsichord were

touring everywhere in Europe, participating in Bach festivals and musicological congresses. From Russia and Spain, she sent to *S.I.M.* delightful accounts of her travel adventures (March 15, 1910, March 15, 1911). In one of them, written in Tiflis, February 3, 1913, she made her first incursion into the domain of modern music and called it "Pourquoi la Musique Moderne n'est-elle pas Mélodique?"

The degree of acceptance of the harpsichord differed as widely as the countries in which Landowska played it. In Spain and Russia, where the national instruments—guitar or balalaika—have plucked strings, harpsichord sonority was readily understood and liked. Yet, the first official recognition of the importance of Landowska's campaign came from the country that had been the hardest to convert—Germany. Hermann Kretzschmar, who in 1909 had succeeded Joachim as director of the *Hochschule für Musik* in Berlin, invited Wanda Landowska to create there a harpsichord class. That was a success Landowska could be very proud of.

In 1913 she and Lew moved to Berlin, bringing along the recently built large Pleyel harpsichord. All went well for a while. The *Bossische Zeitung* of May 24, 1914, published a short article by Landowska on the renaissance of the harpsichord, which was an up-to-date version of the last pages of *Musique Ancienne*. Then tragedy began—war, during which Landowska and Lew were held as civilian prisoners on parole in Berlin. Landowska was allowed to continue teaching at the school and occasionally to give a concert. But no more of her writings would be published for many years.

As soon as the war ended, Landowska and Lew, free at last, prepared to return to France; then, shortly before their departure, Lew was killed in a car accident. Deprived of the companion who for nineteen years had worked and fought with her for the renaissance of the harpsichord and its literature and having lost most of her earthly possessions, Landowska returned to Paris. With admirable courage, she began to rebuild her life, devoting herself more than ever to the music she was born to serve and glorify. A livelihood had to be earned through concert tours and teaching. Little time was left for writing, except for the preparation of the lectures Landowska delivered in various European cities. *Musique Ancienne* had long been out of print, but the publishing firm of Sénart in Paris put out a new edition of this work in 1921.

In the fall of that year an International Congress on the history of art was held in Paris with great pomp and ceremony. The fourth section, devoted to the history of music, included a lecture by Wanda Landowska at the Sorbonne, followed by a concert in the Galerie des Glaces at the Château de Versailles. A passage from a review of these events should be quoted here:

Saturday, the first of October, there was a crowd at the Sorbonne, a chosen public, the elite of the Congress, including many members of the Institut de France, to hear a lecture of a very special interest on Bach and the French harpsichordists. A great artist to whom no harpsichord virtuoso can be compared today and one who has devoted herself to the erudite, though passionate, study of the masters in order to penetrate and interpret their thought better—who would not recognize Wanda Landowska?—kept under her spell an audience of academicians and amateurs by her erudite explanations illustrated at the harpsichord.

Another reviewer said:

. . . the Quinet amphitheater was overcrowded at the expense of the other amphitheaters of the Sorbonne where scholarly dissertations were being read before empty benches. . . .

Unfortunately, and for unknown reasons, the actual text of Landowska's lecture was never printed in the *Actes du Congrès*.

That same year, Wanda Landowska, who was giving master classes for pianists at the *Ecole Normale de Musique* in Paris, wrote "How to Interpret Bach's Inventions" for *Le Monde Musical* in July 1921, and gave an enlarged version in the same periodical in September 1922. The study of two-part music had always been the basis of Landowska's teaching, and in these two articles she also exposed the reason why pianists trained for the romantic repertoire are so utterly perplexed when they attempt to play polyphonic music.

Turning to criticism, Wanda Landowska reviewed Marc Pincherle's book, *Les Violonistes*, in *Le Monde Musical* of October 1922. More than a critical essay, this paper is a beautiful homage to musicologists, in whose ranks Marc Pincherle was taking a prominent place. In the same vein she reviewed Emile Vuillermoz's *Les Musiques d'Aujourd'hui* for *La Revue Contemporaine*, October 1, 1923. Vuillermoz was also one of France's best music critics. Although it was surely unintentional, Landowska's description of Vuillermoz's style could apply perfectly to her own! Her comparison of sixteenth century lute music to jazz and to Ravel is one among many examples of Landowska's uncanny sense of *rapprochements*, of detecting affinities between things no one else would ever think of bringing together.

In August 1923 *La Revue Mondiale* in Paris and *La Tribune de Genève* published simultaneously Landowska's recollection of a speech on Chopin delivered by Paderewski in Lwow in 1910. Her juxtaposition of Paderewski the orator (the title of the article) with Paderewski the pianist makes for a striking portrait of her glorious compatriot.

Again in 1923 upon the occasion of a concert in Geneva in which Wanda Landowska played at the piano Mozart's Concerto in E Flat, K. 482, the *Tribune de Genève* printed her notes on this work (January 7 and 8). In them Landowska not only analyzed the concerto, but she also drew the attention of the readers to one of the most baffling problems of Mozartean interpretation, the improvisation of ornaments. Landowska was as much an authority on the interpretation of Mozart's keyboard works as she was on Bach's. Her numerous performances of Mozart's sonatas and concertos, her recordings of some of them, and the cadenzas she composed for several concertos (Broude Bros.) are her legacy in this domain.

That same year saw three more important steps in Landowska's career. Thanks to her influence, the harpsichord was introduced in a modern work for the first time by Manuel de Falla. Wanda Landowska played this new harpsichord part in the first performance of *El Retablo de Maese Pedro* in Paris on June 25. Three years later she played the first full scale modern work for her instrument, Falla's concerto for harpsichord, flute, oboe, clarinet, violin, and violoncello dedicated to her. This inspired Francis Poulenc to write for Wanda Landowska the *Concert Champêtre*, in which the harpsichord is opposed to a large orchestra. Landowska played it many times. With these three modern compositions, Wanda Landowska had succeeded in reviving the harpsichord not only as a vehicle for the music of the past, but as an active participant in new music. Since then many composers have written new works for harpsichord solo or in combination with small and large groups of instruments.

In the fall of 1923 Wanda Landowska sailed for America. "I arrived there like a lion tamer," she said, "dragging along four large Pleyel harpsichords." She introduced her art and her instruments to many cities of the New World, and at Camden, New Jersey, she made her first recordings for Victor. On the occasion of her appearances in America *Musique Ancienne* was translated and published by A. A. Knopf under the title *Music of the Past*. It came off the press in 1924.

For four consecutive seasons Wanda Landowska shared her time between Europe and America, touring constantly. There was no time for writing.

After so much traveling, Wanda Landowska felt the growing urge to create a permanent home, a center for this music to which she had devoted her life. She bought a conventional suburban house at Saint-Leu-La-Forêt, a few miles north of Paris, and transformed it into a home of exquisite charm and comfort, filled with mementos of her travels and souvenirs from the many personalities who were her friends. There she made room for her library, which had become quite extensive. In the back of the garden, designed in the spirit of the classical *jardins à la française*, she had a small concert hall built of modern and sober design. Besides two modern pianos and two Pleyel harpsichords it housed the precious ancient instruments she had been collecting over the years—clavichords, spinets, a 1642 Ruckers harpsichord, pianofortes, violas, even a small organ dated 1737, etc.

Wanda Landowska inaugurated the concert hall in the summer of 1927 and subsequently gave concerts there each Sunday afternoon from May to July. Musicians, writers, painters, sculptors, lovers of music from all parts of the world converged toward the small temple to witness the resurrection of masterpieces of long ago. In this ideal atmosphere Wanda Landowska could give free rein to her inspiration and communicate to a choice audience her unquenchable enthusiasm for the music of the past. At St-Leu, Landowska also founded her own *Ecole de Musique Ancienne*. From many lands came not only harpsichordists and pianists, but organists, singers, violinists, flutists, and musicologists as well. Landowska gave private and public master classes, explaining the works performed by the pupils and playing herself music of various epochs. With an extraordinary sense of *le mot juste*, she made the most intricate music take shape, meaning, and emerge full-blooded and alive before delighted and amazed disciples and listeners. What a pity that tape-recording was not in current use yet! These master classes would have yielded material for several books. All was not lost, though, because some pupils and secretaries took notes, as I personally did, from that day in July 1933 when I had the good fortune of becoming Landowska's pupil.

Although Landowska still toured during the winter, she was able at St-Leu to resume writing. Now that the battle for the revival of the harpsichord had been won, she could channel her energies increasingly toward the elucidation of deeper and more subtle problems of interpretation. Returning to a favorite theme, reciprocal influences, Landowska wrote "Chopin et l'Ancienne Musique Française" for *La Revue Musicale* in 1931. Her style by then had become truly her own, free, enriched with experience, refined by constant reading of the best French literature. From then on, Landowska's writings were to be closely related to each particular masterpiece of music on which she chose to concentrate. For instance, she had been studying sporadically throughout her life Bach's *Goldberg Variations*. Now she decided to perform them in their entirety, a thing that had probably not yet been attempted in modern times on the harpsichord. For months she of course worked at the keyboards on these devilishly difficult variations, but she spent just as much time studying their history, their relationship with other works, exploring far beyond the cold facts of technical analysis in quest of the poetic and human meaning of this music. The results of her discoveries were penned in an essay soberly titled "Sur les Variations Goldberg." It was published by *La Revue Musicale* at the time of the first complete performance of the work at St-Leu in May 1933. Of this event, it was said, "When Wanda Landowska reconstructs with her infallible hands and her lucid soul, the edifice that is the *Goldberg Variations*, this monument of ancient music becomes a temple open to all mankind. . . ." (René Lalou, *La Revue des Vivants*, July 1933).

Every one of Landowska's concerts at St-Leu was accompanied by extensive program notes offering erudite and original views on the many gems of music she was resuscitating. They also added interest to the albums of recordings she made from 1933 on. There was, for instance, the revelation of Scarlatti in 1935, when Wanda Landowska dared to devote an entire program to his sonatas. There were Couperin, Rameau, Mozart, and all the

French, German, Italian, Polish music of the past to play and to write about. There was a lecture for the literary society, Les Annales, on the music of Shakespeare's time. It was published in *Conferencia* April 15, 1936. The celebration of a glorious trinity— Bach, Handel, and Scarlatti, born the same year—called for a short article in L'*Art Musical* December 25, 1936; the recording of five Handel suites was accompanied in *Radio-Magazine,* January 1937, by one of Landowska's most fascinating articles.

Parallel with these specific writings, Wanda Landowska was planning a new book, one that would begin where *Music of the Past* left off; it would be a history of her discoveries in the domain of interpretation. Much documentation was gathered, not only from specialized works on music, but also from classical and modern literature, of which Landowska was an avid reader. But before the book could materialize, another tragedy struck—the Second World War. St-Leu had to be abandoned with all its treasures. In our hasty departure we could only attempt to save what three small boxes would hold. In them went a few indispensable books and music scores and some notebooks. Landowska wanted to take along a collection of priceless manuscripts of Karl Philipp Emanuel Bach's concertos. I insisted instead upon filling the space with the notes from the master classes. She protested. Despite my deep respect for Wanda Landowska, I threw in the notes and left the Karl Philipp Emanuel manuscripts. I was later to hear about that in no uncertain terms, but I never felt sorry for my disobedience. Other manuscripts of Karl Philipp Emanuel Bach's concertos existed in libraries and could be photostated. Of the notes, there was no other copy in existence; they represented fourteen years of Landowska's teaching.

After spending eighteen months in the south of France, where Landowska was told that St-Leu had been thoroughly looted by the Nazis, we were finally able to sail for America, reaching New York on Pearl Harbor Day. For the second time, and with the same indomitable courage, Wanda Landowska started rebuilding her life, as she had done twenty years before. In February 1942 she played *The Goldberg Variations* in Town Hall. The endless ovation she received from both the audience and the press after her stunning performance will remain engraved forever in the annals of music in New York. Before this memorable concert and each of the next three she gave, the

New York Times and the *Herald Tribune* printed articles written by Landowska. They were "A Note on Bach" (*New York Times*, February 15, 1942), "Tribute to Rameau" (*New York Times*, October 18, 1942), "Strings Plucked and Struck" (*Herald Tribune*, February 28, 1943), and "Notes on a Great Neopolitan" (*Herald Tribune*, October 24, 1943).

A busy schedule of concerts, recordings, and teaching left little leisure for writing. Yet in the summer of 1947, having realized her dream to live again in the country—she had discovered an ideal house for rent in Lakeville, Connecticut—Wanda Landowska completed extensive commentaries to accompany her recent recording, *A Treasury of Harpsichord Music* (RCA Victor). They were illustrated with numerous pictures and interesting reproductions.

In 1949 the Grolier Society asked Landowska to write a short history of the revival of the harpsichord for their *Story of Our Time Yearbook 1949.* Two years later the *Saturday Review of Literature* enticed her to review a book on Couperin and to publish her "Recollections of Paderewski" on the tenth anniversary of his death.

To celebrate her seventieth birthday, Wanda Landowska decided to undertake one of the most ambitious tasks ever—the recording of Bach's complete *Well-Tempered Clavier.* As with *The Goldberg Variations,* thorough research and study of the work went along on a par with the preparation at the keyboard. Five years later, along with Landowska's recorded performance, came her detailed analysis of *The Well-Tempered Clavier,* about which she said, "It is simply the story of my experiences as a worker in music, a worker who jots down her impressions, prelude after prelude, fugue after fugue."

Although relatively few writings by Wanda Landowska were published during the last fifteen years of her life, it was perhaps the time she wrote the most. Notebooks of all shapes and sizes, small pieces of paper, old envelopes, anything that could be written on, were covered with annotations. To while away many sleepless nights, or during her walks in the countryside, at almost any time, Wanda Landowska would jot down or dictate her thoughts and reflections on musical subjects as well as those about nature, people, and her philosophy of life. She wanted very much to publish a revised version of *Music of the Past* together with her most significant articles. In view of this she made a number of corrections and suggestions. The idea, conceived in St-Leu, of doing another complete book was never abandoned. Yet around 1955 she said, "This book I want so much to write, this book I bear in me, about which I dream, and that has always been in my thought . . . will I have the strength to do it?" Alas, this wish was not to be granted. Landowska was past seventy-five; a choice had to be made between recording or doing the book. Naturally, and we may be thankful for that, recording came first.

One summer evening as I was reading aloud to Wanda Landowska some notes she had just dictated—they were, as I remember clearly, a description of the salient features of her interpretation that she wanted to discuss in the planned book —she suddenly said, "It is for you to do it." Too stunned to find any better reply, I mumbled that I would never feel capable of undertaking such a task. Still ringing in my ears is the indignant and sonorous *"Idiote!"* that followed my cowardly statement. "How I wish I were in your place," she added. "What a wonderful work I would do!" And to boost my courage, no doubt, she inscribed a copy of her commentaries on *The Well-Tempered Clavier* with these words: "For my cherished companion, Denise, without whom these commentaries could not have been written." Finally she made clear in her will that I was to be the recipient of all her notes and documents on music as well as of her musical instruments and library. This and, above all, the unique experience of having been closely associated with Wanda Landowska for twenty-six years are my credentials for presenting this book. During those marvelous and too short twenty-six years Landowska taught me the secrets of her harpsichord technique, she guided me through the intricacies of contrapuntal music, and clarified with infinite patience so many problems of interpretation. From her I learned how to listen, how to work, how to teach, and I might add, how to live. Watching her own practicing was the most revealing lesson. Taking notes while she was teaching others opened new vistas; working with her on the preparation of an essay or an article meant to be invited to follow her in a fascinating voyage of discovery. Landowska's generosity was such that she never kept from her pupils any part of her incredible knowledge and experience.

On August 16, 1959, Wanda Landowska died. The world seemed to come to an end for me. Yet, when I began to recover from the initial shock of grief, Landowska's words, engraved in my memory, kept rushing insistently into my mind. I found myself surrounded by her heavily annotated books and music scores and by a staggering number of notes and documents—in short, the legacy of Landowska's entire life work. I knew how inseparably connected all this was with her keyboard performances. Thanks to recordings, a representative part of her playing is available. Therefore, it was unthinkable to keep the counterpart of her achievements locked in a safe. It was all the more imperious to bring these out because none of Landowska's writings—except for a few record jackets—was in circulation. *Music of the Past* had long been out of print; the essays and articles were scattered and buried in the periodicals in which they had first appeared in France and elsewhere. Besides, there was the wealth of unpublished material, perhaps the most significant of all. Aware as I was of Landowska's desire that her writings, the old as well as the new, be published, I decided to overcome my misgivings and to plan for a book that would include most of her writings on music. In conformity with her wish, I worked on the idea of presenting a revised edition of *Music of the Past*, observing the corrections and occasional deletions she had indicated and blending into it the articles that treated more extensively identical subjects. Then the articles and essays she had earmarked for re-edition would follow, revised and edited in order to avoid repetitious passages. As for the numerous unpublished notes, their destination remained to be considered. After thorough examination and classification, I came to the conclusion that the manner of utilizing them was two-fold; those which completed or had a bearing on a subject treated in *Music of the Past* or any of the other essays should be added where they belonged. From among the rest of the unpublished material a selection had to be made. The notes which in my judgment represent the best expression of an idea had to be singled out and grouped with others according to subject matter. When necessary, I would link these together with a few sentences of my own; and that would constitute the last part of the complete book.

Once this outline was made, I had to consider the practical aspects of the realization of my project. I visualized the tremendous amount of work involved. Beside editing, revising, and organizing all this material, most of it had to be translated from the French language in which Landowska wrote, although she was fluent in several others. I could not even use the translation of *Music of the Past* made in 1924, because it had been done with hardly any consultation between Landowska and the translator hired by the publisher. It did not convey the characteristics of her style and would not compare favorably with, for instance, Landowska's commentaries on *The Well-Tempered Clavier*, which she had written in close collaboration with her own translator.

But the most forbidding obstacle was the precariousness of my situation now that I was left alone. And here enters the man who made possible what seemed a hopeless dream, Robert Hawkins, master in English at the Hotchkiss School in Lakeville, Connecticut. It was with him that Landowska had worked on the English version of her commentaries, not only those on *The Well-Tempered Clavier*, but also on Mozart, Haydn, and others. He had become our friend, and his respect and admiration for Wanda Landowska were limitless. Robert Hawkins was keenly aware of the importance of publishing Landowska's writings, and he understood my predicament. He took it upon himself to approach in my behalf admirers of Wanda Landowska who immediately sponsored a part of the project so that I could start to work. To these generous friends who have requested to remain anonymous go my most grateful thanks.

Later Robert Hawkins introduced me to the directors of the newly established Deerfield Foundation, and I was privileged to receive the first grant they bestowed. It enabled me to go on with the work, and I am happy to express to them my deep gratitude.

After a year of work much remained to be done. I applied to the Ford Foundation and was awarded a fellowship in 1963. It is difficult to describe adequately my thankfulness.

As for Robert Hawkins, his role did not stop there. With complete devotion and indefatigable zeal, with his authoritative knowledge of the complexities of the English language, he has been assisting me constantly in my endeavor to convey not only the exact meaning of Landowska's original texts, but their flavor and spirit as well.

Without Robert Hawkins this book could never have been attempted. No words could express properly the extent of my indebtedness to him.

In planning her book Wanda Landowska often wondered, "Whom will it concern?"

At one time she said, "It will be a bitter answer to musicology." Obviously dryness and pedantry are often the appanage of that science rather than art. Yet Wanda Landowska praised highly the work of musicologists. In the best sense of the word, she herself was one of them.

Would her book rather be addressed to professional virtuosos? She confessed, "I really don't know what I am doing among them; I have no contact with them. They are on their guard with me, thinking that I am a 'learned' musician. But I, aware of the little I know, feel ill at ease with them. For this reason, I live apart. They take it for aloofness."

Will it attract teachers? "They expect a vade-mecum with recipes for every ornament and registration," she once said wearily. But who more than herself loved to teach? ". . . My destiny might well have been that of an educator. I was made to initiate. . . ."

Revealing her true feelings, she said, "I do not want this book to be meant exclusively for musicians; they are not the only ones who interest me." She hated the limitations of categories. The audiences she loved best were composed of writers, painters, sculptors, actors, lovers of beauty in all its forms, as well as of musicians. But, above all, it was youth whom she addressed, "those who search and wait, often discouraged by the tyranny of virtuosity." She often told them, "Do not be apprehensive of the severe aspect and heavy wig of Father Bach. Let us gather around him, and feel the love, the noble generosity that emanates from each one of his phrases. They will create strong and warm bonds between us all."

The miracle with great human beings is that they do not cease to live when their hearts stop beating. So much of Landowska's genius remains alive, so much we can enjoy, learn from, and so much that will be an inspiration to future generations. This imperishable attribute emanates from every one of the recorded performances and every one of the writings of Wanda Landowska. With Scarlatti let us say,

"Live happily!"

DENISE RESTOUT
Lakeville, Connecticut
February 1964

PART ONE

Foreword to Part One

To appreciate fully the spirit of Wanda Landowska's writings on music, especially those dating from the first fifteen years of this century, one must be conscious of that which distinguishes them from the works of the musicologists of her time. One must be clearly aware of her motivation.

If Landowska was drawn to scholarly research, it was because her intuitive and compelling love for the music of former epochs provided the impetus for her inquisitive mind to find out all she could about it, since so little was known in this domain. It did not stem from any special inclination toward historical or technical studies as such.

Another important factor that shaped her personal approach to the subject was being a performer of great ability. It provided her with a constant, practical, intimate, and complete contact with music itself, an advantage very few musicologists possessed at that time. Also, being engaged in concert tours, she was exposed directly to the reactions of the public and critics; she did not suffer from the isolation and limited communication to which most musicologists were then restricted. Therefore she was able to feel, hear about, and evaluate at first hand, so to speak, and in various parts of Europe, what music lovers knew or, rather, ignored or misunderstood about the music of former times. She said in

1905, "Music of the past has become a distant and vague country where everything is totally different from our surroundings, our life, our art, our impressions, and our concepts." This is why she felt that her mission was to expose and refute misconceptions and to enlighten people on the true characteristics of the forgotten music she played for them. That was a staggering task because ignorance was appalling, distortions were numerous, and prejudices firmly entrenched.

Some of the facts and ideas for which ·Landowska had to fight sixty years ago are widely accepted today; her defense of them may appear to us somewhat quixotic. It was not so then. And for this very reason Landowska's pre-World War I writings provide us with a retrospective view of the attitude of that period toward the music of the seventeenth and eighteenth centuries. We may pride ourselves rightly for being so much more enlightened now that performances of works from far more remote times are no longer rarities. Yet, for those who are too prompt to take things for granted, it is worthwhile remembering that had not Landowska fought so vigorously her twin campaign—writing and playing —our present knowledge of two centuries of music might be much poorer.

Reading what Landowska had to say half a century ago is also very sobering because in many instances we have to admit that, despite the fact that the number of initiated musicians and listeners has greatly increased, many of the old prejudices continue to linger among us. And while musicological investigations are now probing the music of the earliest epochs, there is still much to learn about that of the seventeenth and eighteenth centuries.

When she wrote *Music of the Past*, Landowska's first objective was to fight the idea of straightforward progress in music. It proved a much deeper truth—namely, that music, at all times, has always been a living organism. As such it had its changes of seasons, its ebbs and flows, its overlapping waves, and most of all, its continuous rotatory motion. Music of past epochs had been too often mummified, neatly tagged, and filed away. Reminding us of the opinions of great men from Seneca to Debussy on the various aspects of music was to bring into focus the eternal fluctuations, the continuous "orbital" motion of this art, perhaps the most vital of all. This approach inevitably aimed at destroying the arbitrary and congealed dogmatism that Landowska encountered so often among her fellow musicians and the public.

Aside from the denouncement of prevalent false ideas, Landowska's treatment of several fundamental problems concerning, for instance, ancient instruments, ornamentation, movements, or the French and Italian influences on German music has remained the basis and springboard for all her subsequent studies.

The first part of the present book contains a condensed and revised version of *Music of the Past* into which the gist of six of the articles written between 1905 and 1912 has been incorporated. In the chapter on keyboard instruments, some descriptions, more complete than the early ones, have been borrowed from later writings.

D. R.

I ⟨ Is Music a Progressive Art?

It is a sign of the age!
I have found, however, time after time, the same facts
with analogous circumstances in old memoirs or in
history books.—Anatole France

So MANY people still believe that music is a pre-eminently modern art born obscurely not very long ago. So many think that today we are witnessing its glory after the magnificent progress made during the past two centuries!

Yet in the middle of the eighteenth century at a meeting of academicians, a musicologist from Lyons read a report on music which began, "It may be truly said that the arts have made considerable progress in the past two centuries. The moderns have improved upon the old masters."

In his treatise on the flute, Quantz, the renowned flutist of Frederick the Great, draws one of the darkest pictures of the state of music in Germany in the seventeenth century. According to him the great evolution was quite recent.

"There are today," said Voltaire, "a thousand people who

know music for every one who knew it at the time of Louis XIII, and this art has improved in the same proportion. Under Louis XIV music was still in the cradle."

Scarcely half a century earlier, however, Bonnet declared, after he too had insisted upon the two centuries of progress, that during the reign of Louis XIV the art of music, on a par with the other arts, had achieved such a triumph that "France was as flourishing as Rome had been at the time of Augustus."

To Berlioz true music did not begin before Gluck; and Brossard, about 1725, was delighted to see this art at its peak of perfection.

If we looked back, I am convinced that we would find each generation proud of having reached the apogee of perfection after one or two centuries of progress. Surely enough, in an ancient book entitled *Sur le Beau*, I find an excerpt from Seneca's letter No. 84 in which he writes: "We have now more musicians in our solemn concerts than the ancients had public at their spectacles." We might then place the birth of music one or two centuries before Seneca. But we are taught that the first poets and philosophers of antiquity were great musicians. We are even told that by the time words were invented men already possessed singing. Then it must be true that at each period of history people preserve some vague notions about the music of a few preceding generations; when their knowledge begins to fail, they place the cradle and tentatively name a father. Josquin des Prés, Jacques Mauduit, Heinrich Schütz, and Bach were, in turn, called fathers of music. And these fortuitous attributes are repeated with each passing generation. In 1905 Vincent d'Indy said, "For me, Bach is simply the father of all modern music." (*Die Musik, Jahr V, Heft* 1, p. 35)

Youth threatens to produce masterpieces which will make us forget all that has been written previously. The elders, those prophets of evil, deplore vehemently the corruption of taste. In their time, everything was better. As for the public, "that voice of God which is never mistaken," it ignores these extremes and celebrates the two or three composers who died during the last twenty or thirty years and whose obituaries are still deeply engraved upon the memory of everyone. Speaking of music, Auber said, "It is a fugacious art which fashion destroys."

Voltaire, Rousseau, and all eighteenth-century writers, except perhaps d'Alembert, entertain us to satiety with the idea that from day to day music progresses miraculously by leaps and bounds. In his article for the *Dictionnaire des Sciences et des Arts*, Cahuzac went even so far as to state it with a certain precision. "Since the compositions of Pergolesi, Handel, Leo, et al.," he said, "are far above those of Carissimi and Corelli, accordingly the works of our good French contemporary masters are much superior to those admired at the end of the last century." Cahuzac's favorite composer was Mondonville, who would thus greatly surpass Handel, Corelli, Lully, and Palestrina. Here you see the value of these classifications and appreciations made in the name of progress.

Forkel, that great admirer of Bach, found passé several works of the Cantor, and he did not believe they could survive. For Zelter, Mozart sums up all by himself J. S. Bach, Karl Philipp Emanuel, and Haydn; as he wrote to Goethe, "I remember perfectly that the music of J. S. Bach from Leipzig and that of his son from Hamburg, both very original and spontaneous, appeared to me almost incomprehensible, although I was attracted by their basic originality. Then came Haydn. Finally appeared Mozart, who epitomized all three."

In the first half of the nineteenth century, Adolphe Adam, the composer of comic operas, prided himself on being a great and expert admirer of the music of the past. After Candeille's revival of *Castor et Pollux*, however, he wrote, "It was probably the last performance of this masterpiece, which is now reduced to the status of a library ornament. . . . Now that better systems of composition prevail, who will ever dream of reading the didactic works of Rameau? Who will search his operas for the melodies that made them successful?"

At all times not only mediocre minds, but some cultivated musicians as well, have imagined that their art surpassed that of their predecessors. I often hear this irritating remark, "If only the ancients had known our music!" and faces shine with pride and self-satisfaction. It is like a maid in her Sunday finery looking at herself in the mirror and thinking, "If only the folks at home could see me all decked out like this!"

In 1908, under the title *Is There a Progressive Party in Music?*, Richard Strauss launched a kind of encyclical pompously called the "Fontainebleau Manifesto." The famous composer was

convinced that music not only advances or rather rushes breathlessly along the road of progress, but also that the best compositions of former times were created to serve merely as stepping
stones for our advent. "Even a perfect masterpiece," he said,
"must be considered just a seed deposited in the soul of posterity
to continue producing greater and more perfect works."

In what respect would modern works be greater, more perfect, and superior to those of Bach, Palestrina, or Beethoven?
Richard Strauss did not care to say. Nor did Cahuzac tell us why
Palestrina, Bach, or Handel were so inferior to Mondonville. To
do that one should know all the music of today—that seems simple
enough—and in addition all the music of the past; and that would
be harder. For a comprehensive view of both, one would need
sufficient perspective, and that is impossible. Moreover, such a
mission could be entrusted only to men of infallible taste; of
those, to be sure, we should find only too many!

Who knows if the certitude of our superiority and that of
having made such spectacular progress over our ancestors will not
in turn become a fecund subject of mirth in future generations?

Richard Strauss went on to say, "The natural and straightforward instinct of the naïve crowd must be defended against the
never ending retrogressive party, always seeking to stifle in people
their lively attraction to progress."

I shall certainly refrain from discussing whether new tricks in
music have such particular attraction for the "naïve crowd." I personally believe that the public prefers repetition and well-known,
hackneyed works. Without insisting upon this, I merely wonder
why we should exterminate the party of the return to the past?
Did we forbid Mendelssohn to propagate the works of Bach, Bach
to copy those of Frescobaldi and Couperin, Couperin to write his
Apothéose of Lully and Corelli? Did we protest Wagner's ecstatic
writings about Beethoven, Beethoven's admiration for Handel,
Berlioz's deification of Gluck, Rossini's zeal in trying to make
Mozart loved in his country, where people still found him too
complicated? All great musicians have committed this redoubtable crime of lèse-progress. Did not Mozart himself admit that he
was less of an innovator than Bach?

One day, when Meyerbeer's admirers said in his presence that
it was no longer possible to hear Don Giovanni after the fourth

act of *Les Huguenots,* he retorted, "So much the worse for the fourth act of *Les Huguenots!*"

Contrary to the poor legislators of taste, all great musicians have been filled with respect and tenderness for their forebears, and they have never pretended to absorb all the past in their radiant glory. Liszt, a romantic musician par excellence, claimed to be merely a faithful descendant of the classics and to seek in the past the origins of the tradition he wished to represent and perpetuate. "I make a daily confession of my sins to that mighty one (Bach), and I endeavor to purify and strengthen myself through him," said Schumann in a letter to Keferstein January 31, 1840.

Enthusiasm for one's forebears never prevented any man of genius from creating new masterpieces. To my knowledge there is only one exception, the composer Porta. Highly esteemed by his contemporaries, he remained sterile for years, believing with a touching modesty that it would be otiose for him to compose new works. "I thought," he wrote, "it behoved me to guard from an unjust oblivion the works which the great composers have left to posterity, so apt as they are to their purpose, so full of beauty, delight, and charm." Let us remember that Porta (1530-1601) lived in the century in which we place the cradle of music or, I should say, at the time we could scarcely distinguish the first symptoms of what might necessitate a cradle. Yet he was speaking of remarkable works of the past which had fallen into an unjust oblivion!

Why fear the seduction of the past so much? Should we, like Ulysses, bind ourselves to the mainmast and plug our ears with wax so as not to succumb to the charm of the ancient sirens' songs? The Renaissance was but a return toward antiquity; yet it does not seem to have been disastrous to the arts. What would we say if poets, painters, or sculptors would demand in the name of an imaginary evolution that the Homers, Phidiases, and Raphaels be hidden from the "naïve crowd"?

Progressionists, as well as reactionaries, lack historical sense. Today out of a thousand musicians you would hardly find ten able to differentiate amidst the compositions of Lully, Rameau, or Gluck; and even if they did, they would have trouble in agreeing upon the superiority of anyone of the three. Therefore, it is a question of taste, not of progress.

Eternal beauty may be immutable, but all the same, it

changes a little every season, fortunately without following a pre-designed path toward an absolute ideal; that would lack charm and spontaneity.

> For time is like a fashionable host,
> That slightly shakes his parting guest by the hand,
> And with his arms outstretch'd, as he would fly,
> Grasps in the comer. . . .

as Shakespeare said in *Troilus and Cressida* (Act III, Sc. 3).

It is incredible how little we know of the history of our art compared to what poets, painters, and sculptors know of theirs. Of the Greek, very little has been investigated yet, but what works from the Middle Ages are familiar to us? Where do we hear the marvels of the Renaissance? And what about the works of the seventeenth century? Do we know them? But this does not prevent our affecting a profound disdain for all this unknown past.

The natives of the Fiji Islands kill their parents as soon as they become old. Such is the morality that governs music. We think that the works of the past have fallen into a deserved oblivion because they did not have the qualities necessary to resist the harsh bite of time. The evaluation of beauty and truth must be left to time, we say—as if time were not ourselves, but a kind of Heaven-sent infallible judge. We are the ones who reject the greatest masterpieces like worn out and outmoded clothes; time is merely our helper in letting them mildew, and its hazardous choice does not betray an expert judgment.

From time to time, on the occasion of a jubilee, we unearth a work with which we had lost contact for centuries; and if this music, after being tampered with, disfigured, and mutilated, still exhales some beauty and accelerates our heartbeats, we are surprised. How come? Beautiful music at that epoch? Three centuries ago? It is unbelievable! Yes, it did exist; I cannot say whether it was superior or inferior to that of today; but it filled with tenderness hearts that were well worth ours. And yet, even moved to tears, we never forget our superiority. "What charming naïveté in these pieces of Couperin!" write his modern admirers. Now, there is as much naïveté in the works of Couperin as in the *Tales* of Voltaire. In the eighteenth century, Couperin was considered a profound composer.

After a concert in which I played some marvelous works of Bach, Handel, Purcell, and Frescobaldi, a good old provincial composer, who later on sent me his compositions (and what compositions!), came to congratulate me. He seemed sincerely moved; "How beautiful," said he over and over; "you would think that these composers had a foreboding of us modern composers. Isn't it so, Madame?"

I do not wish to disparage the present, nor do I consider associating with certain eulogists of the past who at every turn find signs of decline in modern art and predict its imminent death. They probably find a kind of consolation in telling themselves that "the universe will end with them." (Anatole France, *Le Jardin d'Épicure*)

"I hope that reason, which sometimes weakens with old age, will keep me from the common mistake of extoling the past at the expense of the present," wrote Voltaire. And perhaps to feel youthful, he preferred to fall into a contrary exaggeration. In a letter to the Marquise du Deffand he said, "Prior to Lully, melody consisted only of cold, drawling, and lugubrious songs, or of a few *vaudevilles* like our modern carols; as for harmony, it was a rather coarse counterpoint. We came late in all respects." Thus, with a few strokes of the pen, Voltaire dismissed Lassus, Josquin des Prés, Goudimel, Jannequin, and all the masters of the French Renaissance, as well as the beauties of folk music with its irresistible tenderness, wit, and charm. Wary of eulogizing the past at the expense of the present, the most serious musicians and writers were led toward an opposite judgment. Ignorance did the rest, whence this disdain for the so-called naïveté and lightheartedness of former masters compared to the splendor and magnificence of ours. "Why should we care about the wrinkled art of our forebears now lying in their graves?" we are asked. "Why look back to try to explore the depth of their works?" No need to encourage people to be ignorant; adaptation to that is very easy and requires no strenuous effort. Dissatisfied with propagating this ignorance, one goes as far as making a dogma of it in the name of a so-called continuous and indefinite evolution.

To avoid being excommunicated by the believers in progress, I am delighted to rest my case on the authority of one of their greatest pioneers, Victor Hugo. "Beauty in art is its immunity to improvement. Art as such does not by itself advance or regress. Transformations in poetry are merely undulations of beauty useful to human motion. Art is not capable of intrinsic progress.

Retrogress as far as you please, from the palace of Versailles to the castle of Heidelberg; from the castle of Heidelberg to Notre-Dame de Paris; from there to the Alhambra; from the Alhambra to St. Sophia; from it to the Coliseum; from the Coliseum to the Acropolis, and from there to the Pyramids; you may go backward in centuries, but you will never regress in art. Art does not depend on any betterment of the future, on any transformation of language, or on any death or birth of an idiom. It is as pure, as complete, as divine amid total barbarism as it is in the midst of civilization. Such is the little known law of Art!"

The strictly ascending line drawn by the proponents of progress, which was supposed to lead us wisely step by step toward an ideal, is transformed into a series of fluctuations, of capricious undulations of diverse beauty, each of them perfect in itself, each unsurpassable. Bach's *Christmas Oratorio* cannot be bettered, nor can a small piece of Couperin. There are works before which we can only bow down because they have reached their supreme perfection. Those who try to go beyond are either illiterate or lacking in taste. They do not realize that "above the very good," as Théophile Gauthier said, "there is the too good," which is nearer the bad than we think. When certain animals slough off their skins each spring, it does not mean the new will be more beautiful than the old. "After Mozart came Beethoven; a new Mozart will be followed by a new Beethoven," said Schumann.

Life is always rich in beauty, the manifestations of which vary. Considered in a certain light, it may appear inferior or superior, but it never follows a predetermined path either toward continuous progress or toward regression. Taste may be refined or become corrupted and may later correct itself. Simplicity is sought after and is found; somebody starts beautiful traditions, others follow them; another tries to outdo them, and finally the exaggerated form is repudiated. In art we may prefer a certain epoch to another; we may find that a particular generation has given birth to more geniuses than has another. But to affirm that an evolved Palestrina would become the equal of Kuhnau, that an evolved Bach would give a Meyerbeer, and that all of them put together, if evolved, would be like any of our contemporaries would be pure ineptitude. Music is not like a schoolgirl who advances dutifully from one grade to the next and who has just successfully passed her examinations.

When a musician says that the harpsichord works of Rameau seem to him inferior to those of Couperin, he may be right, their genre, form, and character being close enough to allow an objective judgment. It would be more difficult to estimate the comparative worth of Palestrina and Brahms, for instance. But what would you say if someone, when asked the difference between Homer and Alexandre Dumas, answered without a moment of reflection, "Dumas is much superior because he came several centuries later"? I would say, "He is a musician!"

It is generally believed that progress is the greatest incentive for artists because they could not create if they did not have absolute faith in perfectibility. If this were true, why not ask us to believe that we smell flowers just to exercise our noses or that the sole aim of loving is to surpass in tenderness our grandmothers in order to attain perfection? One loves because one is in love, and one cultivates art because one loves it; even the most elevated speculations have nothing to do with that. The peasants from my Polish countryside sing admirable ancient folk songs and create new ones; they practice art without being poisoned by the vain pride of progress. Everything advances, everything progresses in life, we are told; the earth itself is not immobile. Yes, but fortunately it does not try with gigantic strides to reach the sun; it seems that while rotating around it the earth gets closer at times, farther at others, only to return to about the same place. Similarly art does not run in the direction of just one preconceived ideal; each generation has its own, and each generation reaches it more or less. From that spring the numerous aspects of beauty in works of art which are perfect in themselves, although different from each other. This is why we enjoy equally Homer and Shakespeare, Sophocles and Molière, Phidias and Michelangelo, Watteau and Rodin. Only with music are we supposed to accept the idea that the sole *raison d'être* of the classical composers was their being the precursors of the romantics, who, in turn, would become the springboard for new geniuses.

If this religion of progress went on, coupled with ignorance, we would read in two hundred years, "Ravel may be considered the father of music because the composers who preceded him, such as Beethoven and Wagner, were still in an embryonic stage and have fallen into a just oblivion."

AN HISTORIAN of music once said to me, "At every epoch the innovators' abuse of strong sonorities is met with disapproval. The eulogists of the past are not aware that in this gradual ascension toward loudness lies one of the greatest elements, if not the essential one, of musical progress." I had known for a long time this widespread theory, but it was the first time I had heard it stated with such clarity and precision. I must confess that I remained impressed.

Yet at various times throughout history the refinement of the music of the preceding period is praised while complaints are made about the violence of that of the day. La Fontaine criticized Lully for the uproar of his operas. Ramists saw Gluck as a German who came to France to harden ears with his constant din. "Since the seizure of the Bastille, music is made only with cannonade," said Grétry in his *Mémoires sur la Musique*. Considered as a prodigal son who, so to speak, threw thunderbolts out the windows, Berlioz in turn raised his voice against the abuses perpetrated by singers and composers; he went as far as to demand the promulgation of an ancient Chinese law which decreed the death penalty for every exaggerated use of tam-tam. Nietzsche said, "With a strong voice in the throat it is almost impossible to think subtly." And Gounod's comment was, "Good makes no noise, and noise does no good."

Despite the constant hostility toward expansion of sonority, our modern music, however, is outdoing that of the past in this respect. If power of sonority is recognized as one of the essential elements of our evolution, why should we reduce it to fit into the narrow confines of the past? Why not offer our progress and our advantages in homage to the ancient masters?

Yet if we wanted for the sake of historical truth to remain faithful to authentic sonorities, all we would have to do would be to decrease them gradually in proportion to the remoteness of the work to be performed. See the great advantages that would have! Unfortunately nothing is perfect on this earth. This theory so easy to adopt, so useful, and so flattering to our civilization has a little loophole; under the guise of correctness it is essentially false.

Is the music of Mozart and Haydn more powerful than that of Bach and Handel? Was eighteenth century music noisier than that of the seventeenth? All to the contrary.

In music history classes we are shown a chronological list of instruments and told that their sonorities increased in the same order, the clavichord being more powerful than the lute, the spinet more sonorous than the clavichord, the harpsichord stronger than the spinet, the square piano louder than the harpsichord, and the grand piano the loudest of all.

Except for the lute, I have played for years all the other instruments mentioned, and I can state that the spinet is not necessarily more powerful than the clavichord and that the square piano has always been weaker than the harpsichord. Here too, instead of an ascending line traced by progress, we see undulations. The idea that sonority was a kind of hardy plant, very feeble at first, which developed tremendously and attained today a strength unheard of in past centuries, is an error, fortunately for our sense of hearing.

Without going as far as to recall the legendary concerts at

Solomon's temple in which up to ten thousand performers took part, we see in the middle of the eighteenth century the famous concerts of Potemkin, the favorite of Catherine the Great. Suffering from neurasthenia, he ordered the bells of all the churches to peal at the same time, and he commissioned performances of works composed to his taste by Italian musicians. These were symphonies of sorts for full orchestras in which artillery salvos replaced ornaments.

At the gigantic concert given in 1615 at Dresden by command of the Elector of Saxony a certain Raposki from Cracow had a contrabass over twenty-four feet high carried on a wagon pulled by eight mules. A small ladder had been built so that the neck could be reached, and on the strings of this monstrous instrument one ran an enormous bow with all the might of one's arm. But this contraption did not seem enough; later came the grandiose idea of improvising a contrabass with the help of a windmill from which big cables were stretched; four men were needed to set them in vibration by means of a large piece of indented wood. On one side of the orchestra there was a great organ on which Father Serapion exerted himself with hands and feet; a few *bombardes* in battery replaced the kettle drums. The performance was worthy of these beautiful preparations; the prima donna Bigozzi from Milano sang so well and so long that she died three days later. G. Scoppio from Cremona, one of the ablest violinists of the time, performed the most difficult pieces of his repertoire holding his violin behind his back. But the applause for the day went to a double fugue depicting the battle of the Assyrians against the Israelites; it was played with such ardor that the foreign singers, who portrayed the Assyrians, fell into a quarrel with the choristers from Dresden, who represented the Israelites; and the chorus ended up in a real battle." (Lavoix, *Histoire de l'Instrumentation*, Paris, 1878)

In the *Currus Triomphalis*, dedicated to the Emperors of Germany by Rauch in 1648, the voices were supported by trumpets, violins, trombones, and horns; in addition, Rauch also used noisy war machinery, and the instrumentation of the concluding movement of his last motet included cannons and musketry. The title page of the original edition represented a concert of angels performing the work; thirteen trumpets and a cymbalist gathered about an organist were vanishing into a cloud of smoke vomited by three cannons ignited by an angel. The Emperor Ferdinand, surrounded by brilliant light, hovered majestically above this orchestra.

And to think that half a century later Wagner wrote only five strokes of cymbal and six rolls of triangle in all of *Tristan und Isolde!* No, let us not flatter ourselves; great noise was not invented by us. Just think of the charivaris of ages past:

> Listen to the sacred canticle;
> Let us hasten, howl;
> Let us have a charivari!
> Resound pots, pans, and cauldrons—
> Popular music.

Nordic people always had a marked predilection for noisy instruments. No festive occasion would take place without kettledrums and trumpets. England too excelled in this account. During Queen Elizabeth's repasts, a concert of twelve trumpets and two kettledrums with fifes and drums resounded in the hall. A manuscript preserved in the British Museum enumerates among the officers of the Crown at the court of Elizabeth in 1587 the following musicians:

10 trumpets	3 virginalists
2 flute players	(the virginal was the favorite
lutes, harps, singers	instrument of the Queen)
1 chief lutenist	3 drums
1 chief harpist	1 viol maker
1 bag-pipe, 1 rebec	1 organ builder
6 trombones, 8 viols	1 regal builder

Henry VIII and Edward IV supported almost as many instrumentalists.

If we rarely encounter these avalanches of sonorities in the music of the eighteenth century, principally in France and in Italy, it was not due to a rudimentary state of that music nor to any weakness of its composers, but to that refinement of taste which rejected all violence and emphatic uproar. "Avoid exaggerated sonorities" is the first advice that great musicians gave their pupils. As Karl Philipp Emanuel Bach said, "Music is meant to touch the heart, and the harpsichordist will not attain this if he thinks only of making noise."

The Baron de Tremont related in his memoirs that Haydn synthesized in a single word, *piano*, the ideal of musical execution; when he had his works performed, especially his quartets, he never ceased to repeat to his players, "Hush, hush!"

And to think that all the gapers at progress are deeply convinced that Haydn and Mozart would be infinitely flattered if they could hear their works heightened by tempestuous sonorities, the fruits of our immeasurable evolution!

It is only toward the end of the eighteenth century that tendency toward loudness can be noticed. The following anecdote about Cherubini is well known; being told of the death of one of his instrumentalists, he replied disdainfully, "Small sound!" Once though he heard himself being rudely reprimanded for one of his works, the *Funeral Pomp of General Hoche*, which was too loud. Bonaparte said to him, "You make too much noise; true sorrow is subdued." And later, at the height of romanticism, we find Chopin writing from Vienna, "One is so used here to the uproar of virtuosos . . . I foresee the criticisms I shall receive in the papers, all the more so since the daughter of one of the editors pounds mercilessly."

In a letter to Clara, Schumann wrote, "Art as you practice it, and as I often do myself at the piano while composing, this beautiful intimate tenderness—I would not give it up for all of Liszt's splendor, in which there is sometimes too much flashiness."

Force of sonority is neither a quality nor a defect for the simple reason that in music the amount of sound is quite a secondary consideration; it is its quality and its judicious use that count. To find our music superior because it is richer in powerful sonorities is like saying that certain modern paintings are superior to those of Watteau or Raphael, whose colorings were less violent. No, the power of sonority is no more a sign of progress than it is of decadence. It is intimately tied up with the taste and esthetic concepts of a generation, or, in one word, the style of an epoch.

3 〤 From Classicism to Romanticism

WHEN the public and even musicians speak of music of the past, they generally mean that of the eighteenth century; they think especially of some minuet, gavotte, or opera aria, which justifies their complaint that composers of that time were superficial.

True, eighteenth-century composers may seem superficial; but they were so out of refinement. Instead of wallowing in muddy waters, they preferred to flutter on the surface. "Seriousness is never gracious, nor is it attractive, being so close to severity, which is repulsive," said Voltaire. Instead of excessive sublimity, they favored pale and fugacious visions sweetly entwining the heart, soft elegance, pretty and piquant nothings, or smooth and happy sounds that cajole the ears. They accepted captivity if their chains, made of garlands of flowers, were not felt too much. To the tempests of the human heart they preferred the sprightliness of life, the gladness of beauty, or the solemnity of majestic spectacles. "Sorrow, you are not harmful," said the stoics. "You are not very beneficial either!" seem to answer the men of the eighteenth century. "Let us avoid it; let us not tire the world with our mourning and our grief!"

Gluck was criticized for his coarseness, his lack of lightness and elegance, but most of all, for his overindulgence in vehement accents and transports of sorrow. The object of art is not emotion alone, but also the pleasure that accompanies it. It is not enough that emotion be strong; it must also be pleasant. The Laocoön suffers, but does not wince. Mozart's ideas conformed with this perfectly. Delacroix quoted an excerpt from one of Mozart's letters which is a credo of a sort: "Violent passions must never be expressed to the point of provoking disgust; even in horrible situations music must never hurt the ears or cease to be music."

Brutalities had to be hidden, shrieks and moans set aside, as well as anything else that could be shocking to men trained to control the manifestations of their emotions. The so-called "vicious imitations," or the representation under gigantic outlines of that which was only great, was avoided. One did not build up to rudeness that which just had a virile character. "Do not mistake baroque for expressivity, nor harshness for energy; do not give a hideous picture of the passions you intend to describe—in a word, do not imitate French opera in which the tone of passion is more like shrieks of colic than like transports of love," said J. J. Rousseau in his *Dictionnaire de Musique*.

The basis of French taste in the eighteenth century was the moderation and serene nobility of Greek art. Romain Rolland was absolutely right when he said in "L'Opéra populaire à Venise" (*Mercure Musical*, January 15, 1906) that "most of the musical controversies—such as Ramists against Gluckists, Debussyists against Wagnerians—stem basically from the important subject of aristocratic art versus popular art." The principal merit of the music that was cultivated at the courts of kings and polished by a society always attentive to conventions and urbanity had to rest upon elegance, flexibility, and purity of taste. Hence its light and divinely frivolous gait, sometimes majestic, but always sparkling with grace and wit.

As Debussy said of *Hippolyte et Aricie* in *Le Figaro*, March

7, 1908, "Why do we not regret the passing of this charming way of writing music? We have lost it as well as the ability to find again the trail of Couperin. That music avoided all redundancy and it had wit; now we scarcely dare have wit for fear of lacking that grandeur toward which we are rushing breathlessly and quite often without success."

Did this music lack grandeur and virile accents? Do not ask a queen of such simple and refined beauty to surprise us by the strength of her muscles or the heaviness of her foot. Let us thank her for having swept by with majesty and divine grace.

But what about Bach? He was an exception; he was the precursor, the prophet who anticipated our epoch and our taste! And this idea that he, who dedicated his works to Frederick the Great and to the princes of his time, was nevertheless composing with today's public in mind is such a consecrated commonplace that I hardly dare fight it.

Has not Bach anticipated romanticism in his *Chromatic Fantasy?* Does not the fiery and tempestuous character of this piece foreshadow Beethoven and the whole sequence of geniuses who came after him? Bülow asserted it; other great musicians proclaimed it also, and now it is repeated almost everywhere. Yet if we must see a happy message in *The Chromatic Fantasy,* it is not Beethoven, Chopin, or Schumann whom it heralded, but composers much newer to us because they are little known, such as Bach's precursors, Frescobaldi, Buxtehude, the lutenists, and others.

Why would Bach have taken the trouble of guessing at the tastes that were to prevail centuries after his death when he could so easily draw all these characteristics, apparently romantic, from the works of his predecessors? He knew their works and copied them with the greatest reverence. Let us not be mistaken; Bach never tried to divine the tastes of future generations, nor did he follow all the ideas considered advanced in his century. Bach was rather conservative. When musicians began to develop a passion for opera in Germany, he preferred to remain faithful to his learned counterpoint and to the taste of masters of the preceding century. And in this may lie the reason for the limited success he enjoyed in his lifetime; his sons sometimes called him "old hat."

The romantics, who scorned ancient French music, appreciated the works of Bach more than those of Haydn or Mozart because they found in them the qualities dearest to them, grandeur and pathos. And yet they would have found the same qualities—with less genius perhaps—in almost all compositions of the seventeenth century and earlier because these qualities were not a modern invention.

If contemporaries of Josquin des Prés said that "no one knew better than he how to excite the affections of the soul through his songs," it must be believed that his music was not an empty aggregation of sounds to set the eardrums vibrating. Bonnet seems to have found in Lully's operas something more than an accumulation of sonorities pleasing to the ears. "Did he want to depict love?" he asked in his *Histoire de la Musique*. "No heart remained unmoved. And what melody! What naturalness! What harmony in his duos! Had he wished to express sorrow, even rocks would have moaned with him. Had he chosen to depict furor or revenge, no heart would have failed to experience secret tremors. If he had wished to create enchantment or to evoke the damned from the Inferno, souls would have been seized with horror and fright, etc."

Romain Rolland in his notes about Lully (*Mercure Musical*, 1907) quoted a story, mentioned in 1779 by François Le Prévost d'Exms, after Louis Racine. Lully, he said, vexed to hear that he owed all his success to the sweetness of Quinault and that he was unable to compose good music for energetic words, once sat down at the harpsichord and improvised a song on these verses from *Iphigénie*:

> A priest surrounded by a cruel crowd
> Will lay a criminal hand on my daughter,
> Tear apart her breast, and with a curious eye
> Consult the Gods in her palpitating heart.

"The listeners," he added, "thought they were witnessing this horrible spectacle, and the sounds that Lully joined to the words made their hair stand on end."

And what about the masters of the Renaissance?

> No, not you, Costeley, who among the best
> Practices the sweet art of selected music,

Who knows how to appease the anxious soul
with beautiful chords,
To excite it when dormant, to express its sorrow.
(J. A. de Baïf to Guillaume Costeley)

And what about the troubadours to whose influence is attributed the perfection of the works of Dante, Petrarch, Ariosto, and Tasso? And what about the bards who, harp in hand, spurred on the armies of Gaul? And we read about the surprising effects of Greek music that made Ulysses weep or incited Alexander to take arms. We may believe that this music was not solely concerned with an agreeable teasing of the auditory nerve.

It is true that the very concept of grandeur and pathos has changed, especially as far as the seventeenth and especially the eighteenth centuries are concerned. Today an emphatic and insistent vehemence able to captivate the attention and to strike it despotically without any reprieve is what is required. Formerly this language was tagged as plebeian and as mere showy eloquence. Quantz, Karl Philipp Emanuel Bach, and, above all, the French continuously advised against it.

About a score he did not like, Azevedo, a combative critic of the second half of the last century, used to say, "This work lacks *gendarmes*; it does not grip me."

In music of the past it was bad taste to indulge in the excessive use of *gendarmes*. As Boileau wrote:

I prefer a brook which slowly meanders
Through a meadow strewn with flowers
To an overflowing torrent which, in its stormy course,
Rolls, full of pebbles, onto a miry terrain.

"Sweet affections, those emotions which are merely touching, belong to the domain of pleasantness, where art has nothing to do. They hardly touch sensibility, applying to external nature only, and not at all to the inner one."

That was said by Schiller at the end of the eighteenth century. Any soil will become devitalized when subjected for a long time to the same culture. Probably those eternal twitterings of birds, those restrained emotions, and those pleasant folderols were becoming tiresome. The public, though, remained faithful to them and preferred to be agreeably titilated by all that was gay or sweetly melancholy rather than to be startled or strongly stirred. At least so Schiller declared in describing a concert audience of his time, a description conceived in an exaggerated romantic style: "All that is tender is favored; no matter how noisy a concert hall may be, silence reappears at once when a sentimental passage is played. Then an expression of sensuality bordering on bestiality ordinarily shows on all faces; eyes are drowned in rapture, gaping mouths are all desire; a voluptuous tremor invades the entire body; breathing is febrile; in one word, all the symptoms of intoxication."

From now on violent accents, insistent and impassioned, will be opposed to those light swoonings, to these caresses and thrills described by Schiller as signs of abominable drunkenness, although they hardly touch the soul. Extravagant or gigantic traits, unrestrained transports, overflows of admiration or outbursts of hatred will be preferred to justness, moderation, and wisdom. Excess always, always paroxysms! The redoubtable step that separates the sublime from the ridiculous was no longer feared; taken boldly, it went sometimes beyond limits. To lose one's head in an impetuous delirium and cause others to lose theirs by crushing their hearts and imaginations—such were the new trends. Breathing became possible only on the summits; grace, pleasure, wit, serenity—all that meant to charm or seduce —was proscribed; on the contrary, an explosive style and the ever-present idea of grandeur and suffering were in order. There was an esoteric contentment in exposing one's wounds and telling about one's scars. It was good taste to exaggerate everything and to fill the world with cries of distress.

Sensitive people bemoaned the corruption of taste; witty men poked fun at the poets who "compose tempests in a happy quietude" and who have "lifted mountains of foam hundreds of times with their pens."

After the presentation of Gluck's *Armide* La Harpe wrote: "I do not come to hear the cry of a man in pain. I expect the expression of sorrowful, not disagreeable, accents from a musician's artistry; I want it to flatter my ear while penetrating my heart and to blend the charm of a melody with the impression I feel. I want to carry away in my memory a harmonious lament which will long continue to echo in my ear and will leave a desire to be heard again. . . . If I hear but clamors of despair or convulsive moans, I may find them very realistic, so realistic in fact that I shall not want to remember them." (*Lettres de Gluck et de Weber*, Paris, 1870)

Later and even in Germany, where this genre was more likely to take root, refined minds such as Goethe's did not submit willingly to this tyranny of grief. On January 22, 1808, he wrote to Zelter: "My little Institution is doing well; but the young people, as you surely know, are very fond of stepping out of the rut, and each one fancies himself better off when he is singing some pitiful or mournful lament of unrequited love as a solo. I allow such things toward the end of each session, and at the same time execrate men like Mattheson, Salis, Tiedge, and the clergy in a body, who show us heavy Germans, even in songs, a path beyond the world, which we leave quickly enough, as it is. Add to this that musicians themselves are often hypochondriacal and that even joyous music may dispose to melancholy." (Translation A. D. Coleridge, London, 1887)

But like children lulled to sleep for so long with pleasant and sprightly tales, one became attracted by stories full of ghosts and terror. And with their eagerness for all that saddens, women were perhaps the first to seek those tragic and heart-rending emotions. "There is one thing in the world that does me some good," wrote Mademoiselle de Lespinasse. "It is music. But others would call it pain. I would like to hear ten times a day the aria 'J'ai perdu mon Eurydice'; it tears me apart, but makes me enjoy all I regret."

Elsewhere, also concerning Gluck, she wrote, "This music drives me insane; my soul hungers for this kind of sorrow." It did not prevent her, though, from retaining the taste of her time nor from writing about a heroic ballet by Marmontel and Grétry, "My friend Grétry should confine himself to the sweet, pleasant, sentient, and witty genre. It would be quite enough for him; when one is well built, although of small size, it is dangerous and certainly ridiculous to walk on stilts."

The abundance of marvelous masterpieces that Romanticism has left us shows once more the fallacy of all the dictatorial precepts of beauty that arbiters of taste want to impose upon us in the name of tradition or of progress. Romanticism most certainly had its incomparable virtues; but like any other esthetic movement it failed by the defect of its qualities. Enlargements that make everything appear great and sublime, as though they were seen through a magnifying glass, can tire us just as much as the refinement and daintiness that prevailed a century before. In the long run, everything becomes blunted. A too complete adherence to the prejudice of grandiosity must produce finally a contrary effect.

I do not wish in the least to deprecate the grandeur of romanticism; we do not demand of Watteau the power of Michelangelo; Wagner has qualities and defects different from those of Mozart or Couperin.

Is classical taste making a comeback? Perhaps. One of the greatest Germans of the nineteenth century, Friedrich Nietzsche, wrote in *The Joyful Wisdom* (Autumn 1886): "How the theatrical cry of passion now pains our ears, how estranged from our taste has become all the romantic riot and sensuous bustle which the cultured populace love—together with their aspirations after the exalted, the elevated, and the intricate. No, if we convalescents need an art at all, it is another art, a mocking, light, volatile, divinely serene, and divinely ingenious art which blazes up like a clear flame into a cloudless Heaven! We, at last, know better what is first necessary for that—namely, cheerfulness, every kind of cheerfulness, my friends!" (Translation Thomas Common, Edinburgh, 1910)

If I am not mistaken, romanticism is departing with a noisy farewell in the person of a few pundits of progress who continue to exaggerate the Wagnerian genre; this, I should hope, will not prevent their creating masterpieces. Let us not emulate those fashionable hosts, of whom Shakespeare speaks, who take leave negligently of the departing guest. Let us bow down, very low. Romanticism gave us strong emotions and unforgettable ecstasies; it awoke in us unbounded ideas and supreme flights of fancy; it flattered our palate with tart and bitter fruit, which seemed so good after an overabundance of sweetness; it brushed our skin with the coarse caresses of a wild beast. May all the centuries to come look with full respect and envy upon its grandeur, which is still hovering sovereignly.

Let us not say adieu, but au revoir to romanticism because soon it will come back adorned with new attractions and under a changed name. Some will call it evolution or a gigantic step forward; others will denounce the corruption of taste; but the crowd will continue until further orders to prostrate itself before yesterday's genius.

ED. NOTE: In the last years of her life Wanda Landowska often said, "What a pity that I shall not live long enough to witness the return to romanticism!"

And on September 8, 1948, she dictated this: "To judge romanticism we must first silence the sentimental jeremiads and all that stupid crowds misunderstood for true romanticism; we must let the voice of the most authentic romanticist, Chopin, pour out in all its purity. In short, there is romanticism, and there is this foam produced by fatuous agitators who contributed in transforming a movement, very beautiful in itself, into an unintelligible and turbid jargon.

"To embrace an epoch in all its splendor and truth, to understand the fluctuations of taste, one needs perspective. Today we are placed far enough away to give romantic effusions and roarings their just value. Let us not forget the contempt of Lully's contemporaries for the polyphonic works of the Renaissance, and let us keep from making the same mistake about authentic romanticism."

4 Innovations

*There is nothing sensible or witty that has not
already been thought of by somebody else;
there remains only to think it anew.—Goethe*

In 1907 or 1908 I attended a lecture on Beethoven. The lecturer
spoke at great length of the innovations Beethoven introduced
into music. "He was the first who dared tear down existing
barriers; he bent all forms; he created the symphony, enlarged
the domain of the sonata, invented new forms; with his *Pastoral
Symphony*, he was the first to introduce the descriptive genre,
thus giving us a foretaste of Wagner," and so forth. . . .

So carried away by his desire to present Beethoven as a kind
of inventor whose first concern was the discovery of some novelty
and whose sole aim was to obliterate all impediments, all molds
of the past, the lecturer almost forgot to tell us that Beethoven
was also an immense musical genius and an incomparable poet.
How fortunate that this genius had other claims to glory than

those mentioned by the lecturer because, as an innovator, he broke away from a very few things, accepting most of the time with indifference the formulas bequeathed to him by tradition. He used the sonata form which had previously exasperated Fontenelle, who said, "Sonata, what do you want of me?" Did he modify it completely? No; the principal alterations had already been made by Karl Philipp Emanuel Bach. But wasn't it said that he added a new movement?

The beauty of Beethoven's sonatas resides in their content and not in the so-called novelty of their outlines; nor does it lie in the evolution from minuet to scherzo. In his first sonatas, and even in the *Pathétique*, Op. 13, the span is only five octaves at a time when pianofortes with five and a half, even six octaves, were already in use; Beethoven could not have ignored that. He preferred to be satisfied with the instrument he had at his disposal and to contain his inspiration within five octaves, even if it meant folding backward a few passages, an effect not lacking in charm. Later he conformed to the new instruments. But at no time do we find in his works this strained search for novelty for which he is so often glorified. The following anecdote must have contributed somewhat to this opinion:

"One day Beethoven, at the organ, played several consecutive fifths; the singer Keller exclaimed, 'It is wrong, it is wrong!'

"Beethoven repeated the musical phrase, and, turning toward Ries, he asked, 'Does that not sound good?'

" 'Certainly,'' replied the choirmaster, 'but successions of fifths are forbidden by the most elementary rules.' All the others concurred.

" 'Then, I shall allow them!' replied young Beethoven."

If he gave in to modifications and innovations, it was necessitated by his inspiration; it was not to effect a premeditated revolution of form.

Palestrina was not an innovator in any genre; he conformed to all traditions, but that did not prevent his being deeply original. The greatest reformer, Wagner, knelt before Palestrina's sublimity and expressive richness.

The apotheosis of innovation in the domain of form has today reached its zenith; every great composer is introduced as a breaker of molds and as the creator of a new genre. In past centuries composers took good care not to parade their innovations. Bach did not try to innovate, and even Gluck, considered a great reformer, said in the dedicatory epistle to the Grand Duke of Tuscany that "he attached no value to the discovery of a novelty, unless it was naturally required by the situation and tied to the expression." It was proof of good taste, on the contrary, not to venture into the alluring glitter of contingency; one would rather use the forms honored by preceding masters from whom, not only the genre, but even themes were borrowed. Twenty masses had been written upon the words of a popular song, L'Homme Armé, before Palestrina composed two more masses, extremely beautiful, on the same subject.

In Musurgia, a theoretical work, its author, Athanasias Kircher, who was greatly esteemed by Bach, wrote in 1650: "Who will ever create anything honorable in poetry, even a born poet, if he has not read and learned to imitate those excellent Coryphaei of Virgil, Ovid, and others? What variety can we expect from our musicians if, neglecting imitation, they go no further than their own personal discoveries? None of the Italian poets can ever hope to attain any distinguished facility in their national poetical language if they have not previously fixed in their minds and in their memories the famous writings of Petrarch, Dante, Tasso, Ariosto, Sannazaro, and innumerable other poets. No one can pretend to any perfection in painting if one has not applied oneself diligently to imitating the works left by A. Dürer, Raphael d'Urbino, Michelangelo Buonarroti, Guido Reni, Rubens, and other princes of the art. Who today can approach the talent and skill of Josquin des Prés, Albrecht, or Cipriano de Rore? Who among the moderns can weave harmonies with the ingenuity of Orlando, Morales, or Palestrina?"

The great merit of Kuhnau, we are taught, was being the originator of the primitive sonata. Now, not only did he refrain from considering that a title for glory, he also stated in his preface that the invention of program music was not his. The illustrious Froberger and other excellent composers had employed it before, and he himself had heard a sonata in the same style entitled La Medica, which was the work of a great composer believed to be Kerll."

Composers of the past never concealed their preference for the formulas of their predecessors, nor did they seem eager to discover new ones. Perhaps they did find, as Anatole France said, that the old prejudices are less pernicious than the new ones; time, in wearing them out, polished them; or, as Jean d'Udine wrote in the *Courrier Musical* (1906), "All forms are equally good for expressing our emotions; it is our emotions that are not equally sharp and profound."

Jean-Jacques Rousseau predicted that the unnatural fad for the sonata would not last and that soon one would be rid of all this trash—another unrealized prophecy, since this trash was just being revived. Today the sonata is loved more than ever; this appanage of musical prose is considered a profound and sublime form, although I cannot say why for sure. On the other hand, the concerto, even Beethoven's or Mozart's, is being thrown off its pedestal. Why? Because it is only an accompaniment intended to bring a soloist into prominence instead of being a collective manifestation. Then let us suppress Hamlet or indeed all of Shakespeare's dramas in which the hero is surrounded by characters intended to set him off; let us suppress all the musical plays, for the concerto is like a small opera in which the principal role is played by the soloist.

The concept of beauty is too delicate to withstand an inflexible adherence to the principles of everyday logic. There is no such thing as a superior or an inferior form; all are superior in the hands of a genius. Innovation in itself is of little interest. Let us say with Voltaire: "Taste may become spoiled in a nation; this misfortune ordinarily occurs after centuries of perfection, and artists, fearing to be mere imitators, look for divergent roads. Innovators bring a change, but not always progress or improvement in taste. The loud criticisms of Wagner's reforms made believe that the world would either collapse or rise to Heaven after this revolution, which, after all, was merely in line with national taste. Musical painting? It already existed before Palestrina. Leitmotiv? It can be found, although in a more modest form, in harpsichord pieces of the seventeenth century. Forms which were previously circumscribed and lacked boldness were simply enlarged and consolidated. This was generally true in the eighteenth century, although greatness, spaciousness, and solidity were not then esthetic terms; only nobility, grace, and sweetness were required in works of art. Brevity was considered a condition of beauty; taste was not being hectored to a degree demanding voluminous productions from an elegant pen. Quantz, in his

Essay, never tired of advocating brevity in composition. "It is better if listeners find a piece too short rather than too long. A concerto grosso should never exceed a quarter of an hour: five minutes for the first part, five to six for the adagio, and three to four minutes for the last movement." Unending works suggesting a feeling of infinity because of their duration were not appreciated. This did not prevent anyone's enjoying spectacles over four hours long, insofar as their constituent numbers were of reasonable length. "With our great sorrows let us make little songs," said Heine, who never was a true romantic. Camille Mauclair, in *Les Idées et le Symbolisme de Rodin*, explained very vividly that "when a thing is well organized, its grandeur lies in the model, not in the size . . . the shape of a pear or of an apple is as great as that of the celestial sphere. The truthful harmony and proportions of surfaces or of volumes are essential notions which obviate the idea of size. Therefore, the resplendence of this truth is such that, for want of a better word to express it, we call it ideal."

Other fallacies about innovations concern the notation of music. If Rousseau had left us masterpieces in the figured writing he expounded, we might have adopted his system and claimed it as evolutionary, just as we now consider modern writing progressive in comparison to that of former times.

In other instances, though, modern musical system has introduced an enrichment of means, as in extending the range of usable musical sounds. In Palestrina's works the compass rarely exceeds two octaves and a fifth. As a general rule, the ancients liked to restrain the motions of their music within a limited space; all that overstepped the average bounds was considered strained. Obviously, our extended system has aerated the congested atmosphere of restricted confines and has permitted new combinations and formerly unknown effects. Yet, "I do not know if we have much reason to congratulate ourselves," wrote d'Alembert in the *Encyclopédie*. "Was it such a great misfortune that ancient music could supply only full and harmonious sounds out of a beautiful medium range? Voices sang without being strained; stringed instruments did not constantly mew toward the bridge. Can the heart be touched by false and muted sounds drawn from the neck or by the yelping of voices stretched beyond their capabilities?"

Timid attempts, however, had already been made in the sixteenth century to stretch the span of voices. "I have no doubt," wrote Costeley, "that your Lordship will find it strange that in some of my songs I have exceeded the precise and more common limits of the tonalities as required by the rules of which I am not ignorant; to that I answer: I did it so as not to leave idle the rare compass of the beautiful voices which our very Christian, very magnanimous and exceptionally well-born King of France has the pleasure of employing in his Chamber, as they themselves have the happiness of going toward him; I did it, however, without straying from the tonality and only to make the music airier."

Italian violinists often exceeded the average span and were criticized for "making the violin whistle up at the neck and for imitating somnambulists who climb on walls; they took advantage of the ignorance and bad taste of the public, who applaud these disorders."

In writing for violin, Handel, Bach, and all the classic masters never exceeded three octaves (the highest note being an F two octaves and a fourth above middle C), save for very rare exceptions—for instance, in the sonata opening the *Trionfo del Tempo*; there, the violin goes up to an A two octaves and a sixth above middle C.

Even Haydn and Mozart remained within this range in their orchestral works.

5 \ Vocal and Instrumental Music

INSTRUMENTAL music has made enormous progress. This is undeniable. Today we are more sensitive to the nuances of timbre,
we understand better the properties of instruments, and we use
them with an ease previously unknown. Orchestral music has
developed in a prodigious way. This is a fact. It ensues that
symphonic and instrumental music in general are considered
the sublimest manifestations of art. Formerly, the same thing
was said about vocal music. "No instrumental music," wrote
Byrd, "can be compared with the human voice." This idea did
not belong exclusively to the great English virginalist. It was
a popular one dating from the Middle Ages; *musica id ars can-
tandi*. It was believed that a beautiful human voice penetrated
the soul more directly and more naturally than did sounds produced by organs, viols, or lutes. Ancient sacred music, extolled
by Wagner for its sublimity, richness, and inexpressible beauty,

had for its unique sonorous expression an ensemble of human voices. Instruments were used occasionally to sustain the voices or to replace those which might be missing.

We find instrumental music in the fifteenth and sixteenth centuries, but essentially it was vocal music performed by instruments instead of voices. Instrumental music did not win a right to equality before the end of the seventeenth century. It was only then that it began to develop its own character.

We know the cult the Italians had for vocal music. As for the Germans, voice was always their weak point. Wagner well acknowledged it when he wrote, "Nature deprived the Germans of this inclination for vocal art, or rather, for this vocalization, full of suppleness and grace, with which the Italians are endowed at birth." This is corroborated by Albert Schweitzer. Speaking of the *aria en ritournelle* in Bach's works, he said, "Unconsciously Bach sinned toward the genius of German music. In siding with Italian art, he stopped German art short on the road leading to the kind of music Wagner eventually realized." Naturally, when the Germans began to liberate themselves from the exigencies of foreign taste, they gave free rein to their national inclination for instrumental music.

Today primary interest is in the orchestra, not in the voice. This is the opposite of the esthetic concept of Lully's time, when voice was always the most important instrument to express deep emotion. "Your hero is dying of love and sorrow," wrote Lecerf de la Viéville, "or so the words say; but if his singing does not concur or is not touching, then I shall not take any interest in his fate. . . . Yes, but the accompaniment would make rocks split. . . . Pleasing compensation! Is the orchestra the hero? No, the singer is. Therefore, let the singer be touching; let his expressive and tender singing depict what he suffers; and let him not delegate the task of moving me to the orchestra, which is there only by grace and accident." (Romain Rolland, "Notes sur Lully," *S.I.M.* 1907)

Doni clearly defined this idea when he said that the orchestra must be adequate to sustain the voice, but should not be so arresting as to distract the listener and prevent his giving complete attention to the singer.

This subject is a breeder of dissension; it attracts unending quarrels from the amateurs of melody.

Toward the end of the seventeenth century the accompaniment and the orchestration of the Italians were found too noisy and too complicated. Fifty years later Italy was praised ecstatically; for there, a voice, even a weak one supported only by a few chords, and without the assistance of a noisy orchestra, carried all feelings to the soul.

"What!" wrote D'Alembert in *l'Encyclopédie*; "this chaos, this confusion of parts, this multitude of various instruments which seem to insult each other, this din in the accompaniment which covers the voice without supporting it—does all this make for true beauty in music? Let us consider our contemporary Italians. See their sobriety in the chords, their choice of harmony! Truly their operas are only duos, and all Europe admires and imitates them."

Rameau is criticized for drowning beautiful song "in a too strong accumulation of chords and ornaments" and Gluck for failing to excel in melody and for making trumpets resound, strings rumble, and voices bellow, so that the faults of his Teutonic modulations were covered by the uproar of the orchestra.

In a letter to M. de La Harpe, a masterpiece of wit, Gluck promised to compose anew all his operas. "I shall scrupulously banish all noisy instruments such as cymbals and trumpets. In my orchestra I want only oboes, flutes, horns, and violins, with *sordini*, of course. . . . I want Armide, in her despair, to sing an aria so 'regular,' so periodical, and at the same time so tender that the most delicate little lass will be able to hear it without the slightest irritation of her nerves. If some ill-intended person dared to say to me, 'Sir, pay attention to the fact that the furious Armide must not express herself as a love-inebriated Armide,' I would answer, 'Sir, I do not wish to offend the ear of M. de La Harpe; I do not want to counterfeit nature; I wish to embellish it; instead of having Armide shriek, I want her to enchant you.'"

A poet of the time, too, pitied the poor opera singer:

> One hundred and fifty instruments, fed with colophany,
> Seem to take pleasure in forcing their tone;
> And these feeble singers, vanquished, annihilated,
> Succumb to terribly roaring tutti.
>
> Berchoux, *La Dance*, Paris, 1808

"Now that instruments are the most important part of music," said Rousseau, "sonatas as well as all kinds of symphonies are extremely fashionable; the voice is merely its accessory, and singing accompanies the accompaniment."

Although he insisted on being regarded as a pupil of Bach, Johann Friedrich Doles took good care to instruct his readers that he had not forgotten in his counterpoint exercises "the sweet and touching melody for which Graun's and Hasse's works were the models."

In the dedication of his first piece addressed to the wife of Gottschec, Johann Ludwig Krebs, the favorite pupil of Bach, professed simplicity in compliance with the taste of the day. Mattheson gave recipes for producing easy melodies. Marpurg, on the contrary, protested the invasion of effeminate songs by fashionable composers and of perpetually jumpy melodies worthy at their best of street singers. He prescribed a renaissance of harmony and a return to fugue and counterpoint, "a word that sounds bad to our modern ears." (*Abhandlung von der Fuge,* Berlin, 1753)

The character of musical poetry resides in the melody, said others; it can be found in all French pieces for viol or harpsichord. The attribute of musical prose is harmony. Sonatas are musical prose.

Some scoffed at Grétry's orchestration where "a six-horse carriage could pass between the first violin and the bass." Others complained of the too bosky, too rich, and too wearisome orchestration of the Germans.

Italy was laughed at because there taste required the sacrifice of verisimilitude for the pleasure of hearing a brilliant voice flutter on a syllable and because the orchestra, according to Wagner's genial definition, resembled an immense guitar. But Wagner was accused of killing the voice; modern lied was deprecated for being drowned in a torrent of harmonies and dissonances, the complexity of which would be sufficient to sustain a symphony; the singer's role would then be limited to accompanying his own accompaniment with a few indistinct cries.

The perfecting of instrumental music lends itself to abuse, as does any effort toward perfection. Past centuries ignored the amplitude of our orchestration, but they possessed other qualities that we no longer have, not to mention that instrumental progress has been accomplished to the detriment of vocal music.

The Eighteenth-Century Orchestra

In the eighteenth century average orchestras were composed of about forty musicians for the opera and twenty for concerts.

The opera of the King of Poland in Dresden, conducted by the illustrious Hasse, was considered by Rousseau to have the greatest number of musicians, distributed in the best manner, and forming the most perfect ensemble; there were thirty-nine instrumentalists, two stands for trumpets and kettledrums, and two harpsichords. Wind instruments were in the same proportion as the strings.

In 1731 the Music Academy of Strasbourg had twenty appointed musicians thus divided: six violins, one alto, two cellos, one bass, two flutes, two oboes, two bassoons, two horns, two trumpets, and with kettledrums in addition.

At the court of Wilhelm Ernst von Sachsen-Weimar, Bach had at his disposal twenty-two performers, including singers, each of whom also played one and sometimes several different instruments. Six boy choristers joined them, and for great ceremonies the *Stadtmusiker* (town musicians) supplemented the court musicians.

In his memorandum of August 23, 1730, Bach himself set the number of singers at twelve and instrumentalists at eighteen, besides the organist. It is interesting to notice the proportion that Bach kept between singers and instrumentalists; he never tried to make the voices dominate. Handel, on the contrary, always avoided covering the voices with the orchestra, although the number of his singers did not surpass that of the instrumentalists; he used the organ more sparingly than Bach did.

In the first half of the eighteenth century, the Treasurer of State, La Boissière, wrote to Mellier, manager of the Music Academy of Nantes, "You are already in business, and you employ twenty-four musicians; it is a great many if they are good. We have only seventeen at our Italian Academy." (Lionel de La Laurencie, *L'Académie de Musique et le Concert de Nantes*, Paris, 1906)

The maximum number of instrumentalists mentioned by

Quantz did not exceed thirty-five. Haydn's orchestra at Esterhazy numbered from sixteen to twenty-two performers: four to six violins, two altos, two contrabasses, one cello. The rest was composed of wind instruments—flutes, oboes, bassoons, horns (often four of them), and later clarinets—almost as many winds as strings.

We certainly can find larger orchestras, even in the seventeenth century, but they are rare exceptions.

Louis XIV continuously added to his body of musicians, which eventually reached a total of twenty-six singers and instrumentalists. This prompted La Fontaine to say in his Epistle to M. de Nyert in 1677:

> All his entertainments are war-inspired;
> His instrumental concerts have the noise of thunder,
> And his vocal concerts resemble the outbursts
> Made by the shouts of soldiers in a fighting day.
> It is no longer the season for Raimond and Hilaire
> To please; there must be twenty harpsichords
> and a hundred violins.

This should not be surprising, because the King's twenty-four violinists had not only an adequate strength of sonority; but those who had listened to them said they had never heard "more affecting or more powerful music" (Père Mersenne). And in his book on the tuning of the spinet, Jean Denis related the miraculous cure effected upon a young girl's melancholy by the powerful bowing of the King's violinists.

With each enlargement of the orchestra, we hear new criticisms and new complaints. Toward 1740 the noise and bad taste of concerts were deplored:

> Our concerts do not affect us anymore,
> Unless the monstrous assembly
> Of twenty superfluous instruments
> Makes of them a bacchic din.
>   *Mercure* 1739.

There were some very noisy spectacles toward the end of the eighteenth century, but they were solemn festivities in which more care was bestowed upon decorative splendor than upon the artistic value of the performance.

In 1786 Bach's successor, Hiller, staged Handel's *Messiah* in the Domkirche in Berlin with one hundred eighteen singers and one hundred eighty-four instrumentalists, an organist, and a harpsichordist.

On December 23, 1797, one hundred fifty-six musicians and as many choristers, with a harpsichordist accompanying the recitatives—in all, three hundred thirteen artists—took part in a solemn presentation of *The Creation* at the Paris Opéra; it was attended by Bonaparte, then First Consul. An infernal machine exploded before the performance, probably to warn the century about to begin of the futility of exaggerated noise and to prove that a can of explosives may produce more din than three hundred thirteen musicians.

Handel was accused of using an exaggerated number of performers, and Quantz wrote in his memoirs that Handel's orchestra was unbearably powerful. But Handel was aware of the number of players he was writing for, and he organized them according to his judgment. He may have displeased Quantz by using more instrumentalists than was customary, but in so doing, he was not altering the ideas, the style, or the character of his own genial compositions.

Today by increasing threefold the ancient instrumentation, the most beautiful thoughts are often disfigured; confusion among the voices occurs, and soloists are overpowered. Instead of being supported, they must fight to make themselves heard. Such unusual enlargements would mean little if only proportions between the various groups of instruments would be observed.

In Italy, in the seventeenth century, instrumentation was reduced almost exclusively to strings, and in the second half of that century wind instruments even disappeared completely. In France, at the time of Cambert, the originator of French opera, the instrumental body was based on the group of strings; a few flute passages were introduced to brighten slightly this monotonous mist and to throw some highlights of color upon this *grisaille*.

Lully, too, built the core of his orchestra around violins, but in his scores we also find, besides the flute, a few trumpets, kettledrums, oboes, bassoons, hunting horns, guitars, bagpipes, and for the ballets, *tambours de basque*, castanets, and so forth.

In the seventeenth century Praetorius left instructions for the different ways of varying the accompaniment of choral singing; they continued to be used until Bach's time. Wind instruments were employed in equal number with strings, and choirmasters alternated them to avoid monotony.

Although we still find a few composers favoring violins in eighteenth-century Italy, it was wind instruments that played the significant role in Germany and France. The importance trumpets had in Handel's orchestra and the vigor of their blaring are well known. The oboe was his favorite instrument; trombones, horns, cornets, flutes—straight and *traversières*, large and small—oboes, bassoons, and contra-bassoons were part of his orchestra. In Rameau's, the winds entered in great number.

Bach's instrumentation was even more varied because of the diversity of instruments he employed. He gave a preponderant place to coloration, relying on the whim of his genius for the use of the various timbres. Sometimes violins were eliminated altogether, sometimes winds. He made a greater use of trombones than Handel did, especially for choral accompaniment. It is regrettable that Lavoix in his book on the history of instrumentation did not indicate the exact number of instruments which comprised the orchestras of Bach and Handel. Fortunately, Quantz told us the proportion necessary to form an ideal ensemble. I have chosen among the examples he quoted one that is average: against eight violins, two altos, two cellos, and one contra-violin there were two oboes, two flutes, two bassoons, and a hunting horn *ad libitum*. Since Quantz always professed moderation concerning the volume of sonority, the proportion of wind instruments he specified would seem rather too modest. As we have seen before, strings and winds were about equal in number in the orchestras of operas and academies.

In our modern performances, strings are doubled or tripled, while the proportion of winds not only remains the same, but often their number is even reduced. I once played a Mozart concerto in which, against twenty violins, there was scarcely one flute; I say "scarcely" because the flutist never failed to miss his entrance.

By depriving the ancient orchestra of the flamboyant sonorities of the oboes, the sweetness of the flutes, the pastoral verdancy of the hunting horns, the jubilation of the trumpets, one destroys its entire coloration, its airy, ethereal, and luminous character. It has already been impaired enough by the suppression of admirable instruments such as the *oboe d'amore,* the hunting horn, and the whole family of viols, whose only fault was to have gone out of fashion, and by the addition of new instruments for the dubious purpose of rejuvenating the work.

We pretend to endow ancient composers with the extraordinary progress of our instrumentation. But Wagner, to whom this progress is largely due, said, "The application of modern procedures of instrumentation would be the surest means of disfiguring the theme and the character of works of the past."

As for Bach, he made small groups of instruments of the same family answer each other and sometimes unite in tutti. The string quartet formed one group, the oboes and bassoons another, the brasses a third, and the trumpets and kettledrums a fourth. By enlarging one group to the detriment of another, we make the work limp, and we deprive it of the entire harmony of its construction as well as of the contrapuntal character of its instrumentation.

I once attended a performance of Bach's *St. Matthew Passion* under the direction of a remarkable conductor who had at his disposal excellent soloists and choirs. While the number of soloists remained evidently the same as in Bach's time, the orchestra was doubled, even tripled, and the choruses were increased tenfold. It was obvious that these immense choruses were crushing the soloists under their weight and that the polyphonic equilibrium was destroyed. Even without probing deeply into musicology, let alone into faithfulness of execution, we know that in Bach's time choristers did not dominate and that they were rather inferior in number to the instrumentalists. I was told that this reinforcement of sonority is a consequence of the large size of our concert halls. If this were true in this instance, why was not the proportion among the various groups observed?

The Sistine Chapel had only a small ancient organ and a very restricted choir; harpsichord accompaniments were heard in the largest churches in the seventeenth and eighteenth centuries. And, after all, who is urging us to favor these abominable "abysses for receipts" as Berlioz called them? "They have always been responsible for the howlings of tenors, bassos, and sopranos at the opera; they have made the most famous singers deserve being called bulls, peacocks, and guinea fowls by simple people accustomed to giving things their rightful names."

If solo voices can be heard even when they are squeezed between immense choruses and smothered by two large orchestras, we certainly would find sufficient the strength of a few dozen beautiful voices singing together; and from among three hundred excellent choristers, a choice of about forty admirable ones could be easily made.

The true reason for the enlargement of orchestras and choruses does not lie in the size of the concert halls. In the musical esthetic of our day, the important term "a·great deal of" presents an irresistible attraction to the masses, and each manager is very happy when he can advertise:

"Great Festival! Mammoth Concert! Five Hundred Performers!"

6　French and Italian Music —
Influence on the Germans

"THE FRENCH have no music and cannot have any, but if they ever do, it will be all the worse for them." Such was Rousseau's solemn declaration in his letter on French music (1753).

In his *Apologie de la Musique Française* (1754), L'Abbé Laugier took an opposite view; he defended the elegant simplicity of Lully which had delighted music lovers for a whole century, as well as the touching quality of Clérambault's recitatives, the meditative charm of Lalande, and the lively and spontaneous spirit of Campra. Dissertations, epigrams in verse and in prose, pamphlets, which either defended French music or attacked the Italian, poured in from everywhere.

To the Genovese who will answer?
The public with vain murmurs,
The writers with insults,
But Rameau with an opera.

To avenge French music of the ridicule that the bilious philosopher had thrown at it, Rameau not only composed an opera,
he also wrote his "Observations on Our Instinct for Music"
(1754). Many others also defended French music. But Rousseau's
authority was reinforced by the whole army of the Encyclopedists.
Although the champions of French art, gathered under the name
of "The Queen's Corner," thought they had won the war over
their opponents, the "Buffoons," the accusations of the Genovese
continued for a long time to weigh upon French music.

It has interested me to investigate the opinions of the Germans of the eighteenth century on this question. To which flag
did they pledge allegiance, the Italian or the French?

With the exception of Gluck, none of the Germans took part
openly in the quarrel between the Italians and the French, who, to
be sure, called it the "querelle d'Allemands" (German quarrel)!
Gluck, who had just arrived from Italy and was still uninformed
about French music, wrote a letter to the editor of the *Mercure
de France* saying, "The study I made of the writings on music
by the famous Rousseau of Geneva and, particularly, the letter in
which he analyzes the monologue of Lully's *Armide* proved to me
the sublimity of his knowledge and the sureness of his taste and
filled me with admiration." But in a letter to M. de la Harpe, a
few years later, he admitted that in reading through the scores of
French operas of preceding periods, he found in them enough
real beauty to believe that the French had in themselves their
own resources.

The war of the Buffoons, which broke out the year of Bach's
death, was not the first of its kind. The fight between French and
Italian musicians had already started at the time of Charlemagne,
who brought back from Rome a group of musicians, thus thoroughly displeasing the French (Bonnet, *Histoire de la Musique*,
1715). In the first years of the eighteenth century, a significant
quarrel, which had some repercussions abroad, broke out during
Bach's lifetime after the arrival in Paris of Italian singers whom
Mazarin had engaged to play the *Orfeo* of Luigi Rossi.

L'Abbé Raguenet having raved about Italian music in his *Parallèle des Italiens et des Français en ce qui regarde la musique et les opéras*, Paris, 1702, Lecerf de la Viéville answered in 1705 by defending French music. Ten years later Bonnet devoted a whole chapter in his *History of Music* to the superiority of the French at the expense of the Italians.

Mattheson knew these writings, and the quarrel stirred him up to the highest degree. French music had in him a devoted and faithful enthusiast. "The Italians may well boast as they please of their voices and of their arts, but let them try to write a real French Overture, and in its true character at that. . . . This means that French instrumental music has something particular to itself; although the Italians make the greatest efforts to excel in their sinfonias and in their concerts, which, truly enough, do not lack beauty, one has to prefer, however, a lively French Overture." He added, "In instrumental and especially in choral music and dance, one must admit that the French are imitated by everybody while remaining inimitable." (*Das beschützte Orchester*, Hamburg, 1777) In spite of this, Mattheson sometimes let his polemical temperament take the upper hand, and he vehemently attacked the successors of Lully. He said: "They seldom have a serious basis, but they do not lack presumption nor stubbornness. They constantly usurp the name of Lully, who alone deserves the glory. But it is not enough to write a few small overtures or a little suite for keyboard with a big Parisian title; whoever wishes for a universal reputation must, at least, be universal in his profession."

Repenting, he apologized later, "A certain great composer has reproached me for having spoken of the French offhandedly in my *Orchester*; I feel obligated to invalidate this insinuation because it does not concur in any way with my ideas since I have the greatest admiration for the French and especially for their instrumental music." (*Das Neu-Eroeffnete Orchester*, 1713)

As for vocal music, Mattheson deplored young French singers' trying too hard to emulate the Italians, thus losing their naturalness and their melodic lightness. He advised composers to take as models Lully and some of his celebrated successors rather than the Italians. But according to him the field in which the French were absolutely unsurpassable was dance music; here he said, "The French model should be law since France was and will remain the true school of the dance. Good dancers aiming to perform on great stages, and theater composers as well, should study this style thoroughly; I am not speaking of the movements but of the music for which the works of Lully are law to everybody." In *Kern Melodischer Wissenschaft* (1736), Mattheson also devoted numerous chapters to comparing French opera, scenery, dances, and interpretation with those of the Italians, Germans, and English. All of this proves that Mattheson and his countrymen knew French music and held it in very high esteem, sometimes preferring it to the Italian. These ideas must have been common at the time, since we find almost identical ones in Quantz, although expressing a somewhat lesser enthusiasm for French art. He reviewed the qualities and the defects of both nations without indicating preference for either one, and he justified the epithet *gusto barbaro* given to German music by the Italians. After having drawn a picture as dark as it was inexact of the past of German music, he spoke of that of his own time with moderate enthusiasm. After demonstrating at length the differences between the two conflicting musical styles, Quantz begged the reader not to accuse him of prejudice; he conceded that he himself all during his life had drawn upon French as well as upon Italian sources. "The French," he said, "are more conscientious in their compositions; their church music has more staying power, but also has much more dryness than the Italians'. They prefer natural progression to the chromatic. Their melody is more straightforward, more touching than the Italian, but poorer in invention. They care more for the right expression of the words than for the charm of the melody."

Although Quantz considered the Italian art of singing superior to the French, he, as well as Marpurg and Mattheson, found French instrumentalists preferable to all others "because they execute their pieces with such infinite neatness and clarity one is sure that, at least, they will not alter the composer's ideas . . . therefore it is advisable for all instrumentalists and especially for harpsichordists to begin their studies in the French manner."

We must not forget that the detractors of French music were attacking not only the music itself, but also its interpretation. "French singing is like an uninterrupted and unbearable barking," said Rousseau; he added that one would hardly find four instrumentalists in France who knew the difference between *piano* and *dolce* and were able to render it. In his *Dictionnaire de Musique* he criticized the orchestra of the Paris Opera for being the first in Europe to have a large number of players but the last in quality of execution; he justified his accusation by saying that the symphonists were not up to their task because of their tedious way of scraping, tuning, and preluding with great noise and because of their lack of rhythm and that disdain they have for anything that has become daily duty. Most fortunately French instrumentalists were judged quite differently by the Germans. Mattheson found the playing of the French *"so admirable, so unie, und so ferme"* that there was nothing superior to it. "They learn everything by heart, and unlike the Germans they think nothing of repeating and rehearsing a piece a hundred times to attain perfection." (*Das beschützte Orchester*, 1777)

As we can see, French music found its true defenders on the other side of the Rhine, and the Encyclopedists were mistaken in thinking that they had all foreigners on their side.

This infatuation for French music abroad probably came about through the influence of three of Lully's German pupils who upon returning to their native country were very much responsible for furthering the renown of their master's art. One of them, Cousser, published in Stuttgart in 1682 a collection of pieces under the title: "Musical Compositions According to the French Method." In 1696 a collection of harpsichord pieces appeared in Germany; they were by Johann Kaspar Ferdinand Fischer, *Kapellmeister* in Baden; they were entitled *Blumen Buechlein*. Then came from the same composer *Musicalischer Parnassus, Ariadne Musica,* and *Blumen Strauss,* all of which were written in the French manner. About the same time, the third pupil of Lully, Georg Muffat, published his *Florilegium Musicum*; in the preface he defended French ornaments against the criticisms of German musicians.

The vogue for French music in Germany began to subside toward the middle of the eighteenth century. Karl Philipp Emanuel Bach in his *Essay* deplored that the youth of his time ignored the music of the French, which had always served as a model to his ancestors.

Quite naturally a question arises. How can it be explained that during so many wars between Italian and French music no one ever thought of opposing German music to either one of them? The answer is that at no time were the Germans considered worthy rivals in the arts. Lecerf de la Viéville mentioned disdainfully that their reputation "was not great in music, their compositions being as harsh and heavy as their genius."

Toward 1705, when Pantaleon Hebenstreit came to play the *cymbalum* for Ninon de Lanclos, he was judged all the more worthy of inciting curiosity because "he came from a country little prone to producing men of fire and genius" (Michel Brenet, *Les Concerts sous l'Ancien Régime*, 1900). While the Germans were so well informed about French music, under Louis XIV the French were completely ignorant about German art. In his *Histoire de la Musique* Bonnet devoted only a few pages to it, relating and describing some festivities given at the court of the Emperor and at the Munich Palace with musicians who came from Italy and "whose great success made Italian music take possession of all of Germany." In 1723 Handel was engaged with his troup, composed of two women, two *castrati* and one *concordant* (bass), for a series of concerts at the *Académie Royale de Musique*, but the contract was never honored. Yet Handel was, I believe, one of the first German composers whose works were performed in France. At a Tuileries concert, on December 24, 1736, Coremans sang an Italian aria by the famous Handel; in 1743, one of Handel's concerti grossi was given at the *Concert Spirituel*. Some of his harpsichord pieces must also have been known, judging by the factitious collection in the Library of Nantes which contains, among others, a Sonata for Harpsichord, a Capriccio, a Prelude and Allegro, and a Fantasia by Handel (L. de la Laurencie, *L'Académie de Musique et le Concert de Nantes*, 1906). And this was about all. The French knew nothing of Johann Sebastian nor of Karl Philipp Emanuel Bach, although Diderot, while passing through Hamburg, addressed the following letter to Karl Philipp Emanuel:

I am French; my name is Diderot. I enjoy some consideration in my country as a man of letters; I am the author of a few plays, among which you may know *Le Père de 'Famille*. I am on my way from Petersburg in my dressing gown and without pelisse, by post and without any clothing; otherwise I should not miss the opportunity to pay a visit to such a celebrated man as you are, whom I beg to send me a few harpsichord sonatas if he has some in manuscript and which have not yet been published; he will be good enough to attach a price to them, which I shall remit to the person who will bring me these sonatas on his behalf. The only observation he will allow me to make is that I have more reputation than riches, an unhappy conformity I have in common with most men of genius without deserving the same title.

The only Bach whose works were played in France was Johann Christian; one of his motets for two voices was performed at the *Concert Spirituel* in 1773, and his opera *Amadis* in 1779. But this brings us to the second half of the eighteenth century. Including a motet by Telemann sung in 1738, we have been through about all the German repertoire known to the French. They could hardly have a just idea of German music from that. Had they known more of it, I doubt they would have enjoyed or esteemed it. The censors from the *Encyclopédie* would certainly have labeled it too scholarly and too complicated for their taste; they would have found it bizarre, dry, cold, and well deserving of these barbaric vestiges which remain only "as in the portals of our gothic churches—for the shame of those who had the patience to build them," as Rousseau said.

But what did the Germans think of their own music, they who had composers such as Froberger, Buxtehude, Pachelbel, Mattheson, Telemann, Handel, to say nothing of the Bachs?

I found at a bookstall on the banks of the Seine a fat old volume entitled *Progrès des Allemands*. After having spoken with enthusiasm of the poets and musicians of his country—omitting Bach, naturally—the author, a highly cultivated German, ended thus: "If the Germans would have raised their ambition to the point of believing that they equaled the Italians or even the French in the perfection of art, they should have had more presumption and less discrimination than they actually have."

The Germans credited France and Italy with being the only nations that had original music; they said theirs was but a mixture of both; there was no German style, only a *gemischter Styl* (mixed style), which the Germans often manipulated with adroitness after the fashion of Lully. Although he was born in Italy, Lully leaned rather toward French taste to please the court of Louis XIV, while the Germans tried to unite the qualities of both nations in approximately equal shares. It ensued that Handel and the Bachs, whom nineteenth-century estheticians later recognized as eminently German geniuses, were considered by their learned contemporaries a sort of composite of French and Italian taste, devoid of any stamp of originality.

This *gemischter Gesmack* (mixed taste) was certainly the fad of that time. Couperin realized a fusion of both styles in his *Les Goûts Réunis* and celebrated the French and Italian agreement in his *Apotheosis* in which the styles of Lully and Corelli were combined. Even rivals of the Buffoons—Mondonville, for example— became Italianized little by little; and a day came toward the end of the century when French music sank into perfect Italianism.

And in the nineteenth century, Wagner wrote, "Italians have an instinct for melody; the French have the pride of the virtuoso; but to the Germans alone belong true feeling for music. Perhaps only a German has the right to claim the title of musician because it is undeniable that he loves music for its own sake, for its divine nature, and not as a vulgar means of arousing passions or of acquiring fame and fortune." Wagner should not be resented for his exaggeration; since the Germans had been formerly much too modest, they had a right to vindicate themselves. To each nation its turn! The influence of Germany all during the nineteenth century and even today is immense and well deserved. The incomparable geniuses she gave us could only make of Germany the cynosure and admiration of the whole world. The real cult she professes for her masters with her profusion of schools and of all kinds of concerts could only draw to her all the true devotees of music. "Never will the Germans have schools as good as the ones that for a long time have existed in Italy," said Quantz. Musicians are usually bad prophets; they know too little of their past to predict the future well. We have now more perspective for embracing the music of the eighteenth century. That does not allow us, however, to utter infallible opinions—those being non-existent in questions of art—but, at least, we can analyze at leisure the judgments, or rather, the edicts of the Encyclopedists.

Was French music deplorable to such an extent? Was Italian music from the same epoch really superior to it? Did the music of Bach and Handel deserve such disdain?

"It is for the poet to produce poetry and for the musician to make music, but only to a philosopher belongs the right to speak well of both." Such is the consecrated sentence. We have seen how *well* Rousseau and the Encyclopedists spoke of French music. And if great philosophers did exaggerate to such an extent in their judgment, what can we expect from the censors whose literary background or musical education are insufficient to warrant their being critics?

In his letter on *Omphale* Grimm said that a nation owes its taste for good music to philosophers and men of letters. I am willing to believe that the Encyclopedists, through their famous quarrels, did incite an interest in the art of music, but that their torch threw more smoke than light on French music.

French Influences on Bach's Keyboard Music

Although Bach did not leave behind any theoretical writings to inform us of his tastes and preferences, his works are in themselves proof of his high regard for French art. It would be difficult to give a complete list of the French compositions Bach knew, but, thanks to Gerber, we know that he admired François Couperin le Grand and recommended his works to his pupils. Although Forkel and others may have judged Couperin's thoughts poor and devoid of power, his pieces contain so much grace, nobility, and elegance, so many melodic beauties, and at the same time, so many harmonic refinements, that they could not have failed to seduce the author of *The Well-Tempered Clavier*. And there is no doubt that Couperin's knowledge of the most intimate resources of the harpsichord must have been thoroughly appreciated by Bach.

For instance, it has often been said that Bach borrowed from the Italians the use of hand-crossing. But there are two different kinds of hand-crossing. In Italy it was a purely technical effect; in the midst of a piece one hand executed perilous jumps over the other at either end of the keyboard. This can be done on our modern piano, with just a little less brilliance. The French, on the contrary, played each hand on a different keyboard at the same level, an effect that cannot be achieved on a single-keyboard instrument. This figuration did not aim at virtuosity, but at certain effects of sonority produced by a very close interweaving of the voices. Bach rarely used the Italian manner of crossing although we find exceptions in *The Goldberg Variations*, in which some variations are conceived in the Italian character, while others are in the French manner.

The Goldberg Variations, the Fantasia in C Minor (Schmieder 906), the Sinfonia in B Minor, and many others are striking examples of Couperin's way of "crossing on the two keyboards." As for the Gigue from the first Partita in B Flat Major, it shows outwardly some affinity with the Italian manner because of the large distance between the jumps in the left hand; but, nonetheless, its character is French because the crossing of the hands is not used as a kind of fireworks in the middle of a piece, but continues steadily from beginning to end, aiming only at an interesting effect of sonority. We find similar effects in Couperin's works such as Les Bagatelles and Les Tic-Toc-Choc ou les Maillotins, to mention but two.

Among the works of the French harpsichordists Bach must have been particularly sensitive to the suave and mysterious voluptuousness sustained by the droning monotony of pieces like L'Angélique, Les Sylvains, or Les Amusements. In certain preludes of Bach, and even in some of his dances, especially the courantes, we find this same character. Just compare the Courante from the B Flat Major Partita with Le Moucheron of Couperin. One finds this also in Purcell's grounds, but I do not believe that Bach knew them. The theme of the A Flat Major Fugue from Book II of The Well-Tempered Clavier is almost identical to that of the Allemande from the first Concert Royal of Couperin.

In the first English Suite in A Major the Prelude offers a variation of descending hexachords that exist also in La Vénitienne of Marchand, in a gigue of Dieupart, and in a gigue of Gaspard Le Roux. (Pirro mentioned these four examples in his remarkable book L'Esthétique de Bach, 1907.) In the same Suite we find a Courante avec deux doubles (courante with two doubles); and in the Suite in A Minor, we see a Sarabande, et les agréments de la même sarabande (sarabande and the ornamentation for the same sarabande), a procedure dear to François Couperin.

Not only were the titles taken from the French, but the form as well. In Couperin's first book of harpsichord pieces, we read: Courante et le dessus plus orné sans changer la basse (courante, and a more ornamented upper part, without altering the bass) or Gavotte, et les ornements pour diversifier la Gavotte précédente sans changer la basse (gavotte, and the ornaments to diversify the preceding Gavotte without altering the bass). These are procedures used by Bach. One could easily find other features in Bach which would indicate a certain relationship to the harpsichordist of Louis XIV.

The copies made by J. S. Bach of Dieupart's pieces and of the organ works of Nicolas de Grigny, organist at Rheims, are sufficient proof that these works were familiar to him.

In Mizler's *Musikalisches Bibliothek* we read that Bach, while still a student at Lüneburg, found occasion to cultivate French taste by listening frequently to the musical group of the Duke de Celle, which, for the most part, was composed of Frenchmen.

In the manuscript notebooks of Bach's pupils there are copies of the works of Louis Marchand, Clérambault, Corrette, Dandrieu, Le Bègue, d'Anglebert, and others, whom Bach undoubtedly knew. In *L' Esthétique de Bach* André Pirro devoted a long chapter to the French composers and virtuosos who could and must have been known to Bach. And even if Voltaire in a chapter of *Les Artistes célèbres du temps de Louis XIV* named only Lully, Colasse, Campra, and Destouches, as French musicians—after enumerating dozens of painters—there is no doubt that Bach knew many more intimately. Lully's music was not foreign to Bach, who owed to it his pronounced taste for French overtures. Specimens of this style are found in the Partita in C Minor and in *The Goldberg Variations*; in both works the title *Overture* is clearly indicated. In *The Art of Fugue*, the *Contrapunctus 6* is accompanied by the following subtitle: *in stile francese*.

In other pieces, although they bear no indication, the general character shows that they belong to the same family. The Fugue in D Major (*Well-Tempered Clavier*, Book I), for instance, is a typical overture; the Preludes in F Sharp Major and in A Flat Major (Book II) are written in *stile francese*—that is to say, in the dotted rhythm peculiar to the French. Being aware of it is very important for the performance of these pieces. In France dotted notes were played in a very special way; their duration was extended beyond their notated value, and the following short note was reduced to a minimum time. Now modern pianists play these rhythms exactly as they are notated. In his edition of the first book of *The Well-Tempered Clavier* Busoni even insisted that the note following the dotted one should not be shortened (see

p. 387). These are not insignificant details because the character of the piece depends on the manner in which it is scanned. In keeping the short note too long, we soften the piece, giving it an uncalled-for heaviness; we deprive it of its haughty, jerky rhythm, and of its radiant splendor, which were the characteristics of the French overture and of the *stile francese*. Couperin insists on this manner of scanning, whereby one does not play note-values as they are written down. "Usage has enslaved us, and we go on," he said. In certain pieces the notes marked in even values had to be *un tant soit peu* (just a little) dotted—for example, as Couperin indicated at the head of his allemande, *La Laborieuse*. He also said, "Measure defines quantity and equality, and *Cadence* is properly the spirit and soul that one must add to them." (*L'Art de toucher le Clavecin*)

How could Busoni imagine that Bach, after adopting the genre and writing of dotted style, would have wanted it to be played in a different and absolutely opposite way?

It is probable that Bach also shared the opinion of his contemporaries who considered France the true school for the dance. It is interesting to note that although the great Cantor had a penchant for Italian titles, he employed French words almost every time a dance was concerned. Thus besides the *Fantasias, Concertos, Capriccios,* and *Praeludia,* we read *Courante, Courante avec double, Sarabande, les Agréments de la même Sarabande, Gavotte, Musette, Passepied, Bourrée, Menuet, Air, Allemande, Anglaise, Loure, Gigue, Rondeau, Polonaise, Sarabande simple, Sarabande double.*

Bach also expressed in French the general title of a series of dances: *Suites pour le clavecin di Mons. Bach,* or *Suite pour le clavessin par J. S. Bach.* It is believed that the title of "French" was given to a series of his suites because of their grace and delicacy. The English Suites, so named according to legend because they had been written for a rich Englishman, are more grave, more imposing, it is true, than the French Suites, but they are related nonetheless to French dances. In the Partitas the French character is even more evident.

All these works are essentially French, and are enriched by the splendor of Bach's genius. He also adopted the ornaments of the French, who were great masters in this art. See the chapter *About Ornaments* (p. 114).

Although I have limited myself to Bach's harpsichord works, we could find just as much evidence of French influence in his choral and instrumental music.

Thus, despite having been belittled by the Encyclopedists, French art, refined and gracious, and which knew how to elevate itself toward nobility and majesty, was held in high esteem in Germany and served as a model to geniuses such as J. S. Bach. This is what I wanted to demonstrate.

ED. NOTE: In 1938, Wanda Landowska wrote:

It is a bad sign that so many keyboard players specialize exclusively in Bach because it is impossible to play and love Bach when one has little knowledge of those he loved and played and with whom his works are tied intimately. Therefore, I distrust those Bach specialists who, submitting to current fashion, have sprung up like mushrooms. What is striking in them is precisely the fact that they do not know the music Bach himself knew and developed. Moreover, they do not even know all the works of Bach. It is evident that they would play differently the Adagio from the D Minor Concerto if they knew well the Entombment from *The St. Matthew Passion*. Their ignorance of the chief works of Bach, and of the music of Couperin, Rameau, Pachelbel, Buxtehude, and others, is constantly felt in their renderings of Bach's keyboard works. How many times it has happened that Couperin or Pachelbel have enlightened for me a phrase of Bach's about which I was anxiously undecided!

I confess that in spite of my fanatical love for Bach I am able to pass naturally from *The Goldberg Variations* to the Passacaille of Couperin without any of these shouts of indignation that I have heard from some musicians.

7 ⟨ Style

THE music of the nineteenth century from Beethoven on is
called "Romantic." Since the beginning of the twentieth century,
it is "Modern." But all that preceded Beethoven has the unique
name of "Music of the Past," and its performance requires what
is known as "style."

When we are told that a work has been performed *with style*,
when we read that an artist *has style*, the same thing is always
meant. It is a kind of indifferent placidity, stiff and pallid. Style
is the contrary of feeling, since we are told by one of the greatest
pianists, Eugène d'Albert, in his preface to *The Well-Tempered
Clavier* that "there are many things in the art of Bach that are no
longer congenial to us. I know there are people who can listen
for hours to his cantatas without showing any apparent boredom.
These people are either hypocrites or pedants. Bach knew nothing

about the gradation of passions, of sorrow, of love, and he did not suspect the possibility of expressing them through music."

As you well know, Bach had two wives to whom he was very devoted and twenty children whom he loved with all his heart; but he "did not know what love was" as was the case, by the same token, with all musicians who lived before Beethoven. Eugène d'Albert was categorically opposed to the idea of rejuvenating Bach; he asked, on the contrary, that his works be performed just as they are, in their true character, that of the cantatas—in other words, in such a way that it would be impossible to hear them "without showing apparent boredom." Eugène d'Albert certainly made no pretense at being the creator of this kind of interpretation; he knew well that for years music of the past had to be interpreted with style, or, as it was also said, "in the classical manner."

I was still a child when my teacher said to me, "Not so much feeling, mademoiselle; more style!" I listened to him obediently, and later I had all the trouble in the world to unlearn this.

Too often the word *style* meant severity or sobriety. Therefore, the radiant solemnity of the first part of the *Italian Concerto*, the overflowing joyfulness of its Presto, the exuberant ecstasy of the Prelude and Fugue in C Sharp Minor from *The Well-Tempered Clavier* and of the chromatic part from the Toccata in F Sharp Minor, the brilliant luminosity—colored like an ancient stained glass window—of Handel's Chaconne in F Major, the restrained rapture of certain pieces by Pachelbel, the *tendrement, affectueusement, galamment, voluptueusement sans lenteur, the fièrement et noblement* of François Couperin—all these had to be performed with a uniform severity, sobriety, and rigidity, in accordance with this alleged one-sided style. The public likes those signposts indicating "straight ahead! no detour!"

It was also said that Bach's music, even in its least important theme, is immense, powerful, and colossal; therefore, these qualities had to prevail without exception in the interpretation of his works.

The prejudice of grandiosity is one of the most widespread today. Light and insignificant pieces are performed in a way that makes them appear grand. That is very bad; a small work must remain small. Enlargement is the business of a photographer; a real artist will know how to appreciate a miniature. What fool would transform a dwarf of Velasquez into a Goliath?

The miniatures of Kuhnau, Couperin, and Pachelbel are marvels in themselves; their worth equals any work of large scope, and size cannot be the only decisive factor. To reinforce or enlarge a piece of delicate and fragile concept is a crime against taste as much as weakening and reducing a great and powerful composition would be. Of course, I speak of true grandeur, not of the deceptive and vain grandiloquence that often takes its place.

Bach wrote minuets and dances of all kinds, as well as many pieces such as the Preludes and Fugues in C Sharp Major, F Sharp Major, or G Major from the first book of *The Well-Tempered Clavier*, in a light and joyful character. The title of the *Clavierübung* means "Exercises for keyboard composed of *preludes, allemandes, courantes, sarabandes, gigues, menuets,* and other gallant pieces, dedicated to amateurs for the pleasure of their minds."

Title page from J. S. Bach's *Clavierübung*

On the other hand we know that *gallant style* was becoming fashionable in Bach's time. It consisted of greater freedom which contrasted with the rigid style of counterpoint. Karl Philipp Emanuel Bach and Quantz spoke of it with enthusiasm and considered it a mark of superiority over the ancients. That must not be taken literally because Poglietti, Froberger, Fischer, Gottlieb Muffat, Kerll, Richter, Purcell, all the virginalists, Chambonnières, Louis Couperin, d'Anglebert, and other French and Italian composers had written gallant pieces before them; and I do not even mention the "expressly careless" style of Kuhnau nor that of Frescobaldi. It may be that Bach wrote his *galanteries* to conform to the taste of the day; he may just as well have done it to continue a genre so magnificently illustrated by his predecessors. No publisher, no patron, no outside influence ever forced him to approach a style that is now considered so foreign to him. Why then perform one of his gigues as if it were a prayer? What relationship is there between some of the arias from his cantatas, those which are infinitely tender or ecstatically sensuous, and the immense and colossal style? This gigantic style might apply to some organ pieces or parts from cantatas, but not to all of Bach. How could his works, so varied in character and genre, be confined to a single style, even if it were considered the highest?

Another concept even more widespread is that Bach's style is always that of the organ. But no matter how far we search, we cannot find a single detail indicating that organ style is necessarily the right one for Bach. Furthermore, it is easy to ascertain that Bach composed twice as many solo works for the harpsichord as he did for the organ, and this of his own volition and for his own pleasure, without coercion or encouragement from anyone. How could anyone explain why Bach, who had both instruments at his disposal, would have written for one pieces suited for the other? How could anyone believe that Bach, known even more for his keyboard performances than for his compositions, would have ignored the individual resources and characteristics of the instruments he played? One needs only to study his harpsichord works to be convinced to the contrary.

It must have been the great respect and veneration in which Bach was held that was responsible for this so-called *organ style*. But how he would have loathed it! "What!" he would have said,

"I have devoted a great part of my life to writing gallant pieces, I have devoutly copied the works of the harpsichordists, I have appropriated for myself the elegance and neatness of the French style, as well as several ornaments from Couperin, and you dare say that my sarabandes are *Pater Nosters*, that the brilliant *Italian Concerto* is like a chorale for organ! But what about *The Goldberg Variations* and all the Suites and Partitas? Would I, like a village organist, have ignored so completely the character of both instruments?"

"Revered Master," we would answer, "we know that some of your contemporaries, such as Scheibe, sometimes criticized you for lacking charm, but today we are too grave to tolerate minuets, gigues, arias with ritournelles, and any light, tender, or jumpy piece." Bach, author of gallant pieces, of almost frivolous music? What a profanation!

"Ordinarily," said Pascal, "one imagines Plato and Aristotle wearing long togas and always being serious and grave. But they were honorable people who, like anybody else, laughed with their friends; and when they made their laws and political treatises, it was with ease and to divert themselves."

Nobody would dare say, of course, that Bach created his great works to divert himself. But may we be allowed to think that his secular pieces at least were written for "the relaxation of the mind," since these were his own words? I do insist on this, because recognizing that Bach most certainly had feelings other than those of grandeur, power, and sublimity does .not suggest depreciating or dwarfing this colossus. "Music has only one purpose," said Bach, "to honor God and recreate the mind." On the first page of the small *Clavierbüchlein* of Anna-Magdalena, he wrote in his own hand: "Anti-Calvinismus and Christian School are also Anti-Melancholy!"

How remote from us is Bach's philosophy—this mysticism, this inalterable quietude, this soothing serenity, and this great faith, naïve and fervent, from which he drew his most beautiful inspirations! Between the recollected, surrendered ecstasy of man before his God and the presumptuous grandiloquence of modern man, what an abyss! And serenity, what a restricted place it occupies now in our feverish life and in the concept of our volcanic art! As with Gothic art, the works of Bach try to reach the infinite through this admirable embroidery of sounds more often than by the grandeur of architectural lines.

I am far from supporting the idea that all secular works of Bach are tender and serene and composed exclusively of passepieds and gavottes. The penetrating sorrow of the Toccata in F Sharp Minor, the large and magnificent solemnity of the Toccata in D Major, the tempestuous passion of the Toccata in C Minor, and the ecstatic sweetness of the Prelude, Fugue, and Allegro in E Flat Major for lute-harpsichord, as well as many other marvels of profundity, are proof to the contrary. I only want to protest against the uniformity to which some people would like to condemn Bach.

Even if the critics of Leipzig blamed Bach for his violence and considered him a sort of long-faced pedant who displayed a disturbing knowledge, one who was ill-tempered and who willingly assumed "the pretentious and lacrymose tone of a village preacher," there is no valid reason for continuing these exaggerations and for searching indiscriminately in all of Bach's works for ascetism, acerbity, and severity. Doubtless these qualities may be found in some of his great works, but they do not at all preclude other attributes, either in his secular pieces or in the cantatas. We discover in them a wealth of arias imbued with tenderness and intimate insight as well as pastorales and choruses—all singing without restraint the happiness of life and all overflowing with a lively, festive joy, as in *The Christmas Oratorio*, for example. In his *Lexicon der Tonkunst* (1790), Gerber tells us that apart from his profound and serious music Bach did not disdain light and pleasant thoughts and that he emphasized them in his playing.

Our education, completely impregnated with romantic ideas, makes any probing beyond Beethoven difficult for us.

Bülow presented Scarlatti in the preface to his edition of a group of sonatas as a precursor whose wit gave birth to the Beethovenian scherzo. Biographers of Karl Philipp Emanuel Bach, of Rust, and of so many others never failed to discover some vague relationship between these great composers and the author of the Ninth Symphony. We are generally so busy finding links from Bach to Wagner or from Palestrina to Beethoven that we no longer see all that separates them. And it is precisely these differences which form their particular character, their individual beauty—in a word, their *style*.

Guillaume Costeley wrote:

Go now, my labors, follow those who will like you;
Go, go, and do not be astounded by those who will say
This fellow Costeley does not have so-and-so's counterpoint;
From another he does not have the same harmony; but
I have something else that neither of them has.

When we know that "something else" which is his alone
and which the others do not possess, then we shall know his particular character, his style.

We have to know the spirit, the feeling, the taste, and the
atmosphere of the epoch to understand the works of any composer and to present them in a more or less exact image. Otherwise when we proceed, having in mind but a unique principle
of sobriety and severity, we produce those uniform performances
in which pieces are all delivered with the same invariably grave
and impassive look.

"You always instruct a reader badly when you make him
yawn," said a great admirer of Bach, whose name was Frederick
the Great.

In romantic music we distinguish clearly between Beethoven
and Wagner; a great pianist does not play Schumann, Liszt,
Chopin, or César Franck all in the same way.

In ancient music—and that encompasses several centuries—
"this morose tyranny of uniformity" has been adopted for all
composers of all countries, as Ecorcheville said so well. In the
seventeenth century, however, it was recognized that the people
of each country had their own turn of mind which formed the
genius of their nation: "Grave and majestic in Spain, free and
cavalier in France, vehement and impetuous in England, delicate
and refined in Italy, solid and firm in Germany." The rivalry between the French and Italian manner in the eighteenth century
is well known (See Pt. I, Ch. 6). The writings of Quantz, for
instance, prove that musicians of Bach's time did make a distinction among the different tastes·of each nation; and this made
for a varied and shaded interpretation.

And before Bach we find this distinction of national characteristics in the *Musurgia* of Athanasias Kircher (1650): "I declare that musicians will profit from such studies without which

they would not produce anything of excellence. They will learn from the French the style *hyperchromaticum et exoticis triplis tumidum*; from the English the symphonic style, in which a marvelous variety of instruments flourishes; from the Germans, the harmonious style with many voices and an ingenious assembly of parts." (Quoted by Pirro in *L'Esthétique de Bach*, 1907.)

At each epoch, in each country, each composer had a more or less personal style. We have a tendency to consider them all as sons of the same mother. It is difficult for us to bring out and distinguish different styles because we are blinded by "eternal beauty," which is nothing else but the "beauty of the day." Compared to other arts, we are far behind in music. While recognizing that Memling was the more pious, more serious artist, painters know how to admire Watteau and Fragonard too. Musicians are only beginning to experience the enjoyment of an historical approach.

8 Tradition in the Interpretation of Music of the Past

UP TO NOW, and save for rare exceptions, there have been but two ways of interpreting music of the past. Either it was cast in a modern mold, altering the movements, the dynamics, and exaggerating the expression; or it was played in what is called *traditional style*—that is, in a heavy, muffled, and monotonous way. Unable to perceive the true beauty of works thus performed, the public looks over these cold remains and thinks, "These corpses are quite dead. Why not leave them in peace?" If one had to choose between the two kinds of interpretation, the first, no doubt, would be favored; it is less yawn inducing!

The so-called traditionalists pride themselves in conforming to the indications given by the authors of the past, ignoring that the meaning of signs and dynamics has changed. The same traditionalists also make a point of adding nothing to the works of the past. But that too is quite wrong.

Bach certainly would not recognize his music made thin and bony by being played scrupulously as written, with blind obedience. Far from being pure, a bass that is not realized is like a cripple on crutches advancing in a vacuum. Even when the orchestra parts are doubled or tripled, the general effect remains; the music is dwarfed because the places that demand to be filled out with chords supplied by the accompanying harpsichord are left empty.

In the seventeenth and eighteenth centuries more liberty was left to performers and conductors than is today. Authors rarely imposed tempi or interpretative markings; they relied on the artist's taste. Even Weber thought that excess of indications made a piece look caricatural.

Interpreters also had to realize the figured bass, to ornament the adagios, to fill in the empty places in passages where the composer had merely indicated a harmonic skeleton. Without these additions the works were incomplete.

This ancient *ad libitum* was equivalent to saying today to a gentleman, "Make yourself at home," knowing that he would not push the indiscretion too far and would not rampage through your household, throwing out the window objects that offended his taste or bringing in others not in conformity with yours.

From treatises of the time and from author's prefaces we can learn the limitations of this freedom which was not supposed to exceed certain boundaries nor to alter the composer's thought. But no matter how much we search, we shall never find any indication authorizing changes like those which certain conductors and virtuosos of today allow themselves to make. Routine and lack of historical sense are the sole guides for their mutilation of the greatest masterpieces.

Although they left performers free to take some liberties, composers of the past were also very sensitive about the exact interpretation of their own works. "The more one is devoted to searching for perfection and truth," said Gluck, "the more precision and exactness become necessary. The slightest alteration of movement or of expression, the misplacement of a detail are enough to destroy the effect of an entire scene, and to transform the aria 'J'ai perdu mon Eurydice' into a marionette song."

In his prefaces Couperin recommended altering not a single note, nor a single ornament; he also taught us how to voice the harpsichord, adding, however, that there are some people who can dispense with these recommendations, since they play equally badly on any instrument.

Muffat demonstrated how a precise execution of Lully's ornaments and the knowledge of his movements were important. In his advice to organists, Viadana begged them to watch closely those singers who "while knowing perfectly all the resources to be extracted from a flexible throat do not take the trouble to observe their text thoroughly; they alter the melody and exceed the boundaries of the written music."

Jacques Dalcroze (*S.I.M.*, 1908) and Jean Huré ("Les Dogmes Musicaux," *Monde Musical*, 1906-08) were certainly right when they poked fun at *trrrraaadition*, because what bears that name is often but a collection of time-honored errors or whims bequeathed by some famous interpreter and taken much too seriously by schoolmasters. There were always and always will be some of those pedants for whom the execution of the tiniest passage according to their own rules is dearer than all the beauties of art. They are rarely scholars, but sciolists; they belong to the species Gluck abhorred and about whom a Hindu proverb says, "Mutual understanding is easy with the ignorant and even easier with the scholar; but Brahma himself could not get along with the man whose stupid vainglory has been swollen by a bit of knowledge."

Dalcroze scoffed at the uniformity perpetrated in the name of an alleged tradition and usually applied to Bach; but carried away by his subject, he went so far as to say that a true artist has no use for, nor does he have to worry about, historical evidence, since "interpretative genius is self-oblivion." As admirable a musician as he was, Jacques Dalcroze would have been unable to perform most of the lute, virginal, or harpsichord repertoire without consulting writings of the period or works of modern historians. Self-oblivion could not have revealed to him how to realize ornaments nor what the tempi were nor how to decipher tablatures.

It is true that the spirit of a performance depends more on taste than on signs, but before saying anything, an artist must be aware of what he has to say in order to subordinate the expression of the sounds to that of the thought. An interpreter must penetrate all the composer's ideas in order to feel and be able to convey the fire of expression and all the refinements of detail. There are a thousand different ways of interpreting a piece without ever getting away from its character.

Besides, the knowledge and perfect rendering of signs, dynamics, ornaments, and particular taste of the period to which the work belongs will never restrain an interpreter nor prevent his daring anything. On the contrary; it is when we follow the same routine for all epochs that we become prisoners, eternally breathing the same air. This is not a question of musicological pedantry, but of a knowledge of the language of the work to be performed. What would you think of an actor who did not try to understand the meaning of certain words in poems from the Middle Ages and who would leave the proper placement of accents to the good luck of his inspiration?

It is wrong to glorify the fallacious idea that inspiration alone is all that an interpreter needs. Unfortunately we are told over and over again that, should we lose our innocence, we would also lose our freshness and our pink cheeks. It is probably feared that after reading Romain Rolland's notes about Lully a virtuoso or a student would suddenly become a philosopher in the fashion of the musicians of antiquity. Think of it! What misfortune to be thus thrown back thirty centuries, we who are racing toward progress! A needless fear; we are still so far from it.

All interpretations must be studied and thought out; and the more they are, the more they give the illusion of spontaneous inspiration. To see Corneille's verses, so pompous, and Racine's, so natural, one would not guess that it was Corneille who worked with facility and Racine with difficulty. Beethoven's manuscripts are illegible because they are so full of corrections; the most passionate and transcendent passages are those which have been the most studied, searched, and tormented.

I am willing to accept Jacques Dalcroze's formula, "The genius of interpretation is oblivion of oneself." Oblivion of oneself, yes; but not oblivion of the work played nor of the style of its author nor of his ideas nor of the slightest detail which he regarded certainly as much as modern composers do theirs.

Too often we are offered the works of the past in the stiffest, most boring presentations, and we are asked to believe that thus they conform to "tradition." But in their time these works were criticized for their excess of passion. If we are now unable to arouse these same feelings in performing these works, it shows that our tradition is false and that we would need a Timotheus to make us unlearn it. The famous Greek musician attached to Alexander made his pupils forget what they had learned under other musicians and in such cases charged a double fee (Burgaud des Marets, *Rabelais*, T.1, p. 172).

On the other hand, conductors and performers who take all kinds of liberties with the texts, priding themselves in ignoring both erudition and tradition, are following—they too—a tradition because their colleagues in Berlin, Vienna, or London, save for a few exceptions, have adopted the same procedure. However, in their case it is not "the hands of chance that bring everything up to the rules of art"; it is not the suddenness of their inspiration which dictates their choice, but routine and a bad tradition.

Like every other art, music presents an infinite variety of style, character, and genre. The past of our art is a magnificent museum in which all epochs and all nations have deposited their treasures, all perfect and each one different. Modern musicians, unlike old-fashioned virtuosos, are no longer satisfied with just a few dozen spectacular pieces. Our art had its Homers, its Shakespeares, its Raphaels, and its Watteaus. We want to know them all, and thanks to the work of musicologists, we are beginning, little by little, to get acquainted with the treasures bequeathed us by our greatest masters of the past, treasures that we have left to mildew far too long in the dampness of archives.

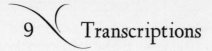

9 Transcriptions

IN 1908 to commemorate the anniversary of Carrière's death, I played the harpsichord in Rodin's studio. The master was a great lover of the music of the past. He had the kindness to show me his collection of antique sculpture. To watch him stop at each carving was a sight to behold. He looked at it lovingly, caressing it with his sensitive hands; he became ecstatic before a woman's torso mutilated by the centuries, "See, madame, the refinement, the suppleness of these lines! Ah! what a pity that parts are missing!" Out of curiosity I ventured to ask, "*Cher Maître*, why don't you try to reconstruct them?" He looked at me, amazed. It was obvious that this idea had never entered his mind; one had to be a musician to have such a thought. "But, madame, I do not feel able to do it; and even if I were, I should never dare." And I thought of all these small virtuosos and schoolmaster-composers who go tooth and nail at tampering, mutilating, and disfiguring our sublime works. If they do not have Rodin's genius, they have more courage; they dare anything. They put Bach, Mozart, and Handel back on the drawing board; and after slandering the most beautiful masterpieces, they dare to juxtapose their obscure names with those of our greatest masters.

Change only one syllable in a verse, and you will make the poem limp. Such precautions are not observed in music. The stamp of genius is removed from marvels of art on the pretext of accommodating them to our modern exigencies. The reason for that often lacks nobility. Every time a publisher suggests reprinting a piece from one of my programs, he always asks me to make some changes "so that the work will become our property." But more humiliating yet is to see a wretched arranger trying to convince us of what he himself believes, that he has improved upon and rejuvenated a work of Mozart that was sparkling with youthfulness in the first place.

What would sculptors say if some plasterer took it upon himself to shave off some marble from the Venus de Milo to give her a wasp waist or if somebody twisted Apollo's nose to give him more character?

What would you say of the person who would replace the authentic jacks and quills of Couperin's harpsichord with new ones under the pretext that the old ones are in bad shape and that the instrument must sound? I would say he is a barbarian.

Unfortunately true is the fact that the admirable Palace of the Popes at Avignon has been used as a barracks for a whole century; frescoes by Giotto have been spoiled with inscriptions such as *Vive la Classe!* and others. But that is an exception. Most masterpieces of music, however, are despoiled by similar outrages; they are covered with vulgar and arrogant marks, not dictated by naïveté, but by a stupid presumption of superiority over our ancestors. Opera directors have often been responsible for tampering with the repertory, producing medleys and making a lyric tragedy, for example, out of the two *Armides*—Lully encased in Gluck, thus reconciling the worst of antagonists.

In a brief essay written with a noble passion and a liveliness seldom encountered in a scholar, Michel Brenet sketched for us a glimpse of these innumerable potpourris that we owe to the fancy of conductors, and sometimes to that of the greatest musicians. ("Le Respect des Maîtres," *Guide Musical*, 1901)

Henry Expert quotes an unusual case of transcription of a work by Jannequin: "The Prince of Moskowa is far from respecting the texts as they stand. Under pretext of ease and convenience, he alters the words here and there to the greatest damage of the form and inner meaning where curious effects of timbre have a preponderant part. The last movement is completely disfigured; the cuckoo seems insolently shameless: it is transformed into an owl! But is it not incredible for the night bird to borrow the song of the cuckoo, otherwise so well known and pleasantly developed? The joyful Jannequin was certainly not being revived in these incomplete restitutions!" (*Les Maîtres Musiciens de la Renaissance Française*, 1898)

Wagner and Berlioz often rose up against this barbaric mutilation of the most admirable productions. Probably prompted by the fear that his own works would undergo the same treatment, the author of *Les Troyens* gave the following instructions on the first page of his work: "The author believes he must forewarn singers and conductors that he has not allowed anything inaccurate to stand in his way of writing. Singers are, therefore, requested to change nothing in their parts, to introduce no hiatus in the verses, to add no ornaments or appoggiaturas in the recitatives or anywhere else, and to suppress none of those which are marked. As for conductors, they are instructed to strike certain accompanying chords in recitatives always on the very beats where the author placed them and not before or after. In a word, this work must be performed as it is. Accompanists are likewise requested not to double in octaves the passages written in single notes and to use the pedal only at the places indicated in the score."

But it is with the rich literature for harpsichord that the champions of transcription take unlimited liberties; and to justify what they do, they invoke the differences existing between our piano and its predecessor. The harpsichord, they say, had only a narrow span of three or hardly four octaves, precluding any great variety of sonority; it was afflicted besides by many other defects. All this proves only one thing: these people have never manipulated and perhaps never even approached a harpsichord. Their absurd explanations show only a taste for faking and a complete lack of historical sense. A whole volume would be necessary to enumerate all these pretentious transcriptions which aspired, alas with success, to supplant the originals. It is really regrettable that even great musicians have committed this crime of lèse-genius.

"The harpsichord works of Bach," said Bülow, "are the Old Testament; Beethoven's Sonatas the New. We must believe in both." And while saying that, he added several bars to the *Chromatic Fantasy*, changed the answer of the Fugue, and doubled the basses; thus he impregnated this work with an emphatic and theatrical character. A true believer must not change anything in the New or the Old Testament.

Zelter, director of the Royal Academy of Singing and the first who undertook to make the music of Bach known, wrote to his friend Goethe: "Old Bach, son of his country and of his time, with all his originality, did not escape, however, the influence of the French, especially that of Couperin. Wishing to prove oneself pleasing results in works that cannot remain as they were produced. Fortunately the removal of these 'amabilities,' of these layers of light gilding will uncover instantly their true value. Thus I have arranged many cantatas for my own use, and in my heart I know that from up there old Bach approves of it with a nod, as did the good Haydn, 'Yes, that is good!' "

In his reprint of Scarlatti's sonatas Bülow admitted changing the titles, grouping the pieces to form suites "because the public," he said, "fear the sonatas." These are rather insignificant details; but it becomes more serious when Bülow said that he transposed the G Minor Sonata (Longo 231) in F Minor and brought a whole series of changes "to clean it thoroughly of all dust." To prove the absolute necessity of this and to give an example of Scarlatti's extravagant writing, Bülow quoted the following excerpt from the Sonata in D Major (Longo 415).

Excerpt from Scarlatti's Sonata in D Major (Longo 415)

It is easy enough to recognize that this is a series of *acciacca-turas* written out in notes instead of signs. Later in the preface Bülow spoke of that "eccentric" ornament and affirmed that it was unplayable on our modern piano. This ornament, however, was commonly used by the ancients; it is one of the most beautiful and can be performed on the piano with the same ease as on the harpsichord.

Tausig transposed Scarlatti's D Minor Sonata (Longo 465) in E minor, thus depriving it of all freshness and pungency and turning it into a flabby and sentimental piece. For what purpose? Could it be to couple it with the Capriccio in E Major?

Bach's organ Toccata which became so popular in the arrangement for piano by Tausig begins with an ornament wrongly realized in a brilliant and spurious passage. From the beginning this lends to the piece a noisy and brutal character.

Who did not give lessons to Bach? Well-meaning people deploring Bach's not being among us to benefit from our progress found it necessary to bring about changes, retouching, or transformations which, according to them, Bach himself would have made. I am willing to believe that these posthumous collaborators are inspired by the best of intentions and that all of them, like Zelter, are certain that from up there old Bach is approving, "Thank you, colleague!" I do not know Zelter's transcriptions, but Charles Widor, who did, said, "O! candor! We visualize Bach's nod. Red with anger, he grabs his wig and throws it at Zelter's face. 'Ah! you have the nerve to alter my music. Beware, or else!'"

I believe that modern transcribers would not be treated differently. Seldom, very seldom do we hear the authentic music of the Cantor of Leipzig. We are given a modernized Bach arranged in today's fashion and fitted to the demands of our time.

In his edition of Mozart's seven great concertos, Hummel slogged away at the creation of his master with an incredible offhandedness; the *Coronation Concerto* most of all bears scars. Often there are series of measures during which one forgets that the work is by Mozart; on the other hand nearly one hundred bars from the original have been suppressed in the finale.

And for what purpose did Hummel take such impertinent license with Beethoven in editing the Seventh Symphony, altering the rhythm in the bass and removing several bars? Yet Beethoven's music was not archaic then.

Several years ago in Warsaw there was a performance of Beethoven's Tenth Symphony, a patching up of parts and pieces from his quartets sewed together by an illustrious unknown. The idea was not even new, for Auber, that man so famous for his wit, had not enough of it to refrain from writing a new symphony by Beethoven out of fragments of his sonatas.

And what would Chopin say—he who could not stand any alteration of his thought—if he were to attend an opera in which Italian singers bellow full throatedly his most delicate preludes? Or if he heard the pitiful rhapsodies which were made out of his works by virtuosos of few scruples?

It is said that a distinction must be made between music and painting, for example, because those who uglify a symphony commit an error in taste, a sacrilege against the masters and an absurdity in trying to alloy gold; but most of the time the original they used remains intact. This may seem true, but it is only so partially. It took many years before an artist dared to play in public Bach's famous Prelude in C Major; many listeners would not have recognized it since they had in their ears the tender romance, the parasitic melodic line of the *Ave Maria* Gounod grafted on this prelude.

When will our masters be freed at last from the tutelage of grammarians? Who has any right to undertake "thorough cleanings" of their perfect masterpieces?

In Poland there is an anecdote according to which a peasant says to his wife, "You know, up there at the castle they love cherry pie. Some day you should bake one for me to taste."

"But butter is expensive."

"Make it without butter."

"What about eggs?"

"We shall do without them."

"And, you know, the cherry season is over."

"Oh! make it without cherries; it does not matter!"

The peasant tasted the pie and exclaimed, "How stupid can these rich people be; they are so fond of something that has no taste at all!"

One takes away from ancient music all that constitutes its

true character. One cuts, transcribes or mutilates it. Either the harpsichord or the winds are suppressed; the strings and the choruses are overburdened; the most beautiful thoughts are torn apart; all that gives life and motion is destroyed in the name of tradition. Then, with some satisfaction, it is stated that this music has little taste and does not compare favorably with the productions of our progressive age.

Ed. Note: Much later, Wanda Landowska added this:
The craze for transcriptions at the end of the nineteenth century and at the beginning of the twentieth is understandable. The harpsichord works of Bach were hardly known except for a few Suites and some Preludes and Fugues from the first book of *The Well-Tempered Clavier*. Bach was known as the organ composer par excellence. This accounts for the transcriptions of Liszt and Tausig and later those of Busoni. Was it also because they felt that Bach's music played on the piano was bare? I have often thought that was a possible explanation.

10   Of Movement and Measure

"Old music should be played slowly." That is one of those current formulas which we have not even invented, for it is encountered in every epoch.

Quantz said that, in the century preceding his, music was performed at least twice as slowly. Partisans of Lully resented Rameau for drowning beautiful melodies in modern speeds. But did not Lully hear his dances, called *baladinages* because of their extreme rapidity? Chambonnières, among others, was cited in opposition to him. Mersenne, however, spoke with ecstasy of the lightness and incomparable swiftness of Chambonnières's hands.

On what grounds have we built the idea of a continuous accelaration of movement?

Instruments were imperfect, we are told. Which ones? The

violin? Is ours more perfect than a Guarnerius, Stradivarius, or Amati? During the seventeenth and eighteenth centuries there were brilliant violin virtuosos who, by the way, were constantly criticized for sacrificing everything to speed, fireworks, and feats of strength.

As for the harpsichord, with the exception of *glissando* effects, one can obtain on it every degree of velocity, permissible or not.

Forkel reported that Bach amazed his contemporaries by the rapidity of the tempos he took when playing his compositions at the harpsichord. "He conducted with great precision and in a very quick movement," said Agricola and Gerber.

Couperin advised playing even tender pieces "without too much slowness." He said that cadence and taste should be preserved at any rate of speed.

The rapidity of Mozart's playing was famous; legend wills it that once in Naples Mozart astounded his audience by the ease with which he played the most difficult passages, especially those for the left hand, on one finger of which he wore a ring. The Neapolitans believing the ring was a talisman responsible for Mozart's prodigious skill, he had to play the same piece again after taking it off. Mozart must have been quite sensitive about quickness of movement, if we are to judge from the letter he wrote to his sister after his competition with Clementi, "He is a *ciarlatano*, like all Italians. He writes *presto* over a sonata, or even *prestissimo* and *alla breve* and plays it himself *allegro* in 4/4 time. I know this is true, for I have heard him do so."

In another letter Mozart criticized exaggerated speed: "The eyes have no time to see nor the fingers to find the keys. Moreover, it is much easier to play fast than slowly. One can miss a few notes in passages without anyone's noticing. But is it beautiful?"

What may have induced the error and brought about a belief in this so-called slowness was the ancient way of writing music. Notation of the vocal music of the Renaissance, for example, in whole and half-notes takes on for modern eyes a solemn and slow character; it did not preclude, however, light and fast movements anymore than heavy Gothic letters disturbed the liveliness and grace of the works of the poets of the Middle Ages, as Michel Brenet said in her book on Palestrina.

The movement *alla breve*, very frequent in Couperin, Bach, Karl Philipp Emanuel, and Mozart, may also have been a cause of this slow interpretation. Performers seldom pay attention to the bar that goes through the C (₵), and they take the usual movement instead of playing twice as fast. French composers replaced the ₵ by the figure 2. This sign should not be confused with the figure 2 that Rameau placed after the clef, indicating simply that the piece was in two beats regardless of the note value of each beat.

Karl Philipp Emanuel Bach admonished virtuosos whose profession consisted in playing fast; they only astounded the eyes without touching the heart and dazzled the ears without charming them.

But I anticipate the routine retort, "What was considered then very fast would be today a most moderate movement." Fortunately, Quantz left us sufficient indications on the subject to obviate this statement. Although he did not have a metronome at his disposal, Quantz had a certain notion of it; he quoted Loulié, who in his *Eléments ou Principes de Musique* (1698) spoke of a machine called a chronometer. Quantz thought, however, that it was simpler to use the beats of the human pulse for checking tempo. Since there is a difference between the pulse of a man "whose temperament is choleric and sanguine" and that of a "phlegmatic and cold" person. Quantz established the number of pulse beats of a healthy man at eighty per minute. This corresponds approximately to the figure 80 on the Maelzel metronome. Quantz devoted a very long chapter to indicating the precise duration of all movements as well as the tempos of all French dances. For a long time I have been experimenting with Quantz's observation, calculating tempos taken from the pulse with the metronome, and I can vouch that the movements of old music are no slower than those of modern music. It often seems to me that these movements are somewhat too fast for Bach's works. Obviously it would be false to adopt Quantz's indications for all music. For instance, secular works were generally performed faster than sacred ones.

Italian and German pieces were supposed to have a lighter and faster pace than those of French composers. Rousseau in his *Dictionnaire de Musique* and Voltaire in *Le Siècle de Louis XIV* spoke of the slowness of French singing, which also affected instrumental music. That was in strange contrast with the liveliness of that nation. But the opinions of Rousseau and Voltaire are exaggerated, since French music had adopted moderate movements, indulging neither in speed nor in slowness.

In vocal pieces it was not always found necessary to inscribe the movement, and speed of dances could also be deduced from their particular rhythms without special markings. But in time composers used dance titles without conforming exactly to their original movements. Since it does not happen too frequently, it would be of great help to modern performers to know the movements of seventeenth- and eighteenth-century dances.

We should not take too literally nor interpret in today's fashion the signs of tempo that we find in old editions, because the meaning of these signs has greatly changed.

Gather a hundred musicians and ask them to play *andante* a piece by Rameau or Mozart; if they have not investigated the matter, they will play slowly; and if the next piece bears the indication *più andante*, they will play even more slowly. And this will be wrong. Why would they all concur in playing in a false tempo? Would that be due to a sudden inspiration? No, but because they would be following tradition, the sole, unique tradition for all music of all epochs, that which ill-advised professors have grafted upon their students and which they in turn carry on.

But even musicians who profess a haughty disdain for any historical research have recourse occasionally to an encyclopedia or to a musical dictionary. Let us see what they would find under the word *andante:*

Le Dictionnaire de l'Académie Française says:
"Andante"—moderate movement.

Littré:
"Andante"—not too fast nor too slow.
"Andantino"—slower than Andante.

L'Encyclopédie:
"Andante"—slow movement.
"Andantino"—faster than Andante.

L'Encyclopédie des Gens du Monde:

"Andantino"—faster than Andante;
but under the word "Movement" we read:
"Andantino"—slower than Andante.

L'Encyclopédie Moderne:

"Andantino" indicates a slower measure and a certain
regularity in the movement, more in keeping with stiffness
than with gravity.

Larousse:

"Andante"—moderate movement with a tendency toward
slowness. "Andantino"—word indicating a modification
of movement [?].

Le Nouveau Larousse:

"Andantino"—more animated. All musicians agree on this
subject!

This alleged agreement among musicians mentioned by
Larousse comes from the fact that movement has changed. In
the eighteenth century *andante* corresponded to the French *gracieux* (gracious) and *sans lenteur* (without slowness); it indicated
a moderate pace "going" (*allant*) from the slow to the fast;
andantino was played in the same movement, but with more
lightness; *più andante* meant faster, not slower. George Sand
gave an almost exact explanation when she wrote: "Autumn is
a melancholy and gracious andante which admirably prepares
the solemn adagio." Only, *andante*, always gracious, was not
necessarily melancholy, since we often find *andante-allegro* in
Handel's works.

One could mention many other indications, the meanings
of which are different today. The erroneous belief in the slowness of old music was the cause of a polemic between Vincent
d'Indy and the *Opéra Comique* after a performance of *Iphigénie
en Aulide*. Saint-Saëns, who took part in the discussion, wrote:
"How could Gluck's work not seem boring with this slowness
which, according to current belief, should be inflicted upon it,
while, in modern music, it seems that one never runs fast enough?"

What we call tradition is the long patriarchal gray beard we stick on the composers of the past. We are so used to saying "old Bach" or "Papa Haydn"—poor Haydn, who was never blessed with children—that we cannot see them in our minds otherwise than afflicted with old age and moving along with an eternally grave and dragging gait.

Grave, incidentally, required an animated, though pompous movement in French overtures.

Thus we see that the concept of slowness in the music of the past is not built on any solid basis.

In travel books we read that leaders of caravans sing certain songs that have the power of quickening the steps of their majestic camels better than a whip would. If we knew their secret, we should use it in almost every reconstitution of old music. Let us keep, however, from exaggerating and from indulging in these *prestissimi* so dear to the virtuosos; I am far from dismissing speed altogether. What shocks me is not so much the speeding of tempo as its quality. The most fiery gallop of a thoroughbred always remains noble, while in the allegros of certain performers there is something which calls to mind the indifferent brutality of a machine or the feverish haste of the commuter who is afraid of missing his train.

Today we value bar lines so much; yet they do not represent an improvement, but rather a simplification for the benefit of the ever growing number of amateurs. It was to facilitate their reading that the most beautiful music was ingeniously cut up into small squares within which the most capricious traits were forcibly enclosed. This brought about the ever-present, and monotonous, recurrence of the strong beat. In her book on Palestrina Michel Brenet said that "the melody of Palestrina, like Gregorian chant, unfolds in supple volutes; within their superimposed voices their undulations succeed one another, unite, and dissolve without abdicating their individual progress. A hidden measure is the discreet and invisible tie which regulates the harmonious unity of the motion. We shall understand the refinement and all the musical wiles to which Palestrina resorted in transforming a theme, such as that of the mass *L'Homme Armé*, only when we compare its original graphic disposition with that of a modern reprint."

Maurice Emmanuel has devoted a very learned study to this

cursed bar line responsible for the strong beat. He wrote in the *S.I.M.* (1908), "Rhythm in modern art has the least dignity. The theorists' and pedagogues' contribution to this subject in their scholarly treatises is about reduced to a decomposition of time and to an inept distinction between 'simple' and 'complex' measures. If Pindar, Aeschylus, Sophocles, Euripides, Aristophanes, and all the composer-poets of ancient Greece had known such treatises, they would have had only contempt for such childish art. Despite the ravages that squareness has exerted on music, it is a constant fact that since the beginning of the sixteenth century great masters have rebelled against the strong beat, although they often had to put up with it. Look for equidistant strong beats in some fugues of J. S. Bach, in the last quartets of Beethoven, or in the works of Wagner since *Tristan;* you will find no more of them in these works than you would in Josquin, Lassus, or Palestrina."

In his *Essay,* Karl Philipp Emanuel Bach praises unmeasured improvisation: "The metric signature is in many cases more a convention of notation than a binding factor in performance. It is a distinct merit of the fantasia that, unhampered by such trappings, it can accomplish the aims of the recitative at the keyboard with complete, unmeasured freedom."

It is clear that our modern way of notating time values— this cross-ruling with its rigid symmetry—can boast of only a few practical qualities; in fact, it has reduced us to poverty as far as rhythm is concerned.

As for tempo rubato, it had at first little in common with what is understood today by this term. It was simply an ornament. Mozart began to speak of tempo rubato in the modern sense of the word and with the same meaning it had for Chopin when he wrote to his father, "People discover now that I am not making faces and yet that I play with much expression . . . they cannot understand that when there is a tempo rubato in an adagio, the left hand must not know it. The left hand cannot yield." One must not believe that our tempo rubato was unknown before Mozart. Frescobaldi and Froberger had already advised performers to avoid too strict a measure; on the contrary, they told them to yield freely to the fluctuations of the movement.

11 ⟍ About Ornaments

WAGNER used to say to his musicians, "Children, pay attention to the small notes, and the large ones will take care of themselves."

In the last century it was considered good taste to ridicule the ornaments in music of the past. Some did it because they found it easier to scoff at them than to play them, an achievement that would have required thorough study. Others wanted to persuade us that these embroideries were only a consequence of the thin sonority of the harpsichord. They said, "Had the seventeenth- and eighteenth-century composers known our modern piano, they would not have indulged so much in this garrishness." Such was the opinion of Marmontel, Le Couppey, Méreaux, and others.

In the eighteenth century the human voice and the violin were as capable of prolonged vibrations as they are today. Why then do we find rich ornamentation in vocal and violin music of that period? The old masters held fast to their ornaments, even more than Wagner did. "Three principal conditions of good execution must be observed," said Karl Philipp Emanuel Bach, "a proper fingering, good ornaments, and good interpretation." He went on, "No one doubts the necessity of ornaments. That is evident, considering the great number of them to be found everywhere. When one realizes their usefulness, they become indispensable. They connect the notes, enliven them, and when necessary, they give them a particular stress and importance; they make them pleasing, and therefore awake special attention to them; they help make their meaning clear; whether the mood is sad or joyful or otherwise, they always enhance it; they can improve a mediocre composition, and without them the best melody is empty and dull."

The idea, propagated by Bülow, that an ornament threatening to obliterate the design of a melodic line should be rejected as a parasite does not correspond very well to the concept the masters of the past held on that matter. They valued their "parasitic" ornaments as much as they cared for neatness of design. They loved this mannered style, bristling with subtle thorns, abounding in affected allusions, coquetries, artifices, and delicate oddities. Although they adopted more severe or grandiose lines for sacred music, they did not hesitate to soften them with beautiful adornments, fine embroideries, and rich attire. It did not in any way diminish their faith nor their enthusiasm, but often harmonized marvelously with the carvings, the gold and enamels of the churches. If the most beautiful idea was not decorated, it seemed like dry bread and prisoner's food to the musicians of the eighteenth century. This is why they rebelled with such energy, not against the complete suppression of ornaments— unable as they were to foresee such barbarism committed by future editors and publishers—but against the slightest alteration of every single ornament.

"I am always surprised," said Couperin, "after the trouble I have taken to inscribe the ornaments that fit my pieces and for which I gave an intelligible enough explanation in a special treatise known as *The Art of Playing the Harpsichord*, to hear people who have learned these pieces play the ornaments without complying with my expressed wishes. This is unforgivable carelessness, all the more so since one cannot put ornaments arbitrarily or at will. I declare that my pieces must be played as I have marked them, and they will never make a definite impression upon persons of true taste as long as all I have marked is not literally observed without additions or substractions."

"A misplaced appoggiatura, trill, or roulade can destroy the effect of an entire scene," said Gluck.

Ornamentation was an art, a great art because the melodic design was not to be overburdened with inappropriate artifices; a beautiful idea, in the hands of a clumsy person who did not know how to use ornaments skillfully, was a reminder of what Diderot once said of a beautiful woman without taste, "One moment, and the dress will spoil everything!"

All composers indicated carefully the manner of realizing their ornaments. To suppress them is a sacrilege similar to cutting off the wings, the gargoyles, and chimeras, or other ornaments, from Notre-Dame de Paris to give it a smooth surface and severe lines.

There were two schools of ornamentation, the French and the Italian. French taste demanded a precise execution of all the *ports de voix*, trills, cadences, mordents, *battements*, *flattés*, and all other ornaments indicated by the composer. No others were to be added. In addition to these, Italian taste also permitted arbitrary ornaments which required a certain knowledge of counterpoint and some personal imagination. They consisted of variants, rolls, arabesques, *groppos* (*Walze* or *Rolle*), *circolo-mezzo*, *firata*, *ribattuta*, and other rolling designs which are numerous and varied. They formed what was called *vermischte Manieren* (mixed ornaments), an intermingling of all kinds of ornaments. Diruta, Praetorius, Mattheson, Leopold Mozart, Quantz, Marpurg, and others gave us detailed explanations of them. Muffat defended French ornaments against the prejudices of some German musicians. He said, "Those who without discretion denounce the ornaments of the French tradition as if they offended the melody or the harmony must have scantily examined this matter, or they have never heard bonafide pupils—but probably some false imitators—of the school of the late Lully."

French ornaments were very familiar to Bach; we know that he himself copied the table of ornaments of Dieupart. In the table he left us in the *Clavier-Büchlein* of Wilhelm Friedemann, we find the following ornaments:

Bach's Table of Ornaments from the *Clavier-Büchlein* of 1720

∿ *Trillo.* A sign we find in Couperin, Chambonnières, d'Anglebert, Le Bègue, Dieupart, Rameau, Le Roux, and Dandrieu. The Italians used a *t*; Bach also used the sign of the Italians, and sometimes others such as *tr*.

∿↓ *Mordent.* The French called it *Pincé*; Bach used the same sign as Couperin, while D'Anglebert, Rameau, and Dieupart marked it as ⁊ , and Kuhnau as ∕∕ .

∿↓ *Trillo und Mordent.* A combination of the two preceding signs. We find it in Couperin with other signs.

∿ *Cadence.* The same sign is found in Couperin, Chambonnières, Le Roux, D'Anglebert, and Rameau under the name of *Double.*

∿ ∿ *Doppelt-Cadence.* (Double Cadence) Bach borrowed these signs and their realization from D'Anglebert, modifying only the name (in D'Anglebert, it is *Cadence*). Rameau and Dieupart never used it. It should not be confused with Rameau's *Double Cadence,* which corresponds to Bach's *Trillo und Mordent.*

∿ ∿ *Doppelt Cadence und Mordent* (Double Cadence and Mordent) is a composed ornament.

ϟ *Accent steigend und* ϟ *Accent fallend* are equivalent to the French *Port-de-voix.* In Dieupart this sign is reversed ⁊ , and Bach must have taken it from D'Anglebert or Le Roux, where we find the identical sign, also adopted by Rameau; Couperin used a note that was to be tied to the main note.

ϟ *Accent und Mordent.* A combination of ornaments greatly ϟ appreciated by French harpsichordists.

ϟ or ϟ *Accent und Trillo.* This second sign is found in D'Anglebert and Rameau under the name of *Tremblement appuyé* with the same realization.

This list is far from being complete. Bach employed other signs also, namely,

 Nachschlag. This last sign, also found in Couperin with the same realization under the name of *Accent,* is not to be confused with the *Accent* of Bach; Walther, a friend of Johann Sebastian, called it *Nachschlag-Aspiration* and gave it the sign ∧ and ∨ , but one must not confuse Walther's aspiration with that of Couperin either.

 Schleifer. This last sign was employed by the French for *Tierce coulée* (slurred third).

{ ⊂ *Arpeggio*. These signs were used by Chambonnières and by
⊂ ⊃ Couperin, while d'Anglebert, Rameau, and Dieupart indicated them with a line ╱ or ╲ .

In his book *Musical Ornamentation* Dannreuther devoted a
thorough study to Bach's ornaments. It appears that he forgot
one ornament. I wish to mention it because it too is of French
origin. It is the *Suspension*, marked thus ⌃ by Couperin. Bach
never used that sign, but realized the ornament in notes.

Italian Concerto, ANDANTE, BAR 12

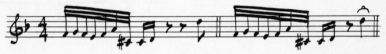

Like French musicians, Bach wrote out almost all of his
ornaments, leaving little to the fancy of the executant, contrary
to what the Italians did. Going even further than the French in
his demand for precision and in order to facilitate execution, Bach
realized most of his ornaments in plain notes. For this Scheibe
blamed him in his *Critischer Musikus* of 1737: "Every ornament,
every little grace, and everything that one thinks of as belonging
to the method of playing, he expresses completely in notes; and
this not only takes away from his pieces the beauty of harmony,
but completely covers the melody throughout."

In 1802 Forkel made this statement: "At the beginning of
the last century it was customary to overload every note with
ornaments, a fashion we are now applying to vocal music. Bach
showed his interest in this fashion and composed some pieces in
this style; but he soon returned to Nature and to pure taste. . . ."

One often refers to the Italian Concerto as a model of ornamental sobriety. Here is how the Andante of that Concerto would
have appeared had Bach written the signs of ornaments instead
of incorporating their realization among the main notes of the
melodic line.

Andante from *The Italian Concerto* as it would have appeared had Bach written the ornaments in signs instead of incorporating their realization among the main notes of the melodic line.

SIGNS USED INSTEAD OF THE
ORNAMENTS WRITTEN BY BACH IN MAIN NOTES

Appoggiatura   from below ⸮ from above ⸮ or small note

Double Appoggiatura   small notes

Trill ∿

Mordent ∿ᛏ

Trill and Mordent ∿ᛏ

Turn ∽

Slide or *Slur*   upward ⌣ downward ⋀

Suspension ⌒

A. *Arbitrary Ornaments* which had no specific signs. Their use was left entirely to the interpreter, who "diminished" at will certain long notes in order to embellish the melodic line with arabesques and variants.

B. *Tempo Rubato, Anticipation* or *Retard*. These had no sign either.

+ Ornaments indicated by Bach in signs or small notes.

Thus we find in the Andante of *The Italian Concerto* more than one hundred ornaments that could have been written in signs or in small notes—Bach used only sixteen of them, two of which are small notes—besides an abundance of arbitrary ornaments in keeping with the Italian character of the piece.

12   Keyboard Instruments

Confusion

THE greatest confusion still reigns in the domain of keyboard instruments. The names *spinet, harpsichord, clavichord, fortepiano,* and their counterparts in French, German, Italian, and Spanish are often used indiscriminately, although the instruments they represent are widely different. The confusion may stem from the fact that during the seventeenth and eighteenth centuries the word *Klavier* was used in Germany to designate any keyboard instrument, including the organ. Furthermore, the harpsichord was interchangeably called *Flügel, Kielflügel, Clavicymbel,* or *Cembalo,* or by its French name spelled *clavecin* or *clavessin.* Uninitiated persons may believe these terms applied to different instruments.

A small one-keyboard harpsichord was called *Spinett* in German, *épinette* in French, and *virginal* in English. Its shape was either rectangular, triangular, or pentagonal.

The question is further complicated by the fact that today in Germany both *Flügel* and *Clavier* mean the modern piano. As for *spinet*, it now designates a small-size piano.

Another cause for misunderstanding arose when Karl Philipp Emanuel Bach's *Essay on the True Art of Playing Keyboard Instruments* was republished. Once at the Bibliothèque Nationale in Paris I asked for a copy of this work. How amazed I was to find in it deprecating comments about the harpsichord! Yet in the original edition I own Karl Philipp Emanuel speaks with enthusiasm of this instrument. I read and read again, until I finally discovered a small annotation, scarcely visible, in which Schilling, who edited the book, said he felt sure that "if Bach were living among us, he would have changed his mind." Therefore, Schilling took the liberty of interpolating some precious ideas of his own, and wherever harpsichord (*Flügel*) was mentioned, he replaced it by *piano*; and he changed clavichord into *pianino*. Few people have the original edition at their disposal, and, unfortunately, the Schilling version was quite widespread. (Even the valuable English translation of W. J. Mitchell, Norton, 1949, contains some discrepancies. For instance, in the introduction to Part I, par. 9, the original word *Flügel* has been translated by keyboard instead of harpsichord [p. 35, 8th line].)

As for the French translator of Forkel's biography of Bach, Félix Grenier, he went even further: everytime he saw in the original *Flügel, Clavicymbel, Klavier,* or *Clavessin,* he translated them by the sole denomination of *clavichord.* What a charming simplification! Thus we find in Grenier's book clavichords with two keyboards, or with registers, or concerti grossi for two clavichords, and other monstrosities that never existed. And to avoid monotony, Grenier introduced here and there haphazardly the word *harpsichord* in English—for instance, in his "revised" title of the *Clavierübung:* "Exercises for the *clavichord,* consisting of a concerto in the Italian taste and an overture in the French manner written for *harpsichord* (in English) with two keyboards." What nonsense!

I chose this example among many others. No wonder that such editions bred confusion in the mind of readers!

The Clavichord

The clavichord, one of the most ancient of keyboard instruments, goes back to the fourteenth century; it is the first in which strings were struck, and this is what makes it completely different from the spinet or the harpsichord, which belong to the family of plucked-strings instruments. The mechanism of the clavichord is simple. In an oblong case strings are stretched horizontally; they are struck by tiny metal tangents fixed at the rear end of the keys. Strips of cloth are woven around the strings to act as dampers. In the early type of clavichord, called *gebunden* (fretted), a single string was used by several keys, producing a different pitch according to the place it struck the string. Builders of clavichords, inspired by musicians, tried to improve upon this limited instrument and gave it an independent string for each key. The enlarged model was called *bundfrei* (unfretted). Daniel Faber and others may already have built such unfretted clavichords at the beginning of the eighteenth century, but they were extremely rare until the second half of that century. Among the extant clavichords to be found in collections and museums, most of those built prior to 1750 are fretted. In 1739 Quirijn von Blankenburg *in Elementa Musica* (s'Gravenhage) complained that the tangents of two or three keys had to strike the same string. Because of this peculiarity, a simultaneous attack of some minor or major seconds was unrealizable.

One of the most characteristic effects of the clavichord, fretted or not, was a kind of vibrato called *Bebung,* an effect exquisite in itself. It was obtained by repeated pressure of the finger on a key without releasing it. But since the amount of pressure increased or decreased the tension of the corresponding string, the pitch was not very pure; in broken chords or held notes this impurity became worse. Used mostly for studies of touch, the clavichord, a small portable instrument, had a timid sound, melancholy and infinitely sweet. It was best suited to expressions of tenderness and meditation. It gave an admirable legato to single melodic lines. All attempts at vigor crush and smother it. Its beauty and poetry reside in the subtle nuances of its varying shades of gray.

In the supplement of the *Dictionnaire des Sciences du 18e siècle* we read, "It is presumed that the clavichord is somewhat more recent than the spinet. It has a very sweet tone and is used to accompany small voices; but it must not join other instruments in concert, because it does not have enough strength to be heard." And elsewhere it says, "Usually the low tones of the clavichord have the sonority of a caldron, while the high ones have none at all; hardly three octaves of this instrument have a pleasant sound."

Despite what the French said, the clavichord is endowed with a fascinating sonority. During the seventeenth century it disappeared from the Latin countries, where it never made much headway. Bonnet does not even mention it in his *Histoire de la Musique* in 1715. Germany was the only country where this instrument played a certain role. There it continued to be used and even underwent a veritable renaissance in the second half of the eighteenth century. The same *Dictionnaire des Sciences* says, "A celebrated German musician named Bach (Karl Philipp Emanuel), at present music director of the city of Hamburg, judges a harpsichord player after having heard him play the clavichord."

The clavichord became the instrument which expressed best the *galant* style from which strict polyphony was eliminated. And Schubert said in *Ideen zu einer Aesthetik der Tonkunst*, in 1806, "Clavichord, instrument of solitude, of melancholy, of unexpressible sweetness. . . . He who does not like noise, outbursts, and tumult, he whose heart seeks tender effusiveness will turn away from the harpsichord and the fortepiano and will choose a clavichord. . . ."

The Harpsichord

As for the harpsichord, which reigned all over Europe from the sixteenth to the end of the eighteenth century, its shape is that of a slender grand piano, generally with two and sometimes three keyboards. Its strings are plucked like those of the lute, the guitar, or the harp; but instead of being plucked directly by the fingers harpsichord strings are plucked by quills or little pieces of leather, each one being a sort of tiny flexible tongue; this plectrum is inserted into an upright thin piece of wood called a "jack," the base of which stands on the rear end of the key lever. When the key is lowered, the jack jumps up, and its tongue plucks the string. A spring in the back of the plectrum allows it to slide under the string when the key is released.

Like the organ, the harpsichord possesses registers which give it richness and versatility. They consist of several sets of strings of varied materials, length, and thickness which are plucked at different points by several sets of jacks. Each set of jacks is encased in a kind of rail that can be moved laterally by manual stops or by pedals. (The function of the pedals of the harpsichord is, therefore, totally different from that of piano pedals.) These various registers give the player the possibility of obtaining on each single key a note at one or two, sometimes even three, different octaves, simultaneously or separately. By analogy with the organ, which has similar possibilities, the harpsichord registers are called eight-foot, four-foot, and sixteen-foot, according to the octave they represent. A few instruments had a two-foot register. Both keyboards can be united by means of a coupler. Other devices produce alterations of timbres. For instance, there is a lute register which sounds like a pizzicato.

Unlike the virtuosos of today, great harpsichordists and organists of the past participated actively in the construction of the instruments they played. There developed a sort of collaboration between musicians and makers. More than once an instrument already constructed was retouched by the hand of the master. Substitution of materials, choice of strings, quality of wood, preference for quill or leather played a great part in these alterations. Such modifications were rarely made for the purpose of increasing the volume of sound, but rather to enrich and vary the tone color. It is not surprising, therefore, to find so many variations among keyboard instruments now in museums and private collections. Although the overall pattern remained fixed, many changes were introduced by individuals.

In 1610 Hans Heyden invented a harpsichord capable of holding the sound; it was presented as a special attraction during the famous mammoth concert given at Nuremberg May 12, 1643, called Origin, Progress, Usage, and Abuse of Noble Music (*Curiositaeten,* 1644, quoted by Lavoix).

In the second half of the eighteenth century the bow-harpsichord created a furor in Germany. The three great potentates of music—Karl Philipp Emanuel Bach, Quantz, and Marpurg—considered it an ideal instrument, superior in every respect to the fortepiano, the clavichord, and even to the harpsichord. In the supplement to the *Dictionnaire des Sciences, des Arts, et des Métiers*, published in 1776 in Amsterdam, someone with the initials of F.D.C. reported having seen such an instrument in Berlin. "The maker had substituted gut for steel for the strings and had put a sort of wheel-bow covered with parchment; a large band of aggregated horse-hair shaped as a ring and tied at one end passed over two cylinders. There was a small bag made of muslin, or some other transparent material, full of resin, which rubbed the horse hair continuously."

Thanks to the use of gut strings, instead of the usual metal strings, the theorbo-harpsichord had a softer sonority, as also did the lute-harpsichord, for which J. S. Bach wrote exquisite pieces.

In the eighteenth century, the harpsichord was the basis of the orchestra. "It is the column which supports the whole ensemble," Mattheson once said. "Its harmonious and warbling sounds have an infinitely beautiful effect on the choir."

Karl Philipp Emanuel Bach and Quantz never tired of insisting upon the importance of the harpsichord in the orchestra. Its role was threefold; while accompanying, it also supported the whole ensemble and led it.

In the seventeenth century and even during Bach's youth some choirmasters conducted by beating time with their feet, others with motions of the head or of the arms, with a scroll of music or with a stick; those who played the violin beat time with their bow. But from 1730 on we see the harpsichordist become the real conductor.

The Paris Opera had a music master who conducted armed with a big stick; this prompted that great disparager of French music, J. J. Rousseau, to say that it was the only theater in Europe where time was beaten without being followed, while elsewhere time was observed without being beaten. Accompanying harpsichords, however, were used.

In Italy and Germany composers of operas conducted not by beating time, but from the harpsichord.

This instrument was already in use in churches in the seventeenth century. Spitta quoted instances from the time of Kuhnau and even earlier periods. Frescobaldi and Buxtehude used it in church too.

It is known that for several years the tuning of Johann Sebastian Bach's harpsichord at the Thomaskirche was entrusted to Karl Philipp Emanuel. Proof that a harpsichord was there! Johann Sebastian played it himself to conduct his cantatas. The harpsichord is expressly called for in the alto aria from the Cantata No. 154, for instance. There is an obligato harpsichord part in the secular cantata *Amore Traditore*; in these the harpsichordist generally realizes the figured bass, and in places he finds his part entirely written out by Bach.

Karl Philipp Emanuel said in his *Essay* (Introduction to Part I, par. 9), "When the harpsichord quite rightly stands surrounded by all the participating musicians, its tone can be distinctly heard by everyone. . . . Already entrusted with leadership by our ancestors, the keyboard instrument is thus in the best position to assist, not only the basses, but the entire ensemble as well in maintaining an even measure. . . . Should anyone begin to rush or to drag, he can be brought back to order most readily by the keyboard player."

For operas there were usually two harpsichords—one placed on the side of the orchestra for accompanying, the other in the center for conducting. In concerts a single instrument filled both roles. Handel, however, had in his orchestra two harpsichords for which he frequently wrote two different basses. Of this dual function, accompaniment was undoubtedly the most important; when "time-beaters" had become the fashion at the end of the eighteenth century, accompanying harpsichordists were kept on. During the performance of the *Creation* in Vienna, as late as 1808, Kreutzer was seated at the harpsichord while Salieri conducted the ensemble. For his performance of Handel's *Messiah* Hiller used an accompanying harpsichord. We still find a harpsichord at the Paris Opera at the beginning of the nineteenth century.

"The harpsichordist is indispensable for any music, large or small," said Quantz. Karl Philipp Emanuel too found a good performance impossible without the accompaniment of that instrument.

The harpsichord was not a separate entity in the orchestra of the past; on the contrary, its plucked-string tone blended marvelously well with the other instruments; it formed a harmonious mortar to link the dispersed voices and to fill out the emptiness of cadences. Moreover, its rustling and warbling sounds, so dear to Mattheson, endowed the instrumentation with a mysterious and light color. Even if the harpsichord cannot be heard clearly in large orchestras or outdoors, it does not matter. It would be heard if people sat high enough; but let it be removed, and its absence will be felt immediately, as if a light had suddenly gone out.

In today's performances of music of the past the harpsichord is often replaced by a piano. I have no prejudice against the modern piano, being myself a pianist, but its beautiful tone has something oily that does not blend with other sonorities; it always floats over the orchestra. This assertion was made by someone who ignored the harpsichord, but who had obviously some notion of the orchestra—Richard Wagner. Albert Schweitzer too stated this fact in his book on Bach. "In ensemble works one discovers how different the sonority of the piano is from that of the harpsichord. When Bach wrote his sonatas for harpsichord and violin, the sonorities of both instruments were entirely homogeneous. Today, with the piano substituted for the harpsichord, they are absolutely different and detach themselves from one another without fusing. A listener who has a good ear and who has in his imagination evoked Bach's works with a beautiful homogeneous sonority cannot help suffering from the antagonism of the two sonorities."

"There is not one instrument," said H. Lavoix (*Histoire de l'Instrumentation*), "with which the sonority of the piano can blend nor one which could entwine its supple lines with the angular outlines of the piano. In short, this familiar and irreplaceable instrument is generally, as a chemist would say, insoluble in the orchestra." This is so true that since its advent the piano has been used in conjunction with the orchestra mostly as soloist or when particular effects are called for, but hardly ever as an accompanying instrument. Kretzschmar's idea of replacing the harpsichord with a harp was more acceptable, since its plucked-strings sound would blend with the orchestra better than would the piano. But the harp lacks the varied richness of the harpsichord, its drone, its fine incisions, its fluted tones, and the superb swishing of its coupled keyboards—all of which add such particular color to the orchestra.

Reviewing a Handel festival in Berlin, Hugo Leichtentritt remarked that the two accompanying harpsichords were not sufficient. It did not surprise me, because I knew the instruments in question. Their maker had not even bothered to find out what a harpsichord was like. Thinking that the ancients were very backward, he built a very small bad piano, sure of making an eighteenth-century replica. No wonder that even two of them were not satisfactory! In another instance I was asked to lend an eighteenth-century pianoforte from my collection for a concert. Having to use it myself elsewhere, I had to refuse. A piano dealer sent to the concert hall a small piano-desk, like those used by the editors of music publishing houses, which are, of course, deprived of sonority or nuances. The next day one read in the papers that the clavichord, the harpsichord, and the ancient forte-piano had little of the brightness of our modern instrument.*

If J. S. Bach and Handel used the harpsichord, it was not to give a musicological flavor to their orchestras, but it was because they realized how useful and indispensable it was. Neither was it used exclusively with small orchestras; in the second half of the eighteenth century a single harpsichord at the Paris Opera had to support ninety instrumentalists. No complaint appeared anywhere about the weakness of its sonority. A good harpsichord should have a large sonority. In fact, this is what distinguishes it from the clavichord and from the fortepiano. One should not judge the sonority of those which now rest in museums; as Anton Rubinstein said, "They can give only an incomplete idea because time alters the sound of keyboard instruments to the point of making them unrecognizable."

In his letter on music addressed to Mlle R. de Saulnier in 1680, Le Gallois asserted that, thanks to his manner of striking the keys of the harpsichord, Jacques Champion de Chambonnières drew sounds of such mellow quality that no other performer could equal him in his art. Jean Denis, in his *Accord de l'Epinette*, 1650, said that "one could not have a more proper instrument . . . it is the most beautiful in the world and the most perfect, since there

---

*ED. NOTE: Today, there are still people who place sheets of paper or tacks in their pianos "to make them sound like a harpsichord"!

is no music which it cannot express and execute all by itself and there are harpsichords with two keyboards to pass all the unisons, a thing the lute cannot do." And La Fontaine, in his Epistle to M. de Nyert, wrote:

> Of this amiable child (La Certain), the unique harpsichord
> Touches me more than *Isis* (Lully's opera) and all its music.
> I do not want anything more, I do not want anything better
> To satisfy mind, ears, and eyes. . . .

We have often been induced into believing that the harpsichord was completely bereft of expression. To prove it, it was enough to use incomplete quotations arranged to suit the purpose. More often than not, Couperin was thus misquoted. Marmontel, Méreaux, Le Couppey, and after them the writers of encyclopedia articles had only to mention this excerpt: ". . . as one cannot increase or decrease its tones. . . ." and delete all that preceded and followed to see in it the disconsolate complaint of those poor musicians of the past lamenting the powerlessness of their harpsichords. But Couperin loved his instrument and never tired of repeating in each one of his prefaces, "The harpsichord has within itself a brilliance and a precision that are seldom found in other instruments" (*Pièces de Clavecin,* 1713). The only drawback of the harpsichord was that unskilled players easily fell into the pitfall of dryness. But this is what Couperin had written: "Since its tones cannot be increased or decreased, I shall always be grateful to those who, thanks to infinite artfulness sustained by taste, will make this instrument capable of expressiveness. This was the goal my ancestors endeavored to attain."

In his preface to the *Inventions,* in 1723, Bach said that he wrote them to teach correct playing and above all to help the student achieve a beautiful *cantilena* (*eine Cantable Art zu spielen*). Following the example of the his father, Karl Philipp Emanuel, with Quantz and Marpurg as well, repeatedly stressed how the attainment of a singing and expressive playing was important for every harpsichordist. Objecting to the reproach of dryness and lack of expression that was sometimes brought against the harpsichord, Karl Philipp Emanuel said that it could only be the consequence of inexpert playing.

Today the main argument used against the harpsichord is its alleged shortness of sound; this is false; the vibrations of harpsichord strings last longer than those of piano strings. I have made the experiment many times. Furthermore, since the touch of the harpsichord is completely different from, even opposite to, that of the modern piano, it obviously follows that a person unfamiliar with the harpsichord will draw from it only part of its real sonority. Truly enough, it is not an easy feat to make the harpsichord sing and produce mellow sonorities. It was considered the greatest art. One of Mattheson's admirers wrote, "Are you no longer pleased to charm the mind, to bewitch our ears, to make a harpsichord speak under your hands?" It was to that quality that Bach referred in his foreword to the Inventions.

Poets like Shakespeare and La Fontaine sang the beauties of the harpsichord, and musicians never ceased to profess high esteem for it, even when toward the end of the eighteenth century the clavichord became fashionable in Germany because it lent itself well to the kind of *galant* music of sweet and sentimental character that was then written, or when the pianoforte began to take root. The perfection of this king of keyboard instruments was so well recognized that no one believed it would ever lay down its scepter.

Organ and Harpsichord

In the eighteenth century the organ was compared to a concert of wind instruments and the harpsichord to a concert of strings, both admirable to an equal degree, although each in its own way. The great ambition of musicians was to excel in the playing of both; that is true of Bach, of his sons, as well as of Couperin, Frescobaldi, and others. Karl Philipp Emanuel said, "The organ is indispensable in church, where it bestows splendor and maintains order. In sacred recitatives and arias, however, and principally when the middle parts have but a simple accompaniment, one must resort to the harpsichord to give the singing voice freedom of variation. Too often, unfortunately, one discovers how bare a performance can be without harpsichord accompaniment. Moreover, this instrument is indispensable in the theater and at concerts."

"The harpsichord and the organ have certainly many features

in common," said Forkel, "but their style and the manner of playing them differ as much as their respective destinations; that
which at the harpsichord produces an excellent effect does not
express anything at the organ and vice versa. The best harpsichord
virtuoso will always remain a bad organist, unless he first familiar-
izes himself with the differences between the two instruments
and constantly keeps in mind the different purposes and objects
of each. I have found only two confirmations of this rule, the
first being J. S. Bach himself, the second Wilhelm Friedemann,
his eldest son. Both were elegant virtuosos at the harpsichord,
but once seated at the organ, it was impossible to perceive the
slightest trace of the harpsichordist. Melody, harmony, movement, everything was different, which means that they knew how
to adapt their skill to the nature of each instrument. When
I had the pleasure of hearing Wilhelm Friedemann at the harpsichord, all was delicate, elegant, pleasing. When I heard him
at the organ, I was truly seized with a religious respect. In the
first instance, all was charming; in the second, all was great and
solemn."

The harpsichord allows half-tint fineness, fluid and light broken chords as evanescent as dreams, or permits mysterious rus-
tlings—effects that are not at all suitable to the organ, on which
they could not even be realized.

The greatest insult to address to a composer or to a performer
was accusing him of writing or playing harpsichord pieces conceived in a character fit for the organ or organ works in harpsichord style. Quantz abused German provincial organists who
were "hardly good enough to play a hurdy-gurdy in a village
inn"; to prove the nadir of their ignorance he said that they did
not know the difference between the organ and the harpsichord.

The Advent of the Fortepiano

How did the phlegmatic fortepiano succeed in dethroning
the dynamic harpsichord? That is a question more complicated
than might be thought. Nobody ever questioned the "perfect
beauty" of the lute, yet this instrument disappeared at the beginning of the eighteenth century.

In *Le Parnasse Français*, Titon du Tillet said that in 1736 he had met M. Falco, a great lute amateur, who assured him that in Paris it would be hard to find more than three or four venerable old timers still playing this instrument. He added, "M. Falco invited me to go up to his apartment where, after having seated me in an antique armchair, he played five or six pieces on the lute, looking at me all the while with a tender expression and from time to time shedding tears on his lute. I could not help mingling a few tears with his. And thus we parted."

Toward the end of the seventeenth century the best lutes were searched out to be transformed into theorboes by enlarging the neck and adding supplementary strings. Somewhat later, the hurdy-gurdy, until then relegated to beggars and village peddlers, suddenly became the fashion. Marchionesses of Louis XV's court were seeking the few remaining lutes, "these gothic and despicable instruments," to have them transformed into hurdy-gurdies.

A teacher of the hurdy-gurdy, the Abbé Carbasus, wrote in a letter on the fashion of musical instruments (1739), "If Madame will glance at all the musical instruments, she will find none perfect except the hurdy-gurdy."

At the mammoth concert, mentioned earlier, given at Nuremberg in 1643, as a demonstration of the abuses of noble music, one heard pieces played on instruments that had become too vulgar or obsolete; among them were hurdy-gurdies, bagpipes, and shawms. In France, though, these instruments had begun to be very *à la mode*.

Hubert Le Blanc in 1740 devoted a whole volume to depicting the strife among the viol on one hand, and the violin and the cello on the other, taking sides with the viol against the pretenses of the coarse violin. I shall summarize briefly parts of this interesting book:

After public opinion had started propagating a mixture of truth and falsehood about the violin, a contest between these two instruments took place before a large crowd. The violin was acclaimed as a miraculous instrument capable of inciting great passions—"What beautiful sound, and so full!" As for the viol, its tender sonority was judged hardly good enough to express pastorales or elegies. To this verdict the viol replied, "What else but the most odious intrigues could make anyone believe that the chief merit of an instrument lies in its capacity for filling the concavity of a vast place? Is it not time that Stentor earned the Greek's esteem with the reasoning of Demosthenes, who had neither an iron chest nor a brazen throat, such as you and the trumpet have?" Shouts and applause arose. The ladies were giving their support to the bass viol, which blends so well with their voices. The violin was beside himself with vexation and had recourse to slander in these offensive terms, "Lady Wig-Box, of great ostent and little effect, between the size of your belly and the sound it produces, there is the same proportion as that between the mountain in labor and the mouse to which it gives birth." "No matter what you do," retorted the viol, "just because you are the strongest, does not mean you are the best in the symphony, etc. . . ." After long disputes, the verdict of the ladies was that "the loud tones and ringing sounds of the violin do not at all denote a person of quality or of noble education; therefore, the viol will remain the share of the gallant man. As for the violin, acknowledged to be the instrument of the multitude, it will be left to public audiences, if not to those who, like sheep, let fashion decide about instruments as it does clothing."

Contrary to modern belief, it was not the merit of filling "the concavity of a vast hall" that made the pianoforte triumph over the harpsichord.

In its primitive form the pianoforte (or fortepiano) was a charming instrument; its crystalline and diaphanous sonorities bore a closer resemblance to the harpsichord than does the modern piano. It also had more varied resources—some of them had a lute-stop or attachments producing the sounds of bells, drums, and kettledrums—but it shone with a feeble and attenuated luster. Up to the first half of the nineteenth century, the pianoforte had a sonority weaker than that of the harpsichord. Quantz and Marpurg acknowledged it in their writings, and Karl Philipp Emanuel Bach said about it in his *Essay*, "The new fortepianos, when they are well built . . . can be played alone well or join a not too strong musical ensemble."

For those who know well the instruments of that time, there can be no doubt about it. Obstinately people refuse to see in the harpsichord anything more than "the little quavering voice of an old man in a jabot," disregarding completely the depth of its low register as well as the ample and massive sonority that can be obtained by coupling the registers. The pianoforte should not be considered an improvement over the harpsichord. Plucked strings and struck strings are two different things. If it represents at all an improvement over a preceding instrument, it would be over the clavichord, which worked on the same principle.

Balbastre, organist of Louis XVI, said to Pascal Taskin, the famous inventor of the buff register, who had just tried out the first fortepiano introduced to the Tuileries, "Whatever you do, my friend, this newcomer will never dethrone the majestic harpsichord." "The fortepiano is an ironmonger's invention compared with the harpsichord," said Voltaire.

In one of his interesting articles Gaston Carraud noted with much perception that there was no cause for astonishment at Bach's rejection of the first fortepiano he saw, because in his time the harpsichord had reached its perfection, while Silbermann's first fortepiano probably was still in an embryonic stage. But almost thirty years later, in 1777, when Mozart met Stein in Augsburg, he described enthusiastically a pianoforte made by this remarkable instrument maker. He mentioned its precision, its lightness, the marvelous functioning of its knee-levers, and the firmness of its soundboard. The instrument Mozart loved and played had a transparent sonority; its middle and upper ranges were rounded and full in *cantilenas*, but were capable of becoming crisp and grained; the bass was ample without ever being heavy. It had none of the opulence of tone, the voluptuousness and stormy basses of the piano. The ideal pianoforte of Mozart never was the instrument of Schumann or Brahms.

While we see all harpsichordists delighted with their instruments, Steibelt, one of the first famous fortepianists, and son of a piano maker, wrote in 1806, "To cover up the monotony of the piano I wish that its own exclusive peculiarities be used toward its glorification." At the time of Steibelt the piano had already reached great perfection according to our modern standard, and yet it was really a monotonous instrument compared with the harpsichord, since it did not have two keyboards nor an equivalent richness of registers. The fortepiano, however, offered great practical advantages; its construction was simpler, its price more accessible, and its tuning was easier and more durable; all these factors could predispose in its favor. Yet in spite of all these qualities, it took nearly fifty years before it was generally adopted. In Bach's time its role was insignificant; at the time of his sons, the harpsichord was still often preferred; and Mozart and Haydn at first used both instruments without showing a preference for either one. Its real triumph did not start before the beginning of the nineteenth century.

What a veritable crossroads of keyboard instruments, and what a transition in esthetics! Nothing describes this better than a letter from Mozart's father dated November 13, 1777, in which he mentions the instruments he saw in the home of a musician at Frankfurt: "You will find at his house a collection of instruments which would mean for you an embarrassment of choice. . . . In addition to his large Friderici harpsichord with two manuals, like our own, he had a perfectly new and very large pianoforte in mahogany, which he described at length and with the greatest enthusiasm. Further, he has a clavichord also in mahogany, which he would not sell for 200 Gulden, as he says that this instrument simply has not got its equal; that the descant sounds like a violin being played softly, and the bass notes like trombones (sic). In addition, he has a number of pianofortes all made by Friderici, as he deals in these."

Thus, while the pianoforte was received with curiosity, although without enthusiasm at first, the harpsichord was bade a fond and lingering farewell. Nonetheless, the day came when the king of instruments which for three centuries had charmed the humors of chatelaines, animated the solitude of cloisters, had been the confidant of Frescobaldi, Bach, and the Couperins, and had reigned as absolute monarch in the theater and in the church was dethroned, disdained, and despised. It ended its days miserably, transformed into desks, dressing tables, or linen chests; or, thanks to the paintings of Boucher, Téniers, or Van Loo that decorated the lid, it was relegated to gathering dust in museums, subject to the scorn of gapers who understood nothing of its elegance, beauty, nobility, and splendor.

Sic transit gloria mundi

This motto is often found on old harpsichords and spinets; it probably meant that their sound would vanish like the glory of this world.

Bach's Keyboard Instruments

Among all the masters of the past, Bach is the most universally revered today. In modern performances of his keyboard works the basic problem resides in the choice of instrument.

Leaving transcriptions aside, Bach's organ works belong unmistakably to the organ. Yet overevaluation of power and force of sonority during the nineteenth century have led to changes or to what many consider improvements in the construction of today's instruments. In his book on Bach in 1905 Schweitzer warned that "the works of Bach could hardly benefit from the sonority of the modern organ. Foundation stops have taken too much importance in relation to the mixtures; they are too numerous, and at the same time they have too much volume. Mixture stops of Bach's time, equal in number to foundation stops, were much sweeter than our modern mixtures and produced an intense, although refined, sonority which illuminated the design of a fugue marvelously." On today's organs these fugues, according to Schweitzer, become heavy and massive, just as engravings would if they were reproduced with charcoal.

As for the other keyboard works of Bach, on what instrument should they be played—harpsichord, clavichord, or piano?

If anyone had dared to ask such a question around 1900, he would have been laughed at. "What! To favor ancient instruments over our perfected piano . . . pure folly! Like a true precursor, Bach obviously foresaw the modern piano, and it is with that instrument in mind that he wrote his magnificent works, unplayable on the 'old boxes' of long ago." Times have changed. This problem is now treated in earnest and with passion by serious musicians and musicologists. Numerous and thorough studies devoted to this subject have been published. But we still find lingering on the old commonplaces that virtuosos, instrument builders, and piano teachers spread all through the nineteenth century. Alone in his generation, Anton Rubinstein did not seem to share the general infatuation with modern instruments in the performance of music of the past. He said, "I cannot help believing that the instruments of the past had sonorous colors and effects that we cannot reproduce on today's pianos. Since the works of the past were conceived for the instruments then in existence, they must have received their complete expression from them; therefore when they are played on today's piano, they sound rather to their disadvantage." Prompted by the best intentions, he searched for means of obtaining the sonorities of vanished eras; "I am always seeking to 'register' the works of Handel, and especially those of Bach by means of various touches and changes of pedals. . . . We cannot have an exact idea of what these harpsichords, clavichords, clavicembalos, and spinets were like, nor do we know the most important thing—that is, the way to manipulate them."

In this he went too far; the seventeenth and eighteenth centuries abounded not only in genial musicians, but also in remarkable theorists. We would rather complain about having too many documents because a lifetime would not suffice to know half of them. We are now beginning to acquire a more precise knowledge of all these instruments and even to discover the way of using them. And if I still happen to encounter accusations such as that made after one of my concerts, "Madame Landowska's clavichord is not, as she announces, a *cembalo*, it is simply a spinet," learned musicians at least no longer throw into the same bag clavichords, harpsichords, spinets, and other confidants of the greatest masters of the past.

What exactly was the instrument for which Bach wrote his keyboard works?

A dissertation read by Professor Buchmayer during the Bach festival of 1908 started a polemic—a too violent one, undoubtedly —which is far from being ended. Buchmayer wanted to prove that Bach's favorite instrument was the clavichord, and he based his assertion on the fondness that Kuhnau, Fischer, and Mattheson were supposed to have expressed for this instrument and on the meager interest they showed in the harpsichord. He backed his arguments on the ideas expressed by Forkel and Spitta, the first biographers of Bach. In spite of my admiration for the knowledge and talent of Buchmayer, I could never share his views; as for his argumentation, it appeared to me quite insufficient and inconclusive.

It is true that Mattheson recommends the clavichord for *galant* pieces, but his suites are quite different from those of Bach; besides he was not an enemy of the harpsichord, as we are led to believe. As for J. K. F. Fischer, he wrote in his dedication that his pieces were composed for the *Clavicordium oder Instrument*. By *Instrument*, he meant precisely *harpsichord*. To dispel any doubts about that, one has only to consult the original title of the volume, which bears in large type *Les Pièces de Clavecin* composed by J. K. F. Fischer.

Even admitting that some of Bach's predecessors favored the clavichord over all other instruments, where is proof that he himself necessarily shared the same taste?

Professor Buchmayer attached great importance to the indication found in the title of J. S. Bach's *Inventions and Sinfonias:* ". . . and above all to attain a singing style in playing . . . *Ein cantable Art im Spielen zu erlangen*). He sees in it an irrefutable proof that these pieces were intended for the clavichord, since that instrument had a more singing tone than the harpsichord. None of this precludes seeing in it proof to the contrary. Bach was not the only one of his time to write expressive music. So many works by French and Italian composers, undeniably written for the harpsichord, bore titles such as *Les Tendres Plaintes, La Reine des Coeurs, Canzone,* etc. Can we doubt Bach's artistry and taste in making his harpsichord sing with expression just as well as Rameau, Couperin, or Frescobaldi did? And since Bach's heart did not indulge exclusively in sweet dreams and as he often did let himself go with force and fury, why then insist that the "timid, melancholy, and infinitely soft clavichord" was his only favorite, his only confidant?

Although greatly exaggerated by Forkel, the love of Karl Philipp Emanuel Bach for the clavichord was a fact; but to assume that the father had shared the feeling of his son is all the more unreasonable, since their own particular epochs represented two completely different esthetics. The clavichord at the time of Karl Philipp Emanuel had become the exponent of the *galant* style, from which a too strict polyphony was progressively disappearing. If Karl Philipp Emanuel had been such a fanatic of the clavichord, would he have written so many concertos specifying clearly *Concerto per il cembalo concertato?* And since these were for harpsichord, his eighty cadenzas (Wotquenne No. 120) could not have been conceived for another instrument. Until 1781 we find in Karl Philipp Emanuel's chamber music sonatas *a cembalo obligato e violino,* or *viola, flauto,* as well as *trios* and *quartettos a cembalo obligato*. Among his solo pieces, the first, written in 1731, when he was seventeen and which he engraved himself, bears the title *Menuet pour le clavessin*. His sonatas published between 1742 and 1744 are called *Sonate per il cembalo*. Only from 1765 on do we find the word *Clavier*, although as late as 1770 Karl Philipp Emanuel published *Six Sonates pour le Clavecin à l'Usage des Dames*. In 1780 the word *fortepiano* appears in his editions. Moreover, had not Karl Philipp Emanuel established in his *Essay* that the clavichord was suited only for solo playing, that the pianoforte could withstand only the company of a few other instruments, and that the harpsichord alone possessed the strength necessary to dialogue with an orchestra?

After Johann Sebastian's death an inventory was made. Here is the section describing the musical instruments found in his home:

1 veneered *Clavecin*, which if possible is to remain in the family	80	rt.			
1 *Clavesin*	50	—			
1 *ditto*	50	—			
1 *ditto*	50	—			
1 *ditto*, smaller	20	—			
1 *Lauten Werck* (Lute-harpsichord)	30	—			
1 *ditto*	30	—			
1 Stainer violin	8	—			
1 less valuable violin	2	—			
1 *violino piccolo*	1	—	8	gr.	
1 *braccia* (viola)	5	—			
1 *ditto*	5	—			
1 *ditto*		—	—	16	—
1 *Bassetgen* (little bass)	6	—			
1 Violoncello	6	—			
1 *ditto*		—	—	16	—
1 *viola da gamba*	3	—			
1 lute	21	—			
1 *Spinettgen*	3	—			
Total	371	rt.	16	gr.	

That is to say, five harpsichords and one spinet, not to mention the three pedal-harpsichords he personally gave to Johann Christian before his death. Anyone who wants to convince us that Bach's favorite instrument was the clavichord should reflect that there is no trace of that instrument in the inventory. On the other hand, notice that the combined value of Bach's harpsichords represents a third of the total worth of his possessions (the grand total of his estate amounted to 1122 rt. 16 gr.).

There is an old anecdote which was very popular in the eighteenth century. A soldier walking through a forest sat down under a tree. He took out some bread and cheese from his rucksack, and he had just begun to eat when he saw two wolves whose famished looks warned him that they intended to partake of the feast. To prevent their approaching too closely he threw out several morsels, but soon everything he had was gone. Not knowing how to escape these creatures, the soldier thought of playing his bagpipe. No sooner had he started to play than the wolves, terrified, fled. Relieved, the soldier said, "Had I known that music would please you so, you would have had it before the meal!"

If the little wolves who wish to tear apart my harpsichord are not satisfied with the crumbs I just threw them, I know certain bagpipe tunes that should send them scurrying; they are Bach's authentic titles.

During his lifetime Bach published only a few volumes of his works, copies of which, revised and corrected by himself, are now in the British Museum. The second volume of these publications bears a very exact indication: *Ein Concerto nach Italienischen Gust und einer Overture nach Französischer Art, vor ein Clavicymbel mit zweyen Manualen.* (A Concerto in Italian Taste and an Overture in the French Manner, for a Harpsichord with Two Keyboards.) There can be no doubt that the Italian Concerto and the French Overture were written for the harpsichord.

In the fourth volume we find a no less precise recommendation: *Arie mit verschiedenen Veraenderungen vors Clavicymbel mit 2 Manualen.* (Aria with Ornamented Variations for Harpsichord with Two Keyboards.)

It was said that the *English Suites* were unsuited for the harpsichord. The autograph, however, which, according to E. Naumann (Bach-Gesellschaft Vol. 45) belonged to Jos. Hauser in Carlsruhe, has the following title: *"Six Svittes avec leurs Preludes pour le Clavessin composées par Jean Sebast. Bach."* (Six Suites with Their Preludes for the Harpsichord Composed by J. S. Bach.)

The autograph of the *French Suites* in the Berlin Library

bears the title of *Sex Sviten pur le Clavessin compossée par J. S. Bach.* We still find further confirmation in the *Clavier-Büchlein* of Anna Magdalena, dated 1722, in which Bach wrote in his own hand above the third Suite *"Pour le clavecin, par J.S.B."* Above the fourth Suite there is *"Suite in Dis pour le clavecin"* and above the fifth *"Suite pour le clavecin ex G-#."*

In the 1725 *Notenbuch* of Anna Magdalena we also read:

> XXX. *Suite I pour le clavessin par J.S.Bach*
> XXXI. *Suite II pour le clavessin par J.S.Bach*
> XXVII. *Solo per il cembalo*

Confronted by such conclusive testimony, by such precise recommendation from Bach himself, it seems to me that all discussion concerning the above mentioned works becomes futile.

As for the Partitas, we lack information, although Spitta himself declared that they were written for the harpsichord, not for the clavichord. They were published during Bach's lifetime in the first volume of the *Clavierübungen.* The word *Clavier,* as we have seen before, was only a general term which applied to any keyboard instrument. But in the second volume of the *Clavierübungen* we find pieces for *Clavicymbel mit zweyen Manualen,* while the third contains pieces designated for the organ. Since Bach demanded the harpsichord for the French and English Suites, there is no reason why the Partitas, whose character and form are close to those of the French and English Suites, should require a different instrument.

The autograph of the *Chromatic Fantasy* is missing, but we are not surprised to find on the oldest copy extant, dated December 6, 1730, the following title: *Fantasia chromatica pro Cimbalo di J. S. Bach* (Chromatic Fantasy for Harpsichord by J. S. Bach).

The first page of the autograph of the C Minor Fantasia is also missing, but we find the indication *per il cembalo* (for the harpsichord) on an old copy.

The Toccata in D Major bears in the Sara Levy copy the title *Toccata-Cembalo.* The Toccata in G Major in Gerber's copy has *Concerto seu Toccata pour le Clavecin.* As for the Overture in F Major, it is entitled *Ouverture per il clavicembalo* in the copy of the Hamburg organist, Westphal.

In the Sonata in G Major, No. 1, and in the third in G minor for keyboard and viola da gamba we find the title written in Bach's own hand: *Sonata a cembalo e viola da gamba*. In other autographs we read:

> *Sonata a cembalo obligato e Traverso solo*
> *Sei Sonate a Cembalo concertato e Violino solo*
> *Sonata a 1 Traverso e cembalo obligato*
> *Concerto a cembalo concertato*.

Generally all the concertos and all chamber music bear, either in the autograph or in the first copies, the indication of harpsichord, which is also found as accompaniment to the recitatives in the Cantatas. In *The St. John Passion*, the bass aria "Betrachte meine Seele" can be accompanied either by the organ or by the harpsichord (*organo a cembalo obligato*). In the trio from *The Musical Offering*, the continuo has been written out by Kirnberger for the harpsichord.

Then in which of Bach's major keyboard works is the harpsichord not clearly mentioned? The two- and three-part *Inventions* and *The Well-Tempered Clavier*; but neither is the clavichord named, nor is the slightest trace of *Bebung*, which was indicated by the sign ⌒ . . . ⌄ to be found in these works. Yet many modern revisors continue to propagate the error of Forkel and Spitta, and—Busoni among them—they go as far as to falsify the title of the *Forty-Eight*, calling this work *The Well-Tempered Clavichord*.*

Bach's autograph title (pp. 146-7) is in itself an eloquent expression of what his concern was. It is well known that for years theoreticians and musicians had been searching for a solution to the dilemma of equal temperament. Bach knew the writings of Werkmeister on this matter. While in Cöthen he had enough leisure to ponder the technical tendencies of the day. His acquaintance with Werkmeister's theory brought to fruition the problem that had long preoccupied him. Riemann suggested that Bach was seduced by the idea of bringing out the characteristics of all the various tonalities. Certainly Bach was not just passively accepting Werkmeister's thesis. That would have been contrary to his nature. Conscious of the

---

* ED. NOTE: At the suggestion of Wanda Landowska, E. Kalmus reverted to the original title of *The Well-Tempered Clavier* toward 1950.

J. S. Bach's autograph title page for *The Well-Tempered Clavier*—1722 minutest research, regardless of its direction, Bach's natural gifts spurred him to exploit any problem of a physical or acoustical order or one connected with instrumental technique. He knew how to reap benefit from the discoveries of the theorists, but he concentrated, first of all, on their musical aspect. The possibility of writing in uncommon keys could only stimulate his inventive mind, and we may be sure that it was not just to prove the veracity of a thesis that he wrote *The Well-Tempered Clavier*. Besides, all arguments of a theoretical or historical order are absolutely superfluous for those who are familiar with both the clavichord and the harpsichord. For them one look is sufficient to realize for which of the two instruments a piece was composed.

Let us see, for instance, the first Prelude in C major from Book I, with its broken chords; the second, in C minor; and the sixth, in D minor, tumultuous, demanding the sonority of a large string orchestra; the third, in C sharp major, with its *batteries à la française*; the eighth in E flat minor with its French rhythm and the fiery gait of its pillars of chords; the thirteenth, in F sharp major, pastoral and requiring a register

Left
BACH'S AUTOGRAPH TITLE: *Das wohl temperirte Clavier. / oder / Praeludia, und / Fugen durch alle Tone und Semitonia, / So wohl tertiam majorem oder Ut Re Me anlan- / gend, als auch tertiam mi- norem oder Re / Mi Fa betreffend. Zum / Nutzen und Gebrauch der Lehrbegierigen / Musicalischen Jugend, als auch derer in diesem stu- / dio schon habil seyenden besonderem / Zeitvertreib aufgesetzet / und verfertiget von / Johann Sebastian Bach. / p.t. Hochf. Anhalt- / Cöthenischen Capell- / Meistern und Di- / rectore derer / Cammer Mu- / siquen. / Anno 1722.*

The Well-Tempered Clavier or Preludes and Fugues through all the tones and semitones both as regards the *tertia major* or *Ut Re Mi* and as concerns the *tertia minor* or *Re Mi Fa*. For the Use and Profit of the Musical Youth Desirous of Learning as well as for the Pastime of those Already Skilled in this Study. Drawn up and written by Johann Sebastian Bach Capellmeister to His Serene Highness the Prince of Anhalt-Cöthen, etc., and Director of His Chamber Music. Anno 1722.

that can evoke the whining sonority of an oboe; the twenty-first, in B flat major with its *roulements à la Rameau*. From the second Book see the sixth Prelude, in which Bach draws wonderful effects of crossings over the two keyboards; the twelfth, again with crossings of parts, this time legato. Are not all these typical harpsichord writing? They make use of the golden dust and luminous facets of its varied sonorities or of the sparkling virtuosity and wild gambols feasible on its double keyboard while they would be absolutely impossible on the single and weak keyboard of the clavichord.

As for the Fugues, the third in C sharp major and the eighth in D sharp minor (while its accompanying prelude is in E flat minor) seem to glorify the victory of equal temperament; the fifth in D major requires the superb plenitude of the coupled keyboards; again in the eighth the plaintive theme asks for the transparent sonority of the upper keyboard, while the inverted theme, at measure 44, is best brought out by the mysterious gravity of the sixteen-foot register. The fourth in C sharp minor and the twenty-second in B flat minor begin with bell-like sonorities and develop into full choruses; the E flat major fugue from Book II is like an a cappella choir. What sad faces they would all make on a "timid and melancholy" clavichord! Rubinstein was absolutely right; Bach's keyboard works demand registers. Could they be those of the clavichord? That instrument has none. Did not Mozart write to his father on June 27, 1781, "We have two *Flügels* in the house where I am lodging, one for *galanterie* playing and the other an instrument which is strung with the low octave throughout like the one we had in London and consequently sounds like an organ. So on this one, I improvised and played fugues."

The rich, colorful, and ever-changing *Well-Tempered Clavier*, with the broad polyphony of its fugues, how could it be confined to the limited domain of the clavichord when Bach had a harpsichord at his disposal? A harpsichord with a variety of registers capable of producing sharp outlines or muted whispers, silvery and fluted tones as well as shifting sonorities and majestic fullness? These preludes and fugues are simply inconceivable on the weak clavichord. They demand imperiously the harpsichord and its architectural planes of sound, its wide, airy horizons which leave us free to erect bold arches within and between which the parts move, float, converge, diverge, and meet in absolute freedom.

The vogue of the clavichord, like its sonority, had a sweet and discreet luster. Why attribute to it soaring and haughty ambitions? Why not let its *Bebung* fade away under the moonlight of adolescent romanticism?

I see the smiles of certain professionals: "What difference does it make whether Bach wrote for the harpsichord or for the clavichord? It is all pedantry!" (To an untidy person, he who washes his hands is pedantic.) "And what do we care," they say, "for which instrument Bach wrote as long as we, anyway, play them on the piano?"

Some interpreters care for virtuosity, others for expression, but few are those who pay much attention to the character, the surroundings, the particular sonorities and style of an epoch. Specialization scarcely exists in the world of interpreters, and we have to be content with country doctors who treat all ailments: Scarlatti, Brahms, Cabezon, Bach, Beethoven, Schumann, Handel or Chopin, as well as the most recent composers. But times will change; they are changing already. While acknowledging the richness of a Louis XV frame, we abstain from setting a primitive painting in it, just as we would avoid placing an eighteenth-century engraving in secession-style surroundings, even if it were very beautiful in itself. Sooner or later we shall feel that the true character and the real beauty of a musical work can be recaptured only when it is played on the instrument which inspired it.

In the course of my travels I have observed that the antagonists of the harpsichord are to be found mostly among pianists. Their reluctance to accept the renaissance of the harpsichord is not based solely on the obvious difficulty of acquiring an expensive instrument, tricky to handle, and of learning its special technique. There are deeper and more serious reasons. When one has heard since childhood certain pieces played on the piano and when the ears have been accustomed all life long to the sound of this instrument, it is natural enough that, at first, one receives a shock of some sort when these same pieces are played with completely different sonorities. Too surprised by these silvery timbres, by these metallic chords, too dazzled by this luminous glitter and by this mysterious drone of the harpsichord, modern ears are unable to follow the melodic idea and to feel its expression. Our taste, ruled primarily by habit, revolts at first; but I could name among today's most fervent admirers of the harpsichord many who at the start rebelled against it. And this is why I am rather sceptical when someone tells me in earnest that he prefers the tone of the piano to that of the harpsichord. Can he be so sure that his taste will not change and that tomorrow his preference will not lie in another direction? Must I remain at the mercy of the mood or fancy of certain musicians or critics? Wishing to prove that the tone of the piano is in itself more beautiful than that of the harpsichord or of the clavichord would be a task as worthless as to fight for the superiority of the flute over the violin. The clavichord, the harpsichord, the early fortepiano, as well as our modern piano, are all admirable instruments. Only one should play on each the works that belong to it; when manipulated with knowledge, each one of these instruments will yield its particular beauty and expression.

ED. NOTE: One of the first musicologists who accepted Wanda Landowska's thesis was Georg Kinsky. In the second volume of his work on the *Musikhistorisches Museum von Wilhelm Heyer in Cöln* (Cologne, 1912) he said (p. 655), "The sentence about Bach in Volume I, third chapter, p. 23, is to be stricken out. Wanda Landowska's campaign, as artist and musicologist, has proved that *The Well-Tempered Clavier* as well as all great keyboard works of Bach were composed, not for the clavichord, but for the harpsichord."

For a detailed and technical study of both harpsichord and clavichord, cf. Lavignac, *Encyclopédie de la Musique*, Part II, pp. 2036 to 2060. This essay is based on extensive documentation furnished by Wanda Landowska.

13 Virtuosity, Now and Then

In their treatises on performance, the theorists of the past often mention the analogy that exists between musical interpretation and various species of eloquence. I secured a *Précis d'Art Oratoire* and do not regret it. I found in it very useful indications, and it is also most charming and instructive reading.

Eloquence is the art of speaking well, while interpretation is that of playing or singing well. It would be wrong to pretend that there is only one interpretation, the right one. What about the thousand bad ones? And the thousand good ones?

Orators recognize many different genres of eloquence according to movements and passions or to the various places at which they speak or in relation to the subject imposed upon them by circumstances. If we musicians wanted to establish a similar classification, we should likewise take into consideration the epoch and the style of the author being interpreted. A book on that subject would be voluminous, although relatively easy to write, because of its great analogies with my treatise on eloquence. We could keep whole pages intact, changing or replacing only here and there technical terms. Let us quote at random:

"One wins confidence through the self-assurance with which one presents oneself to the public, by a gravity that seems a token of wisdom, and by long preliminary meditations. Sometimes, however, contrary ways lead to the same goal, and severity, abruptness, and bluntness incite confidence in the highest degree. A strong and sonorous voice is no less a necessity. In fact, perfect silence never reigns in assemblies, and yet the orator must be heard. . . ." This corresponds to what Chopin said to Liszt, "To play for the average public, one must have the means, as you do, to knock them out."

"Cicero wanted speeches to begin and end with the strongest argument because, he said, one must take hold of the mind at the start and conquer it at the end. Some want to begin with the weakest statements so as to be able to rise gradually to the strongest and come to an end with the decisive ones."

The two systems are in use in musical interpretation. Virtuosos particularly like the first, either preluding with transport, making the basses rumble, or giving in impetuously from the start to an irrepressible feeling of passion, of sorrow, and of indignation so as to strike, electrify, and sweep the audience along while they warm up. Others of a more dreamy nature prefer to go lightly over the keyboard from top to bottom, to begin timidly, and graduating the passions, to arrive at an apotheosis, not out of breath like the former type of virtuoso, but in full strength.

The *Manuel d'Eloquence* contains a mass of recommendations and recipes to awaken the senses; like Phrygian chants, they have the power of arousing passions; they explain how to frighten, irritate, or mollify the audience. With some practice we can obtain all these effects and, afterward, shed tears of joy for having been able to incite so many bitter ones to flow.

I shall not be mistaken, I believe, in comparing the interpretation of virtuosos to the eloquence of plebeian orators or, even better, to military eloquence. "The proper characteristics of military eloquence are rapidity, brilliance, and enthusiasm. It is no

more a question of these slow and respectful forms, of these ora-
tory circumlocutions, and of this subtle argumentation. It must
not be forgotten that in this case the orator is in command;
and whoever commands with boots and spurs commands with a
despotic accent. One may add that a skillful general never hopes
for nor suggests victory; he is sure of it, he decrees it. . . . Therefore, brilliant and varied figures of speech, a swift and pompous
style, the greatest vehemence in accentuation, and the constant
presence of the idea of glory must constitute military discourses."
As to popular orators, their language must contain more human
accents, be more moving, and have more tears in the voice while
remaining exciting and pompous.

Interpretation in virtuoso style oscillates between these two
genres of eloquence, but has less dignity. Acrobatic feats, glares
of defiance shot at the instrument, exaggerated rallentandi accompanied by ecstatic motions of the head, swoonings, skyward
gazes to command emotion, arrogant arpeggios, a boldness too
close to insolence, false brilliance, pianissimi after long crescendi,
routine transports toward the end of a piece intended to stop the
oscillations of the audience and achieve victory, and all kinds of
monkeyshines to picture great ebbs and flows of the soul have a
little *je ne sais quoi* of charlatanism.

Virtuosity was not invented yesterday; most of the composers
of the past were great virtuosos. Bach owed his fame during his
own lifetime more to the perfection of his organ and harpsichord
playing than to his compositions. Handel, Mozart, and Haydn
were great virtuosos. Father Mersenne spoke with enthusiasm, in
his *Harmonie Universelle*, 1636, of Jacques Champion de Chambonnières in whom the harpsichord had "met its last master,"
although Chambonnières affected to be a man of the world who
played the harpsichord only for pleasure.

English virginalists must have had astonishing ability; their
works present sometimes difficulties greater than those encountered in Liszt's Rhapsodies.

In general, the utmost importance was attached to good
execution. When he found fault with a violinist, Lully would
snatch the violin from the hands of the culprit and break it on
his head. He rehearsed the orchestra up to thirty times before
the performance of one of his operas. Karl Philipp Emanuel Bach
said that even with the best orchestras one has to hold several

rehearsals, no matter how simple the work may be, just for the sake of a few notes.

Bach dreamed of hearing Handel play; he traveled far afield to listen to Reincken; he himself played for the aged Reincken, who exclaimed afterward, "I thought that this art was going to die with me, but I see that you are reviving it."

Frescobaldi could play the harpsichord with upturned hands, a tour de force difficult to imitate. Hiller said that Bach executed with his feet pedal passages that others would have had trouble playing with their hands. Bruhns (1665-1697), a pupil of Buxtehude and the author of excellent organ works, often executed pieces on the violin while playing the bass on the organ pedalboard.

The demands made upon harpsichordists were manifold. They had to know how to improvise in various genres, to develop a given theme according to the severest rules of counterpoint, and to transpose *prima vista*. Besides playing solo, they had to master the realization of the figured bass and had to fill it out when it was not even figured. Karl Philipp Emanuel asserted that it was not enough for a performer just to do all this after established rules, as any pedant would. Taste, fantasy, and inventiveness were also expected.

The demands made upon organists were still greater (see Tobias Norlind, *Was ein Organist im 17. Jahrhundert wissen musste*).

At that epoch, coordination of mind and fingers was astonishing. That was technique and not what it has become today, the polishing and repolishing of more or less difficult passages. In the seventeenth and eighteenth centuries an artist could not indulge exclusively in a sportive game of technical prowess; although people were very sensitive to the merit of overcoming difficulties, it was not to be a total absorption in the cold calculations of pyrotechnics. A soloist had to be a good musician, and that is not always true of today's virtuosos. In our art nurseries, music is casually grafted upon wild stock hardly fit for it. Following strenuous and stubborn work and despite a nature not always very musical, a zealous pupil may acquire what is called "magnificent fingers"; by constantly practicing the same two or three dozens pieces which form the trousseau of every virtuoso, he can become a great violinist or a great pianist without being either a musician or an artist. Since the repertory has scarcely changed for the last fifty years, interpretation causes no trouble; small virtuosos imitate the great, overdoing their style; and when they, in turn, become great, they are imitated by their pupils. The artistic mottos are always the same: "Better strike hard rather than accurately!" and "Never shy away from anything capable of producing an effect!" "The more I play in public," wrote Clara Schumann, "the more I hate pure virtuosity."

I believe that the first virtuoso in the modern understanding of the word was the famous pianist Steibelt. He toured extensively in England and Germany and visited Vienna, where he entered into competition with Beethoven; in the opinion of one group of amateurs, he seemed to have surpassed him. His detractors criticized his immoderate use of tremolo, the unevenness of his playing, and the weakness of his left hand. His favorites were the fantasias with variations, the *rondos brillants*, and the bacchanals with accompaniment of tambourin played by his wife. Norvins pretended that "he dethroned Dussek by the charlatanry of his pedaling." He admitted himself that his activity with the pedals made everybody accuse him of showing off, but that this opinion had been reversed. Perhaps he was the initiator of this *mise en scène* since used by so many pianists. In any case he brought to it the consummate knowledge of a man who ignored none of the foibles of his contemporaries (Paul d'Estrées, *La Musique depuis deux siècles*). Norvins had witnessed Steibelt's antics at the home of his cousin, Madame de la Briche. "In these magnificent salons where aristocrats by birth and by fortune congregated in a kind of literary and musical academy, frequented by the elite of intellectual France—poets, artists, savants—Steibelt presented himself, preceded by his reputation as an amazing and whimsical virtuoso, bearer of a dark and fatal look, his brow burdened with clouds, his gait inspired. He walked straight to the piano, sat down like a conqueror, and preluded with a brilliant improvization, which brought him a storm of applause. Then he retired within himself for a few seconds; and in a stern voice, with an imperious gesture, ordered all lights out, even the two candles affixed to the piano. The fireplace alone lighted the room, and its reddish glow danced on the anxious faces of the ladies seated in the first row. Everyone intrigued by these preparations, unusual before that time in the world of artists, exchanged a few words with his neighbour in hushed tones. Suddenly a series of swift and jerky arpeggios imposed silence. Then, a new pause. Finally when he could no longer hear the slightest murmur, Steibelt smacked formidable chords on the keyboard and let loose a real musical tornado that made all heads bow and all hearts shrink."

This display was enough for Madame de la Briche's curiosity. The lady left to those more enamored of fantastic harmonies than herself the privilege of receiving this demoniac musician.

Oscar Commettant in *Le Piano et les Pianistes* tells a seemingly unbelievable story, which he swears is absolutely true. A certain pianist, as admirable a performer as he was a clever booster, hired women for twenty francs a concert to simulate fainting in the midst of his playing of a fantasia attacked so fast that it would have been humanly impossible to carry on at that speed to the end. Once in Paris the hired woman, having fallen soundly asleep, missed her cue; the pianist was playing Weber's Concerto. Counting on the fainting of this woman to interrupt the finale, he had started it in an impossible tempo. What to do? Flounder like a vulgar pianist or simulate a lapse of memory? No, he simply played the role of the hired woman and fainted himself. The audience rushed to the help of the pianist, who was all the more phenomenal, since he added to his lightning performance a fragile and sensitive nature. He was carried backstage; men applauded frantically, women waved their handkerchiefs, and the fainting woman, waking up, really fainted, perhaps in despair at having missed her cue.

Bonnet tells an anecdote drawn from Greek history which might well have happened today; a famous flute player named Harmonide asked his mentor, Timothius, what he could do to win the musical prize offered at public festivities in Athens. Timothius demonstrated to him the difficulties of this enterprise and among other things that "those who ordinarily judge at festivals and spectacles are often those who know the least, but who are, however, the most stubborn, the most obstinate and those who shout the loudest." Harmonide reflected on this advice and thought he could win by playing one tone higher than usual; but the very first time he performed on stage, he expired from having played at a pitch too high.

And at all times we encounter this striking fact: to meet the taste of the vulgar, artists resort to turgidity, to forced and exaggerated accentuation. In the eighteenth century there were many virtuoso singers for whom everything in art was reduced to canary roulades and nightingale sighs or who forced their voices to show off the power of their lungs.

Complaints were made also about instrumentalists. "Today music is only the art of performing difficult things," said Signor Pococurante in Voltaire's *Candide*, "but what is merely difficult ceases to please in the long run."

"How much better it would be to observe a restraint in keeping with the simplicity of perfect justness rather than indulging in this kind of playing I call brazen—not bold—which, ignoring observation, never fails to lie with self-assurance about justness; it deceives only those people for whom audacity of eloquence has always been imposing." (Hubert Le Blanc, *Défense de la Basse de Viole*, 1774)

Gluck's witty remark is well known. During the rehearsal of *Orpheus* at the Académie Royale de Musique, Legros insisted, as he always did, on shouting the phrase of the entrance into Tartarus "Laissez-vous toucher par mes plaintes" (Let my lamentations move you). Finally one day the exasperated composer interrupted Legros in the middle of the phrase and shouted at him: "Sir, sir, will you please moderate your clamor! By Satan, one does not shriek like that in Hell!" (Berlioz, *Orphée*)

Italian virtuosos were the prototype of these note-jugglers. The public relished them as a delicacy, but people of taste found that the "passions enacted by these beardless men were too suspiciously false and that their voices lacked naturalness because they were like an instrument from which some wood had been chopped off to make it produce sounds." The modern virtuoso, with his muscles exaggeratedly developed through mechanical practice, is somewhat in the same situation.

The "law of fist" which reigns now in the keyboard empire has given rise to different aspirations and new ambitions. I cannot forget the article, or rather the ingenious publicity, which appeared in the *New York Music Trade Review* concerning a very great virtuoso:

"The master stopped a moment and suddenly fell into ecstasy. He ran his fingers through his hair, turned up his sleeves, flung back his coattails, brought the seat closer, and bending forward, he threw himself with all his might on the piano. It roared like a lion, trilled like a nightingale, and whistled like an engine. But the implacable master never took his hands off. Having reached the bass, he dug into it way down to hell, and thunderbolts were bursting everywhere in the subterranean cavern. Then, with his left hand, he gave chase to the right, pursuing it up to the highest summits of the descant, and from there all the way up to the sky, where notes became sharper than pins. But he did not let go yet. He led the left wing to the attack, then the right wing, and then the center. He ordered 'fire' to his artillery; bombs, schrapnel were bursting on all sides; explosions of mines, the hall shook, the chandeliers danced, the floor heaved and fell back with all his weight and all the strength of his fists on the keyboard. The piano broke and shattered into 75,542 trills and half trills!"

Women virtuosos, they too, insist upon being up to it; they do not wish to be left behind, since the greatest compliment one can give them today is to say, "With closed eyes one would swear it were a man!"

The taste of an epoch, what a fragile caprice! Not so long ago it was the custom at the pope's court to submit men to painful sacrifice to give their voices the sweetness, clarity, and charm of a woman's voice. The last century offered us the contrary—virile women.

14   The Return to the Music of the Past

I HAVE insisted on the fallacy of progress in music because I consider it to be the principal cause of ignorance about our past and of most errors in the interpretation of our ancient masters. Because of this prejudice, blown up almost to the importance of a religion, the true beauties of music—as numerous as those of other arts—are still very poorly revealed. We remain deaf to these miracles of beauty, so marvelously remote; yet they should uplift the soul by their melodious echo, and, from century to century, they should link sympathetic hearts with a divine tie.

If sometimes we tire of grandiosity and if we lack air in the thick atmosphere of exaggerated romanticism, we need only to open wide the windows on our magnificent past; it will refresh our soul. We wish to participate in all emotions, in all ecstasies at the whim of our fancy. No longer shall we believe that while all the arts flourished marvelously in the past, music alone, although admired, was like a frail and sickly plant that could hardly break through the ground. Even supposing that music was in its cradle, we may be as sensitive to the charm of a prattling child as to the most skillful speech of a seasoned orator. If, on the contrary, music is afflicted with old age, we know how to admire the beauty of a lined face. No, the genius of the composers of the past was not a mere flash in the pan; it is an eternal flame, softly warming. It will never perish.

Yes, but one must go along with one's own time. Let new beauties be created, and we shall like them; but, at the same time, let us not relegate to darkness the works of the masters who were our models. They are not wolves; they will not, as Gounod said, devour the new masterpieces.

And in the name of what prejudice shall we continue to be suspended from the tiny spot we occupy in space instead of extending our view afar, instead of being contemporaries of all men? Only when we are strong enough to withstand that prejudice shall we really belong to our epoch. The great merit of the last half of the nineteenth century was that it awakened a taste for retrospection, a sense of comparison, and made us delight in that which is old, an "old" that is often newer than the new. A passion has been kindled in us; it does not encompass superior civilizations alone, but also those that our computer of taste had rated childish, decadent, or barbaric.

There is an evergrowing interest in the music of the past. But this would prove little in itself, since at all times the greatest musicians bowed before the works of the geniuses that preceded them. "We are not recapturing the masterpieces," said Jules Janin; "the masterpieces themselves are recapturing us." Sooner or later, everyone will understand that a work of Josquin des Prés is well worth a Breughel. People of refined taste will feel that a Magnificat of Pachelbel, a chanson of Jannequin, a cantata of Bach, and a motet of Palestrina are worth more than the songs of modern sirens and of all the machines of speed. Then they will help us to erect a museum where we shall be able to hear and admire all our Titians, our Velasquezes, and our Raphaels, just as painters are able to admire theirs. And then we shall be able to enhance our lives with the memory of times that are gone.

PART TWO

Foreword to Part Two

WHEN Wanda Landowska ana-
lyzed a piece of music, she described it as one would a drama.
Themes, countersubjects, episodes, etc., became as many characters. Following the evolutions of a melodic line or of a harmonic progression, Landowska made us discover the plot. She
was able to penetrate so totally the core of the mechanism of
music as well as the thoughts of its authors that for her each
piece of music was a living experience.

Problems of interpretation are met right when and where
they occur amid the musical context. Their technicalities are
explained in the light of their historical, psychological, and
expressive meaning, in themselves, and in comparison with other
works. We are never subjected to dry and pedantic coaching,
but led into an enchanted world. Our enjoyment of the musical
compositions we instinctively love is greatly enhanced by discovering what makes them "tick," thanks to Landowska's vivid
introductions.

Of her own commentaries Landowska wrote:

I read with profit time and again the analyses written by various commentators and musicologists. They always refer to the structure of
the works, rarely to their character, to the atmosphere that pervades
them, or to the nature of their elements. I agree with many of the
statements I read and disapprove of others. In writing my own com-

mentaries, I am not spurred on by a vain desire to uncover hitherto unknown facts, but by a wish to penetrate the composer's thoughts. If I happen to be struck by a different aspect, unnoticed by others, but obvious to me, I mention it—no more. I know that other researchers may disagree, argue, and try to prove me wrong by crushing me under a mass of quotations and documents. Would that be sufficient reason to abstain from saying what I see in these works, what fifty years of uninterrupted companionship with Bach, his predecessors, and his contemporaries has taught me?

I know the danger of using poetic evocations or literary descriptions in writing about music. I know the fragility, the ephemeral quality of the images that certain kinds of music suggest to us. A Bach prelude described by Riemann as "a balmy spring night" may have a completely different meaning for me. One could write volumes on this subject; no doubt they would make us laugh or cry. Aware of this—and God knows how much I hate romanticized literature —I tried to remain sober in writing my commentaries. Yet when I study documents thoroughly, they become flesh and blood; they suggest visions that haunt me. What am I to do? Stifle them the moment they form? Or let them live and pour out? Through the atmosphere I create in playing, the choice of my registration, etc., am I not imposing these visions on the listeners? Yes, but there is freedom in the realm of music, and everyone's imagination may wander at leisure. Nonetheless it is a puzzling dilemma. How fortunate that in many instances the character of a work is unquestionably established by the composer himself!

I On The Interpretation of
Johann Sebastian Bach's Keyboard Works

Cantable Art

WHY DOES IT happen that a pianist who plays a Liszt transcription of Bach with much brilliance and assurance will stumble meekly when he is confronted with the original version—usually unknown to him—of the same work? His uneasiness does not diminish with a three-part prelude, and the fewer the number of voices, the more his embarrassment grows.

How can we explain this progression in *motu contrario*—the difficulty increasing as the piece becomes simpler? It is because the contrapuntal network becomes clearer and more spiritualized when the number of voices is reduced. This deprives the interpreter of the weapons he handled with shattering strength before. Stripped of all artifices, the performer remains bewildered. A two-part invention will drive him to purgatory and give him a glimpse of the essence of polyphony—note against note, hand against hand. The purity, logic, and independence of the voices prohibit all subterfuge, all confusion. They demand absolute clarity and loyalty. Noisy virtuosity, thick sonority muddied with too much pedaling, exaggerated tempi, contractions, and distortions of the lines—all this irreverent ignorance is banished from the realm of polyphonic music. To be allowed to approach it one should be provided with quieter but stronger weapons. Unfortunately it seldom happens.

Two-part music is of fundamental importance. It is the basis and point of departure of all polyphonic music. Besides the two-part inventions, a great many of Bach's works—concertos, preludes from *The Well-Tempered Clavier*, suites, partitas, etc.—are written in two parts. The immense diversity of these pieces and above all the richness of their character are undeniable proof that Bach considered them on the same plane as he did his more elaborate works. Bach's two-part pieces are as beautiful, as difficult, and as significant as the four- or five-part fugues.

Bach was not prodigal in literary effusions; and, unlike his contemporaries, he left us—aside from a few letters and dedications—only a single written document concerning interpretation. It is the preface to the 1723 autograph of the Inventions and Sinfonias. Short and concise, it guides us admirably toward Bach's idea. It says:

Proper Instruction wherein the lovers of the clavier, and especially those desirous of learning, are shown a clear way not only (1) to learn to play clearly in two voices, but also, after further progress, (2) to deal correctly and well with three obbligato parts; furthermore, not only to have good *inventiones* (ideas) but to develop the same well, and above all to arrive at a singing style (*Cantable Art*) in playing while acquiring a strong foretaste of composition.

Provided by
Joh. Seb. Bach
Capellmeister to his Serene Highness
the Prince of Anhalt-Cöthen
Anno Christi 1723

What interested Bach obviously was a singing and expresive playing—*Cantable Art*, in his own words. This idea was not Bach's alone. We find it in all treatises of the time. Johann

Gottfried Walther, a pupil of Johann Bernhard Bach, writes in his *Lexicon*, "*Cantabile* refers to a vocal or instrumental composition which is easily sung in each of its parts." Telemann insists on the importance of letting oneself be inspired by the human voice: "Whatever piece one writes, vocal or instrumental, all in it must be *cantabile*." Mattheson exclaims in his *Grosse Generalbasschule*, "He who does not know the art of singing will never be able to play."

What is this *Cantable Art* so much sought after, to which all musicians aspired? It is just the contrary of what is understood today by "playing with feeling"; it is the opposite of an overflow of saccharine sentimentality, of swooning in the rallentandi, aiming to prove the "depth of soul" of the virtuoso. *Cantable Art* meant, in composition and in interpretation, the right manner of bringing out the independence and the beauty of a melodic line, the expression being controlled by the spirit. It was the art of phrasing and of bringing out voices, individually or simultaneously. To understand the esthetic of Bach, so different from that of the romantic period, and to revive this *Cantable Art* according to Bach's spirit, let us study closely, with reverence and passion, an invention or a two-part prelude. Let us interrogate the voices separately; let us never defend one to the detriment of the other; both are of equal interest. Let us plunge into each of them, impregnating ourselves with their soul, absorbing their substance. Let us watch their slightest motion, follow their fluctuations. And lo and behold, before the quest of our indefatigable love, a miracle takes place; the inspiration of Bach and the mystery of his melodic line reveal themselves. This melodic line has nothing polished, nothing uniform; it is perpetually alive, agitated, even when it seems to lull. This inner animation, which is not feverish in nature, derives from the overflowing vitality of Bach's inspiration. Exuberant and fiery, penetrating and incisive, this melodic line digs such deep grooves that it becomes polyphonic all by itself. In order to comprehend this—if you have not studied a voice singled out from among Bach's choral or instrumental works—steep yourself in the beauty and liveliness of the music Bach wrote for one voice alone, such as the cello suites or the sonatas for solo violin *senza cembalo*.

How can one do justice to this polyphony resumed in a single voice, to this line of unbroken length which seems to continue beyond the last bar?

First of all, through touch and phrasing, which on the harpsichord are of prime importance in bringing out the life and eloquence of contrapuntal writing. The widespread belief that it is impossible to modify the sound of the harpsichord by touch alone without the aid of registers is completely false.

The development of touch is not a modern discovery. Its invention has been wrongly attributed to the masters of our modern piano, on which exclusively "one is capable of shading, graduating, and making a sound sing." Musicians of the past, such as Diruta, Frescobaldi, and Benedetto Marcello, have discussed this question with gravity and passion and have devoted to it detailed chapters in their treatises. The advice of François Couperin in his *Art de Toucher le Clavecin* is invaluable. The means through which this sonority was obtained differed as much from today's means as the sonority itself does. Harpsichordists, and even the first pianofortists, played with the fingers and did not resort to the use of arm strength, as is done today.

Here is what Rameau said in his *Méchanique des Doigts:* "The perfection of touch on the harpsichord consists principally in a well-conducted motion of the fingers. The wrist joint must always be supple; a suppleness which, after spreading to the fingers, gives them all the necessary freedom and lightness. The motion of the fingers is taken at their roots—that is, at the joint by which they are attached to the hand—and never elsewhere. The motion of the hand is taken at the wrist joint, and that of the arm, assuming that it is necessary, is taken at the elbow joint."

All these laws are in absolute contrast with those of the modern school of piano playing, which calls for thick and strong sonorities to be drawn from the arms and even from the shoulders and to be spread out over the keyboard. Whereas Rameau considered motions of the arms superfluous, the strength of the modern pianist is concentrated precisely in the arms and the shoulders; and it follows that too often it is with arm and shoulder strength that he will play Rameau just as he plays Liszt.

"Never weigh down the touch of your fingers by an effort of the hand," Rameau went on. "On the contrary, let your hand sustain your fingers and thus make the touch lighter; this is of great consequence. Observe a great evenness of movement between each finger; but above all never precipitate these movements; often one misses what one is looking for by hastening too much."

And Bourdelot wrote: "Of the three qualities to which I restrict the merit of instrumentalists, neatness is the principal one, especially for performers of instruments which are played directly by the fingers without bow. Out of five hundred performers on the lute, the harpsichord, etc., not ten of them are able to play with as much neatness as one should rightly expect. And without neatness what is a lute or a harpsichord piece? A noise, a din of chords of which one understands nothing. I might as well listen to a hurdy-gurdy. After this precious neatness comes delicacy. It is to instruments what cleanliness is to singing; it is to the attainment of this delicacy that all these little observations with which your masters burden you are also aimed. Then finally comes the ability to draw enough from one's instrument. An instrument must speak; and it is true that to make it speak well is an art and a very important talent; but let us not forget the capital axiom—a happy medium. The Italians truly did push too far this desire to draw a large sound from their instruments. My spirit, my heart, and my ears together tell me that they draw an excessively high and violent sound."

Absolute legato was a *sine qua non* of a perfect touch. The contemporaries of Chambonnières and Couperin always referred to it in praising these two incomparable virtuosos of the harpsichord. This legato aimed at welding the sounds together, thus forming a broad and smooth line without break. In contrast, the skillful harpsichordist had at his disposal a rich palette of colors which could be obtained only by means of a refined and varied touch that could be staccato, heavy or light, *louré, martellato, espressivo, portamento,* sparkling, whispering, or roaring. All these emerged from under his expert hands, his ten fingers thus giving the impression of being multiplied *ad infinitum.* In that epoch, only he who had mastered the art of touch was considered accomplished.

Brought up to the sound of the modern piano, nurtured by the feeling that emanates from it, today's interpreter is impregnated with a cultural esthetic which takes its roots in romanticism. The result is that we hear the *Chromatic Fantasy* played with the same touch as that given to Schumann's *Carnaval.*

The trouble with many interpretations of Bach on the piano is that the tonal volume is dilated, yet spineless and flabby. The basses which should truly represent the foundation upon which the whole structure is built generally swim into a gray mist. They lack equilibrium and contrasts of heavy and light phrasing; they are not delineated and are much too weak. Even if they were stronger, it would not help because they are not etched.

In opposition to that, the right hand dominates, sustaining the melody. This is the principle of romantic pianism in which bel canto plays the main role, the rest becoming accompaniment relegated to the background. It produces a lack of balance, and we clearly see Bach's admirable construction falter. It gives an increasingly sickish feeling; one expects to see the whole structure tumble.

We should read Mizler, Forkel, and Gerber, who spoke with such enthusiasm of Bach's touch. Clarity and precision, rhythm and lightness made of his playing something unique. Gerber said that despite his serious character, Bach was susceptible to sprightliness and grace. Those of his pieces generally considered very difficult seemed trifles to him; he played them with such perfection and ease that they appeared to be nothing more than simple bagpipe tunes; all his fingers were equally developed and capable of the greatest refinement.

The Two-Part Inventions

(SCHMIEDER· 772-786)

On January 22, 1720, while living in Cöthen, J. S. Bach began a little music book for his eldest son, Wilhelm Friedemann, who was then nine years old. On the first pages he wrote with the utmost care and precision a table of the different clefs covering the span of each one of the four vocal registers, an explanation of the principal ornaments, and exercises to teach fingering to little Friedemann. It was followed by a collection of short pieces, among which we find the first version of the *Two- and Three-Part Inventions*, bearing the title: *Präambula* and *Fantasie*. After three years of teaching these pieces over and over again to his son and his pupils, constantly revising, improving here and there, adding ornaments, Bach wrote another version, entitled this time *Inventio* for the two-part pieces and *Sinfonias* for those in three-part.

Why do we see today the Inventions and Sinfonias—these masterpieces which require a culture of the mind, of the ears, and of the fingers—in the hands of beginners, often very gifted, but always ignorant? Why do we see them in these thoughtless and cruel little paws, which scratch more out of awkwardness than out of malice? Is it because Bach wrote them for his son that it has been concluded that they are music for children? One forgets that Friedemann, a musical prodigy, lived with his father. He had the supreme good fortune of hearing him play the harpsichord and the violin; he helped at the organ and attended rehearsals. But above all, he was instructed constantly by his father. Friedemann did not need to read Schweitzer, Pirro, or Terry to understand the art of Johann Sebastian. What today is for us erudition was for him daily bread and life experience. Far away, as we are now, from that period and its musical conventions, we must try to reconstruct as devotedly as possible the way in which these works should be played. That is why these pieces demand scholarship in addition to independence of fingers. They should not be relegated, as they too often are, to beginners' classes, alongside the *Grande Vélocité* of Czerny.

In interpreting Bach's Inventions, I tried to create a single and vast piece because they derive from each other even when there is contrast. I followed the leading thread that ties one Invention to the next. In so doing I was inspired by the incomparable wisdom with which Bach linked the separate parts of his cantatas. In them what strikes us is Bach's way of distributing the tonalities, of tying the various parts together either by keeping the same mood from part to part or by breaking it up to create contrasts. Recitatives, arias, choruses, with their tempests and lulls, unfold with such an infallible logic that their succession becomes evidence itself. Let us compare that with the Inventions; in the first in C Major, let us follow the course of the two voices answering each other sweetly in a pastoral vein. Was not this mood chosen to throw in more obvious relief the passionate canon of the second in C Minor?

The third Invention in D Major is a light dance with the rhythm of a *ländler;* it is followed by the tempestuous fourth in D Minor. What an extraordinary contrapuntal skill there is in the spirited fifth Invention in E Flat Major! And who would not surrender to the charm of the exquisite E Minor seventh Invention, a solo for *oboe d'amore?* The tenth in G Major is a light gigue. The twelfth in A Major is in 12/8, a measure dear to Bach. Here he delights in the crossing of hands over the two keyboards. Observe the violent contrasts between the third and the fourth, the tenth and eleventh, the twelfth and thirteenth Inventions. The one in G Minor and that in A minor are agitated and impetuous. Listen to the last one in B Minor, in which trills, like tiny drum rolls, pass from one hand to the other, while eighth-notes sustain them with heavy drops.

The Well-Tempered Clavier*

(SCHMIEDER 846-893)

Ever since Bach's monumental work has been known to the musical world, it has aroused the most impassioned curiosity, interest, and admiration. Even ardent romantics bow before the "Forty-Eight."

The bibliography concerning *The Well-Tempered Clavier* is vast. Authors deal mainly with a general analysis and with the structure of the fugues.

All during my campaign in favor of the renaissance of the music of the past, I have devoted myself particularly to the study of Bach's *Well-Tempered Clavier.* The chief aim of my research has been to approximate as nearly as possible Bach's intention.

In the chapter on Keyboard Instruments (Part I, Ch. 12) I have refuted the idea that the forty-eight Preludes and Fugues were composed for the clavichord. A detailed analysis of the work

---

* ED. NOTE: In addition to a revised version of Landowska's commentaries on *The Well-Tempered Clavier,* originally printed as a liner to her complete recording of this work (RCA Victor LM 6800), this chapter contains much hitherto unpublished material.

will further demonstrate, I believe, why these pieces are simply inconceivable on the timid clavichord.

Bach's fugues and also the preludes are masterpieces of counterpoint. One cannot enter, it goes without saying, into the world of pure polyphony with the same casualness as into that of accompanied melody. The fugue, a high and involved art form, appeals to musicians who know how to listen, to those who are able to single out a voice and detach it from the others, even when that voice happens not to be the subject. For the subject by its melodic character, its rhythmic contours, its continual reappearance can be discerned, indeed, even by the inexperienced. Those without professional training should not, however, be less happy than the experts. The poetry, the atmosphere, the intensity of expression, the beauty of the preludes and fugues grip, overwhelm, and stimulate us. Contrapuntal writing is Bach's natural language—a language so natural that it is with "note against note" that Bach sings the love of God or merely love. One must be aware of this because it will dispel some misunderstandings. One should not be surprised to discover that these erudite fugues may become poems, mystical or secular.

The principles of counterpoint, "note against note," and imitation—were they the brain children of some Benedictine monk of time immemorial? Or did they not rather spring from the sounds of nature, like diaphanous echoes with their multiple reverberations? Or like the replications of the wind howling in the depth of the thickly timbered forests? Augmentations and diminutions in contrary or retrograde motion—all these voices mixing their individual parts contribute to the polyphony of the universe. Consciously or not, Bach had watched, heard, and absorbed them. Are not *The St. Matthew Passion*, the burlesque cantatas, *The Art of Fugue*, *The Goldberg Variations*, and *The Well-Tempered Clavier* transcriptions, reforged by a hand of genius, of this universal polymelody?

What has destroyed the human relationship between us and the fugue is having valued only the skill with which it is constructed and having denied it all capacity for emotion and expression. Thus we see musical amateurs, even the most fervent, bent on discovering the subject, the countersubject, the episodes, the stretti, etc. Needless to say, a fugue makes use of all these devices. But one seems to forget it is a hand of genius that directs it and that to a genius every device is a reason for giving free rein to his inspiration.

That which has most corrupted the listener's ear and taste and rendered him incapable of following simultaneously the three, four, or five parts of a fugue is the manner in which interpreters usually trumpet the entrance of the subject. They proclaim it with pomp, and having done this, they let it sink into a mist. But this voice that has been the subject, does it not continue to live on as a countersubject or as counterpoint? Should not these have the same place in the sun as the subject? Moreover, the interest of a Bach subject lies not only in its existence, but in the boundless possibilities to which it gives birth. In truth, it is only a pretext for arousing magnificent conflicts of harmonies, thanks to its encounters with the other voices. We must not think only of the subject; we have to follow all the voices and listen as they sing, despairing or jubilant.

The expressive richness of a fugue by a great master lies precisely in its unlimited variety—a variety that stems from the harmonic shocks the subject undergoes every time it encounters the evolutions of the other parts. It is fascinating to observe how a modulation, sudden or prepared, the appearance in major of the theme of a fugue in minor, or a chromatic motion can change the expression of a subject.

This phenomenon of transformation in the expression happens even in the simplest imitations. Great masters are perfectly aware of it and use it knowingly for our delight. And this is why it is a misconception to phrase the subject consistently in the same way throughout its most contradictory adventures in the course of a fugue. Besides, a Bach theme is rich; it lends itself to many different phrasings by means of various breathings and accentuations. It is hard to believe that there are so many ways to treat a theme. Each version has its logic and its right expression. Moreover, it is often advisable to phrase the answer differently to give new life to the subject itself.

As Spitta rightly said, Bach cultivated the prelude as a form in itself. We should give to all the preludes of *The Well-Tempered Clavier* the importance they deserve. Most musicians and music lovers have a predilection for Preludes 1, 4, 8, and 22 from Book I, and 12 from Book II, probably because of their lyrical character. But one should not forget all the others which are masterpieces of skill and inspiration.

Were the preludes composed with the intention of coupling them with the fugues of the same tonality or as independent pieces? Bach's biographers have busied themselves with this question without reaching a conclusion one way or another. Yet the relationship between these preludes and fugues is often undeniable. Even admitting that these pieces were composed separately at different periods during his life, it is ·plain that Bach selected and coupled them because of a very subtle affinity, which might escape those who look only for literal resemblance.

We do not know if it was Bach's wish that the forty-eight preludes and fugues be performed in their entirety in the same order in which he bestowed them on us. In my integral recording of the work, the order of the preludes and fugues has been retained as it was planned by Bach because it makes clear his guiding thought, according to the original title:

Preludes and Fugues through all the tones and semi-tones, both as regards the *tertia* major and as concerns the *tertia* minor.

The first Fugue is an apotheosis of the key of C major. In every prelude and fugue that follows one always feels this same will to plunge into each tonality, major or minor, thus glorifying the victory of equal temperament. In this way we see clearly that chromatic march of tonalities; it has an imposing simplicity that disdains all attempts at contrast and climax—a preoccupation certainly alien to Bach.

BOOK I — 1722

What was Bach's intention in leading us to his monumental *Well-Tempered Clavier* through a gate of such dream-like atmosphere as we find in the first Prelude in C major? Yet this prelude is simply a chain of broken chords called by the French *harpègements*; they represent one of the high points of harpsichord technique and display the infinite resources of that instrument; they also enrich it with some characteristics of the lute. The various ways of breaking chords—an art in itself—set off the richness of imagination of the composer as well as the ability of the performer. Bach, like the French harpsichordists, was a supreme master of this art, and he devoted innumerable pages to it. One of the most beautiful examples appears in the *Chromatic Fantasy*. Many of the preludes, and even certain fugues of *The Well-Tempered Clavier*, deal with broken chords. In the C major Prelude, Bach presents them as bare chords given to the performer to be spread out note after note.

The first fugue is magnificent and triumphant. Whoever has devoted any attention to the keyboard works of Bach knows that there are two versions of the theme of that fugue, one with a dotted eighth-note, the other without a dot. It is also known that the first version is believed to have been corrected by Bach himself and therefore is recognized as the only right one in all modern editions.

While studying the various manuscripts of *The Well-Tempered Clavier* around 1910, I noticed that this particular fugue, in the autograph which belonged formerly to R. Volkmann in Budapest and is now at the Royal Library in Berlin, shows retouching in fresher ink. We know that this manuscript was damaged during a flood of the Danube. Indeed, the writing has been blurred in several instances. All the same, it is undeniable that the corrections are more recent than the rest of the text. That can be discerned not only by the fresher ink, but also by erasures at the controversial places. More convincing is the fact that the two thirty-seconds—if thirty-seconds were ever intended—should have been written *after* the eighth note in other voices; on the contrary, they fall exactly with them, as sixteenths should.

It seemed to me very doubtful that these so-called "improvements" could have been made by Bach himself. This is why I began to search for a clue in the other manuscripts and first editions of *The Well-Tempered Clavier*.

The first six pages of the second autograph—which is also at the State Library in Berlin and had been previously acquired by the organist Müller from Wilhelm Friedemann Bach—are unfortunately missing. They were copied by Müller, however, with meticulous care. And we find there the original text of the C major Fugue, i.e., a non-dotted eighth-note followed by two sixteenths.

The third manuscript, known as the Fischhof Autograph, has the same non-dotted values.

And while these three autographs give the same version, we find the so-called "improved" formula in copies made by pupils of Bach and also in the first editions of the work. More precisely, the Kirnberger manuscripts—No. 57 at the Amalienbibliothek of the Joachimsthal Gymnasium of Templin as well as No. 49 in the same library—have the dotted eighth-note followed by two thirty-seconds. On the other hand, the Hoffmeister and Kuhne edition has no dot and two sixteenths. In Simrock and Nägeli, the dot and thirty-seconds are there. Identical to them are the French edition of Imbault and the English one of Lavenu.

We find the theme in its primitive version, though, in Marpurg, in the first volume of his treatise on the fugue (1753, Table 10). It is interesting to notice that Schumann, as well as Marpurg, played the uncorrected version as we can see in his collection of essays on music and musicians (1891). Bischoff adopted the correction in his edition and considered it authentic, stemming from Bach himself. A similar example of rhythmical alteration is given us, he said, in the introduction to Bach's Partita in B Minor especially at the beginning and in the last phrase of the overture. In the original manuscript—considered by Rust to be an authentic autograph, but believed by Spitta to be in Anna Magdalena's handwriting—most of the thirty-seconds that we find later in the engraved edition are still marked as sixteenths. Some of them are even written out as simple eighth-notes. But the situation is not the same. We have here a French overture, which required dotted rhythm. Even if sixteenths or eighth-notes were written, the duty of the interpreter would be to shorten their value. The character of gallant pieces, and especially of French overtures, demands it. In certain allemandes of François Couperin—*La Laborieuse*, for example, where no dotted notes are written—we find an indication from the author to the effect that the sixteenths must be *un-tant-soit-peu pointées* (somewhat dotted). But what surprises me is that Bischof did not choose a more proper example, such as, let us say, the allemande from the first French Suite, where

the autograph shows ♪♪ in the eighth bar, while Gerber's copy

presents ♪.♪ at the same place. In this case, Bischoff remained

faithful to the autograph and rejected Gerber's variant. This is of no great importance because in the instance of the French

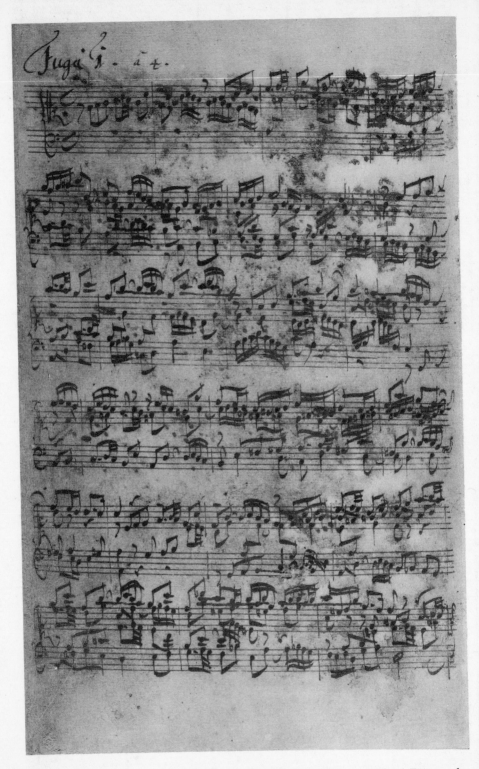

J. S. Bach's autograph of Fugue 1 from

Book I of *The Well-Tempered Clavier*

Suite the rhythm does not apply to the main theme, but simply to a figuration and in an allemande in French style at that.

Therefore, what would be the reason for altering the theme of the C major Fugue and making its rhythm sharper and more trenchant? If one carefully studies *The Well-Tempered Clavier* and *The Art of Fugue*, it becomes obvious that Bach avoided the jumpy rhythm of a dotted eighth-note followed by two thirty-seconds because it did not fit the character of his fugues. There are, however, some rare exceptions—for example, the Fugue in D Major from Book I. But it is written entirely in the character of a French overture. As for Fugue VI of *The Art of Fugue*, Bach himself entitled it "in stile francese." In opposition to this, we find often among the fugues of Bach rhythmic designs similar to that of the non-dotted theme of the C major Fugue. For example:

BOOK I FUGUE 16   or BOOK II FUGUE 2

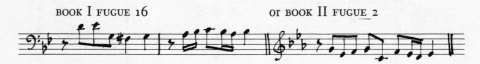

or even better: BOOK II FUGUE 17

They correspond closely to the rhythmic design of the C major Fugue:

Forkel placed the C major Fugue among those "which show the immaturity of youth but which later received many changes." Although one must approach the assertions of Forkel with the greatest caution, it would be interesting to learn why the change from non-dotted to dotted rhythm would represent an improvement dictated by maturity of judgment!

Nothing really proves that the correction was made by Bach himself. Rather, we can be sure of the contrary. Most probably, this correction came from Kirnberger or from Altnikol, who were under the influence of the gallant style that flourished in their time. But more likely it was made to avoid a few parallel fifths or some dissonances. Yet, in measure 20 of this Fugue the primitive text has been kept in the bass without change; no doubt that was to escape even stronger dissonances. But we should remember that Bach was not at all pedantic in such instances. As always, his pupils showed themselves more Catholic than the Pope. It would be easy to find licences of this kind in many works of Johann Sebastian. Moreover, in the two fugues mentioned above, dissonances are in no way weaker than those of the C major Fugue, and it would have been just as easy to avoid them with similar corrections.

I hope to have proved sufficiently that:

1. the correction does not stem from Bach himself;

2. there is no good reason to consider the correction introduced in all modern editions a necessary and indispensable improvement;

3. this so-called improvement is absolutely foreign to Bach's fugal style.

I do not know if it has occurred to other musicians, but every time I play the C major Fugue, I think involuntarily of the overture to *Die Meistersinger*, and the jumpy character the dotted rhythm gives to the fugue always disturbs me. Aside from historical truth and our reverence for Bach's intention, the authentic version possesses a simplicity and a nobility which compensate largely for the glitter, the pungency, and the paltry pedantry of the retouching.

Does not Prelude II in C Minor suggest a full string orchestra of somber color advancing impetuously until its tumultuous billowing stops brusquely on the dominant?After a lull of several measures a presto enters—an indication given by Bach himself, as are the succeeding adagio and allegro—breaking into passages and bringing us to the adagio. Here Bach remembers his admiration for Buxtehude, and gives us a recitative combined with passages which lead to an allegro on a tonic pedal-point.

The Fugue indulges in various kinds of double and triple counterpoint. The two countersubjects are important and of great beauty. They have to be played with a *cantabile* touch. Interpreters must not forget to breathe at measures 7-8 and 27-28 in order to emphasize the imitation of the two voices.

Among the five episodes the second is remarkable. It enhances the subject by assuming its rhythm in the two upper voices. The very expressive melodic line of the left hand has to be played too with a *cantabile* touch. In the third episode this melodic line moves to the soprano. The last two episodes combine the rhythm of the subject with fragments of the first countersubject. This Fugue, usually regarded as graceful, has boldness and undeniable virility.

Prelude III in C Sharp Major is a beautiful version of broken chords, called at that time *batteries*. Here again we seem to hear a string orchestra, but now golden and bright. It makes us think of a Spanish dance, especially from bar 63 on, when a special kind of *batteries* suggests the guitar. Do not be surprised; Bach knew everything—Italian, French, Spanish music. This Prelude, sparkling, gay, and witty, prepares us for the Fugue.

The joyous and glittering subject of the Fugue reminds us of the aria "Mein glaübiges Herze frohlocke, sing' scherze" from Cantata 68. The same mood prevails in both pieces, and at the end of the aria we find, as well as at the end of the subject of the fugue, the same jump of a seventh from the leading note to the tonic below.

There are two countersubjects; the first is joyous also, but more tender. The second is in sustained notes—the only ones in this Fugue.

Among the six episodes, we are seized by the beauty of the fifth toward measure 30. The subject and the two countersubjects lead independent lives, and yet they are in complete agreement. The inversions which they undergo emphasize their exuberant happiness. The triple counterpoint does not weigh them down.

The marvel of this fugue is in its richness and in its variety, which are always renewed despite relatively modest material. The miracle is accomplished thanks to the genius of Bach, who enjoys the play of all kinds of inversions. One can almost hear him laugh and say, "And now let the soprano leap into the bass!" The last measure of the fugue contains, encased in chords, the end of the subject. Do not ignore it!

Prelude IV in C Sharp Minor is an eloquent avowal of Bach's love for Couperin and French music. It is a kind of *courante à la française* with neither upbeat nor repeat. The rhythm—dotted quarter-note followed by an eighth-note and a quarter-note—has to be played rather sharply and with a certain lightness. It is this rhythmic design, both fluid and incisive, that gives a unique and distinctly secular character to the Prelude. Motives pass from one hand to the other, arpeggios are thrown here and there, ornaments of French origin enhance the melodic line in true lute fashion, although transposed for the keyboards of the harpsichord. The whole piece seems improvised; yet a mind conscious of its aim conducts these volutes.

To determine the tempo of a prelude or of a fugue requires thorough study. It should be based on comparison with other pieces of similar character among Bach's instrumental and vocal works as well as among the works of other composers known to him and by whom he was influenced. Of great importance is the fact that very often a prelude or even a fugue is positively a dance, although not indicated as such at the beginning of the piece. For those who are familiar with the instrumental dances of Bach's time, it gives a clue to the tempo, and this is of great help.

We notice a very interesting point; this Prelude, so secular in character, is coupled to a Fugue that is considered *absolute music*. This five-part Fugue, one of the longest of the "Forty-Eight," is of matchless grandeur. It is composed of three contrasting subjects. The main one, in sustained notes, solemn with its interval of a diminished fourth, carries in itself the germ of the tragedy which is going to unfold. From the moment it appears, it establishes the mood of the entire Fugue IV. The second subject, in flowing eighth-notes, which enters at bar 35, has profound tenderness. The third subject (measure 49) has a rhythmic vigor which contrasts with the two preceding subjects. Bach manages these three themes with his supreme art, leaving to each its own character.

In company with the third theme the principal one sounds for the last time on a pedal-point, and this grandiose Fugue ends on a Picardy third.

Prelude V in D Major is played by all students the world

over, doubtless because of its technical difficulties. Probably the turbulent sixteenths in the right hand make one forget what takes place in the left. Indeed, this left hand, with its wild leaps, now light, now overwhelming, gives to the whole piece its impelling character, its wit, its spirit, and its humor. In the twenty-seventh measure there appears in the bass a pedal-point on the dominant. Bach then recalls the tumultuous improvisations of Reincken and ends the Prelude with a stream of scales and arpeggios. It is thus that Bach prepares us for the Fugue.

I shall never forget the astonishment, quizzical and incredulous, of those to whom I said in 1906 that Fugue V was none other than a French overture! "What," they said, "a fugue being abstract and absolute music, lowered to the status of secular music!"

Yes, it is a gorgeous and dazzling *ouverture à la française*. In playing it one must exaggerate the sharpness of its dotted rhythm according to the French tradition of that period. (See p. 387)

Prelude VI in D Minor is, once more, an example of broken chords. We are struck by its stormy atmosphere and are reminded of the Sonata, Opus 31, of Beethoven.

At the twenty-fourth bar, Bach brings forth in gusts a succession of diminished fifths, stops on the tonic, and closes on an imperious final cadence.

Fugue VI is somber and authoritarian. In the second measure the slur above the three sixteenths, the dot above the B flat, and the following trill are given by Bach himself—indications all the more noteworthy, since he was not generous in providing interpretation marks. These particular markings are important because they indicate that we must snatch the B flat and consequently attack the trill vigorously. This gives to the phrase a deliberately aggressive character. There are, however, a few moments of tenderness sneaking in here and there, in this otherwise harsh piece.

Bach indulges in a number of stretti and inversions in this Fugue. One should bring out, beginning with the thirty-fifth bar, the progressions in thirds of the inverted theme in the bass and in the middle voice. The Fugue ends actually on the D of measure 43. But as a kind of farewell Bach gives us once more the theme and its inversion, both doubled in thirds, thus forming a succession of four-part chords ending on a Picardy third.

Intense and quiet at the same time, Prelude VII in E Flat Major—a lofty meditation—has much in common with Prelude XI in F Major from Book II, and with the Allemande from Handel's Suite in E Major. There is great significance in the nature of these long phrases, which are not dynamic, although they are perpetually in motion. Their power is entirely introvert, thus giving all the more intensity to their expression. Everywhere in this Prelude reigns a steady light, sweet and enveloping, without sudden outbursts. Its beauty lies in the never ending ebb and flow of waves which, from beginning to end, bestow upon the whole piece a calm grandeur, something eternal that goes beyond the last bar.

It requires much thought to discover the tempo suitable to this Prelude. It is built in three sections—preamble, fugato in the spirit of a chorale, and a double fugue. In the preamble, over a pedal-point, appears a theme in sixteenth-notes; and in the fugato another of sustained character, two themes upon which Bach builds the double fugue that forms the third section of this piece. Both must be stated with clarity and logic.

It is of the greatest importance to realize that the theme in sixteenths is the one which from the beginning of the preamble reveals the tempo of the whole piece. At the sight of sixteenths, many performers rush, believing that they should play fast. They forget that sixteenths—they too—know moderation, if not slowness. Here, it is their gentle, continuous motion that throws into relief the sustained-notes theme and emphasizes its austere beauty. Thanks to a unity of tempo from beginning to end, these three sections merge into one vast piece.

Almost all commentators are slightly scornful in their treatment of Fugue VII. After the grandiose Prelude they expect a piece of imposing dimensions. But no. Here is a Fugue, babbling along, light and carefree. Bach, as though relieved after the overwhelming Prelude, is happy in the midst of voices that chatter back and forth, pursuing and teasing one another.

Supported by columns of arpeggios striking the three beats

from the opening to the closing measures, a regal melody unfolds in dotted rhythm *à la française* in Prelude VIII in E Flat Minor. Here there is no polyphony. In the fourth measure the bass joins with the soprano, and a veritable duo begins which grows in intensity. From measure 25 it assumes the poignant accents of a recitative.

Then Fugue VIII appears, and we have a theme which has something of a folk tune heard in the midst of a vast plain— immense solitude and endless melancholy. The entrance of the inverted theme in the low register at measure 44 is stunning.

After the boundless and despairing phrase which leads up to measure 52, the Fugue abates and pursues its course—with its inversions, stretti, augmentations, and dialogues between voices— and moves toward its climax. Before concluding this deeply melancholy fugue on a major chord Bach offers us in the coda a phrase of intense expressiveness.

Prelude IX in E Major is bucolic, a mood Bach loves: azure and crystal, flute and oboe, impossible to realize on the clavichord.

Above a pedal-point the soprano, conversing with the middle voice, flows along in sweetness and happiness. It reminds us of the Pastorale in F Major for Organ.

After the plenitude of the Prelude with its rich harmonies, the almost perpetual chatter of sixteenths in Fugue IX brings an exquisite vivacity and freshness. Follow the expressive suspensions in the middle voice (bars 13, 14, 15), the flute in the soprano (measure 17), and starting at measure 25, the theme, a truly delightful warbling.

Prelude X in E Minor appears in the *Clavierbüchlein* composed by Bach for his son Wilhelm Friedemann. It has been deduced from this fact that the passages in the bass were designed to develop the virtuosity of the left hand. Now if Bach had had a pedagogical object in mind at all when composing this piece, would it not rather have been to teach his son the art—the great art indeed—of how to treat broken chords, how to improvise them, how to enrich them with passing notes?

The interpretation of this Prelude has puzzled many commentators. It is found disparate. One sees in the melodic line some affinities with Chopin, and we are told that cautious rubati might be in order. But there is more to it: this is a four-part piece; the first note of each two-beat group of sixteenths represents the fundamental bass. It demands to be realized with chords which are indicated by Bach, although they are not always completely filled out. The sixteenths in the left hand are a kind of figuration of the bass notes. Above all this floats a melody that would be more suitable to the flute than to the violin.

This Prelude is divided into two parts. The second bears the indication presto in Bach's own hand—an indication particularly significant because it introduces us to the tempo of the Fugue, also written in sixteenths.

Of the entire collection, Fugue X in E Minor is the only one in two voices. The episodes—four in number—are rich in invention, sparkling with wit and humor. Played on the *grand jeu* of the harpsichord, this Fugue assumes a dynamism unexpected in a piece of only two voices.

One of the most outstanding examples of the importance Bach gives to the dance is found in Prelude and Fugue XI in F Major. Take the Prelude and examine the eighth-notes in the left hand in groups of three. As we follow the rise and fall of these three notes, let us recall the dance motive from *Die Meistersinger* (Act III, Scene 5), which bears the title "Mässiges Walzer-Zeitmas" and was written by Wagner in ¾ time. It becomes obvious that these three notes are the leading rhythm in Bach's Prelude and strikingly clear that the Fugue also is built on the same rhythm, light and graceful in the Prelude, sturdy and ponderous in the Fugue.

Is this Fugue a typical peasant *Walzer*, like the overture to the cantata *Mer hahn en neue Oberkeet?* Or is it one of those numerous *passepieds*, like that of the B Minor Partita (Schmieder 831)? One wonders. The influence of dances was so deeply rooted at that epoch that sometimes it is difficult to define their origin. Differences between closely related ones fade, and the piece becomes androgynous. When felt by the Thuringian peasant that Bach was, this *passepied* becomes a robust, vigorously accented waltz.

The short trill at the end of the subject makes a lovely contrast with the long scintillating trill in the Prelude.

Prelude XII in F Minor is a kind of allemande in lute style with broken chords and sustained notes. Recall the Allemande from the French Suite No. 5 in G Major. If we forget the tonality of G major and transpose this Allemande into F minor, inverting the voices, we will then find an outline identical to that of Prelude XII. It is in four voices of a harmonic and melodic richness that anticipates the Fugue.

Bach knew the refined skill with which French harpsichordists made their instruments resound with amplitude and expression, thanks to an absolute legato from which the slightest rupture was excluded. It made everything sound full, rich, and smooth; notes flowed and interlaced, vibrations were prolonged. The Prelude in F Minor is a magnificent example of the art of playing on the vibrations, of exploiting all the resounding possibilities that a chord, broken or not, a held note, or one brushed by in passing, may produce. This was one of the secrets of *style luthé* on the harpsichord.

Fugue XII has the majesty of a cathedral. The three countersubjects emphasize the power of the subject and its intense expression. The episodes, seven in number, give sweetness to this austere and grandiose piece.

In listening to Victoria's Kyrie *Orbis Factor* we will understand the grandeur of the Fugue in F Minor. We will also understand that an instrumental piece may have the exaltation of a page from *The Passions*.

Prelude and Fugue XIII in F Sharp Major are unified by a similar pastoral atmosphere. In the Prelude Bach indulges in triplets in sixteenths. How delightful is the gentle rocking arpeggio figuration throughout the whole piece! Syncopation is the feature of this Prelude. Enjoy its motion, over the long notes of the bass. The writing, in two parts, is so pure and of such subtle artfulness that sometimes we are under the impression that it is a procession of chords. But no, Bach continues with his consecutive triplets.

The appearance of C sharp minor brings a tender melancholy. Soon Bach abandons it and resumes the swinging motive in the soprano, sustained by long notes in the bass.

The subject of the fugue, with its warbling trill, is enchanting. It seems created for the flute. The countersubject is of infinite tenderness.

In the seventh measure Bach introduces a new idea which he keeps on until the very end, paying no attention to the trouble it gives us to play it in a clear and precise manner. It is with this new motive, now in the soprano, now in the bass, and finally in the alto, that Bach ends this delightful pastorale.

The aria "Buss und Reu" from *The St. Matthew Passion* will help us understand the character of Prelude XIV in F Sharp Minor. It is an aria for alto with two flutes, organ, and continuo. The autograph of the Passion, showing the remarkable care with which Bach wrote it, is priceless. It tells us the importance Bach attached to phrasing, slurs, and detached notes. The middle part of the aria is particularly significant. Bach introduced there a descriptive motive to depict tears, providing the two flute parts at this very place with staccato dots. In Prelude XIV the same dots should be applied to all the short notes in the bass and in the soprano, and equally to the chords of bar 15 and similar ones. The separated eighth-notes in the first bar remind us of the Invention in B Minor.

Fugue XIV, a kind of sarabande, is an apotheosis of the appoggiatura. In Fugue XXI in the Second Book, the slurs in places similar to those of Fugue XIV are provided with ties in Bach's own hand. But above all, read the final chorus of the first part of *The St. Matthew Passion*. It is marvelous to see how carefully Bach has indicated the slurs, preceding them by dots. All this proves how important phrasing is in Fugue XIV. Breathing, short notes, and slurs give to the phrases their right aspect and expression.

Prelude XV in G Major, another in broken chords, is one of those powerful two-part pieces, like Fugue X, in which Bach displays his *joie de vivre* on the *grand jeu* of the harpsichord. Cut out in large strokes, this Prelude calls to mind the rustling of a string orchestra. Therefore, let us renounce small effects in registration.

Observe in the left hand the alternation of leaps and sustained passages. After reaching the dominant, Bach offers a witty, mischievous dialogue between the two voices, during which the right hand drops a seventh-chord, as if grain by grain, and resolves it with an appoggiatura, while the left hand jumps from one D to another.

May I make a confession? This Prelude has been my companion since the time I first touched the keyboard. It is difficult, but how invigorating! I have spent hours attempting to master bar 13 and the following ones. Have I succeeded?

Sometimes Bach devotes a piece to an ornament and to the manner of interpretating it. In Fugue XV it is the turn—four notes which wind around the principal one. This turn becomes the core of the subject. It gives to the entire piece its character— that of a dance. This Fugue is rich in inversions, stretti, and episodes. The first three are made of identical elements in triple counterpoint. But at measure 77 there is a surprise. On the dominant, the inverted theme arises, first in the alto, next in the bass, and then in the soprano, with which the alto and the bass are finally combined; and there we seem to hear Pogner with Hans Sachs in Scene 5, Act III, of *Die Meistersinger.* How can one explain this? Probably because both Bach and Wagner employ at these particular places the same harmonies. Is it not amazing that these two men, separated in time by over one hundred years, expressed the same thought in such different contexts? Beginning innocently on a waltz step, the Fugue grows into fullness. Hammering the theme in thirds, it ends in overpowering joy.

Here again in Prelude XVI in G Minor Bach dedicates a piece to the demonstration of ornaments and their interpretation. For this Prelude he selected the slide and the turn. Generally Bach and the French harpsichordists indicated these ornaments with signs; but in the G minor Prelude Bach realized them as main notes, thus giving us a priceless indication of the manner in which they should be scanned and incorporated in the melodic line.

These ornamented phrases are supported by sustained pedal-notes, now in the soprano, now in the bass. The vibrations of some of them are kept softly quivering with a long trill.

The subject of Fugue XVI is noble and meditative; like all musical thoughts in minor keys that begin on an upbeat, it expresses torment and grief. It is of such complexity that all the ideas which are found in the course of the Fugue are derived from it. The stretto in measures 28 to 30 summarizes magnificently the intense expression of the entire Fugue. Full justice is due the last two bars, in which Bach gives the soprano a melody of supreme beauty.

We will find the theme of this Fugue in the Andante "Es ist der Alte Bund," in F minor, from Cantata No. 106.

Prelude XVII in A Flat Major opens with broad, consonant chords, like a lively overture—not of the French type—for a full string orchestra. It is cheerful and crisp. Imitations zigzagging between the two hands, an effect dear to Bach, give to this piece an exuberant life and an extraordinary relief. In bars 39 and 40 *batteries* in sixteenth-notes join in both hands, and a reminiscence of the theme in bars 41-42 brings to a close this victorious Prelude, in which an unadulterated joy reigns throughout.

The contrast with the meditative, quiet, and serene Fugue XVII that follows is all the more striking. Listen to the episodes and observe how generously they sing. As a farewell the theme appears for the last time in the soprano. The alto joins it with an intensely affecting phrase.

The theme of Prelude XVIII in G Sharp Minor is entirely contained in the first measure. Its expression of innocence and timidity touches us. Bach imitates it in the bass, carries it along by progressions in the soprano and, supporting it by dotted quarter-notes, joins to it an undulating dancelike motive in the middle voice. The slurs, Bach's own, confirm this dance movement, which is continued throughout the whole piece. Imitations, inversions, slurs—thus the piece unfolds. Enjoy the reappearance in the next-to-the-last measure of the initial motive inverted in the middle voice.

Fugue XVIII is somber—all the more impressive after the tenderness of the Prelude. The "step"-motive becomes increasingly threatening as the Fugue advances. Bach emphasizes its power with short and violent chords. It is generally assumed that this is a youthful work. And yet it is very mature.

Prelude XIX in A Major is one of those frequent instances in which, thanks to Bach's genius, the character of the piece speaks of grace and innocence while being the product of the highest knowledge. It is a kind of light, transparent dance in which each voice suggests a different idea. The whole is held together by the most refined triple counterpoint.

The theme of Fugue XIX progresses in ascending fourths, a pattern somewhat rare in Bach's works. At measure 20, on the dominant, the bass stops, while the soprano and alto go on, still in fourths, in happy leaps.

A new theme in conjunct sixteenths appears at bar 23; it forms a sharp contrast with the opening subject, which goes along with it. One is keenly aware that Bach felt the need for these sixteenths to oppose them to the intervals of fourths. Almost all commentators consider these sixteenths a countersubject. What is certain is that the contrast of the opening theme with the motive in sixteenths, together with their interplay, inspired Bach to say exquisite, tender, and mischievous things. It must be noted that this Fugue escapes conventional analysis. All commentators admit this.

Prelude XX in A Minor is a gracious and playful dance. Commentators are surprised that, being so light and carefree, this Prelude could be rightly coupled to an imposing Fugue with a grandiose ending. But who knows? Perhaps it was the contrast of grace and power that pleased Bach. Commentators also have little enthusiasm for Fugue XX. Probably they have been influenced by Spitta, who found it pedantic and lacking in imagination. In their miscomprehension they dare to accuse it of being deficient in rhythmic energy—this piece so full of ardor, of fire, and of extraordinary drive! The appearance of the pedal-note, bar 83, crowns their dissatisfaction. I understand that the unrelenting anapestic rhythm may become exasperating. But it is precisely its insistence that gives the Fugue its Teutonic furor. And, of course, if the beginning is played in a monotonous and weak manner, it may kill the character of the piece. One must lash at this anapestic rhythm and establish sharp contrasts of forte and piano throughout the entire Fugue. The savageness of the rhythm, suggesting steely steps, is the main feature of this stubborn, violent, and very long Fugue.

Prelude XXI in B Flat Major is composed of three different elements—large broken chords in a pattern that Bach has not thus far used in *The Well-Tempered Clavier;* rolling scales, which Rameau called *roulements;* and clusters of chords in dotted French rhythm. It is a dazzling and bold piece which makes demands on the virtuosity of the harpsichordist. Follow the inner voices, so beautiful and expressive, that insinuate themselves into the seventeenth measure.

In Fugue XXI, Bach calms down and makes cheerful play among the subject and the two countersubjects. And listen to the bell-like repeated note in the countersubject in measure 7 and all similar passages.

Prelude XXII in B Flat Minor is sublime. Despite its lofty complexity it can be enjoyed even by a layman. How can we explain this? Is it because of the great simplicity of the melodic element that reigns in this piece? Is it because of the regular motion of its rhythm? Or is it the overwhelming richness of the chords that brings fullness and bliss to this Prelude?

From measure 20 on the melody soars, enriched with harmonies, toward a pedal-point. In the last measure a phrase of intense expression in the tenor suggests a farewell.

It is noteworthy that this Prelude, so simple in its immense richness, is coupled with a five-part Fugue of consummate contrapuntal skill. Bach states the subject imperatively. Starting on the tonic, it drops a fourth below and then leaps boldly over a quarter-rest to reach the ninth above. This rest does not interrupt the train of thought; on the contrary it breathes into it an increase of life. The *durezza* produced by the dissonance of a ninth arouses passion and breaks the uniformity of the half-notes. These half-notes reign imperiously, indeed, from beginning to end, somewhat softened by the quarter-notes.

There are five episodes, several stretti, and beginning at measure 67, an admirable *stretto maestrale*.

Now Bach is in a diatonic mood. Prelude and Fugue XXIII in B Major form a unified whole. The same bucolic atmosphere pervades both pieces. The Prelude opens on a pedal-point and announces a motive whose first notes will become the subject of the Fugue.

All is serenity and sweetness in this Fugue. The voices engage in a tender dialogue, and even the minor passes by lightly without leaving a trace of sadness. At measure 16 an innocent flute appears and disappears. It returns, happily, at measure 31, and the Fugue closes in perfect bliss.

Prelude XXIV in B Minor is admirably organized. Composed of forty-seven measures, it is divided into two parts by a double bar. From the beginning the soprano and the alto progress as a duo in the purest two-part writing and so continue until the very end of the piece. This duo is supported by a bass of uninterrupted eighth-notes. Compare this bass with the violin and alto parts in the fifth measure of "So ist mein Jesus nun gefangen" from *The St. Matthew Passion*. See in the one as well as in the other the continuity of the movement, in common time, the restlessness, the insistence of the eighth-notes.

And when one is faced with phrases like those at bar 43 and following ones, with their collision of harmonies, and their accumulation of dissonances, it becomes evident that they demand easing up the tempo.

The indication Andante at the head of the Prelude is Bach's. Likewise are the Largo at the head of Fugue XXIV and the slurs over the eighth-notes of the subject. These slurs make us think of the recitative "Ach wer doch schon im Himmel wär!" from Cantata 146, when the soprano sings "Mein Gott das fällt mir schwer."

In this Fugue the four voices clash with dissonances of terrifying beauty. But see! Here come the episodes—eight of them—which bring the tender warmth of conversing voices (soprano and bass). The third, bars 17-20, is the most impressive.

At bar 44 the freshness of D major comes as a balm amidst the desolation of B minor. The ties in the theme are Bach's. Because they require an emphasis on the first note, they give us a magnificent example of the manner of interpreting appoggiaturas. In the course of the Fugue Bach subdivides the design into sixteenth-notes, which then become the leading motion of the piece. It goes without saying that these sixteenths, too, must be phrased like the eighths, with the tie indicated by Bach, and with a leaning on the first note. These appoggiaturas in sixteenth-notes provide a background for those in eighths, thus giving organic unity and an admirable quietude to the Fugue.

It is significant that Bach ends the first book of *The Well-Tempered Clavier* with a Prelude and a Fugue having the gravity and depth of *The Passions*.

BOOK II — 1744

The second book of *The Well-Tempered Clavier* opens with a Prelude which proudly displays the key of C major.

The melodic motive in the upper voice is grounded on a pedal-point. This short, always interrupted motive, stated fractionally, is the nucleus of the condensed and intricate writing of the Prelude. It expands from one single voice into many voices by means of broken chords enriched with passing notes. Three measures before the end the pedal-point reappears, and the Prelude concludes in sonorous splendor.

Fugue I is of extreme simplicity. It contains none of the devices we might expect after the refinement of the Prelude. But its dynamism is extraordinary; its gait vehement, yet not feverish. The close repetitions of the subject drive us along. The end is abrupt—a high-strung horse which pulls up short in full gallop. By all means, no *allargando!* Let us respect the noble pace of a thoroughbred.

The theme is a glorification of the mordent. The first one is realized in main notes; the second is indicated by a sign.

Prelude II in C Minor is written entirely in two voices and reminds us of the Inventions. It is divided into two parts by a double bar. The upper voice states a motive in sixteenths sustained by a bass of light eighths. This motive is imitated by the bass in the second bar while the light eighths go over to the soprano. A chain of progressions follows with mordents that should be played rapidly and lightly without encumbering the passage work. Modulations lead to the relative major, where Bach ends the first section with a brief arpeggio. In the second, Bach takes pleasure in the effect of inversions. The soprano presents the motive in sixteenths slightly modified. The bass contradicts it in the following measure, inverting the motive. How teasing it is! It surprises the more, since the following Fugue is grave and mystical.

In spite of its conciseness, Fugue II contains a subject in augmentation and inversion, two stretti, etc.—devices generally found in fugues of greater proportions. Its character is inspired by the Magnificats of Pachelbel, a precursor of Johann Sebastian and a friend of the Bach family. It is Pachelbel who indicates the tempo of this Fugue. It is also Bach, as we imagine him at the organ of St. Thomas, expressing resignation as well as the courage and confidence that faith alone can give.

Even though a rest is missing in the alto, Prelude III in C Sharp Major is entirely in four parts. The murmur of arpeggios intermingled with passing notes continues throughout. Listen to the tireless beats in the tenor and to the low repeated notes in the bass; they remind us of the ticking of a clock. A pedal-point supports the whole edifice. A light and gracious *fughetta* of twenty-six bars, marked allegro, ends the Prelude. Who would have expected this allegro in ⅜, which comes as an exquisitely cool shower after the dreamy Prelude? No doubt Bach knew what he wanted; if we do not at once understand his intention, we must keep searching. As short as it is, this allegro constitutes a piece in itself and necessitates a well-defined tempo, that of a slow waltz. It contains problems; one of them concerns the execution of the mordents, bars 28 and 29. Should they be beaten with a half-tone or with a whole tone? Passing by swiftly, the phrases brush on several tonal possibilities. Musicians could debate this without ever agreeing. In such instances, I always call on Bach himself to help me; I search for similar cases realized by him in main notes. But one should not rely entirely on this method, because Bach is sometimes unpredictable and may interpret differently situations that appear similar.

With bouncy steps Fugue III itself appears, restrained at first, but soon becoming triumphant. From the second measure Bach inverts the subject. Augmentations, diminutions, and stretti follow; for Bach is in high spirits and enjoys himself royally. In the midst of indescribable tumult—a tumult governed, needless to say, by the imperious grip of Bach—the eighths roll, the sixteenths rumble, the thirty-seconds crackle. At measure 27 the subject in augmentation thunders in the bass and imposes order in this supreme Fugue. Bach likes to oppose detached eighth-notes, like heavy drops, to a plan of sixteenths. His evident intention is to use the difference in character of the parts to set them off from each other.

The three-part Prelude IV in C Sharp Minor is deeply influenced by the French school and most of all by Couperin. All in it is French—the lute-style of writing, the manner of treating appoggiaturas and mordents, and the character of the melodic line, which calls for the whine of *oboes d'amore* or *da caccia*, instruments dear to the French. The Prelude is crowded with ornaments of every kind; at first we are uncertain and confused about their realization. But happily the paternal foresight of Bach reassures us. Each of these ornaments is made clear by Bach himself in the course of the piece. Thus we can play the Prelude, certain that we are following his intention.

The first bar of this Prelude is identical to that of the Sinfonia No. 5 in E Flat Major. In both, over a broken chord in the bass, Bach throws an ascending cantilena of infinite tenderness; its outline is exquisite.

Fugue IV unrolls in triplets. Avoid treating it like a gigue. The mood of this Fugue is incontestably serious and demands a moderate tempo. The triplets proceed gently, but should be played with a certain weight in order to express the value of each note. They should not be hurried.

Prelude V in D Major reminds us of the opening chorus of *The Christmas Oratorio* and of the Allegro from the Overture to the Partita for Harpsichord in D Major. In spite of the difference in type and time signature, the same D major and the same powerful drive dominate these three pieces. We imagine this jubilant and triumphant Prelude played by trumpets. It should be performed in that spirit.

When a triplet of eighth-notes is placed over or under a dotted eighth-note followed by a sixteenth, I play the sixteenth after the third eighth of the triplets, as Quantz advocates. This sets the triplets into relief, and it is in accordance with the exultant fanfare character of the piece.

Of vast scope, divided into two sections by a double bar, this Prelude prophesies the sonata form. Imitations in like and contrary motion sparkle throughout the piece.

After the jubilation of the Prelude comes a meditative Fugue. Why this contrast? Bach did it on purpose to enhance the absolute serenity and plenitude of Fugue V.

Prelude and Fugue VI in D Minor send us once more into a world of affinities. The Prelude is a virtuoso piece demanding the double keyboard of the harpsichord. Its flow is torrential and reminds us of the Concerto for Harpsichord and Strings in the same key. Compare the first measure of the Prelude with the first measure of the Finale of the Concerto. Besides, we find in the Prelude, as well as in the first and third movements of the Concerto, one of the most characteristic effects of double keyboard, the *batteries*.

The Fugue is grave. The triplets of the subject, as in the C sharp minor Fugue, flow smoothly, but with a certain weight. To understand this Fugue we must study *The Art of Fugue*— namely, *Contrapunctus 13, Canon alla Ottava, Canon alla Decima, Canon alla Duodecima,* and *Fuga a due Claviere*. There we find, among other resemblances, the flowing triplets, the opposition of these triplets to the same values in groups of two, and the chromaticism. The study of *The Art of Fugue* helps us understand the deep beauty and the art of this Fugue in D Minor.

Compare this Prelude VII in E Flat Major to the Prelude in the same key from *Prelude, Fugue,* and *Allegro* (Schmieder 998). Certain tonalities inspired Bach to a particular style of writing, thus creating ties between pieces in the same key. This Prelude, influenced by lute-style, is a dreamlike soliloquy followed by a concise and powerful Fugue which evokes an a cappella choir. In the magnificent episode from the forty-third to the fifty-eighth measures the voices converse with humor. Fugue VII concludes in overwhelming joy.

Prelude VIII in D Sharp Minor is divided by a double bar into two parts of nearly equal length. One might be tempted to consider the initial motive as a sort of formula. We find identical ones at the beginning of several Scarlatti sonatas (Longo 127, 385, 390, 500). It is in the jump of a fourth which follows this formula that the flavor of the whole Prelude resides. This becomes clear when the fourth reappears at the second half of bar 15 and at the beginning of the last measure. This Prelude is a cantilena veiled with melancholy. Its very nature is revealed by a motive in the last two measures of the first and second sections. A surprise! This motive is a gavotte, a French *bergerette* of the eighteenth century. I used to sing it as a child.

The thirty-seconds which intermingle with the sixteenths are indisputable proof that the tempo should be moderate; for they must not be rushed, but played with a clear and expressive touch.

Fugue VIII is as meditative as that in D major, but is pervaded by the melancholy of the Prelude. Starting at the end of bar 40, Bach introduces clusters of chords which sustain the structure and give impressive grandeur to the whole before the final entrance of the theme in the treble.

Prelude IX in E Major, divided into two parts by a double bar, is written strictly in three voices, with the exception of the last two bars. I hardly dare apply the term "strict" to writing so warm and affecting. The sixteenths converse from voice to voice. Notice the rocking movement of the eighths from measure 18 on, as well as in similar places of the second section.

In measures 32 to 34, 41 and 42 we find the ornament "turn" written out, as if Bach were taking us by the hand to warn us: "Above all, play it on the beat, and not like those performers who, taking advantage of my absence, anticipate it!" True, this warning would have been superfluous to a contemporary of Bach, who would have known how to carry out the turn.

The essential difference between the fugues of Bach built on subjects similar to those of Froberger's or J. K. F. Fischer's fugues —the present one being a case in point—does not lie in the importance of that subject. It resides in the way these composers deal with the conversations among voices and how these voices participate in the unfolding of the drama that a fugue represents. For Bach the smallest motive is important. He exploits it, treating it mostly in imitations. There is never any stagnation in the conduct of voices. The promptness of their ripostes is responsible for the prodigious liveliness of Bach's contrapuntal texture. The appearances of the subject are not the most important events in the unfolding of a Bach fugue. Cecil Gray calls the subject of Fugue IX "a noble theme." No, it is not noble in itself. It hardly exists. It is the Fugue that is noble and magnificent because Bach made it so.

This four-part Fugue is of incomparable magnificence. Its complex artfulness is handled with unbelievable ease by Bach; glowing with the key of E major, it is one of the most perfect works of music.

I always dreamed of hearing the E major Fugue sung by an a cappella choir, for I felt it was more vocal than instrumental. Years ago in Paris my dream was fulfilled. A few of my friends from among the Chanteurs de St. Gervais sang it for me. It confirmed my belief.

Prelude X in E Minor is a kind of two-part invention in binary form with a double bar. Though only in two voices, the writing is rich and complex. This Prelude has strong affinities with the Prelude from the A minor Partita. It represents a beautiful example of the way in which Bach treats progressions; in itself, this device has too often tendencies toward easy emptiness. But when Bach takes hold of it, we can only marvel at the stimulation it brings. Bach's progressions extract the utmost intensity from the expression of a phrase.

The trill, measure 33, starts with a C sharp, not C natural, as certain editions erroneously have it. This C sharp is justified because the note preceding the trill is a C sharp, as are those appearing in the bass voice under the trill.

This quiet and peaceful Prelude does not announce its Fugue, a combative one. The staccato dashes are Bach's own. They are of great importance because they confer on the piece a character of vehemence, and they underline the rhythm of the triplets.

From bar 68 on, Bach announces a climax which he extends into imposing dimensions for eighteen measures. Yet, the tempo must maintain its moderation. This can only give greater intensity to the power of the entire Fugue.

The phrase in the eighty-second bar reminds us of Béla Bartók's indication *parlando-rubato* for a folk song. This rubato is indispensable. The storm abates at bar 86, and the Fugue ends on a Picardy third.

Written in five voices, Prelude XI in F Major is a poem which opens to us horizons of infinite space through stages of succeeding modulations. But who would expect what Bach prepares for us? For after a Prelude which soars high, comes a terrestrial and lively Fugue.

Most editions indicate "grazioso" or "scherzando." Yet Fugue XI is just a gigue. It does not have the violence of the finale from the G Minor Concerto for Harpsichord and Strings, for instance; but it retains nonetheless the marked features of a gigue. Though not grazioso, and not scherzando, it must have the verve and the character of a gigue.

From the seventeenth measure on, the motive in the bass— the tail of the subject—imitated by the middle voice, then by the treble, and in the following bar once again by the bass, contains a surprise. I recognize this motive in the third measure of the Prelude from Bach's English Suite in A Major. It is not marked "gigue" in the English Suite, but we find the denomination in Dieupart, Le Roux, Marchand, et al., above pieces whose motives are analogous to that of the English Suite. This motive was dear to the French harpsichordists (cf. Pirro, *L'Esthétique de Bach*).

Does not the motive in the bass of Prelude XII in F Minor (in two parts with a double bar) remind us of Beethoven's *Eroica* in measures 1 and 2 and again in measures 8, 9, 28, and 29? Above the bass comes a procession of appoggiaturas. Bars 4 to 8 and 16 to 20 clearly reveal writing for the two keyboards of the harpsichord. This has escaped the notice of commentators. Even worse, how could this weaving of broken chords, so characteristic of the harpsichord, be mistaken for an accompaniment of an imaginary sentimental melody? Or turned into rapid passage work? Appoggiaturas, broken chords, measures 20 to 24, the entrancing progressions at bars 36 to 39—all these are proof enough that the piece ought to be played, if not slowly, at least in a moderate tempo. And what can be said of the last two bars? Are they not almost an implied recitative?

The Fugue in F Minor sways us by the continuity of its sharp dancelike rhythm. This *perpetuum mobile* has the monotonous intoxication of a whirling dervish. The obstinate anapestic rhythm augments this character.

Like the Fugue in E Minor from Book I, this one does not display any device of counterpoint. Listen to the beauty of the bass in the last eight measures.

Compare the beginning of Prelude XIII in F Sharp Major with the opening measure of the Praeludium to the St. Anne Organ Fugue; both have the same melodic impulse. Throughout Prelude XIII Bach makes use of a dotted rhythm *à la française*, but it never gives an impression of angularity. It glides gently and with fluidity. In contrast to the dotted rhythm there is a network of broken chords in even sixteenths. They should be played with a sostenuto touch, since they provide the harmonic background. The end, with its added full chords, gives us a glimpse of the free manner in which Bach must have played this Prelude—as if improvising. But leave this speculation to the realm of daydreams.

In Fugue XIII, the trill of the subject must start on the upper note. I know it is almost too much to ask of interpreters today. If necessary, they will agree to a trill on the upper note in the course of a piece. But to start with it!

The countersubject, with its irresistible gavotte rhythm is as important in this Fugue as the subject itself. Bach elaborates it in the episodes.

Prelude XIV in F Sharp Minor is entirely in three-part. The treble is a cantilena full of love and tenderness, a true aria for *oboe d'amore*, interspersed with triplets and broken syncopations. It is escorted continuously by a dyad made of the bass and middle voice. This manner of writing, one of Bach's most beautiful, is analogous to that of the Andante of *The Italian Concerto* and of the thirteenth and twenty-fifth *Goldberg Variations*. It also reminds us of the aria "Aus Liebe" from *The St. Matthew Passion*. When tenderness is overwhelming, Bach suspends the melodic flow under a fermata.

Fugue XIV is built upon three subjects. To each Bach gives a different character. The main one which opens the Fugue announces the epic of a soul, heroic, grave, and deeply tender. After its exposition, the second subject enters in the second part of bar 20. Slightly dotted, this one starts on the upbeat, like a speech interrupted and renewed. The third subject, which comes in the second half of measure 36, is entirely in sixteenths. Softly murmuring and monotonous, it provides a background against which the eighths stand out and acquire their full meaning.

Imitations and allusions to subjects and countersubjects appear and reappear perpetually. The three subjects combined fill the second half of the Fugue. The construction, the mood, and the third subject of this Fugue show an undeniable resemblance to those of the C sharp minor Fugue of Book I. The miracle of this music is that in creating it Bach did not concern himself with construction alone. The liberties he took prove it. Otherwise, how could he have been so divinely inspired?

When Bach writes of sorrow, it never crushes us. Perhaps because there is no trace of bitterness. This music, even if it describes rebellion or anguish, fortifies us.

Oh, the malefactor who decided that Prelude XV in G Major should be played very fast! For it is the way we generally hear it, "executed" in the literal sense of that word. Really it does not deserve this fate. Tranquil, bucolic, and grounded on a pedal-point, it whispers gently as if to warn us, "Enjoy the calm; you will see the Fugue is quite different!"

And here is Fugue XV briskly dancing a 3/8 rhythm. Waltz? *Courante à l'Italienne?* It is difficult to tell.

In approaching the minor, from the twenty-fifth measure on, the Fugue becomes lighter, but not for long. More brilliant than ever, it rings with trills in the treble, middle voice, and bass. A bravura passage in thirty-seconds rolls across the keyboard and leads to the theme, which appears for the last time in the middle voice.

The indication Largo above Prelude XVI in G Minor is Bach's own. The Prelude, in strict four-part and written in the purest *stile francese*, reminds us of Couperin, particularly of *La Ténébreuse* (*Ordre* 3). Do not look for a literal resemblance; but we find in this Prelude the proud magnificence, the gravity, and the atmosphere of Couperin's incomparable piece. It has also some affinities with Kuhnau's Biblical sonata *Saul*.

When Bach takes possession of a certain rhythm, he does not let go. The Fugue in A Minor, Book I, proves it, as does this G minor Fugue. Even those of Bach's biographers and commentators who admire him without reservation blame this Fugue for what they call its rhythmic insistence and its stiffness. But we need not make the same mistake if we listen to this piece with the reverence it deserves. Obviously a knowledge of counterpoint is indispensable to do justice to this extraordinary work, in which Bach delights in multiple combinations of inversions.

Let us not be misled by the chords in the first measure of Prelude XVII in A Flat Major. It is written entirely in two-part. This is indeed Bach's way of imposing the tonality from the beginning with full harmonies and then enjoying the refined elaboration of the parts.

Commentators often mention the paucity of Bach's thematic material. Is it not rather the richness of Bach's inventive mind which accomplishes wonders with motives that might appear simple? This Prelude, like the one in F Sharp Major of Book II, and so many other pieces, proves it eloquently.

Between phrases in which the bass, sustained by chords, affirms the dotted French rhythm, Bach interrupts, modulates, and bestows upon us a kind of recitative whose intense expression is very moving (bars 32, 37, 38, 52, 53, 54, 74, etc.). This comes as a surprise in the midst of a piece that advances with such a quiet pace.

The luminous and gentle character of the subject of Fugue XVII is only slightly veiled by the chromaticism of the first countersubject. Subject, countersubject, and another countersubject undergo slight variations as they unfold. They intermingle peacefully without any tour de force except that of invertible counterpoint. But isn't that enough?

With each appearance of the subject—fifteen times in all— we experience a new happiness. The uninterrupted motion of the sixteenths, which forms a background for the subject, pervades the whole piece with an atmosphere of grandeur and majesty. This is a four-part fugue. Notice the last three measures in which the bass branches off on the last beat while the tenor brings forth the theme as a farewell.

Something unexpected strikes us at the beginning of Prelude XVIII in G Sharp Minor; passages, meticulously uttered in the right hand, evoke five-finger exercises, while in the left hand they make us think remotely of Alberti basses. But soon, the purest counterpoint in two voices appears. The captivating poetry of the key of G sharp minor, the plaintive accents of the appoggiaturas— to be played as eighth-notes—fill us with delight. The London autograph is marked *piano* and *forte* in bars 3 and 5, a notation all the more precious, since Bach rarely indicated dynamics.

The first six notes of the subject of this noble and grave Fugue XVIII are identical with the opening phrase of Scarlatti's Sonata (Longo 413). In spite of its being written in 6/8, this Fugue is not a gigue, a fact important to notice in order to choose a rather moderate tempo. The chromaticism of the countersubject prepares us for the second subject, which comes at bar 61 on a half-cadence. Eleven episodes enrich the glowing life of the Fugue. The two subjects meet on the dominant toward the end (bar 135). The bass rings like a bell (bar 136), and the Fugue ends with a tender appoggiatura like an expressive aria from a cantata.

Bach was particularly fond of 12/8 time. Think only of the last movements of *The Brandenburg Concertos* No. 2 and No. 6. They are dances, light or vigorous, in which the skipping motion plays a vital role. This 12/8 time inspired Bach to write not only dances, but also many pieces in a quiet mood. Prelude XIX in A Major, ending on a pedal-point, is a pastorale whose bucolic atmosphere continues in the Fugue in 4/4 time. Notice the dotted counter-subject, which should be articulated sharply, somewhat in *stile francese*.

Prelude XX in A Minor, whose chromatic bass supports delicate melismas in the treble, is divided into two sections by a double bar. This chromatic bass, which symbolized grief, was much loved in the seventeenth and eighteenth centuries. Inspired by it, Cavalli, Purcell, Couperin, and the German composers, among others, wrote marvelous works. Bach often employed it, as in the Crucifixus of *The B Minor Mass* and in the Adagissimo of the *Capriccio sopra la lontananza del suo fratello dilettissimo.*

The powerful and commanding tone of the subject of Fugue XX, swooping down on a diminished seventh, forms a most impressive contrast with the gentle and affectionate Prelude. This diminished seventh does not, however, belong solely to Bach. We find it in Handel's *Messiah,* in the chorus "And with His Stripes," in the Fugue of Haydn's Quartet in F Minor, in the Kyrie of Mozart's *Requiem,* etc.

The Fugue contains twenty-eight measures. Only Bach could create in such a limited space a piece of such grandeur.

Prelude XXI in B Flat Major is in two sections divided by a double bar. Follow in measures 13 and 14 the triplets; the fourth in each bar spreads a chord up to an interval of a tenth. Does that not remind us of Chopin's writing? What is fascinating in this piece, in which commentators see the sonata form presaged, is the adolescent freshness of the gallant style; I would even say that here Bach goes beyond Karl Philipp Emanuel or Mozart. The dotted eighths in the crossed-hands passages should not be played staccato in the virtuoso manner of Scarlatti, as it is usually done. Their purpose is to sustain the harmony.

One would like to linger on the D flat of the second beat of bar 75 and on the C flat, a Neapolitan sixth, in bar 85. Do not glide by; give due regard to this C flat; it is beautiful; and it foretells the end of this delightful piece.

The Preludes and other pieces divided in two sections with a repeat sign invite the interpreter to change registration for the second time around. It is just a suggestion, however, not an order. It happens that the initial choice of registration may correspond perfectly to the character of the piece. In this case there is no reason to offer another registration for the repeat. In Prelude XXI the four-foot register seems to evoke ideally its bucolic character. I tried vainly to find another suitable registration. Therefore I decided in favor of keeping the same registration both times.

Fugue XXI is in 3/4 time. The slurs in the third and fourth bars are by Bach. Once having imposed them at the beginning, he found it unnecessary to mark them everywhere. Obviously they must be observed in all similar phrases. These slurs are significant; they reveal the origin of the appoggiatura. It would be advisable for every interpreter to study the way in which this ornament has to be played or sung. It is particular, and among other difficulties it requires emphasizing the first note and playing the second *morendo*.

Prelude XXII in B Flat Minor opens with a tender and sorrowful cantilena. At the third measure the familiar theme of the Prelude in the same key from Book I appears unexpectedly. Is it deliberate or not?

Bach weaves both motives together and creates a work rich in polyphonic possibilities. Fugue XXII, somber and imperious, needed this preamble in which the human soul sings of its distress, not with cries of despair, but with restraint.

The subject of the Fugue opens on the tonic, rises on the first two notes of the scale, and before continuing its upward motion, is interrupted by a rest. This rest is of vital importance. It does not stop the ascending motion of the subject, but on the contrary breathes into it an increase of life.

The countersubject is chromatic. There really is, however, another countersubject which is not generally mentioned. It appears at the thirteenth measure, in detached quarter-notes, like heavy drops, which we find again all throughout the piece; they set forth clearly the design of the eighths of the subject.

The stretti, direct and inverted, are numerous. The twelve episodes bring tenderness into this powerful and somber piece. They are so well incorporated that their entrances are never surprising. The Fugue ends on a Picardy third.

In Prelude XXIII in B Major, sixteenths roll upward, then downward, passing from the right hand to the left. Perhaps because of its perpetual motion this Prelude has been characterized as a bravura piece. Well, it is not. It is a work strongly influenced by lute-writing; not the flexible, undulant, and wandering writing of the sixteenth century, but that of the end of the eighteenth century, that of an Ernst Gottlieb Baron or Sylvius Weiss. Bach had a great fondness for the lute. He knew thoroughly the technique and resources of this instrument, which he taught to his pupils and for which he wrote solo pieces and notable parts in *The St. John Passion* and in the *Trauer Ode*.

Fugue XXIII is a triumph of workmanship, achieved, however, without employing all the devices of counterpoint. The subject advances with solemn strides, which impose from the beginning the nature of the whole Fugue, a majesty full of jubilation.

Commentators draw attention to bar 35 of this Fugue, in which the second theme appears but is not completed. Fuller-Maitland sees in it a "touch of humor," Tovey, "a ghost-like appearance," and Prout, "an abortive entry." As for me, I see in this Bach's indefatigable inventiveness. For him a subject is not an irrevocable pronouncement. He states it fully, but a moment later he will present just a fragment if he so pleases.

Bach wrote down Prelude XXIV in B Minor in two different notations—in common time and *alla breve*. The London autograph is *alla breve*. An example of the most perfect writing for two voices, this Prelude reminds us of the Inventions. Often pupils ask, "Which of the two voices should be brought out?" I answer, "Both." Indeed, in this soulful Prelude each note of each voice should be brought out with expression. And here lies the difficulty for interpreters educated in the manner of romantic music, where melody prevails.

As for Fugue XXIV, it startles us by its vigor and spirit. Compare the design of the subject with that of Fugue XI, Book I, and see the striking rhythmic similarity. Is it not a dance? Could it not be a *passepied*, the dance which Madame de Sévigné describes so beautifully in her letters (1671)? "It is something quite extraordinary, this number of different steps and this cadence short and exact. I have never seen any man dance it as well as Lomaria . . . with what lightness and precision he takes off and puts on his hat . . . !"

We are reminded at this point that the young Bach had heard French instrumental ensembles at the court of the Duke of Brunswick-Lüneburg, whose wife, Eléonore Desmier d'Olbbreuse, was a native of Poitou. Yes, it is probably a *passepied*, and like Fugue XI, Book I, this French dance becomes a robust, vigorously accented *ländler* in the hands of the Thuringian peasant Bach was.

Would not one expect Bach to end this prodigious work, *The Well-Tempered Clavier*, with a dazzling display of his skill in counterpoint? But indeed no. Here is the last Fugue, deceptively carefree and entrancing in its apparent simplicity. Yet underlying it all is Bach's consummate artistry.

The Goldberg Variations
(SCHMIEDER 988)

On July 27, 1733, while in Dresden, Bach submitted to the Elector of Saxony, Augustus III, a Kyrie and Gloria, fragments of *The Mass in B Minor*, with a significant dedication. In it he complained, among other things, of the injustices he had to endure in the course of his professional duties at the churches of St. Thomas and St. Nicholas in Leipzig; he besought the Prince to engage him in his chapel. After waiting three years for an answer, Bach repeated his request, this time with success. The decree which named him "Composer to the Royal Court of Poland and Saxony" appeared on November 19, 1736, and was entrusted to Count Kayserling to be handed personally to Bach. To celebrate this nomination, so very important to him, Bach announced he would play on the Silbermann organ of the Frauen-Kirche in the afternoon of December 1. The news of this concert spread rapidly. The church was filled with high dignitaries from the court and with many famous artists and musicians who happened to be in Dresden at that time as well as with amateurs, among whom was Kayserling.

Baron Hermann Karl von Kayserling was born in Courland in 1696. His large family, with whom he kept in close touch, lived in Königsberg, where he had been educated. A great art lover, he was vastly cultured; he entered the diplomatic service, in which he rapidly rose to a very important post. As Ambassador to Russia from the court of Dresden, he enjoyed considerable influence in both countries. The Elector of Saxony, who esteemed him highly, bestowed upon him the title of count. But, despite his success as a diplomat, he devoted the greater part of his time to the arts, especially to music, which he loved passionately. Famous instrumentalists were at his service, and the greatest musicians of the time, such as G. J. Pisendel, Franz Benda, and Wilhelm Friedemann Bach, honored with their presence the renowned musicales given at his home in Neustadt. One could meet there the extraordinary lutenist Sylvius Leopold Weiss, a friend of J. S. Bach, whose "art of expressing passions, of improvising fantasies and fugues, and whose refinement and grace in cantable art were incomparable." Walther and Gerber described enthusiastically the virtuosity of Weiss, and quoting the lutenist Baron, they declared that he was unrivaled. Weiss could sightread entire scores of violin concertos and play them on the lute; while listening to him, one imagined hearing an organ or a harpsichord being played by a great artist.

Kayserling's entourage was a curious and attractive assemblage of men of taste and of refined artists; each of them had brought, in addition to the perfection of his performing skill, the peculiarities of his nature, or the exoticism of his native land. There was a young Circassian named Beligradsky, who was an excellent musician endowed with a lovely soprano voice. The Count had engaged him as a pandora player and made him study lute with Weiss.

But it is the strange figure of another young boy that particularly commands our attention. He is slim and nervous with melancholy and passionate eyes. Shy and uncommunicative, he remains apart, although attentive, in the midst of this brilliant company. When the Count asks him to sit at the harpsichord, there is a sudden silence, and a circle of listeners surrounds him. Wilhelm Friedemann Bach steps forward, suggesting a theme to develop, and the young man begins to improvise. The moment they enter in contact with the keys, his hands—which up to now looked like any other hands—instantly undergo a transformation; they stretch and expand; they encompass both keyboards, uniting them into a single entity. Strict polyphony or free preambula with their unexpected curvatures, broken chords dripping gold, or passages crossing over the two keyboards with the speed of lightning, intersect, chase one another, and roll toward the abyss of the low bass notes. Yet, a logical mind guides and dominates this rich and impetuous improvisation. One feels that this young prodigy has been brought up by a master into the highest principles of art.

Born in Danzig in 1727 of Protestant parents, Johann Theophilius Goldberg by his fabulous gifts drew to himself the attention of Count Kayserling. An enlightened patron, Kayserling cared vigilantly for the child's musical education and entrusted it to Johann Sebastian Bach, for whom he had always had a limitless admiration. Very pious himself, Kayserling wanted Theophilius to become impregnated with Bach's profound faith.

Kayserling's only son, Heinrich Christian, was a student at the University of Leipzig. Both he and Theophilius were fourteen at the time and became friends. They were often seen together in Leipzig when Goldberg, who lived in Dresden, came for his lessons with Bach. The great hopes the master had for his pupil and the marked preference he had for him quickly spread the growing fame of the young prodigy. Tales of the marvelous feats he performed went from musician to musician. Gerber, Hiller, Reichardt, and Forkel related his miraculous prowesses, and Marpurg exclaimed, "I hear all the time fantastic praise of this indefatigable and prodigious Goldberg." They went as far as to say that he could sightread the most difficult pieces, even when the score was put upside down on the desk.

Wilhelm Friedemann Bach often came to Dresden with his father. He was a regular attendant at the musicales held at the court and at Kayserling's, and he became organist at St. Sophia's in 1733. In the dedication of his E Minor Concerto to Princess Maria Antonia of Saxony, we read the following passage: ". . . when a certain young man named Goldberg, who is attached to the Count of Kayserling, Ambassador to Russia from the Court of Dresden, had the honor of giving proof of the perfection of his art, which he learned from my teaching. . . ." Does not this claim of being Goldberg's teacher undermine once again our confidence in Wilhelm Friedemann? Had he not taken upon himself to sign his name on one of his father's beautiful manuscripts—a transcription of Vivaldi's Concerto in D Minor—a work which subsequently became known all over the world as Wilhelm Friedemann's?

Gerber called Goldberg "one of Johann Sebastian's best disciples in composition and harpsichord playing." Forkel, Reichardt, and Mizler all mentioned Johann Sebastian as Goldberg's only teacher. Furstenau, however, and with him Spitta, considered the possibility that Goldberg might have studied first with Wilhelm Friedemann and might have come to Leipzig only after 1741, when his devoted protector introduced him to Johann Sebastian. But even admitting that Goldberg might have taken some lessons from Wilhelm Friedemann, it remains nonetheless an irrefutable fact that he owed everything to Johann Sebastian. Strangely enough, there was a haunting similarity of nature between the eldest son of Johann Sebastian and Theophilius; both were marked by genius. Misanthropic and whimsical, they were consumed by a profound and incurable melancholy.

Music was Kayserling's passion, his refuge, and his consolation. Harassed by constant traveling and the heavy responsibilities of the missions entrusted to him by Catherine the Great of Russia, the Count suffered from insomnia. During these interminable nights the young Goldberg played for him. But how could the tumultuous and nostalgic improvisations of this child appease Kayserling's constant restlessness? Kayserling sought in vain for some magic formula that would fill in his hours of anguish with carefree images. In desperation he called upon Bach, asking him to compose a piece that Goldberg might play for him during his sleepless nights. More than happy to prove his gratitude to his friend and protector, Johann Sebastian set to work with joy, his enthusiasm heightened by the knowledge that his work would be placed in the hands of the most extraordinary of all harpsichordists. A short time later, Bach offered Kayserling a composition entitled *Aria mit verschiedenen Veranderungen vors Clavicimbal mit zwei Manualen* (aria with ornamented variations for harpsichord with two keyboards). Gratefully, Kayserling sent Bach a snuff box filled with one hundred *louis d'or*.

Thus runs an anecdote according to documents of the time. "The only enduring works are those that are circumstantial," said Goethe. Anatole France commented on this thought saying, "All considered, every work is circumstantial because everyone depends on the place and time it was created. One cannot understand or love intelligently any work if one does not know the place, the time, and the circumstance of its origin." But it also happens that there may be an almost grotesque disproportion between the occasion and the work. Compare, for example, the mediocrity of Doctor August Friedrich Mueller's sympathetic, but insignificant, personality with the depth and scope of the cantata *Der zufrieden gestellte Aeolus* written for his birthday. Breathing unexpected poetry into the description of this banal life, Bach created a work of universal significance.

Should one bless Kayserling's insomnia for having given us one of Bach's masterpieces? I think not. The occasion does not engender a work of art, nor is it responsible for its birth. The occasion is merely used as a pretext by a genius who will always find, or if need be, invent this pretext. Had Kayserling been a victim of sleeping sickness, Bach, in all probability, would have composed a cantata glorifying sleep and dreaming, a subject very much appreciated at the time, by the way. Handel wrote admirable slumber arias, as Lully and others had done before him.

The little story attached to *The Goldberg Variations* affects in no way their true grandeur. Along with *The Art of Fugue* and *The Musical Offering*, this work stands as a dazzling secular temple erected in honor of absolute music.

What an extraordinary psychological clairvoyance Bach had! Instead of a suite of dances in which an obstinate rhythm might have aggravated the Count's insomnia, he wrote for Kayserling a composition which, in the richness of its elements, kept shifting and diverting without ever becoming enervating. Bach understood what was needed to dispel the melancholy of a refined gentleman of extensive musical culture. One can almost visualize this neurasthenic aristocrat, a lover of music, in the large room of his palace, lighted only by the pale glow of candelabra, as he watched and listened intently to the adolescent musician bent over the keyboards. One by one the variations diffused their phosphorescent light and graceful arabesques, like delicate corollas, to the fascination and delight of the Count. He knew, indeed, how to follow the thread of each voice in its complete individuality, and how to encompass the complex musical web with its distinct nervures.

The principle of the variation, as practiced by the Virginalists, or by Sweelinck and Frescobaldi, could not suit Bach's nature. The progressive division of the note values of the theme into an increasing number of smaller units represents a somewhat automatic and set process; it precludes inner life. The fecund vitality of Bach's melodic line opposes that violently. Therefore we understand why his *Aria alla maniera italiana* is the only example he left us of a procedure so contrary to his nature. To obtain a progressively increasing liveliness, Bach discovered much stronger and more complex means. Just compare *The Goldberg Variations* with Handel's aria known as *The Harmonious Blacksmith* or with Rameau's *Gavotte et Doubles*, and you will perceive immediately the basic differences among these three men in their concept of the variation.

Counterpoint, Bach's basic culture, became for him an organic function. Other musicians who were brought up in the same tradition adopted this language too, but without incorporating it. Bach did not have to adhere to counterpoint; he sprang from it; he was counterpoint incarnate. It is through the medium of contrapuntal language that he depicted life and death, and it is in this language that he forged the thirty *Goldberg Variations*.

The Aria, the theme of the Variations, appears as a sarabande copied in Anna Magdalena's hand in the 1725 *Clavierbüchlein*. The fact that this sarabande precedes the aria "Schlummert ein ihr matten Augen"—later incorporated in Cantata 82—proves, according to Spitta, that it was written before the Cantata. Therefore, the Aria, probably composed for Anna Magdalena, had existed for at least ten years when Bach used it as the theme for his variations. We are impressed by an important detail which seems to sustain the idea that the sarabande had not been intended as the theme of a set of variations; beginning five bars before the end of the Aria, the bass abandons its tranquil gait, becomes animated, and never returns to its initial design. Above it the evenly swaying sixteenth-notes bring the theme to a close and pursue their course in the first variation.

Let us examine this bass carefully in its entirety. Immutable, it remains the foundation upon which Bach elaborates his thirty variations, rarely breaking its original gait. Even in the twenty-fifth Variation in G Minor, the bass remains in G major, a tour de force accomplished by Bach through the use of chromaticism enriched by extraordinarily daring harmonies. Sometimes he takes pleasure in making the bass jump an octave upward or downward, according to the direction imposed by the variation in which it occurs. At other times Bach introduces this bass line into the middle voice, or in the manner of chaconnes, he places it in the top voice as, for example, in the first bars of Variation 18. And all of this is done just in passing! Therefore it is not the melody of the sarabande, but its bass, with all its harmonic possibilities, that Bach elaborates and develops. Thanks to an inexhaustible inventiveness, the unchanging harmonic progression reappears with a perpetually renewed freshness every time it passes through another variation.

Great architect that he was, Bach planned the Variations so that each third variation would form a canon, beginning with *canone all'unisono* and on through to a *canone alla nona*. Many of them are in *moto contrario*.

After the Aria, grave and serene, though vibrating with inner life and following the measured swaying motion of the first variation, the second and third variations pass by in a tranquil and pastoral mood. Variation IV is a series of jocose imitations, and Variation V—in which the voices cross each other over the two keyboards—is an outburst of irrepressible joy. Calm returns; Variation VI, smooth and swift, glides into a *canone alla seconda*. Variation VII has the frolicsome and capering spirit of an Italian *forlana*. In Variation VIII the playfulness of crossing voices resumes and then halts abruptly to make way for Variation IX, a meditative and quiet *canone alla terza*. Variation X is a youthful and exuberant *fughetta* which follows the bass while developing according to the strictest rules. Variation XI is like an exquisite duo for *oboe d'amore*, and, in contrast, Variation XII, a *canone alla quarta*, unfolds with a majestic self-assurance. Variation XIII is a delicately wrought cantilena which bears a certain resemblance to the Andante of *The Italian Concerto*. But while the famous second movement of the Concerto is wrapped in the somber tonality of D minor, the delightful Variation XIII unfolds in the most radiant luminosity of G major.

Variation XIV resumes the frolicsome mood with hand-crossings over the two keyboards; a dance rhythm alternates with motives suggesting the fluttering of butterflies.

Variation XV, a *canone alla quinta in moto contrario*, is the first of the three variations in G minor. These diatonic steps, ascending and descending, seem to be the very motion of anguish and despair. The ascending motive in the last bar remains suspended in mid-air, like a question mark. If Bach leaves us in suspense at that moment, it is only to affirm his power and his certitude in Variation XVI, an overture *à la française*. Variation XVII, all along its course, is like a cascading waterfall, tumbling and foaming. Variation XVIII, a *canone alla sesta*, is like a well-scanned march in which the parts converse with gaiety and humor. In contrast, Variation XIX swings along in the manner of a smooth barcarolle. Wild flights return in Variation XX, in which bold dialoguing voices run into an increasingly vivacious pursuit.

Like a caryatid slowly moving with stony steps, the bass of Variation XXI, the second in G minor, poignant and tragic, supports two voices in canon. This chromatic bass reminds us of the Crucifixus from *The B Minor Mass*. Oh, the anxiety of this interrogation, the sobbing of the answer which sums up the whole expression of the phrase, then accepts, becomes resigned, and concludes! In opposition, Variation XXII is a monument of certainty; massive in stature, its voices interlace after the fashion of Palestrina. In Variation XXIII, written according to the principle of *La Joyeuse* of Rameau, Bach uses the short phrase which we also find in Alessandro Poglietti's variation *Baiselemens* (hand kissing). A carefree cheerfulness characterizes the twenty-third variation, in which scales and thirds ride in an unbridled cavalcade. With Variation XXIV Bach sobers us, and there comes a *canone all'ottava*, marking the rhythm of a *siciliano*.

Variation XXV, the third and last in G minor, is the supreme pearl of this necklace—the black pearl. In its somber shimmerings, all the restlessness of the romantics may be already discerned. This richly ornamented adagio is overwhelming with the poignancy of its feverish chromaticism. Is not this nostalgic and plaintive curve toward the sixth the same as that later to be rediscovered by Chopin and the Wagner of *Tristan?*

In Variation XXVI we hear a scintillating passage, flying in double triplets around the sarabande theme. Variation XXVII presents itself as a *canone alla nona*. Only Bach could bring to this scholarly form so much mischievousness and humor. In Variation XXVIII it seems that small bell-like tinklings are tracing a light melodic web against an uninterrupted fluttering of trills. Opening like *The Christmas Oratorio* with joyful drumbeats— these *batteries* Rameau thought he had invented—Variation XXIX overflows with a tumultuous exaltation, expressed by hammerings on the two keyboards, figured in rolling triplets, dense and heavy. In reducing these figurations for a single keyboard, Liszt drew from them one of the most brilliant effects of his technique. These jubilant accents prepare us for the last variation, a quodlibet. As a kind of musical joke, it had enjoyed considerable popularity for two centuries before Bach's time. There were various ways of composing a quodlibet; it could be either a medley of popular songs of opposing character succeeding one another (the more disparate the words and the music, the more enjoyable the effect), or it could consist of several folk tunes, as different as possible from each other, intoned simultaneously. This last formula, which contains interesting contrapuntal possibilities, was chosen by Bach. The quodlibet of *The Goldberg Variations* is composed of two folk-songs: *Ich bin so lang nicht bei Dir gewest* (I have not been near you for so long) and *Kraut und Rüben* (cabbage and turnips). The words of these two songs have been preserved thanks to a copy made by Kittel, a pupil of Bach. The first one, which Spitta sought in vain and believed lost, was very popular in the streets of Leipzig in 1696, a half-century before Bach used it. According to tradition, Bach split the two motives, interchanging them in inversions and imitations. In the first bar he gives the lead to the tenor. It seems that Bach by ending his imposing work with a joyful quodlibet meant to symbolize the patriarchal tradition which ran in his family from generation to generation. Forkel described how the Bach clan—composed of cantors, organists, and town musicians—was in the habit of gathering upon a given day. They began by singing a chorale. After this pious start, they went on to jesting and singing facetious and salty tunes, improvising all at once. In the midst of laughter shared by everyone present they succeeded, thanks to their musical skill, in composing learned quodlibets, although the words were different for each part. (Quoted by Elsa Binenfeld, *I.M.G.* VI, Part I.) After this culmination in pure joy, there is a silence. Then the Aria returns, grave, noble, and serene. This affecting repeat of the sarabande incites us to look back upon the entire path trodden since its first inception. Such was Bach's wish undoubtedly.

Some variations have the poignant beauty of a page from *The St. Matthew Passion*; and between the somber torsades of the variations in a minor key, intervene the freshness of rolling cascades and the gaiety of uninhibited laughter. Our god Bach is in high spirits. The devilish crossing of hands on the two keyboards fascinates him. He yields to it with a total joy. All this liveliness startles us. Is that counterpoint, said to be so severe? But since we know that Bach is counterpoint incarnate, it is obvious that we are never confronted by a demonstration of skill as such; thanks to Bach, we understand the *raison d'être* of polyphony. Others have made fugues and canons just as perfect as his; but he alone can tear our hearts apart and give us mortal anguish, only to appease us immediately with so much loving vigilance. Is it possible that a canon *per moto contrario* may contain within itself a whole world? That a fughetta may give us a glimpse of infinite bliss?

Today Bach's dynamism fascinates young people. But who among them takes the trouble of dismantling, one by one, the ensemble of voices, the polyphonic complex in order to plunge into each isolated voice and extract all its flavor? It seems that what appeals most to them is the dynamic bloc. This kind of dynamism can be found in a concerto of Hindemith or of Falla because their density does not stand to be disassembled; there it exists through accumulation. But Bach's dynamism is of a very different nature.

There is no other work which, like *The Goldberg Variations*, leaves such a vast field for interpreters to display qualities of imagination, skill, and virtuosity, while giving the most substantial nourishment to musicians. How can one explain, then, that this masterpiece, unique in keyboard literature, yet available in print, remained forgotten for so long? (Ed. Note: This was written in 1933!) First of all, because Bach wrote at the head of the piece *Vor Clavicymbel mit zwey Manualen* (for harpsichord with two keyboards). Above each variation that must be played on two keyboards, we read *à deux claviers* (for two keyboards). Others bear the inscription *à 1 cl.* Those marked *à 1 ovvero 2 cl.* may be played either on one or both keyboards. Written in two or more parts, often invertible, intercrossing and constantly entwining each other, this music demands an instrument equipped with several registers representing different colors and levels of sound. Various ways of performing the Variations at the piano have been devised to remedy its lack of registers. Once it was attempted with the help of a two-piano transcription; this at least permitted distributing the text between the two instruments. But the piano, which has no more than a single eight-foot register, goes contrary to the needs and nature of overlapping voices. Besides, the blunt-ness of sound produced by the impact of hammers on the strings is alien to the transparency obtained with plucked strings, a trans-parency so necessary to polymelodic writing. By interchanging parts on various registers of a two-keyboard harpsichord, we dis-cover the secret of this foolproof writing which is similar to a hand-woven rug with no wrong side.

But choice of the proper instrument is not all. The thirty Variations which follow the majestic sarabande are tyrannical in their exigencies; the relentless contrapuntal speculations require a mathematical distribution of light and shadow. The technical difficulties which, from Variation to Variation, accumulate and multiply, demand a complete independence of each hand and finger. In calling forth this world of polyphony, his alone, Bach remains the god who diverts himself and makes child's play of everything. But we, poor creatures, where can we find brain, heart, and muscles *à la hauteur* to such a degree?

A revelation awaited me as I studied the work of a composer seventeen years older than Bach. Gallant, with almost frivolous allusions, *Les Folies Françaises* of François Couperin le Grand are considered light in character. And yet, a close examination of their structure unveiled for me a striking affinity with the monumental *Goldberg Variations*. In both works there is the same principle of an immutable bass, the same succession of unchanging harmonies passing from one variation to the next. Both composers show their scornful nonconformity to the laws of scholastic variation form. One point, however, and not the least, sets apart one piece from the other, making each one even dearer to us because it underlines the salient features of its author; while Bach's inexhaustible inventiveness moves in the sphere of contrapuntal speculations, the inspiration of Couperin moves toward an extremely refined psychological elaboration.

The absolute music of Bach and the gallant music of Couperin meet and interlace on the same level—a level above our prejudice about superior or inferior art.

The Fantasias

As has already been mentioned on page 49, there are many who find in Bach's *Chromatic Fantasy* (Schmieder 903) an anticipation of romanticism. Yet in this rhapsody, rather than fantasy, with its fiery recitatives (see p. 396) interrupted by chords spread out in a skillfully built disorder, we find the surviving spirit and influence of the great French lutenists of the sixteenth and seventeenth centuries. We are reminded especially of the *preambula* written without bar lines and which were to be played "with discretion"—that is, freely without observing any definite measure. While retaining the nostalgic and wandering qualities of this style, Bach strengthened and established it.

Like Mozart's C Minor Fantasy (K.397), *The Chromatic Fantasy* is perfectly symmetrical. No matter how much we search, there is no trace of "spur of the moment" improvisation. Divided into sections, solidly grounded, its ordonnance tells us about Bach's nature—Bach the architect who planned everything and liked surprises only when they were well prepared.

The Chromatic Fantasy fell victim to numerous transcriptions. In many modern editions, the answer to the subject of the fugue has been altered. These editions have adopted the version of Forkel, who, following the already doubtful tradition of Friedemann Bach, attired the end of the Fantasy with arbitrary and bombastic variants.

The Chromatic Fantasy acquires its full meaning only when it is played on the harpsichord. With its double keyboard and its multiple registers, now organlike, now comparable to an immense lute, the harpsichord permits recreating wonderfully the pathetic intensity of the recitatives, the splendor of the arpeggios, and the polyphonic majesty of the fugue.

Another Fantasia and Fugue by Bach is that in A Minor (Schmieder 944). Here the Fantasia is only a brief preamble made of a few tumultuous broken chords, the free realization of which is left to the interpreter. It launches immediately into the immense Fugue, two hundred bars long, a fugue unique among the works of Bach for the amplitude of its proportions, the power of its surging stream, and the uninterrupted unfolding of its inspiration.

Bach wrote other fantasias in a completely different style. For instance, that in C Minor (Schmieder 906), the autograph of which is in Dresden. It would be important for every performer to know it because it reveals how certain ornaments should be played. Instead of indicating them with signs, Bach wrote them out in measured notes. What an eloquent lesson!

Although this Fantasia can be played on the modern piano, the passages for crossed hands obviously call for the two keyboards of the harpsichord. The character is stormy. The two voices run, sometimes in contrary motion, sometimes together; but at other times they clash and interweave—magnificent effects intended for two keyboards.

Another Fantasia in C Minor (Schmieder 919) is written in the style of the Inventions. Only twenty-five measures long, it is a superb example of Bach's mastery in writing for two voices. One ought to have two right hands to do justice to it and not be like those pianists who follow the Biblical dictum, "Let not thy right hand know what thy left hand is doing."

The Keyboard Suites

Bach's works known as the French Suites were thus named because of a supposed similarity in their writing to that of the

French style. And yet, the English Suites are more French than the French. As for the Partitas, claimed to be the German Suites, they are the most French of all. (See p. 83)

The Partita in C Minor (Schmieder 826) is one of Bach's most eloquent homages to French music and especially to the tradition and style of French interpretation. "We write differently from what we play," said Couperin in his *Art de Toucher le Clavecin*. Bach proves and demonstrates this postulate in the C Minor Partita.*

It opens with a Sinfonia which is a French overture condensed into seven measures. A narrative solo, gentle and expressive, follows, evoking an *oboe d'amore*; the Sinfonia ends with a powerful two-part fugue.

The Allemande, the Courante, and the Sarabande bring us close to Couperin. In the Rondeau and Capriccio, Bach delights in jumps bouncing from one hand to the other. One feels he is in high spirits, and the outburst even increases in the Capriccio.

Bach himself published the six partitas, one by one. The second in C Minor first appeared in 1727.

In the Suite in B Minor (Schmieder 831), the Overture is grandiose because of the intensity of the two elements that confront each other—the menacing and tragic Grave and the unleashed and furious Fugato. It stops abruptly to let the Grave conclude with appeased chords, although the mood is still somber and tragic.

The Toccatas

Bach's toccatas are like large decorative panels. Their structure is immense, their expression overflowing. They have no sacred implication, but they are full of pathos and impassioned transports.

---

* ED. NOTE: Wanda Landowska was convinced that the Sarabande of the C Minor Partita, as it came to us with the even motion of its sixteenth-notes, was in fact a *double*. Inspired by other instances in which Bach himself wrote both the "simple" version and its ornamented *double*, as well as by Chambonnières's *Moutier* with its *double* by Louis Couperin, and other examples among French music, she reconstructed a "simple" version for the Sarabande in C Minor. Following the same train of thought, she also provided a *double* for the Sarabande of Bach's English Suite in E Minor.

At first sight they look incoherent and disparate. What strikes us above all is the unrelenting insistence with which Bach holds on to a motive, repeating it indefatigably on every step of the scale, as, for example, in the C Minor and F Sharp Minor Toccatas. In them, the chosen motives are rather short-winded. Is it to entice their repetition? Or is it to enhance the feverish character of the work that they are so brief and panting?

In the toccatas there is a ceaseless progression, climbing with implacable tenacity toward the culminating point. But this climax is illusory because beyond it there is something that we cannot grasp, something that floats around the theme and its development. The gradation never seems to stop.

Obviously the constant repetitions account for the difficulty of interpreting these toccatas. The only way to treat them is to build them up in large planes corresponding to their apparent monotony. In this way one may achieve the barren effect of vast expanses. (See p. 397)

As for the D Major Toccata (Schmieder 912), it contains within itself all the elements of Bach's genius: the spontaneity and force of his improvisation, the ineluctability of his contrapuntal elaboration, and his unique sense of architecture. Bach's masterly hand unites the varied elements into a magnificent triptych. Flanked on both sides by brilliant D major parts, a tragic but tranquil F sharp minor fugue forms the supremely beautiful center piece.

For the Lute-Harpsichord:
Prelude, Fugue, and Allegro in E Flat Major
(SCHMIEDER 998)

The Prelude, Fugue, and Allegro is a magnificent example of what can result from the interest of a creative genius in the construction of an instrument. This composition came to us from the estate of Karl Philipp Emanuel and bears an autograph title: *Prelude pour la luth o cembal.* The ambiguity of this title was, and continues to be, the subject of controversies. Is it for lute or for harpsichord? We do not know for sure, but probably it was for lute-harpsichord (*Lautenwerk*), a combined instrument, in the construction of which Bach took great interest.

The *Lautenwerk* was a harpsichord with gut strings introduced in it for the purpose of imitating the sonority of the lute and of the theorboe. A pupil of Bach, Adlung, gave a very detailed and enthusiastic description of this instrument in *Musica Mechanica Organoedi*, 1768; he mentioned that he knew only the *Lautenwerk* built by Johann Nikolaus Bach, a cousin of Johann Sebastian. This instrument was not a new thing. The fact is that lute-harpsichords had been built successfully since the sixteenth century. Bach's friend Walther mentions in his *Musicalisches Lexicon* (1732) makers who excelled in the construction of these instruments; among them he named Fleischer and Gleichmann. We know that Bach himself while in Cöthen ordered a *Lautenwerk* and later another one from the organ maker Hildebrand of Leipzig. Two *Lautenwerke* were listed in the inventory of Johann Sebastian's estate.

Bach was tempted by the idea of combining the grandeur of the harpsichord with the gentle silvery tone of the lute and the mysterious depth of the theorboe. Thanks to its keyboards, this instrument offered unlimited possibilities and enabled skillful harpsichordists to enrich their interpretation by new effects of sonority. Bach was fully aware of this.

Let us now consider the work as a whole. The first piece, Prelude, and the last, Allegro, are two-part music. The Prelude, announced by a low E flat, like a bell, is a *récit*, every note of which is rich in meaning. Fervent and chaste, it makes us think of the beautiful tenor aria *Sehet was die Liebe thut* in Cantata 85. Between these two *bicinia* the Fugue rises grandiose and simple. Calm at first, it advances with majestic steps and unfolds in an overwhelming choir. Interrupted by an episode, the Fugue reappears exactly as it was first exposed. It makes for a true triptych, the two wings being represented by the Fugue and its repeat and the central panel by the episode. In it the theme of the Fugue comes, goes, and passes from one voice to the other against the incessant murmuring of the lute stop.

The Allegro is a soliloquy sustained by a bass scanning the

triple meter with humorous vigor. Bach's art is so masterful that we think we are hearing not two, but many voices pursuing one another, multiplying, discussing, questioning, now heated, now calm. And underlying it all there is that bass leaping joyously, participating eagerly in the play of echoes and delighting in chiaroscuro effects.

The Prelude, Fugue, and Allegro is of incomparable beauty. Inspired, spontaneous, without a moment of arduous elaboration, it is unique among Bach's works.

Notice that this composition, written for lute-harpsichord, sounds admirably well on a modern grand harpsichord furnished with a lute stop.

A Descriptive Work:

Capriccio on the Departure of His Beloved Brother

(SCHMIEDER 992)

This piece, originally called *Capriccio sopra la lontananza del suo fratello dilettissimo*, was composed at Arnstadt by the nineteen-year-old Johann Sebastian in honor of his elder brother, Johann Jakob, who enlisted in 1704 as oboist in the army band of the Swedish king, Charles XII.

In the Arioso, tender and graceful, the friends of Johann Jakob try to cajole him into abandoning the voyage.

The Andante Fugato which follows is a polyphonic description of the various misfortunes that could happen to him en route.

The Adagissimo is a general lament of his friends. The descending chromatic bass, so dear to Bach and his predecessors, reminds us of the Crucifixus from *The B Minor Mass*.

But Johann Jakob is adamant, and his friends wish him farewell. Then comes the Aria di Postiglione followed by a spirited fugue, an imitation of the postilion's horn, overflowing with gaiety.

This descriptive piece—almost unique among the works of Bach—was inspired by Kuhnau, whose descriptive *Biblical Stories*, in sonata form, had been composed four years before.

A Transcription: The Sonata in A Minor

(SCHMIEDER 965)

This Sonata is a transcription from Adam Reincken's *Hortus Musicus*. Bach reduced for harpsichord the work of Reincken written for two violins, viola, and bass. But how can one term "reduction" that which has been amplified, extended, and enriched? An examination of both texts—Reincken's quartet and Bach's sonata—enlightens us about the intentions of the author and about the will of the transcriber. The original is full of ideas, but the hand that drew them was timorous and unconscious. Reincken had little knowledge of his own richness. Bach discovered it, set it according to its real worth, and revealed it to us in the light of his own genius.

The Adagio which opens Reincken's quartet is awkward and apparently incomplete; it stands magnificent at the head of Bach's sonata, ornamented by him with variants and arabesques in the most refined Italian taste. Thus it is to Bach that we owe not only the salvation of Reincken's work from oblivion, but also our understanding and love of it. This transcription escaped the attention of Spitta, who mistook Bach's sonata for an original work. The discovery was made only in 1881.

Bach and the Italian Concerto Grosso

Bach traveled very little in his lifetime; he never once left the confines of his native country. At most he would, upon occasion, quit his home and his work and go to hear Reincken or Marchand improvise. Yet, though withdrawn from the world, he kept in complete touch with musical movements in foreign countries. He knew the French masters thoroughly, and he delighted in reworking the compositions of the Italians. A burning curiosity to learn everything, to read and hear everything consumed Bach from his earliest childhood until the last day of his life. There is a familiar anecdote, told by some of his biographers, to prove this. Orphaned at the age of ten, Johann Sebastian was sent to Ohrdruf to the home of his elder brother Johann Christoph, an organist, who devoted himself to young Sebastian's musical education. In a very short time the ten-year-old Bach had mastered all the compositions his brother had given him to learn. For some unknown reason, however, he had been forbidden the use of a collection of music by celebrated masters of the time. Johann Christoph had locked it up in a cabinet. Yet, in spite of his brother's orders, Bach succeeded in extracting the paper-covered book through the lattice door of the cabinet; when everybody in the household was asleep, he copied it furtively by moonlight. At the end of six months, this musical booty was his. But Johann Christoph came upon it and mercilessly deprived his little brother of the copy which had cost him such work and devotion. All in vain! While bending over his work in the midst of the silent nights, the boy of genius had understood and absorbed the music he was copying. It consisted of pieces by Kerll, a pupil of Carissimi, by Pachelbel, a pupil of Kerll, by Froberger, a pupil of Frescobaldi. That is how Bach, when a mere child, became acquainted with Italian music through musicians who had studied with Italian masters.

From that time on, Bach never ceased to live intimately with the compositions of Legrenzi, Albinoni, Corelli, Marcello, and Vivaldi. He used their themes to build up fugues; he transcribed, reconstructed, and amplified their works. Why? For the joy of steeping himself in the spirit of creators of a foreign race, of familiarizing himself with new musical concepts, and of quenching his thirst by extracting the substance that he needed to assert his own powers.

The concerto grosso had a peculiar fascination for Bach. He knew this form of art born in Italy, he followed its evolution from composer to composer, and it was in the concerto grosso of Vivaldi that Bach found complete satisfaction. He was attracted by the flowing spontaneity and uncomplicated naturalness of Vivaldi's Mediterranean inspiration, which aimed only at pursuing its unbridled course. With his tormented nature, his inventive mind always on the alert, Bach found Vivaldi's music restful, if only for a moment, because his inspiration, spurred and quickened, would soon retrace the path trod by the Italian. Then he would begin to create obstacles, to provoke conflicts, to disrupt the joyous cavalcades, and to gather clouds which would burst into storms.

Bach extended the limits of Vivaldi's form and enriched its content by countless complexities of harmony and counterpoint. But above all, it was Vivaldi's architecture of the concerto grosso which Bach decided to adopt. Therefore, let us not be surprised by his transcribing for solo harpsichord Vivaldi's concertos originally written for solo violin and strings; let us rather consider it an urge to re-create splendid materials which seemed to him insufficiently developed. This preparatory work gave birth to masterpieces such as *The Italian Concerto* and *The Brandenburg Concertos*.

Antonio Vivaldi was probably born in 1678. For more than thirty years he fulfilled the functions of composer, violin maestro, and orchestra conductor—either from the harpsichord or at the violin—at the conservatory of the Ospedale della Pietà. This conservatory was the most famous of the four musical institutions in Venice.

"The passion of this nation for music is amazing," wrote President De Brosses in his *Lettres familières écrites d'Italie* (1739-1740), in which he gave us a very vivid glimpse of the musical life in Italy.

"The transcendent music here (Venice) is that of the Ospedale. There are four of them, all devoted to illegitimate or orphaned girls, or those whose parents cannot afford to rear them. They are brought up at the expense of the State and are trained exclusively to excel in music. They sing like angels and play the violin, the cello, the bassoon; in short, there is no big instrument which can terrify them. They are cloistered like nuns. There is nothing more fascinating than to see a young and pretty novice, clad in white with pomegranate blossoms nestled in her hair just over the ear, conducting the orchestra and beating time with all the grace and precision you can imagine. Among the four Ospedale, that to which I most often go and enjoy most is the Ospedale della Pietà. It also is first in the perfection of the Sinfonias."

We know positively that Vivaldi was appointed to conduct a great number of rehearsals there. "Vivaldi made himself one

of my intimate friends, perhaps to sell me his concertos at a very
high price," continues De Brosses. "He is *uno vecchio* who has a
tremendous passion for composition. I have heard him claim that
he could compose a concerto with all its parts faster than a copyist
could write them down."

De Brosses noted with regret that Vivaldi no longer enjoyed
in his own country the consideration he deserved, a country in
which "fashion is the dictator . . . and in which the music of the
previous year no longer attracts."

How can it be? This music full of life and passion, with its
impetuous rhythm, the noble grace of the slow movements, its
architectural grandeur, its inexhaustible melodic richness—this
music neglected, forgotten?

We can hardly believe that the death of Vivaldi passed unnoticed, and we did not even know, until 1938, that he died in
1741 and was buried in Vienna.

But it is Bach who honored his memory. By transcribing his
works, he raised an imperishable monument to Vivaldi.

Vivaldi's Concerto in D Major, for instance, is in its original
version the ninth of a series of twelve published about 1700 under
the general title *Estro Armonico*. It consists of three movements,
an Allegro, a Larghetto, and an Allegrissimo. When we hear this
sumptuous and magnificent Allegro, this Larghetto which is a
suave Italian cantilena accompanied by streaming arpeggios, and
this finale overflowing with the joyful rhythm of a dance, we can
understand the fascination the work of Vivaldi, the Red Priest
of Venice, had for Bach.

The essential feature of the concerto grosso is the opposition
between tutti and soli. After having transcribed for solo harpsichord the concerti grossi of Vivaldi and other Italian composers,
Bach accomplished an extraordinary tour de force; he composed
his *Concerto in Gusto Italiano*, a complex work containing within
itself all the elements of the concerto grosso. With regal authority,
Bach attacked and settled this question of tutti and soli, and in
bestowing upon a single instrument the rendering of this opposition, he elucidated in decisive fashion the structure of all eighteenth century concerti grossi and the manner in which they were
performed at that epoch.

The Italian Concerto is in fact a concerto grosso for solo harpsichord. It is the most living of documents, the most eloquent of all explanations. With its double keyboards and varied registers, the harpsichord has the multiplicity of an orchestra, or it can transform itself into a soloist, according to the fluctuations of the work being performed. It is on the harpsichord that *The Italian Concerto* achieves full reality. The contrasts between tutti and soli, the dialogues passing from group to group, the juxtaposition of light and shade—all this mosaic of richly varied tones can be brought back to life only on the instrument for which this music was created.

The Keyboard Concertos

Between 1730 and 1733 Bach wrote seven concertos for harpsichord and strings. Most of them are transcriptions from his violin concertos. Consequently it has been said that the violin, rather than the harpsichord, was better suited to the inspiration and expression of Bach's ideas. One seems to forget Bach's passion for transcriptions, a passion that prevented his ever being satisfied with any definitive version of his own compositions, whether they were vocal or instrumental. His versatile and restless spirit refused to be limited to the use of any one particular instrument or even to instruments in general.

I wish to call particular attention to a possible confusion between Bach's idea of transcription and that which is called transcription today. They have nothing in common. Bach reshaped and recast his own works constantly because, thanks to his inexhaustible wealth of invention, he did not like to stop at one possibility. The transcriptions of today, however, are generally a deformation of a great master's work. They deprive it of the purity of its character by playing false to the tradition.

An example of Bach's transcription of one of his own works is found in the Concerto in G Minor for Harpsichord and Strings (Schmieder 1058). In this instance the original was his Violin Concerto in A Minor. The slight disparities between the two versions are most interesting to examine, since they demonstrate Bach's feeling for the peculiarities of each instrument, violin as well as harpsichord.

The first movement is dynamic and charged with the power of opposing rhythms. In the second movement, Bach, with imposing architectural simplicity, presents alternately four measures of tutti and four measures of solo. The tutti consists of majestic arpeggios supported by a continuous bass in French rhythm. In the soli, the rich, although attenuated, arpeggios accompany a cantilena which unfolds with indescribably delightful smoothness. The final movement is a gigue of furious activity. From time to time, Bach intersperses it with witty and light touches.

Some musicologists have doubted the authenticity of the Concerto in D Minor for Harpsichord and Strings (Schmieder 1052). But who else, at that time, could have conceived a work of such grandeur, skill, and might? We find parts of this concerto in Cantatas No. 146 and 188.

A few of Bach's keyboard concertos are not transcriptions. For instance, the Concerto in C Major (Schmieder 1061) is an original composition for two harpsichords and strings. It unfolds in a streaming contrapuntal display. Its unlimited breadth does not stop at the last bar; it goes beyond, victoriously Jupiterian. A beautiful autograph of two of its parts is in the Berlin State Library.

As for the D Minor Concerto for Three Harpsichords and Strings (Schmieder 1063), there is no extant autograph. Five manuscript copies are, however, in existence. Four of them are almost identical, therefore trustworthy. These copies bear the title *Concerto à 3 cembali concertante, due violini, viola e basso continuo dal Sr. Gio. Sebast. Bach.*

This work, more than any other, demands to be performed with three harpsichords—not pianos—because each instrument is like an orchestra in itself. These three orchestras, joined by the group of strings, skirmish, approach each other, recede, or unite without ever merging. In this lies one of the most important conditions of Bach's tonal esthetic. Each voice taken separately must float into space; and when all of them unite, they either join forces, pass by, cross, or interlace, but they never crush one another.

How can one reconstruct Bach's triple concerto, build up

the framework, organize, and spread out the effects of light and shade? Or trace the immense arch of a tempo which, in keeping with the firmness and logic of Bach, will vibrate to the pulsation of his great heart? The problem is serious and complicated by the traps that are set for us by the three harpsichords themselves; we are too easily inclined to treat them as three solo instruments. In fact, if one considers only the importance Bach gave to the individual cadenzas, one would be all the more tempted to go along with this hypothesis. But nothing of the sort is intended here. It would be a profound error to employ three different ways to depict three subjective characters. In this work, constructed on the principle of the concerto grosso, none of the three harpsichord parts should be left free to run at the whim of its fancy or to follow independently the particularities of its temperament in the manner of soloists. In Bach's concerto grosso, each harpsichord part—a complete world in itself— submits to the others. The autonomous orchestra comes along as an obedient servant to associate itself with the three harpsichords. In concerting fashion, the four groups join to form a single unit, a fourfold, independent, and complex unit. It is with this unity in mind that the registration and the tempi should be planned. While respecting the independent life of each instrument, I try to embrace the whole in a single "one" so as to give Bach's triple concerto a single brain, a single soul, and a single body equipped with a baton and six hands.

In the *Brandenburg Concerto* No. 5 in D Major (Schmieder 1050)—the original title of which is *Concerto 5to à une Traversière, une Violino principale, une Violino à une viola in ripieno, Violoncello, Violone à Cembalo concertato*—the *flauto traverso* and the *violine principale* converse almost continuously; the *cembalo concertato*, without pausing for a moment, now assumes the role of accompanying harpsichord, following Bach's instructions, and now concertizes with the tutti, or joins in the dialogue between the flute and the violin. Suddenly, in the first movement, after a *fermata* above the violas, we come upon the direction *Cembalo solo senza stromenti* (harpsichord solo without instruments). All instruments disappear and the harpsichord launches into an overwhelming cadenza which has all the power of *The Chromatic Fantasy* or of the Toccatas.

The second movement, entitled *Affettuoso*, is devoted entirely to the three solo instruments. Wrapped in a somber B minor, it proceeds in French rhythm, suggesting the dignity of a funeral march for a hero.

The last movement is a dance of exultant vitality. The harpsichord jumps from solo to accompaniment with broad, rich chords.

The Sonatas for Harpsichord and Violin

(SCHMIEDER 1014 TO 1019)

A manuscript of these sonatas, not entirely in Bach's own hand, bears the title *Sei Suonate à Cembalo certato e violino solo col basso per viola da gamba accompagnato se piace, composte da Giov. Sebast. Bach* (Six sonatas for concerting harpsichord and solo violin with optional bass accompaniment for viola da gamba, composed by J. S. Bach).

It is important to stress the distinction between harpsichord *certato* and harpsichord *accompagnato*. The former was worked out by the composer himself, while the latter was to be realized by the performer. The six sonatas for harpsichord and violin belong to the first category. In spite of this fact, there are many important places which have to be elaborated by the harpsichordist. Some performers have gone to exaggerated lengths in extending this function. Bach's pupil Kirnberger even went so far as to employ another harpsichord to accompany his own; while the obligato part was played on one instrument, the bass was reinforced and the harmonies realized on the other. If we followed blindly every precedent in the performance of these sonatas, the bass would then be played first by the harpsichord *certato*, second by the viola da gamba, and third by the accompanying harpsichord. Consequently this bass would be multiplied not just three times, but at least five, since the most limited harpsichord possesses a minimum of two strings for each note. It follows, therefore, that the bass, multiplied and re-multiplied in this fashion, would weigh down the ensemble and create a perfect lack of balance. Bach knew precisely what he wanted when he suggested the *se piace*, or optional, accompaniment of a viola da gamba. Since a harpsichord grand is equipped with four strings for each note, one of them being a versatile sixteen-foot register, it renders the participation of a viola da gamba superfluous and even irritating. In any event, these speculations may comfortably be left to theorists. Paper is patient and puts up with everything; but to the ears of a musician versed in the music of the past, its style and methods, these complications offer little suspense. The sonatas for harpsichord and violin display not only Bach's profound knowledge of these two instruments, of which he himself was a master, but an architectural grandeur comparable to the most inspired pages of *The Passions*.

The Universality of Bach

In the nineteenth century one liked to see in Bach the severity of the Gothic. But what about the Prelude in B Flat Major, the Fugue in D Major from Book I of *The Well-Tempered Clavier*, or the cadenza from the fifth *Brandenburg Concerto*?

Today one likes and sees in Bach only the Baroque. The Gothic has been forgotten.

The truth is that Bach never ceases to be human. Too much so? No, completely human, sometimes with overpowering intensity, often in all simplicity. And this is why we love him. The aria "Ach mein Sinn" from *The St. John Passion* has truly the feeling of a poor human being distraught by remorse and losing his mind at the idea of having betrayed his master. In *The St. Matthew Passion*, "Aus Liebe" is moist with tears, while "Golgotha" provokes a shudder of horror.

Bach understands everything; he is sensitive to everything, the pastoral life as well as the atmosphere of village kermises, the mighty Gothic as well as the humility of the sinner kneeling to confess his faults. Everything is close to Bach, and everything in Bach's music is close to us, is part of our own life of misery, despair, or bliss. Bach never climbs on a pedestal to preach or to admonish.

Let us not forget that Bach was a peasant and that this

peasantry can be felt in every note of his music, despite his profound skill. Yes, he is a learned peasant. That is why his art suffocates in conservatory classes and in concert halls.

Why does a melodic line, as beautiful as it may be, even a melodic phrase of Chopin, for instance, become tiresome while the melodic line of Bach can withstand more severe tests? Because there is something eternal in Bach's music, something that makes us wish to hear again what has just been played. This renewal gives us a glimpse of eternity.

2 George Frederic Handel

IL SASSONE FAMOSO, as Handel was called during his sojourn in Italy, was born at Halle and died in England, where he spent a great part of his life.

The breadth of Handel's genius and the variety of his inspiration alternately overflowing with joy, melancholy, or wittiness, can be felt in just a few strokes of his leonine imprint. He was not only one of the most powerful composers of his time, but he was an incomparable virtuoso at the organ and at the harpsichord as well. This double faculty, however, was very common among all great composers of that period. That is why their works were written with such perfect knowledge of the instruments for which they were intended. Handel made the rich qualities of the harpsichord seem to blossom as though touched by a magic wand. Passages and scales roll brilliantly, chords and arpeggios have the flamboyant sonority of dripping gold, and the basses have the depth of bells.

Too often in the performances of his operas and oratorios Handel is smothered under monstrous choral masses. One makes of him a giant of stone. The last aria of *Acis and Galatea* reminds me of the last chapter of Colette's *La Naissance du Jour*. Both proceed with slow steps; each of which is charged with meaning and leads ineluctably toward the end. And yet *Acis and Galatea* is just a pastorale, "a charming pastorale," as the average listener would say. Yes, but Handel's genius made it divine. To give but one example, the motive depicting Acis being transmuted into a brook is a murmur of sensuous serenity.

The Harpsichord Suites

The first collection of Handel's harpsichord suites bears this title in French:

Suites de Pièces pour le Clavecin, composées par G. Fr. Handel Premier Volume. London. Printed for the Author.

Published in 1720, ten years after Handel had left Italy, this first collection is the only one which was engraved under the personal supervision of the composer. Because of this fact, it constitutes a unique document, all the more precious, since numerous pieces and other suites were engraved in 1733 by Walsh, unknown to Handel, under the apocryphal title of *Deuxième Recueil* (Second Collection). In a brief foreword to the first collection Handel said: "I have been obliged to publish Some of the following Lessons because Surreptitious and incorrect Copies of them had got Abroad. I have added several new ones to make the Work more useful, which if it meets with a favourable Reception I will Still proceed to publish more, reckoning it my duty, with my Small Talent, to serve a Nation from which I have receiv'd so Generous a Protection."

The Suite in F Major (First Collection No. 2) opens with an Adagio. Never did Corelli or Vivaldi write a more divinely terrestrial cantilena. Luminous, it unfolds voluptuously between slender columns of thirds. With loving care Handel realized the ornamentation of the entire piece, leaving no opportunity for the interpreter to add the slightest grace note.

Let us bring together for a moment this page inspired by Italy and the Andante from *The Italian Concerto*. Bach too endeavored to enrich the melody in the Italian manner. But the entwining of his ornamented melody has the logic of axioms, and his garlands the solidity of wrought iron. While tracing arabesques, Bach's graving tool digs grooves so deep that they reach unsuspected nerve centers and provoke collisions, shocks, and harmonic cataclysms of extraordinary richness. It fills us with delight and often with anguish. It is thus that Bach's ornamentation, substantial and dense, goes beyond the musical laws of his epoch. By bringing together and soldering distant points of a melody, this ornamentation softens the angles and enriches the outlines. It raises itself to the summit of a creation; it lays the foundation of a new realm in an already established kingdom.

But let us go back to Handel. Trills, appoggiaturas, *circolo* (cadences), and arpeggios warble, murmur, and bewitch us. Vocal rather than instrumental, translucid and animated as a brook, Handelian ornamentation intoxicates and lulls us with its sweet enchantment. Its skill will not crush the layman, who will be able to abandon himself with beatitude. It will relieve a dilettante from "trying to understand" while flattering his taste by the purity of its lines and the refinement of its curves. It will give him the relaxation his whole being craves. Perhaps Handel alone is able to lavish it with such generosity. Listen to the aria "Hush Ye Pretty Warbling Choir" from *Acis and Galatea* (second version, 1721, written at Cannons). A piccolo and two violins bend over the soprano, enlacing it, twittering and imploring with amorous tenderness. This aria, a marvel, springs forth from the same quality of inspiration as that of the Adagio of the F Major Suite, although here slowness enriches the Adagio with a deeper ecstasy.

From the eighth measure on, Handel proceeds toward areas in minor keys. Having passed from one to the other, he stops under the vault of a fermata in A minor. Is it to settle there? No, only to give more brilliance to the F major, which appears again in the next part, a light, sparkling, and playful allegro. It is written in two parts, and not a single note of filling out is required, because Handel is a master at mixing and grinding a complex harmony, at scattering it in small consecutive notes which he lets ripple off, or sparkle, so as to give us—together with the transparency of two horizontal, bouncing voices—the feeling of a vertical harmonic plenitude. And herein lies the secret of the irrefutable contrapuntal art of a Handel or of a Bach.

The lovely Allegro, like a thoroughbred, stops abruptly in the midst of its wild gambols, scorning any rallentando. The Adagio follows, a brief interlude veiled by the minor tonality. This cloud, which suddenly darkens the radiant luminosity of F major, is somewhat startling. Contrary to what he did in the first Adagio, Handel in this page allows the interpreter the liberty of extemporization. And with nostalgia we think of the *Sassone famoso*'s own improvisations. The grandeur and dignity of his style, the majesty of his chords, the grace and the unexpectedness of his cadences were incomparable. "When Handel sat at the harpsichord," said one of his contemporaries, "the most profound silence resulted, and life itself seemed suspended."

The somber Adagio stops, and the Fugue appears without any vain preliminary. The first note of the subject, a lively exclamation, hails us and brings us a whiff of salty air blowing from the open sea. This subject is joyous and sturdy. But the countersubject surpasses it in robustness and good humor. Both pursue each other teasingly, chattering and bursting into laughter. The parts converge, diverge, clash. The air floats and passes through the voices; *ohs!* and *ahs!* throw back at each other their multiplied echoes. Overflowing with joy, the fugue acquires toward the end an unsuspected grandeur. With its last appearance in the bass, the subject stops on the dominant, a pedal-point against which the last word of the large and beaming countersubject buttresses itself. The supreme art of Handel and the generosity of his nature unite in this fugue, which ends in splendor the Suite in F Major.

Handel loved French music, but it was not only the sumptuousness of the overture which attracted him. Undulating curves of the melodic line, refined and sensuous, as well as harmonies full of flavor—in short, all that we cherish in Couperin—that was what Handel relished, cultivated, and developed. Listen to the Allemande which opens the Suite in D Minor (Second Collection No. 3). Is it not twin to *l'Exquise* of Couperin, a sister hardly more robust who expresses the same melancholy in her smile, the same tender abandon in each one of her inflexions?

The Allegro which follows is shorter, but no less explosive than that of the Suite in G Minor. Handel, who loved violent contrasts, appeases us without transition with a brief and concise Air, which has the proud gait of a sarabande .This piece bears an inscription in French: *Lentement* (slowly). A gigue persists stubbornly in its irate rhythm while diverting itself with playful imitations. The Suite ends with a very simple Minuet on which Handel grafts three variations in the Italian manner.

The Suite in G Minor (First Collection No. 7) begins with a French overture. Imposed by Lully and carried into Germany by his pupils Cousser, Muffat, and Fischer, this French overture triumphed in all the courts of Europe. The sumptuousness of the beginning, the brilliance of the *fugato*, the jumpy tremors of the dotted rhythm stamp this instrumental form with a resplendent character which could only seduce Handel. This is why he left us overtures of such sovereign beauty. An interesting detail is that Handel's first opera, *Almira*, which he wrote at nineteen, begins with an overture; under a revised form, this overture is used again, sixteen years later, in this G Minor Suite.

The festive whirlwind vanishes. Introspective and surrounded by silence, the Andante enters. But who can describe the profound solitude and the ineffable beauty of this page, one of the most inspired in all music? It is often said that "the art of Handel is cold and conventional," and that "his formalism satisfies reason more than sensibility." *Indifferent* is the qualificative we like to apply to that which we do not understand. The pathos of Handel is overwhelming because of his way of expressing it—naked and scornful of any ostentation. The capacity of this colossus for isolation—he before whom the court and the public trembled—gave depth to the inner life of his music and augmented its intensity in sorrow as well as in appeasement. Think only of the Christ's aria, "He Was Despised," in *The Messiah*; written in a radiant major tonality, it attests to an inner peace that hurried people mistake for apathy. But are we well enough aware that Handel was sobbing while he composed it?

The Andante vanishes. An Allegro in triple-time suddenly springs forth. Robust, light, or fierce, this rhythm, with its well-defined features forcefully vital, dominates the entire eighteenth century. Handel and Bach employed it with passion and prodigality. By mixing the *furor teutonicus* with a dionysiac joy, both extracted from this rhythm a prodigious dynamism.

How soothing is the Sarabande which follows this unleashed page! Like the Overture, it too appeared in the youthful opera *Almira.* The theme of this Sarabande was dear to Handel. He took it and revised it again and again. But it is in the famous aria "Lascia la spina" from the opera *Il Trionfo del Tempo* that Handel brought to an apogee the magnificent bearing, noble and passionate, of the Sarabande in G Minor. A short, flashing gigue intervenes and defers to the passacaille. This piece is built on a *basso ostinato* and unfolds proudly, unyielding and full of pathos.

Flanked by a French overture and an Italian passacaille, the Suite in G Minor has the superb proportions of an edifice erected to the glory of the musical and gallant Europe of the eighteenth century.

Although Handel's *Harmonious Blacksmith* is familiar to a large audience, the entire Suite in E Major (First Collection No. 5), of which it forms only a part, is almost unknown. Yet it deserves attention for its beauty and perfection. It opens with a Prelude with improvised passages and broken chords establishing the luminous color of the key of E major. The Prelude is followed by an Allemande, a slow dance of elegant and graceful pace, and by a sparkling Courante. It is after the Courante that the Air and Doubles, known as *The Harmonious Blacksmith*, appears.

One day, while walking in the outskirts of Cannons, England, Handel was overtaken by a storm and took shelter in the smithy of a man named Powell. The blacksmith, in the midst of his work, was singing a tune to the accompaniment of his anvil. Enchanted by the performance, Handel immediately took both the tune and its accompaniment for his own and christened them *The Harmonious Blacksmith*. This little anecdote may be found, amplified and embellished, in various monographs on Handel. The famous anvil, elevated to the rank of a heroine, after manifold adventures was sold for its weight in gold to a Handel enthusiast at a London auction.

In 1915, the ex-tenor and musicologist, Dr. Cummings,

offered another version of this story. An apprentice blacksmith of remarkable musical talent gave up his first calling and devoted himself to the study of the harpsichord. The title *Harmonious Blacksmith* passed quite naturally from him to the Air and Doubles, of which he was particularly fond.

Then, another devotee, probably stimulated by this onslaught of legend, offered an even more seductive revelation to a public which had hardly adapted itself to the latest version. The hero of the anecdote on this occasion was a young singer and not an apprentice blacksmith at all!

None of these endearing stories, invented after Handel's death, is confirmed by any historical evidence. We would do well to forget them. And first, forget the mass of chords above which Handel placed his theme. We may hum this theme to ourselves, very softly—not too slowly—and with a certain lightness of inflection. Stripped of all harmonic content, it now emerges revivified and bare, transformed into an *ariette*; the solemn cadences assume the ingratiating quality of a gavotte *à la française*.

On the twenty-sixth day of July, 1756, the Fair of St. Laurent was in full swing in Paris. Situated in the once rustic and gay section between the Faubourg St. Denis and the Faubourg St. Martin, its vendors of jewelry, sweet cakes, and lemonade, its tightrope walkers and dancing bears, its cabarets and marionettes attracted festive crowds. On this particular night, a comedy by Anseaume set to music by Lefèvre de Marcouville was being performed. A gavotte sung in one of the leading roles became an instant success. The gavotte was none other than the Air of the phantom blacksmith.

It has been suggested that the popularity of Handel's Air caused its introduction into this French *opéra comique*. Would it not be more natural to suppose that, on the contrary, this Air, French from the beginning, picked up by Handel and reworked for the harpsichord, returned to the country of its origin?

Handel was obviously fond of it because we find the initial fragment of the Air—a succession of intervals and identical rhythmic patterns—in his youthful work *Almira*, composed in 1704, and also in the first movement of the Concerto for Organ or Harpsichord in B Flat Major, Opus 4, No. 6.

I regret to say, at the risk of disillusioning the legend-loving devotees of *The Harmonious Blacksmith*, that it is neither har-

1. Wanda Landowska, the young pianist-composer, soon after her arrival in Paris in 1900.

2. Wanda Landowska and her husband, Henri Lew, at the time they wrote *Musique Ancienne* (1909).

3. *Right.* Wanda Landowska playing the harpsichord in Auguste Rodin'
studio in 1908 on the occasion of the anniversary of Eugène Carrière'
death. Rodin is standing behind Landowska. Among the audience ar
Charles Morice, the biographer of Carrière, and Pierre Paul Plar
historiographer of J. J. Rousseau. The boy is the son of the compose
Maurice Moszkowski.

4. Reception at the Pleyel Salon in 1907.
Seated L. to R.: Mrs. Harold Bauer, Mme Koussevitzky, Chaliapine,
Felia Litvinne, Saint-Saëns, Blumenfeld, Rimsky-Korsakov, unidenti-
fied, Mme M. Casadesus. Standing L. to R.: F. Casadesus, unidentified,
Paul Vidal, Harold Bauer, Enesco, Alchewsky, Casella, Koussevitzky,
H. Casadesus, Rachmaninov, Gustave Lyon (Director of Pleyel),
Gabrilowitch, M. Casadesus, Safonov, Wanda Landowska, unidenti-
fied, unidentified, Mme Lénars-Tournier.

5. Landowska playing in the Hall of Mirrors at Versailles in 1921 during the Congrès International de l'Histoire de l'Art.

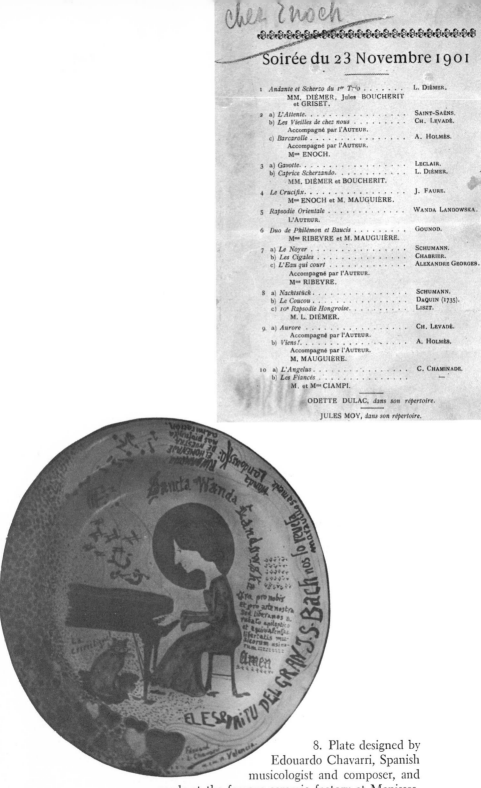

chez Enoch

Soirée du 23 Novembre 1901

1	*Andante et Scherzo du 1er Trio*	L. DIÉMER.
	MM. DIÉMER, Jules BOUCHERIT et GRISET.	
2	a) *L'Attente.*	SAINT-SAËNS.
	b) *Les Vieilles de chez nous*	CH. LEVADÉ.
	Accompagné par l'AUTEUR.	
	c) *Barcarolle*	A. HOLMÈS.
	Accompagné par l'AUTEUR.	
	Mme ENOCH.	
3	a) *Gavotte.*	LECLAIR.
	b) *Caprice Scherzando.*	L. DIÉMER.
	MM. DIÉMER et BOUCHERIT.	
4	*Le Crucifix.*	J. FAURE.
	Mme ENOCH et M. MAUGUIÈRE.	
5	*Rapsodie Orientale*	WANDA LANDOWSKA.
	L'AUTEUR.	
6	*Duo de Philémon et Baucis*	GOUNOD.
	Mme RIBEYRE et M. MAUGUIÈRE.	
7	a) *Le Noyer*	SCHUMANN.
	b) *Les Cigales*	CHABRIER.
	c) *L'Eau qui court*	ALEXANDRE GEORGES.
	Accompagné par l'AUTEUR.	
	Mme RIBEYRE.	
8	a) *Nachtstück.*	SCHUMANN.
	b) *Le Coucou.*	DAQUIN (1735).
	c) *10e Rapsodie Hongroise.*	LISZT.
	M. L. DIÉMER.	
9	a) *Aurore*	CH. LEVADÉ.
	Accompagné par l'AUTEUR.	
	b) *Viens!.*	A. HOLMÈS.
	Accompagné par l'AUTEUR.	
	M. MAUGUIÈRE.	
10	a) *L'Angelus.*	C. CHAMINADE.
	b) *Les Fiancés*	
	M. et Mme CIAMPI.	

ODETTE DULAC, *dans son répertoire.*

JULES MOY, *dans son répertoire.*

8. Plate designed by Edouardo Chavarri, Spanish musicologist and composer, and made at the famous ceramic factory at Manisses.

e Commemorate Bach This Year - -

But let us not forget the music he studied. Let us imagine Bach in his musical environment. To know the composers who have influenced him, composers he loved, helps to understand Bach more profoundly. To study the Italians, the French, predecessors or contemporaries, and even the Germans — in their turn influenced by foreign music — often throws a true light and reveals the very core of Bach's art.

*PRELUDE IN E FLAT MINOR. FUGUE IN D SHARP MINOR . **J. S. BACH**
*PRELUDE AND FUGUE IN D MAJOR 1685-1750
From Book I of the Well-Tempered Clavier

*THE TWO ITALIAN CONCERTOS
Concerto in D major . . . . **A. VIVALDI**
transcribed for harpsichord by J. S. Bach 1678-1743

Italian Concerto . . . . **J. S. BACH**

INTERMISSION

PASSACAGLIA . . . . **J. K. F. FISCHER**
1650-1746

*LES BERGERIES . . . . . . **FR. COUPERIN LE GRAND**
1668-1733

DIALOGUE . . . . **N. DE GRIGNY**
1671-1703

BOURREE . . . . **G. PH. TELEMANN**
1681-1767

LAMENT composed in London to dispell Melancholy
to be played slowly and with discretion . . **J. J. FROBERGER**
1620?-1667

*CHROMATIC FANTASY AND FUGUE . . . . **J. S. BACH**

*RCA VICTOR RECORDS   HARPSICHORD PLEYEL. PARIS

Tickets: $3.60, $3.00, $2.40, $1.80, $1.20; Loges, seating six $21.60 (tax incl.)

Kindly make mail orders and checks payable to Town Hall Box Office
and send with stamped self-addressed envelope to:

6. *Far left.* The program of one of Landowska's first public appearances in Paris in 1901. She played her own composition, *Rhapsodie Orientale,* on the piano. (Chez Enoch)

7. *Left.* A typical Landowska recital program, Town Hall, April 4, 1950.

9. Seventeenth century fretted clavichord from the Landowska Collection.

10. 1737 Swiss organ from the Landowska Collection. Photo H. Landshoff.

11.
Sixteenth century Italian
harpsichord from the
Landowska Collection.
Photo H. Landshoff.

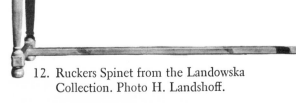

MVSICA MAGNORVM
SOLAMEN DVLCE LABORVM

12. Ruckers Spinet from the Landowska
Collection. Photo H. Landshoff.

13. Nordquist Fortepiano from the Landowska
Collection. Photo H. Landshoff.

14. a. Landowska's Pleyel harpsichord on which she recorded Bach's *Well-Tempered Clavier* and many other works.

b. Inscription on the bar of the Pleyel harpsichord:
"*The lower register, called sixteen-foot, was incorporated in the Pleyel harpsichords beginning in 1912 at the request and according to the suggestions of Wanda Landowska.*"

grave (dit par les Anciens) de 16 pieds fut introduit dans Les Clavecins Pleyel à partir de l'année 1912, sur La demande & les suggestions de WANDA LANDOWSKA

a. "You may take liberties, but with hands full of respect and reverence for the work you play."

b. "Here are two autonomous parts, but they are guided by a single soul."

c. "This is an exquisite bucolic; play it with lightness."

16. Wanda Landowska at the entrance of her concert hall at Saint-Leu-La-Forêt, France. Photo Lipnitzki.

d. "We are seeking repose in the sweet quietude of this serene, lucid, majestic, and divinely naïve music."

17. Landowska's hands.

a. and b. Playing Bach's
Goldberg Variations,
Saint-Leu, 1933.
Photos H. Landshoff.

c. In 1943.
Photo Ralph Kestly.

d. In 1951.
Photo
Denise
Restout.

18.
Landowska demonstrating one
of her technique exercises.
Photo H. Landshoff.

19. Wanda Landowska at her desk, Lakeville, 1949. Photo Denise Restout.

20. Landowska autograph.
"*Don't worry about the devices, about the science of counterpoint. Relax! and just listen to this fugue which is a marvel. This is a prayer, mystical and yet human. Bach understands our grief, Bach gives us relief, he helps us in our sorrow. Fugue D sharp minor.*"

21. A page from Landowska's work-score of the
Well-Tempered Clavier, Book I, Fugue XXIII.

22. *"Oh, the burning delights, the mortal anguish I experience in playing!"* Lakeville, 1951. Photo Denise Restout

23. Landowska's hands in repose.
Photo Denise Restout

24. Autograph of a few of Landowska's notes on music.

a. "*After my death—perhaps even before—someone will discover that the* Courante *should be dotted . . . while waiting for the musicologists to agree on this—there is little chance that it will ever happen—let us take advantage of this precious moment of respite, and let us play the* Courante à la Française *as a* basse *dance, glided. Yes, let us glide it . . .*"

b. "*How many days and nights of unrelenting work, of deprivation, of indescribable efforts to succeed in playing with insouciance, with careless ease. Fugue III, for example.*"

25. Landowska annotating a Bach Fugue (1951). Photo W. Eugene Smith

monious nor a blacksmith, but simply an air with doubles, which means "variations."

To enlarge the frame of each piece, to widen its established limits, to extract from each dance, one by one, its essence, such was Handel's will in the Suite in G Major (Second Collection No. 8). In the preceding suites, he had allowed us to penetrate the most intimate recesses of his inner life, but here he is completely and dashingly in an effusive mood. Amplifying the Allemande, he adjoined to it a varied annex; he pushed forward the development of the Courante; he breathed into the Minuet a power and authority which are in contrast with the fragile and tender minuet in fashion at the time. Truly a man of the theater, conscious and sure of his plans, Handel here erected a sumptuous spectacle hewn from the substance of choreographical material.

Allemande, Courante, Minuet, Gavotte, and Gigue—barely interrupted by a very brief Air—march past in a festive whirlwind. Is it the stage that Handel brought to the double keyboard of the harpsichord, or is it the black and white keyboard that yields to the stage? Curiously enough, as a curtain raiser, Handel displayed his own image. Listening to the Allemande, how could we not evoke the gigantic structure, the legendary immense wig, the fiery and ponderous gait of the glorious Saxon? Written in the purest French style, strewn with its scintillating dotted rhythm, the beautiful Allemande which opens this Suite proclaims with pride Handel's passion for French music.

The Concerto in B Flat Major

The original manuscript of this concerto is in the British Museum. It bears the title *Concerto per la Harpa*. It was intended for the harpist Powell, a celebrated English soloist. Nevertheless, Handel's publisher, Walsh, advertised in the London *Daily Post* in September, 1738, the forthcoming publication of six concertos by Handel for the harpsichord or organ, and the B Flat Major Concerto was among them. It consists of three movements: Andante Allegro, Larghetto, and Allegro Moderato. It is written in cantabile Italian style. The instrumentation, in which we encounter frequent pizzicati and sordini, is of an incredible transparency and grace and therefore never overshadows the solo instrument. It allows, on the contrary, the display of the full brilliance and variety of the harpsichord. In the first and last movements, one may hear imitations of the cuckoo's call. In accordance with the tradition of Handel's time, a cadenza has to be improvised in the second movement, a beautiful larghetto.

The entire concerto has—like the G Minor Suite—the architectural grandeur of a monument dedicated to the gallant Europe of the eighteenth century.*

* ED. NOTE: Wanda Landowska's cadenza for the second movement of this concerto has been published by Broude Bros.

3 ✕ Domenico Scarlatti

Domenico, son of Alessandro Scarlatti, one of the great Italian composers, was born in Naples in 1685. In a letter preserved in the archives of the Medici in Florence, dated May 30, 1705, and addressed to Ferdinand de Medici, Alessandro says, "This son of mine is an eagle whose wings are grown; he ought not to stay idle in the nest, and I ought not to hinder his flight." Domenico was then twenty years old.

Curiosity about distant places and love of the unexpected made him leave Italy in 1719 for London, where his opera *Narciso* was performed the following year. From London he went to the Iberian Peninsula. In Lisbon he was appointed Maestro of the Royal Chapel, and he guided the musical education of Princess Maria Barbara. A desire to see his father again took Scarlatti to Naples in 1724. While there, he played the harpsichord for the great composer Hasse, who was delighted and amazed. Domenico left Italy and went back to Portugal, where he resumed his position and his harpsichord lessons with the Princess Maria Barbara. It was for her that he composed harpsichord pieces which he called *Esercizi*. Maria Barbara worshiped her Maestro and invited him to join the royal suite when she went to Madrid in 1729. From this time on Scarlatti did not leave Spain. He was now thoroughly established at the court and had become the center of its musical life. He stayed there twenty-eight years, until his death in 1757.

This period spent in Spain must be regarded not merely as a pleasant sojourn, but as one of the most profound musical experiences in Scarlatti's life. Indeed, his Neapolitan birth and spirit may be described as the most propitious preparation for the fecund influence Spanish folk music and dancing were to have upon his art. When we hear Scarlatti's music, we know that we are in the climate of sunlight and warmth. It is Italy, it is Spain—the spirit of the Latin countries and the god of the Mediterranean; we are in the presence of that deity who has been truly called "the god who dances."

Spain fired the imagination of the great Neapolitan; Spanish music, with its Moorish influences, inspired him to create masterpieces of inexhaustible originality and boldness. We can almost see Scarlatti in one of those sumptuous royal palaces in Madrid, La Granja, or Aranjuez. We picture him at the harpsichord in the midst of this magnificence and pomp—Scarlatti, who had no fondness for the *grandezza* of princes. And yet, he is oblivious; he is at home because his pupil, Maria Barbara, a gifted musician, understands him and surrounds him with affection; because her husband, King Ferdinand VI, who made him a *Caballero del Habito de Cristo*, admires him and lavishes favors upon him. So the atmosphere at the court is warm and responsive; and when Scarlatti gives free rein to his improvisations, a miracle takes place. The palace salons, built for solemn receptions, vanish. Through the huge rooms with their much too high ceilings, dancers with guitars and castanets, peasants, beggars in rags, pretty girls are so vividly evoked that their rough, languorous, and piercing voices seem to vibrate and echo. Scarlatti feels happy. The queen and the king, the princes and princesses—the whole court listens, captivated and full of wonder.

The Sonatas

Though Scarlatti called his sonatas *Esercizi*, let us not be misled by this word being applied to his spirited and imaginative work. The term should be construed in much the same sense as the *Etudes* of Chopin. It is interesting to read what Scarlatti had to say in the preface to his sonatas:

Reader,

Whether you are a dilettantè or a professor, do not expect to find in these compositions any profound intention, but rather, an ingenious jesting of the art, to prepare you for bold playing on the harpsichord. No motive of self-interest, no ambitious aim, but obedience alone, spurred me on to publish these pieces. If they prove agreeable to you, then even more willingly shall I obey other orders to please you with an easier and more varied style. Show yourself more human than critical, and thus you will increase your own pleasure. To teach you the disposition of the hands, be advised that "R" indicates the right hand, and "L" the left. Live happily!

Thus prepared by the author himself and relieved of all preoccupation of having to discover a new world, we approach the first volume of Scarlatti Sonatas. As of today (1935), there are eleven volumes in all, representing 545 sonatas. Who knows if new research will not uncover more?

"An ingenious jesting rather than a profound intention," a laconic warning, indeed, the irony of which unveils its strength as we explore the work. Surprised at first, but then falling more and more under its spell, we marvel at the richness of invention, at the harmonic flavor and boldness of these sonatas. We are captivated by the unexpected diversity of the images they offer.

The form created and adopted by Scarlatti is one of the simplest. We know what a Couperin did within the narrow confines of the rondeau and couplets. With Scarlatti, one might almost be tempted to believe that he purposely reduced all architectural luxury to the strictest minimum in order to have free rein and, being relieved from all obligations, to abandon himself to folly and casualness.

The way Scarlatti wrote his music is very curious. Evidently he knew counterpoint, and he could be a polyphonist when he pleased. But what he liked and that in which he excelled was to throw a voice and at a certain point to divide it fork-fashion. This gives the illusion of the entrance of a second voice. Yet it does not lead to anything. The divided voice soon merges again into a single one. At other times, Scarlatti stated a theme and answered it in a second voice. We expect the elaboration of a fugue, but instead Scarlatti dropped the answering voice with a jump and made the initial theme reappear. This simulated, elusive polyphony, which derives its strength from being deliberate, is both learned and full of careless ease.

Scarlatti depicts neither the sumptuousness of palaces nor the ostentatious magnificence of princes. It is the people whom he loves; it is the street that attracts him above all—the motley and swarming crowd. Stirred by the frenzy of the dance, by sobs and desire, this tender, mischievous, and unbridled music takes its nourishment from perpetual motion. Flames spurt and disappear; major and minor tonalities follow one another with a swiftness that takes our breath away. Even in bucolic pieces, those pervaded with melancholy, even when Scarlatti the poet seems to be meditating or contemplating, life keeps its intensity. We always perceive the quick and regular beat of an uninterrupted pulsation.

Scarlatti is often considered merely the author of sonatas of insuperable technical difficulty. But no! His real power lies in his dynamic strength, one that gushes forth in runs, *batteries*, passages, and cascades.

Quite often in Scarlatti's sonatas the first few bars are like the entrance of a dancer with her mantilla and fluttering fan. She introduces herself and then disappears. It is only when she returns that the dance begins.

Scarlatti is the only composer who reminds me of the playfulness of a cat, and he does not suffer from this comparison. We all have seen a kitten play with a twig. It is impossible to describe its grace, charm, vivacity, and inventiveness. For a very serious man, these puerile marvels are, of course, useless, to say the least. After all what is the cat's aim in playing with a twig? If only it were on the lookout for a mouse, it would be useful to the household and therefore acceptable.

Among all the Scarlatti sonatas which appeared the most beautiful to me, I chose to play those which according to their affinities and to my fancy form a chain and pursue a single tale of love and wild adventure. To fix my choice in this world of marvels, taking some sonatas, rejecting others, was difficult. I consoled myself with the idea that the abandoned sonatas may have their revenge later. And since there are almost six hundred of them, the enchanted thread of Scarlatti's incantations can be spun almost ad infinitum.

Here follows Landowska's description of each link of such a chain:

Opening with the Sonata in E Major (Longo 23), we find ourselves on a radiant morning. The hammering of horses' hoofs, the ringing of silver bits, and the jingling of spurs come to us from a distance. A magnificent and martial procession approaches. It is before us. Fifths ring out and pursue one another in imitation; trills carry on a dialogue and vibrate in echo. With its unchanging minuet rhythm the procession passes before us, and little by little vanishes in the distance. In spite of its worldly splendor there is something eternal about this piece.

The Sonata in F Major (Longo 474) is a dance which maintains a rocking rhythm in triple time. The alternation between major and minor underlines its sensuous and provoking nonchalance, while the simple and naïve Sonata in F Major (Longo 479) plays and jests. Triplets reflect themselves in echoes, and crystalline passages glisten, break up, and scatter away.

As for the Sonata in C Major (Longo 102), it presents striking affinities with certain mazurkas of Chopin. Because of that, should one launch into research to establish proof that Chopin might have known Scarlatti's works? After all, it could be perfectly possible, were it only through Czerny's edition or Tausig's transcriptions. Yet is it absolutely conditional for Chopin to have known Scarlatti in order to write certain phrases which, by their curve, harmony, or modulations, compel a Scarlatinian vision? Aren't there more subtle encounters?

The Sonata in F Major (Longo 384) consists entirely of bantering dialogues which are interrupted by the ringing of bells. The final phrase is delightfully roguish.

In contrast the fiery and rapid Sonata in F Minor (Longo

475) passes by like a flash of lightning, while the Sonata in E Flat Major (Longo 142) begins with a dance. Light and coquettish at first, it suddenly takes on a passionate character. Sobs and supplications alternate with the nonchalant accents of the beginning.

Passing to the somber and martial Sonata in G Minor (Longo 338) we hear a distant drumroll which approaches gradually like a storm and then fades away. Once more Scarlatti displays a grandiose effect of perspective.

Calm returns with the Sonata in G Major (Longo 257). Bell-like sounds, large and small, weave, note by note, a light melodic web which vibrates and disperses in the clear blue sky.

There is nothing melancholy about the B Minor Sonata (Longo 263). It moves forward with a quick and resolute step; and although not polyphonic, it surprises us by its animated dialogue.

As for the Sonata in D Major (Longo 463), it is obstinate in its softly rocking triple time. Its final bars recall the echo of a hunting horn fading in the distance.

Passion, amplitude, and contrast of light and shade give the F Sharp Minor Sonata (Longo 294) the scope of an orchestral work.

In contrast, and with an aristocratic grace, the Sonata in D Major (Longo 208) is a light and ethereal dance. Now a couple appears, now others, and soon they vanish.

Of a pastoral character the Sonata in G Minor (Longo 488) creates a spell with its rhythmic monotony and lightly veiled melancholy.

With its unbridled triplets, repeated in echo and punctuated by jerky chords, the short melody of the G Major Sonata (Longo 232) conjures up visions of a dance with guitars, castanets, and clapping. As for the exuberant E Major Sonata (Longo 375), it abandons itself totally to the *joie de vivre* and the caprice of leaping from one keyboard to the other. Voices chase one another; thirds roll; octaves gallop. Everything sparkles in a whirlwind of luminous sonorities.

This is in sharp contrast to the Sonata in F Minor (Longo 438), which tells serenely a sweet and serious narrative.

With its carefree gambols in the left hand, so characteristic of Scarlatti, the light and fresh Sonata in C Major (Longo 104) marks a dance rhythm as much in the nature of a gigue as of a Siciliano.

In the F Major Sonata (Longo S.20), we encounter an obstinacy of tempo branded derisively by Western people as "monotonous." Yet it is very significant and indubitable that the dances from Spain and the Orient bear in themselves this monotony which gives them a character of fatality and of gravity, thus enlarging their meaning in depth. Of course, very refined minds and ears will perceive the deflections and minute rubati which but reinforce the unrelenting insistence of the tempo.

I am very sensitive to Scarlatti's bucolic mood, to his rustic jauntiness. I like these winged rhythms that do not touch the ground. I also like the elementary strength and the richness of his rhythmical power, as well as all that is Moorish in him. I am amused by the brevity with which Scarlatti escapes into dreaming as, for example, at the beginning of the development section in the sonata in D Major (Longo 418) when an E is repeated in the right hand over chords in A major. Modulating suddenly in C sharp minor, Scarlatti surprises us with a phrase that is a glimpse into a dream world. After a few nonchalant progressions, he brings us back quickly to the sparkling motive of the beginning.

Scarlatti has the genuine nobility, the heroism, and the audacity of a Don Quixote. The second motive of this sonata admirably evinces this chivalrous aspect. In my imagination I see a proud Hidalgo in rags.

As for the very short D Minor Sonata (Longo 423) tinged with melancholy and yet serene, it moves us with its appealing simplicity.

The Sonata in A Major (Longo 132) glides suavely like a barcarolle, momentarily interrupted by the ringing of bells. A descending passage brings back the first sweet and irresistible rhythm.

Veiled and meditative in its expression, transparent and precise in its writing, the Sonata in C Sharp Minor (Longo 256) has an exquisite elegance and a great purity of workmanship. Listen at the beginning of the second part to the beguiling Moorish echoes.

Finally, the Sonata in E Major (Longo 257) is, no doubt, one of the most beautiful and significant of all. At first glance it appears heterogenous because Scarlatti introduces a love theme and then interrupts it abruptly with a motive that suggests an energetic decision. But these mystifying interruptions and the opposition of the two themes are explained by their arrangement and alternation. They emphasize the accents of the drama which is about to unfold. In fact, we are witnessing a little opera. The first bars create the atmosphere of the piece: a vibrant aridity in which floats the heady scent of flowers. In the silence a woman's voice rises, sustained by arpeggios on a guitar. No sooner have we heard this tender entreaty than it fades away. A decided theme springs up like a man's footstep resounding on the pavement. This theme in its turn is interrupted. A silence . . . Then once more the woman's voice rises, more imploring and more voluptuous. The theme of decision mingles with the increasingly passionate accents of the woman. Their dialogue becomes a struggle in which the theme of decision triumphs. Fate ordains that the man will depart. Again the footsteps are heard, near at first, then fading away—an effect of perspective so dear to Scarlatti. The woman remains alone. The last four bars, as a pathetic summary of this tragedy, express the poignant farewell of the deserted woman. Does not the ending of Chopin's Polonaise in E Flat Minor, Op. 26, No. 2, come to mind?

4 \ A Glorious Trinity

1683, 1684, 1685—blessings on you, constellated years so rich in geniuses!

Rameau was born in 1683, and Watteau in 1684. A new era was dawning; it flourished in 1685 and enriched humanity with a glorious trinity: Handel, Bach, and Scarlatti, no less.

Handel was born on February 23, at Halle; Bach just a few weeks later, on March 21, at Eisenach; and Scarlatti came into the world on October 26, in Naples.

Did these three men know each other?

Handel went to Italy for the first time when he was twenty-one. Dazzled by the sunny climate and the music of Venice, Florence, and Rome, he soon found himself in contact with everybody who, in Italy, was illustrious in arts and in society. He became a friend of Alessandro and Domenico Scarlatti, of

Lotti; he regularly attended the musical evenings of Cardinal Pietro Ottobuoni, that generous Maecenas who was madly in love with music. John Dryden exclaims in his prologue to the opera *King Arthur*, set to music by Purcell:

> Indeed, it were a bargain worth our money
> Could we insure another Ottobuoni.

During one of these Monday evenings which became famous as much for the refined taste of the Maecenas as for the quality of the artists—Corelli, think of it, was the first violinist!—Ottobuoni proposed a tournament between Handel and Domenico Scarlatti. While the *Sassone famoso* displayed his sovereign art at the organ, the demoniac Neapolitan made child's play of prodigious difficulties on the double keyboard of the harpsichord. Forgetting its function, the spellbound jury became an enthusiastic audience with only one fear—that the fascinating duel would stop. Their ardor increased and their inspiration stimulated, Handel and Scarlatti continued to surpass, to outdo each other. The bout remained undecided. Generously, Scarlatti was the first to concede victory to Handel at the organ. Later, in 1720, both met again in London on the occasion of the presentation of *Narciso*, Scarlatti's opera, which obtained only a moderate success. But still much later, forty years after, the brothers Plas, famous oboists who were on their way to Madrid, said that every time homage was paid to Scarlatti for his playing, Domenico evoked the name of Handel and made the sign of the cross.

"Bach had great esteem for Handel and often expressed the desire to meet him personally," wrote Forkel in his biography of Bach. "Like Handel, he too was a great master at the harpsichord and at the organ, and therefore numerous music lovers from Leipzig and vicinity wished to hear these two great men side by side. But Handel never could find time for such a meeting during his travels from London to Halle, his native city. During his first visit, which took place around 1719, Bach was still in Cöthen, about twenty miles away from Halle. As soon as he was informed of Handel's arrival, Bach did not lose a moment and went to pay Handel a visit. Handel had, however, already left Halle by the time Bach arrived there. During Handel's second visit—between 1730 and 1740—Bach was detained in Leipzig by an indisposition. But scarcely had he learned of Handel's arrival in Halle than he immediately sent his eldest son, Wilhelm Friedemann, to extend an invitation to Handel, who replied that he was unable to accept it."

The rather tendentious way in which Forkel related this incident has misguided public opinion. To blame Handel for indifference toward his great contemporary would be unjust. It remains only to regret that this meeting, which could have been a significant one, did not take place.

Let us bring together these three great- men born the same year. How could they be more contemporary! Two of them were of the same nationality, and yet so different. Handel, the pro-Italian German, Scarlatti, the pro-Spanish Italian, and Bach, the universal man. Persevering and impassioned Titan, sagacious, and indefatigable, Bach was attentive to nourishing his genius; he took this nourishment from wherever it seemed to him good enough to enrich and consolidate his own nature. Although he was removed from the tumult of the world, Bach absorbed all the substance of the universe.

FRENCH music of the past has always been weighed down by certain prejudices. It has been called *trifling, elegant,* or *quaint,* and regarded as a sort of coquette endlessly humming the *Bergère légère* and pivoting through the steps of a perpetual minuet, charming and vivacious it is true, but incapable of experiencing profound thought or emotion.

One seems to forget the prodigious heritage of the masters of the French Renaissance which includes such names as Goudimel, Jannequin, and Josquin des Prés; the admirable school of French organists, Titelouze, Nicolas de Grigny, André Raison, Le Bègue, Marchand, to enumerate just a few; the extraordinary scope of the French lutenists, the Gaultier dynasty, particularly Gaultier le Vieux and Antoine Francisque, who engendered the imposing work of the composers for the harpsichord; and finally the French harpsichordists themselves — Jacques Champion de Chambonnières, d'Anglebert, Louis Couperin, Gaspard Le Roux, Dieupart, et al. We arrive at a magnificent culmination in François Couperin le Grand and Jean Philippe Rameau.

How could Couperin's pathos, richness of feeling, and perfection of form ever have led to such a misinterpretation of his implicit values as the term "miniaturist" suggests?

How could Rameau's dramatic force, architectural grandeur, and unique descriptive power ever have been misconstrued for anything less than the qualities of universal genius?

For several centuries French music had an incommensurable influence upon the music of other countries. We know (see Part I, Chapter VI) Bach's admiration for the style, the ornaments, and the refinement of writing of the French masters. Organ works of Nicolas de Grigny, harpsichord pieces of Dieupart, and others were copied in Bach's own hand. *Les Bergeries* of Couperin are included in Anna Magdalena's *Clavierbüchlein* of 1725. Between Bach's harpsichord style and that of Rameau one can detect significant affinities.

The French masters of the seventeenth century possessed the supreme art of saying much in a few words. That is why their pieces are short without being small. Concentrated and often consisting of only a few measures, these compositions possess a greatness and an intensity much more *pathétique* than many of those symphonies whose exaggerated length tries both our patience and our receptivity.

Jacques Champion de Chambonnières

Jacques Champion de Chambonnières may be considered the founder of the French school of keyboard music. Almost all leading harpsichordists of the second half of the seventeenth century were his pupils. The renown of Chambonnières spread beyond France; his scholarly and inspired art had a profound influence on German musicians.

He used to spend winters in Paris in the Rue St. Claude and

summers at his estate of Chambonnières in the vicinity of Plessis-feu-Ausoult. On July 25, 1650, the feast of St. Jacques, Chambonnières was celebrating with friends. In the midst of the festivities musical sounds were suddenly heard in the distance. Wondering who was playing this concert, the excellence of which was immediately noticed by Chambonnières and his friends, they left the table to investigate. They discovered, gathered in front of the house, a group of young musicians who had come to offer an aubade to Chambonnières on his name day. They introduced themselves; they were three brothers from the neighboring village of Chaumes—the eldest, Louis, then François, and the youngest, Charles. Their family name was Couperin. Delighted to make the acquaintance of such remarkable musicians, Chambonnières invited them at once to sit down with his friends and partake of the refreshments. He assured them that they should be in Paris rather than in this small village, and he offered to introduce them at court. This spontaneous generosity of Chambonnières was the beginning of the fame of the Couperin family. From that time on, the Couperin dynasty was to spread the glory of French music throughout the world.

In 1670 Chambonnières published a collection of his harpsichord pieces in order to make them known in their correct and definitive text, since many of them had been in public circulation for years in disfigured versions.

Among the works of Chambonnières that I like to play, *Le Moutier* is an allemande resplendent with a majestic and quiet joy. Imitations above pedal points are numerous. Bathed in the clarity of C major, this beautiful piece, also called *The March of the Bride and Groom*, remained famous long after the death of its composer. The *double* of *Le Moutier* by Louis Couperin is an homage paid by that great musician to his master and protector.

The Chaconne in F Major (No. 116) moves along with a peaceful serenity and radiates an air of inner bliss. What infinite variety and resourcefulness are contained in its apparent simplicity! And in the Sarabande in D Minor (No. 88) Chambonnières establishes from the very first phrase the passionate yet restrained mood of the composition. It is like a magnificent poem by Racine in which every word evokes an emotional response.

François Couperin Le Grand

An amplitude and nobility of line, bold and ingratiating harmonies, an intensity of atmosphere and expression are characteristic of Couperin's music and distinguish it from that of all other composers. Although Couperin composed many works for voice and various instruments, as well as sacred music, he devoted the greater part of his talent to pieces for the harpsichord, and it was for this instrument that he reserved his most intimate and inspired thoughts. An extraordinary performer, he knew the most secret resources of the double keyboards. Couperin was, indeed, the Chopin of the harpsichord.

He also was a simple man, a sort of *bourgeois gentilhomme*. The low-ceilinged house in which he lived and died, with its little peasant garden, had nothing of Versailles. Couperin knew the aristocratic ordonnance of Le Nôtre; he was admired by Louis XIV and by the Duc de Bourgogne; he moved about in their salons certainly with modesty, but also with ease. He was not indifferent to the title of *chevalier* which he received, but his nature, his outward moderation, and his politeness formed a smooth surface enveloping hermetically the man and his inner life. To say that his music depicts only the court and its manners is to misunderstand it. After a day spent at Versailles, Couperin came home to his low, intimate little house.

The aristocracy of Couperin's spirit lived in complete unawareness of its superiority. While the magnificence of Louis XIV was all on the outside, that of Couperin's music lies in its inner richness. For music was the center of his life. This is proved by the concentrated attention he devoted to his pupils, amateurs as well as professionals, by the loving care with which he prepared the publication of his works, which he provided with signs of his own to clarify his intentions, and above all by every note of his music.

When did I first understand that Couperin's music touches the subconscious?

One evening I was prey to a profound and indefinable anxiety. I started to play *Les Vieux Seigneurs* from Couperin's twenty-fourth *Ordre,* and this music espoused my mood and corresponded so exactly to it that it appeased me. In the inner recesses of my mind so many perplexities, so many question marks were encircling me, gripping, strangling me; and yet the rhythm of Couperin's piece did not irritate me, but rather suited my anxiety. These desolate torn harmonies responded so well to my inner state that I felt relieved. Why is this music which depicts our despair so comforting too? It is not because it expresses our sorrow, but because it is a sublimation of our distress, and in this sublimation lies the consoling power; it liberates us by loosening the block of anxiety that is suffocating us.

Desperate as I was, if I had been seeing a realistic play by Strindberg, for example, in which beyond sorrow hovers nothing, it probably would have crushed me. On the contrary, the part of sublimity in Couperin's music gives us wings. I have the definite sensation of a fluid matter infiltrating under the skin, penetrating not the heart or the soul, but the world of the subconscious; it makes us vibrate with an anxiety that is mixed with a mysterious joy.

Couperin's language differs entirely from that of Bach or Handel. In theirs everything is precise, and even when chiaroscuro occurs, no misunderstanding can subsist. It has something direct, a nearness that reassures us like a human language, sublime though ritual; it moves us in a wholesome way, grips us with its poignancy, and appeases us. We return toward life steeled and stronger, able to withstand more easily everyday misery. But what is this elusive anguish that Couperin provokes in us? He does not speak of love, sensuousness, or sorrow in the same manner as does Bach or Handel. Couperin's music permeates our subconscious, agitating its levels. It cannot be called exotic, because it goes far beyond the meaning this word implies and because it burrows into the depth of our inner life. Whence comes this strange language? Is it not simply that it is a forgotten tongue very much like that employed by the lutenists in their unmeasured preambula?

Certain titles of Couperin's pieces, such as *Les Délices, Le petit Deuil ou les trois Veuves, Le Coucou, Le Rossignol en Amour,* etc., are not the only reason for giving the impression that this music is merely charming. There is also the fact that Couperin's most commonly used form of composition, the rondeau and couplets, may seem to preclude any possibility of throbbing life. Therefore it is understandable that the romantics, accustomed to the bombast of post-Beethovenian development, found the structure of Couperin's pieces poor and devoid of resources. Yet, does this really matter? A composition form has no intrinsic value; a genius may turn the simplest one into a powerful weapon. The Passacaille in B Minor (8th *Ordre*) proves this eloquently. Among Couperin's rich output, it is the queen of all his harpsichord pieces. The initial theme, the rondeau, is only four bars long, twice repeated. Its gait is proud, its character deeply tragic. The relentless return to this initial theme endows the piece with a fatality and a monotony in which the pathos increases as the piece unfolds.

There are eight couplets, each of which offers a different aspect. The first continues weaving the motive of the rondeau; the second is a bitter and disillusioned soliloquy; in the third, a sorrowful soul searches and despairs; in the fourth, the storm rises with cries of revolt, abating suddenly and dissolving into muffled thirds. In the fifth couplet, Chopinesque cadences of a plagal flavor, pass back and forth like white shades; the sixth couplet is an impetuous cavalcade ending on a trill. heavily hammered. as if it were wrought iron. In the seventh couplet, the menacing storm bursts out; here is a choir of supplicants, imploring. All hands join, all voices clamor; flaming *acciaccaturas* pass through immense arpeggios. In the final couplet, an orchestral tutti, almost objective, summarizes the entire work in a kind of impassive and grandiose cortege. Despite the frequent reappearance of the rondeau, we welcome it every time with renewed emotion, not solely because it is in itself sumptuous and beautiful, but because each return, so differently inspired, spurs our sensibility and quickens even more the enjoyment of again meeting this rondeau laden with a new meaning. Couperin's Passacaille has the majesty of a cathedral.

Les Folies Françaises ou les Dominos are part of the thirteenth *Ordre* in B Minor, which opens with *Les Lis Naissants* and *Les Rozeaux*, their frail stems and delicate corolla being depicted in terms of sound. As for *Les Folies Françaises*, they are composed of twelve couplets, each of which bears a different title. A multicolored and lively procession unfolds; allusions to courtiers and courtesans succeed one another. With a sharp sense of color

Couperin opposes the blue of *La Fidélité* to the linen gray of *La Persévérance;* he makes vivid the purple of *Les Vieux Galants,* only to soften it into the shade of dead leaves. Against the yellow background of *Les Coucous Bénévoles* appears the stormy gray shadow of *La Jalousie Taciturne,* which finally turns into the black sputtering of *La Frénésie, ou le Désespoir.* A chatoyant tress meanders and blazes out before us. Mixed, opposed, or subdued, the colors reinforce the expressive value of the neat and sharp design. Out of this tumultuous flood, among silhouettes full of grace or of haughtiness, and grotesque or bizarre profiles, there emerge, furrowed by sorrow, maskless faces and naked souls.

As I mentioned elsewhere (see p. 219), a close examination of the structure of *Les Folies Françaises* unveiled for me a striking affinity with the monumental *Goldberg Variations* of Bach. Let us compare the bass of *The Goldberg Variations* with that of *Les Folies Françaises.* Both are in triple time and follow a tracing that bears a strong family resemblance. But while Bach's bass evolves, spreads out, and gathers amplitude, the destiny of Couperin's is resumed in a very simple and brief period which is repeated to underline and set into relief his purpose.

Bach's theme is a sarabande, all wisdom and voluptuousness. It seems to be bathing in the light of a Leonardo da Vinci. Couperin too could have built a noble and grave sarabande over his bass. Yet, he preferred to give it the character of a light dance, a kind of minuet, and he placed it at the head of the work under the name of *La Virginité.* But is this *Virginité* really the cell-theme of *Les Folies Françaises?* Is it not rather already a first variation on an unknown theme, one we are trying to guess in following the hint given in the progress of the bass? It is fallacious though. How could anyone have the audacity to imagine a theme that Couperin himself did not write?

La Pudeur continues tracing this minuet step. Unprepared as we are for a large scale work, it gives the impression of being just a trifle. Yet nothing could be more deceptive. Without trying to seize us from the beginning with severe expressionism, Couperin leads us gently from one variation to the next. It is only from the third one on, *L'Ardeur,* that he decides to unveil the importance and the vigor of the bass with all its dramatic possibilities. The fiery peaks of the French rhythm hoist themselves; the call of the Gallic rooster warns us that action is in full swing.

Above a cortege of harmonies passing from one couplet to the next—a cortege that remains unchanged—Couperin, psychologist and refined poet that he is, displays an imagination rich in discoveries. Attentive to the least effect of a decorative order, he makes supple little chains of triplets meander and glide in *L'Espérance*. These light jumps from one keyboard to the other explain the anxious dialogue, and give relief to the questions and answers which follow more and more hurriedly; they illuminate the beautiful last phrase, a quivering, passionate exclamation. *La Fidélité* is an admirable soliloquy long sustained. But whence this poignant and restrained sadness? The straight and loyal gaze of Couperin tells us that he was one of those men born to be faithful; this virtue was natural to him and implied no effort or sacrifice. Therefore let us find the explanation of this sadness not in *La Fidélité* itself, but in the couplets surrounding it—the feverish *Espérance*, which in its last phrase hangs on to a glimmer of hope. *La Coquèterie*, under different dominos, personifies not just one woman, but a thousand and one who are capricious; they spring forth from everywhere and disappear, leaving behind a haunting memory. *L'Ardeur* is sparkling, youthful, and irresistible. Listen to *La Langueur* with its funereal bell-tolling and to the plaintive accents of *Les Coucous Bénévoles*. There is no caricatural intention whatsoever, but a feeling of emotion, all the more significant, since *La Jalousie Taciturne*—the writing of which recalls so clearly that of *La Fidélité*—pursues its desolate monologue, heaving with muffled anxiety. Only *La Persévérance* and *Les Vieux Galants* march pass in an atmosphere of good-natured jesting. Everywhere else, there is this affectionate cordiality, this melancholy tinged with nobility. The somber glint of *La Frénésie ou le Désespoir*, under a black domino, summarizes, in heavy sixteenth-notes the intimate tragedy of *Les Folies Françaises*.

This masterpiece must have been known by Schumann, who may have derived from it the inspiration for his own *Carnaval*.

Couperin already showed himself a great creator of atmosphere in *Les Sylvains* (*Ordre* 1), a bucolic piece. But do not expect to find in *Les Bacchanales* (*Ordre* 4) the imposing dimensions of Nicolas Poussin or the Aristophanic flavor of Claude Gillot. These are simply pleasant drinking feasts, gay pastorales in the midst of the vintage. From among the russet vines emerges the whiteness of a marble statue, a Bacchus smiling at the couples dancing the tambourin, the dance with which Couperin opens this gallant and light triptych, impregnating it from the first note with the tang of the soil.

Couperin's melancholy, which is, like that of Chopin, of a perfect nobility, is reflected in *La Favorite* (*Ordre* 3), a most lofty piece. This melancholy does not pursue any materialistic aim; it is not derived from an earthly discontent or from a specific deception; it is melancholy for melancholy's sake, for its beauty, its poetry, and also for the enveloping and sweet happiness it gives.

How is it that *La Bandoline* and *Les Ondes*, from the fifth *Ordre*, are so rich harmonically, although they are written almost entirely in two voices? It is because the melodic line, passing through space in all directions, strikes on its way harmonic centers, thus producing unexpected rapport, intervals of a ninth, prepared or not, as well as harsh and luscious false relations.

Among the pieces included in the sixth *Ordre*, *Les Moissonneurs* is a peasant gavotte which reminds me of *La Gavotte des Moutons* by Padre Martini (1706-1784). In *Les Langueurs Tendres*, of a restrained though ardent sensuousness, we find another example of this melodic line which goes on uninterrupted, pregnant with thought and always reinforced by delightful harmonies.

As for *Le Gazouillement*, it is a sonorous mosaic of bird calls, alternately tender, plaintive, or happy. It forms an unexpected contrast with *Les Barricades Mystérieuses*, in which Couperin reveals his love for the mysterious play of hands crossing over the two keyboards, the interlacing of voices on the same level. Thus brought together, the voices murmur voluptuously, flash tenderly, and flare out of the double keyboards in tiny dancing flames. In one of the variations from his *Gavotte et Doubles*, Rameau gives an example of this kind of writing.

The light chatter of *La Commère* multiplies as it goes along, developing into laughter and the bursting voices of gossipy women. As for *Le Moucheron*, the last piece of this *Ordre* 6, it is, with its monotonous buzzing, a masterpiece of descriptive music.

All that Couperin was able to express about nobility and human nature, about tenderness and pathos, is displayed *"noblement et sans lenteur"* (nobly and without slowness) in *La Régente ou La Minerve*, the Allemande which opens the fifteenth *Ordre*.

It is a portrait of Françoise Marie de Bourbon, wife of Philippe d'Orléans, in which Couperin described the princess's noble and yet impassioned character.

Le Dodo ou l'Amour au Berceau (Sleep, or Love in the Cradle) follows, with hands crossing over each other on the two keyboards. A popular tune, *Le Dodo*, unfolds over a background of monotonous eighth-notes passing from major to minor. It is a lullaby hummed by a mother to her baby in the crib.

The writing of *L'Evaporée* (The Feather-Brain) in two voices, is sharp and incisive and sets into relief a light and bouncing dialogue. As an abrupt contrast, *La Musète de Taverni** brings its exuberant joy, slightly veiled by a shadow in the minor part, in which two flutes engage each other in a light dialogue.

In *La Douce et Piquante* (The Sweet and Saucy One) major and minor alternate, but the delightful swaying of the 6/8 time remains constant. As for *Les Vergers Fleuris* (The Orchards in Bloom), it carries us on a warm afternoon into a fragrant orchard. The shawm recites a tune in a minor key, and then, during the second part in major, the drone of the bagpipe—so well suggested by the harpsichord—goes on with a ceaseless insistence. The whole fifteenth *Ordre* unfolds in a shadowless felicity, inundated by the sunny quality of the tonality of A major.

Instead of opposing each other, couplets and refrain unite in a single poem of chaste love in *La Soeur Monique* (*Ordre* 18). This piece casts a spell upon us with the tenderness and refined sensuality of its melodic line.

In the middle part of *Les Calotins et les Calotines* (*Ordre* 19) a waggish fife appears. It is a satirical piece with a droll, jerky, and sparkling humor.

In the short preface to the fourth volume of his harpsichord pieces, published in 1730, Couperin tells us that "these pieces were completed about three years ago, but since my health is growing poorer daily, my friends have advised me to stop working." This admission, so simple, moves us deeply, and it is with

---

* ED. NOTE: Taverni is a village close to Saint-Leu-La-Forêt, where Wanda Landowska founded her *Ecole de Musique Ancienne* in 1927. Built on the outskirts of the forest of Montmorency, Taverny (as it is now spelled) possesses a splendid thirteenth-century church. Who knows if Couperin did not play on its organ? According to Wanda Landowska's wish, her ashes are buried in the peaceful little cemetery that surrounds that church.

some apprehension that we open the volume. Yet, from the very first piece—a vigorous peasant gavotte—we are reassured. Couperin was ill, but music was his escape, his happiness, and his cure. *Musètes, Tambourins,* jesting pieces with indications such as *gayement, gaillardement, amoureusement,* overflowing with joy, follow one another, interrupted only rarely by pieces of a serious character.

L'Arlequine (*Ordre* 23), the portrait of a feminine Harlequin, bears the indication *grotesquement* and is a marvel of mischievous grace and witty verve. Delicate, but in no way fragile, she suggests a Spanish dance. We find the same rhythmic pattern in *L'Espagnole* from *Les Nations, Sonades et Suites de Simphonies en Trio,* composed by Couperin in 1726, and in *La Muse Victorieuse* from *Ordre* 25 of the *Pièces de Clavecin.* This rhythm is almost that of a true *jota.* Let us not forget the constant intercourse between the courts of France and Spain at that time and the engagement of Louis XV to the little Infanta Marie Anne Victoire, who was Couperin's pupil. In *L'Arlequine,* Couperin reinforced the rhythmic pattern with bold harmonies. He enjoyed making the multicolored patches of Harlequin's costume sparkle by means of a clash of dissonances leaping forth joyously.

L'Arlequine was one of the favorite pieces of Ravel. I often played it for him.

Carved with a sharp and flawless burin, a bizarre and grotesque silhouette, a face furrowed by pain emerges in *La Pantomime* (*Ordre* 26). This satire, in which pathos is mixed with irony, is a masterpiece.

In *L'Art de Toucher le Clavecin* and in his prefaces, Couperin took infinite pains to explain his ornaments, fingering, phrasing, his particular signs, the way notes *inégales* should be played, etc. He was as meticulous and authoritative as Bach. He offered directions that a careful interpreter should try to follow as closely as possible. But when the explanations were exhausted, Couperin appealed to taste, to *le goût,* this final arbiter, a sort of *deus ex machina.* In his *Rossignol en Amour* (*Ordre* 14) we have some particulars. "Slowly and very tenderly, although measured," wrote Couperin at the head of the piece. Here we can proceed with some assurance. But in the double, or variation, that follows Couperin said, "One should not pay too strict attention to the tempo in this double. One must sacrifice everything to taste, to the neatness of the passages, and to give much tenderness to the accents marked by mordents." Here, once again, this famous *goût* intervenes.

What is this taste that Couperin, St. Lambert, Rousseau, and many others never tire of mentioning?

We think we know what bad taste is. We also say "perfect taste," meaning that the interpreter possesses this discrimination —a gift from Heaven—that tells him what he has to do or to avoid. We even have "perfect bad taste," that which nothing in the world can prevent some interpreters from exposing and pouring forth. But what is this "good taste?" Is there a standard? What is good taste to one is bad to another. This becomes all too clear when one deals with pupils of differing natures and training and also in launching records into the world. Where I find a rubato called for, a listener says, "Mme Landowska takes inadmissible liberties." When I feel that sentimental displays must be avoided, another objects, "How cold! I should like more feeling."

I wonder if Couperin and his contemporaries were not searching in vain to explain the inexplicable, that *je ne sais quoi*, that unforeseen, that something that depends on a moment of inspiration of the interpreter. This good taste—what is it if not liberties taken with rules that are strictly established and observed?

Jean Philippe Rameau

Amusingly enough, Rameau has never suffered from accusations of frivolity, but, on the contrary, for his dry intellectualism. He is the author of many famous treatises on musical theory; and while establishing his reputation as a scholar, they almost overshadow his fame as a creative artist. Indeed, his prestige as a learned musician is not to be questioned, but it shows only the cold and theoretical aspect of a man of genius who was otherwise inspired and impassioned. How else is one to describe the power of the author of *Les Fêtes d' Hébé, Hippolyte et Aricie, Les Indes Galantes, Castor et Pollux,* and of so many other masterpieces? Where else to find prosody of such sincerity and passion or such an acute sense of the picturesque and of rhythm in their most varied manifestations? Rameau blends the choral and instrumental masses and then contrasts them both with the opposing lightness and buoyancy of the human voice singing alone or in concert with an *oboe d'amore* or a *flute douce*.

Even in his compositions for the harpsichord, Rameau, without forgetting for a moment the true character of the instrument for which he is writing, still retains his remarkable architectural sense of the theater, and in keeping with its laws, he paints his frescoes with bold sweeping strokes in order to delight not only our ears, but also our eyes. These harpsichord pieces are, in fact, almost visual, evoking images in turn grave or gay and of rich and constantly shifting colors.

What is perhaps most characteristic of Rameau's art is his extraordinary awareness of the value of the least effect he wishes to obtain, whether it be on the boards of the theater or on the double keyboards of the harpsichord. If any proof of this awareness is required, it may be found in a letter dated from Paris, October 25, 1727, addressed by the composer to the librettist Houdard de la Motte. In it Rameau explains his own artistic creed. "One must study nature before depicting it," he said. With an honest appreciation for his own talent he added, "I, more than anyone else, understand color and nuance. The others are merely confused by them, and if they use them appropriately, it is only the result of a happy accident."

Although he followed the taste of his time and composed light descriptive pieces, Rameau remained faithful to his nature— clear and mercilessly logical. In the same letter he called the attention of Houdard de la Motte to the accuracy with which he characterized *Les Tendres Plaintes*, *Les Cyclopes*, *Les Tourbillons*, *Musette*, and *Tambourin*. He said, "You will see that I am not a novice. I do not parade my knowledge; I try to conceal art by art itself." He also said, "It is up to you to come and hear how I have characterized in *Les Sauvages* the songs and dances of the savages as they appeared at the Italian Theater." (Two Indians, tall and handsome, had come from Louisiana to perform in 1725 at the Italian Theater a peace dance followed by a war dance and, after a simulated combat, a victory dance.)

Musette, *Tambourin*, *Le Rappel des Oiseaux*, and many of Rameau's harpsichord pieces figure in his operas as well—a fact of singular importance, since it reveals the dramatic and picturesque elements which must be brought to the keyboards in the interpretation of these compositions. Even when Rameau deals with a subject as homely as *La Poule* (The Hen), this hen suddenly becomes transformed into a Wagnerian personality uttering shrill cries, now aggressive in tone, now tender.

Certain pieces of Rameau, always the same ones and played singly, are known to everybody; but the public at large is ignorant of the other pieces that form the rest of the suites from which the well-known compositions are taken. It would be of great interest to play these suites in their entirety. Are not the Allemande and Courante from the E Minor Suite or *Les Triolets* and *L'Enharmonique* from the G Minor Suite as rich and beautiful as the famous *Tambourin, Rigaudons,* or *La Poule?*

The Suite in E Minor is perhaps one of Rameau's most poetic pieces for the harpsichord. It opens with an Allemande, which in its somber martial processional establishes the mood of what is to follow; it is a magnificent portal through which we are offered immediate entrance into the Suite. This is succeeded by a Courante *à la Française,* a *danse basse,* horizontal, slow, and gliding. Its use here touches us all the more, since at that time it began to be neglected. Rameau himself soon abandoned it for the *danse haute* with its *entrechats,* its leaps and gambols. Vigorous and robust in character, the *danse haute* corresponded admirably to Rameau's virile sense of rhythm, and thus after the Courante we find *Gigues en Rondeau, Rigaudons* and *Tambourin—danses hautes* overflowing with joy. In the midst of these dances Rameau interposed peaceful, bucolic images—*Le Rappel des Oiseaux, Musette en Rondeau,* and *La Villageoise.*

Curiously enough, although he was a thoroughly urbane person, morose, and even misanthropic in his habits, Rameau could render all of the sweetness and warmth of the countryside. He delighted in the calls of birds, a motive of which he evidently was fond, since we find it not only in the Suite in E Minor, but also in the third act of his opera *Le Temple de la Gloire,* where it is carried by the flutes.

The *Musette en Rondeau,* together with the *Tambourin,* occurs again in the third act of *Les Fêtes d'Hébé;* it evokes the festive scenes of grape-gathering in provincial vineyards. We may imagine a peasant seated on a wine barrel, his eyes closed, his expression flushed and suffused with joy, his nostrils dilated; he is crushing under his arm a wheezing and droning bagpipe. Monotonous as intoxication itself, the initial theme of the *Musette*, clear and incisive, returns sustained by its insistent pedal-point.

In *La Villageoise* Rameau resumes the refrain for the last time with innocent and tender embellishments in order to underline once more the fragile grace of the theme. Thus the dynamic Suite in E Minor is concluded, not with a display of virtuosity, but with a pastorale pure in line and of enchanting naïveté.

A lack of information precludes any precise dating of the publication of Rameau's *Nouvelles Suites de Pièces de Clavecin*. An old copy bears the date 1736, but these pieces may have been published earlier, between 1726 and 1731. Some of the pieces from these suites are found in Rameau's operas. The Sarabande from the A Minor Suite is reproduced in E minor in *Zoroastre* for the ballet-pantomime in which genii of the elements are distributing talismans to Zoroaster to protect him (Act III, scene 9, of the 1749 version and Act II, scene 3, of the 1756 version). Here this dance takes on a kind of religious significance. Religious? Let us even dare say ecstatic. If during the eighteenth century the sarabande could be as grave and chaste as that of *The Goldberg Variations*, for example, it also knew love and passion as well. Think only of the Sarabande from Bach's French Suite in E Major or that from the Partita in B Flat Major and of the passionate tenderness they radiate.

Rejecting all superfluous effects, Rameau's Sarabande in A Major, condensed and so rich of substance, is only twenty-eight bars long. Yet it is the queen among Rameau's works for the harpsichord. Its unrestrained surrender, its ardor, the rustling of its immense arpeggios, the irresistible sweetness of its melody, and its regal deportment give a most shattering denial to those who see Rameau only as a calculator and a maker of treatises. If only they knew how to listen! But the charm of this Sarabande must not cast such a spell on us that we forget the noble melancholy of the Allemande and of the Courante nor the refined grace of *Les Trois Mains*, the brilliancy of *La Triomphante*, as well as the admirable order of the *Gavotte et Doubles*. Candid and naïve at the beginning, the Gavotte grows, thanks to Rameau's dramatic power, into a heroic song of liberation. This piece has been the victim of numerous arbitrary transcriptions. I have always played this work according to Rameau's original version.

What strikes us above all else in Rameau is the solidity of his structure, the breadth and perspective of his plans. The least important of his gavottes is unfailingly strong. Yet Rameau knows how to preserve their innocence and lightness. While Couperin's music has a light and elegant structure, Rameau's framework is robust and apparent.

Concerning *L'Enharmonique* from the G Minor Suite, Rameau wrote: "The effect that can be felt in the twelfth bar may not at first satisfy everybody's taste. One gets accustomed to it, however, if one is willing to lend oneself to it somewhat; and after surmounting the first repulsion that lack of habit may produce in this instance, one may even feel all its beauty. The harmony which causes this effect is not thrown there haphazardly; it is founded upon reason and authorized by nature itself. For the connoisseurs, it is the most piquant; but the execution must sustain the intention of the author by softening the touch." (*Remarques sur les différents genres de musique*)

Also in the G Minor Suite *Les Tricotets* is a kind of dance clicked out with alternate taps of the heels and toes; it was very popular in France during the sixteenth and seventeenth centuries. Henri IV performed *Les Tricotets* admirably and with such passion that it was soon known at court as "King Henri's dance." Despréaux even said, "After nine times twenty years, the joyous *Tricotets* and Henri IV's steps still adorn the ballet." *L'Indifférente*, which precedes the two *Menuets*, is also a minuet.

As to *La Dauphine*, it is an isolated composition which does not appear in any of the four volumes of *Pièces de Clavecin* published by Rameau during his lifetime. It remained in manuscript until 1895, when it came out for the first time in the *Oeuvres complètes de Rameau*, edited by St.-Saëns and published by Durand in Paris.

Who was Rameau's dauphine? She was the Princess Marie Josèphe, daughter of the Elector of Saxony, Frederick Augustus II, crowned King Augustus III of Poland in 1733; in 1747 she became the fiancée of the eldest son of Louis XV.

In one of his reports (1746) the Count de Vaulgrenant, who served as French minister to Saxony, portrayed the Princess, then scarcely fifteen years of age, emphasizing "her noble bearing, excellent character, gentle manners, pious and religious nature, the abundance of her sweet graces. . . ."

This is a conventional portrait by a prudent courtier anxious to assure Louis XV of the virtues of the future dauphine. There are numberless descriptions of the same sort of innumerable princesses, descriptions which mean nothing and in no way reveal the true nature of their subject.

Let us now listen to Rameau's description. From the first measure, by means of a rhythm *à la française*, he sets forth a personage of authority and passion. Broken chords, *passagii, batteries* run over the two keyboards from one end to the other; *La Dauphine* tears along its course, more and more intense, losing all restraint, barely interrupted by a short lull in the middle of the composition. There is not a trace of the "gentle manners" so esteemed by the count.

Rameau's creative genius was extraordinary in its scope and variety. If Marie Josèphe had appeared to him in the "abundance of her sweet graces," he would have depicted this quality just as he did in *La Villageoise* and *La Follette,* masterpieces of tenderness and grace. How then does one account for the impetuosity and dynamic features of his portrait of the dauphine?

Marie Josèphe was the descendant of a line of kings who loved the arts, war, and romantic adventure. Her grandfather, Frederick Augustus I, the despotic and warring Elector of Saxony and King of Poland under the name of Augustus II, was also known as Augustus the Strong; he was a man of extravagant and luxurious tastes and extraordinary physical prowess. He shared the family fondness for art, was a patron of artists, and contributed to the beautification of the city of Dresden.

Augustus III, his son and the father of Marie Josèphe, was a less ambitious and aggressive soldier. Nonetheless, he waged war against Frederick the Great. He enriched the collection of art treasures in Dresden considerably and was passionately devoted to music. It was to him that Bach in July 1733 dedicated the Kyrie and the Gloria of the B Minor Mass.

But it is in the uncle of Marie Josèphe that the outstanding characteristics of the dynasty of the Saxons reached their climax. Maurice, Comte de Saxe (1696-1750), Marshal of France, was the illegitimate son of Augustus the Strong and the beautiful Countess Aurora Königsmark of Sweden. He was one of the greatest generals of his century. The fame of his extraordinary deeds and romantic adventures resounded throughout Europe. Conquests followed one another with dizzying speed.

The regent, Philippe d'Orléans, conferred upon him the title of *Maréchal de Camp*, and so from 1720 on he served France exclusively. This young hero, who could break a horseshoe in two as easily as one would a cracker, this Don Juan, whom women resisted no more effectively than did towns, suddenly turned to study and invention, buried himself in mathematics, and wrote a book on the art of war with the title *Mes Rêveries*.

Maurice de Saxe met Adrienne Lecouvreur in Paris and fell deeply in love with this great actress. It was Adrienne, who, with spontaneous generosity, sold her diamonds, jewels, and silver for a sum of 30,000 *livres* to save her lover during a moment of misfortune.

A captivating figure—this warrior and poet, this impetuous and fiery Maurice de Saxe! Is it not he who reveals to us the real nature of Marie Josèphe, his niece?

Rameau, contemplator of nature, penetrating psychologist, divined this. He understood the real nature of Marie Josèphe and what was hidden under the "gentle manners" of this child princess. With a boldness which defies conventions, the descriptive power of Rameau contradicts in a striking way the colorless description of the courtiers.

The marriage of the dauphine took place in March 1747. In the midst of brilliant entertainment and plays Rameau, at the harpsichord, improvised *La Dauphine*. The tumultuous agitation, the sudden stops, the skillfully organized disorder are indeed in the rhapsodic style of an improvisation. Noble and proud, the rhythm *à la française* dominates the entire piece. It symbolizes the magnificence of France and celebrates the union between the dauphin of France and a faraway princess.

La Dauphine is not only an admirable composition; it is a page of living history from the reign of Louis XV.

Chopin and French Music of the Past

Whoever lives intimately with Chopin's music will discover that its constitution needed the substance of Bach. Thus, if Zywny, and later Elsner, had not been his mentors, Chopin would have been driven intuitively to find the nourishment indispensable to his nature.

Besides Bach, Chopin was under the influence of Mozart. Mikuli mentioned Handel and Scarlatti also. Of the French harpsichordists there is no trace.

I long hesitated to acknowledge openly something that had always haunted me. Trained to submit everything to the objective examination of logic, I refused to admit what was appearing to me with increasing clarity. I tried to justify these revelations with unassailable proof. In vain. I could find no evidence that Chopin while in Paris had known and studied any of the pieces of the great French composers of the past or had received their direct influence. Nothing of the sort. In France, between 1800 and 1850, musicians had scarcely any interest at all in the harpsichord and its masters. The first volume of the *Trésor des Pianistes* appeared twelve years after Chopin's death. The musicological works of Fétis—despite the inclusion of the "Three New Etudes" in the *Méthode des Méthodes of Fétis and Moscheles*—also remained unknown to him. Otherwise, we know the composers Chopin cultivated and which of their works his pupils studied. Therefore it is almost certain that Chopin was ignorant of Chambonnières, Couperin, and Rameau, save perhaps for a chance encounter with an isolated piece by one or the other.

What is, then, this profound and mysterious affinity, with its innumerable ties, between the Cantor of Poland and French music of the past?

I see some of my friends smiling: "Yes, if you wish, Chopin's music has this touch of aristocratic elegance, of fineness, of sensibility that are the appanage of French music." But I feel that inwardly they resent my daring to draw analogies between this poet, whose soul was filled with passion, and the "superficial" musicians of the past.

"True French music always addresses itself to the mind more

than to the feelings. It has a logical construction, and more often than not it is a portrait reproducing a precisely considered object," said André Tessier in his *Couperin* (Laurens 1926).

Evidently titles such as *Les Délices, La Princesse de Sens, Les Bacchanales*, etc., in exciting the curiosity of common people contributed to popularizing the names of a Rameau or of a Couperin. The average listener prefers a ready-made formula, an order given to the imagination, to an effort of the mind to which he has not been accustomed. It is much easier to find *Le Petit Deuil, ou les Trois Veuves* "charming," and to smile while listening to *Les Coucous Bénévoles* than to follow the melodic line of a Louis Couperin, to understand the harmonic boldness of a François Couperin le Grand, or to grasp the dramatic intentions of a Rameau.

It is inconceivable that this prejudice still militates against Couperin and Rameau, whom we persist in seeing only as small miniaturist masters. And yet this music is here, all open to us, asking only to be understood. Let us forget the piquant labels which were glued to these pieces, and let us try to penetrate deeper.

Let us bring together Couperin and Chopin particularly. The predilection of one for the harpsichord and the exclusiveness of the other for the piano caused them to extract from keyboard instruments, either with plucked or struck strings, the most human, the most elevated, the noblest music. The ties which unite Couperin and Chopin appear before our surprised attention. Here they are in their harmonic nature, with their ramifications and consequences; in their rhythmical complexity; in the phrasing of the melody; in the ornamentation; last but not least, they are evident in the esthetics of both composers.

The fundamental trait of the harmony in Couperin as well as in Chopin is the consubstantiality of this harmony with the melody; it does not seem that harmony takes priority over melody, but that these two elements, hermetically welded, always come together and form a unique entity. Couperin, like Chopin, does not accompany his melodic texts with a series of chords. This is why it is impossible to suppress the slightest retard and to change the placement of an imperceptible passing note without altering the logic of the harmony or the expressive truth of the phrase. Couperin and Chopin both knew, consciously or intuitively, that harmony is what stirs the passions and gives expression and truth-fulness to melody; in breathing into it its own life harmony brings us closer to nature.

Chopin, Couperin, and especially Rameau revel in large "exorbitant" intervals, ardent chains of ninth-chords sometimes intensified with *acciaccaturas*, and chords that they disassemble and tighten anew, like radiating spokes, multiple and spread apart, though deriving from the same center. In his beautiful Prelude which has no bar lines, Rameau observed the strictest logic while employing this procedure of writing; it appears careless be-cause of its scattered voices, unfinished, abandoned, or taken again.

The burning chromaticism which tortured and ravaged Cho-pin left him longing for the snowy freshness of diatonic harmonies. He plunged into them to quench his fever; one feels the appease-ment brought to him by the consonance. The immaculateness of a simple triad takes on a striking value in Chopin as well as in Chambonnières, whose chaconnes sparkle with this radiant and fleshy diatonism. The same impulses induced Chambonnières and Couperin to use blocs of major triads with plagal inflections. These consonant periods generally follow those in which the increasing expression has reached its climax—glades after the somber forest or the freshness of an oasis after the burning heat of the desert. And if we encounter analogous cases in J. K. F. Fischer, it is through the influence of French music that they have come to us.

One of the most efficient means of dramatic music, one which contains great possibilities of movement and energy, has always been the progression. No wonder that the ancients used it as profusely as the romantics did. Certain progressions of Cou-perin and Rameau present in their processes and character a striking affinity with those of Chopin. Rameau's magnificent Sara-bande in A Major contains the most eloquent example of an eighteenth-century sequence in Chopin's purest manner. (See p. 270) You sceptics who hesitate to follow me in my hazardous exploration, please be willing to give particular attention to bar 13 of this Sarabande and those following it. They deserve it for the revelation they have in store for us.

Couperin wrote *La Bandoline* and *Les Ondes* almost entirely in two voices. In spite of it, these pieces are very rich harmonically, just as Chopin's voices are. This is the privilege of natures born polymelodic and brought up in the invigorating training of counter-point and folklore.

Couperin and Chopin liked melodic lines that stretch—sustained soliloquies pregnant with thoughts and interrupted by caesuras.

Couperin, using his favorite sign, *'* demands a breathing with the same insistence Chopin exerts when he traces an arc above a phrase and wants it to stop at a certain point, and no-where else. In both composers there is the same uncompromising will.

The phrasing of Chopin and that of Couperin show astonish-ing similarities. Only Mozart punctuates with this extreme care—for example, in his manuscript of the A Minor Rondo (K. 511). And what about the prosody of the phrase, its outline and its swing? And what of its legato, which in Couperin as well as in Chopin, is so hermetic and so intense?

There is as little naïveté in Couperin as there is in Chopin. It is surprising how both are devoid of it. Even the pieces at the head of which Couperin wrote *Naïvement* are not really naïve; they are fresh, young, simple in appearance, but not naïve.

For Chopin, the erotic, as for Couperin, the sensuous, pas-sion has not always amorous reasons; it is stirring and naturally dramatizes their phrases; it makes them rebound with fiery ac-cents. With pathos Chopin rebels against the oppression of the enemy, while Couperin, the amiable harpsichordist of Louis XIV, utters cries of revolt in his sumptuous and magnificent pieces such as *La Favorite* or *La Passacaille* dedicated to the King and to the Queen.

As mentioned earlier (p. 264), the melancholy of Chopin is very much akin to that of Couperin.

Chopin's ornamentation is a fusion of original inspiration, of influence received from Polish folklore as well as from Bach and Mozart. But we also find in it suggestions of Couperin and Rameau, especially the kind of ornamentation in the Italian man-ner that Couperin used in *Le Rossignol en Amour* or the para-phrases of his *Bergeries, Les Rozeaux,* or *Soeur Monique,* as well as the broken chords crossed by the lightnings of passing notes of Rameau's Sarabande. Is not the insistence on a certain note, dominant or tonic—and its being encircled with diminutions, melisms, lively arabesques, and passionate caresses—the same procedure that we find both in the Mazurka in A Flat Major (Op. 41, No. 4) of Chopin and in the Chaconne in D Minor of Louis Couperin? This could surprise us if we did not know that ornamentation has always been an organic necessity of the phrase, which needs to pour out, to rise, to tense, and to relax, to repeat itself with insistence in order to live. This is why we find in folk songs the world over embellishments identical with those of Couperin, Bach, and Chopin.

The numerous affinities between Chopin and French music of the seventeenth and eighteenth centuries are evident. But what is their origin?

Once, during a concert tour in Spain before the first world war, I stopped at Alcazar de San Juan to change trains. It was four in the morning. "When does the express for Valencia leave?" I asked. "Oh, that depends on the number of passengers," replied the conductor. I was alone. What was I to do? The dawn was delightful. I went wandering through the town, breathing in the atmosphere of Don Quixote. Houses were gray-blue, the sky, stone gray. The town was asleep; there was no one in the streets. I was returning toward the station, when from afar I noticed two male silhouettes: handsome lads superbly built, with dark curling hair, wearing vests of black velvet on which shone magnificent silver buttons. The men were gesticulating and talking. My heart stopped short. I did not believe it was possible; they were speaking Polish. . . . Coming closer, I greeted them in Polish. Astounded at first, then joyful, they answered with hand shakes. "Where do you come from? What are you doing here in Spain?" I asked. "We are gypsies. The chief of our *tabor* is Polish too. Will you come with us?" I followed them, marveling at this encounter and impatient to see their companions.

Behind the station, in a field surrounded by hedges, was the odd and colorful encampment. Beautiful tanned girls with long disheveled braids, children like crawling black balls, samovars, musical instruments were strewn all over the place. My two gypsies ran to inform their chief that a compatriot, vagabond, and musician like themselves had come to pay a visit. A tall and handsome fellow appeared in front of me, snatched his cap, threw it on the ground, in the ancient Polish custom, raised an arm, and received me with a joyous yell, "Be welcome! Catherine was only a strumpet!" I understood the delicate attention; the chief wanted to assure me of his patriotic feeling in cursing the great Russian Empress. Girls, children, women, horses and dogs—all greeted me with exuberant cordiality. Tea was served on the ground. They brought me peasant bread and sausage from Cracow. A gypsy with her nursing child was whining a lullaby. The chief rolled his drum and said, "Play something for us, since you are a musician. . . ." But at that moment a clerk from the station called to let me know that there were a few passengers and that the express could leave. The farewell was as cordial as if we had been old friends. I promised the chief to come back, and I left. As I went away, I heard the voice of a woman rising in a song from the region of Lublin, vibrating, filling the atmosphere. A beautiful complaint profoundly Polish was floating over the arid earth of Castile, impregnating it with its nostalgia.

Beyond the direct, palpable influence received by a particular artist, influence that can be identified by immediate testimonies, there is the perpetual and slow migration of reciprocal influences among nations. Brought forth by men, they come back to them and engender them anew. The study of these eternal recommencements, their relations, their respective evolutions, their unusual interdependence bring us every day new light without which we could not understand certain phenomena in an isolated artist. Thus we find very simple the rhythmical similarities and other relationships between a minuet of Rameau and a popular mazurka, or between a theme of Buxtehude and a Norwegian motive of Grieg. What could seem an amusing coincidence or an inextricable problem is only a natural and fatal consequence of this "perpetual rotation."

And I wonder if the mysterious ties which unite Chopin and French music of the past are not of the same nature as those which connect a ground of Purcell to a Portuguese *fado*, a *bourrée d'Auvergne* to an *obertas* from Cracow.

La Bourrée d'Auvergne

Many years ago the Auvergne colony of Paris asked me to take part in a festival of the music and dances of Auvergne. Mario Versepuy, a scholar who devoted himself to the folk music of

Auvergne, knowing my fondness for folklore, sent me a collection of authentic *bourrées*. As I read them, the motives of these dances fascinated me, and I was struck by their resemblance to certain Polish dances. I composed a chain of bourrées and transcribed them for the harpsichord. But their resemblance to the Polish *oberek* continued to obsess me, and I wondered if, in playing this dance, I were accenting it in the true Auvergne spirit. At that time I was living in Paris in the Latin Quarter in an eighteenth-century building where there was a large fireplace in the music room. Every week a man from the bistro across the street brought me a sack of coal. In Paris many bistros sell drinks in the front of the store and coal in the rear, and they are almost all owned by Auvergnats.

"I shall put to the test my way of playing the *bourrée*," I said to myself as I sat at my harpsichord, awaiting the arrival of the coal man. A knock at the door, and there he was with a sack of coal on his back. I broke into the *bourrée*. The man stood still and looked around to see where this music which he knew so well was coming from. Putting his sack down, he began to dance. Content, I gave a sigh of relief.

During the festival my friends from Auvergne enthusiastically showed their gratitude. Since that time, reassured by the Auvergnats, I often played the *bourrée* at my concerts. But, then, why do the Poles who attend these concerts come to me, moved, to thank me for playing an *oberek*? A puzzle. . . . Oh! that exquisite, that versatile *bourrée* d'Auvergne! Paderewski adored it.

6 Polish Music of the Past

Polish Composers

MUSIC has always been a vital part of Polish life among the people as well as at court. Poles are naturally musical. Music is part of their work, love, and pleasures. The peasants sing while working, scratch the fiddle while drinking at the inn, and blow the flute while herding their cattle. The reapers go to the fields and return singing. Singing, they bring in the last cart load. They sing while threshing the grain. The girls who go berry picking in the woods sing. All farm work is done with songs; everybody in the villages sings.

Since the beginning of the fifteenth century the movement of the Humanists profoundly inspired the music of Poland. It developed in a prodigious way during the sixteenth and seventeenth centuries. Great was the love for music of certain kings of Poland from Sigismond I, the Elder (1506-1548), to Ladislas IV (1632-1648). Organs, a cappella choirs, military bands, instrumental ensembles, and, above all, the lute echoed through the palaces and private chapels of kings and noblemen. King Stefan Batory was too preoccupied with preparations for war to devote himself primarily to music. He gave, however, his patronage to artists. The list of his court musicians included—besides choir boys and a military band of twelve wind-players and two drummers—as many as six organists and ten cantors, as well as numerous composers, instrumentalists, and singers.

To be surrounded by great musicians, to discover newborn talents, to attract artists from foreign lands who brought with them new luster to native music—such was the benevolent role of Polish princes enamored of this art. This is why, at the beginning of the seventeenth century, we see at Polish courts Italian, French, and Polish musicians working side by side.

Marenzio Luca, Asprillo Pacelli, Francesco Anerio, Marco Scacchi, and others brought to Adam Jarzebski, Mikolaj Zielenski, Andrzej Chylinski, Bartolomiej Pekiel, et al., the resources of their refined art as well as of their highly developed skill. In turn they absorbed the fresh and lively sap of Polish native music. This made for a fecund and marvelous exchange, giving birth to masterpieces of which Poland may be justly proud.

Among these musicians was Diomedes Cato born in Venice about 1570. He came to Poland in his youth and was engaged as a lutenist by the generous patron of the arts, Stanislas Kostka, who had a magnificent chapel and celebrated Italian singers attached to his court. Diomedes Cato was so deeply influenced by the music, native life, and customs of Poland that he remained there the rest of his life. Poland became his beloved adopted country.

From among his works I often played a *Chorea Polonica*, a dance in which the participants, hand in hand, formed a circle. It was usually danced in the open, often around an ancient oak tree. It is a processional dance of grave and serene character.

As for Jacob Le Polonais, he was born about 1545 in Poland. As a child he went to France, where he was known as *Le Polonais*, rather than as Jacob. "He never played so well as when he was drunk," said Sauval in his *Histoire et recherches des antiquités de la ville de Paris*, 1724. I love his *Gagliarda* with its rhythmic subtleties and mischievous grace.

One of the most outstanding Polish composers, Marcin Mielczewski, was born around 1600. He died in Warsaw in October 1651. He mostly wrote ensemble music or for voices a cappella. He tried to merge the two styles into one. Like many of his contemporaries, he had a predilection for basso voice surrounded by an instrumental ensemble. In his beautiful concerto *Deus in nomine tuo*, which is part of the *Cribrum Musicum* of Marco Scacchi, published in Venice in 1643—proof that Mielczewski was already appreciated in his lifetime—he gives himself to the joy of presenting at its best a beautiful male voice. Could it have been that of Agostino Eutitio, an admirable Italian singer of whom Ernst Ludwig Gerber said in his *Lexicon* that he was attached in 1643 to the famous chapel of Ladislas IV as singer and composer? It would not be the first time that a great composer had been inspired by a great virtuoso and had composed especially for him. Had not Bach composed his gamba sonatas at the time he often heard the celebrated gambist, Ferdinand Abel, at the Cöthen chapel? Other masters who were influenced in the same manner have proved how admirable reciprocal inspiration can be between two artists, one of whom, considered simply as a virtuoso, becomes in turn a creator by fecundating the imagination of a composer.

Among the works of Mielczewski there is a sonata, the manuscript of which is one of several sonatas for two violins and continuo in the collection of Sébastien de Brossard at the Bibliothèque Nationale in Paris. The name of the author is disfigured. This happened often with Polish names in copies of that time. In the addendum to her remarkable thesis, *Polish Elements in German Music up to the Time of the Classic Viennese* (Zurich 1916), Dr. Alicja Simon quotes a few bars from this work which seemed to her disparate and without interest. In the preface of the editions of the Society of the Friends of Ancient Polish Music in Warsaw a great musicologist, Professor Adolf Chybinski, mentions the existence of this sonata. We owe to him and also to Dr. Jachimecki and Dr. H. Feicht detailed studies concerning the bibliography, biography, and analyses of Mielczewski's works. Yet the Paris manuscript, although mentioned by all of them, never retained their attention. These few sheets seemed probably so negligible beside the important and substantial other works of Mielczewski. Therefore, it was with some misgivings that I began a close examination of this manuscript. Covered with rust spots, half burned, it was not very appealing. A constant change of measure gave, at first, the impression of a disquieting lack of continuity. But that is the case with a great number of works of the past; performance practices of these remote times are so different from ours that the meaning of the works escapes us. It seems that they have been locked away and the magic key thrown to the bottom of the sea.

The first part of Mielczewski's Sonata, on three staves, is for two violins and basso continuo. If we compare it to sonatas for two concerting instruments of the middle of the eighteenth century, Mielczewski's procedure evidently appears quite poor. The constant interruption of dialogues hardly begun are deceptive. But let us not be fooled by that. The awkward aspect of this piece, with its short-winded melodic line, is solidly built. It follows an idea which, little by little, takes shape with growing clarity before our very eyes. Our eyes? Certainly, because we are in the presence of one of the most exquisite choreographic subjects. The Sonata starts with a miniature overture in D major which seems to announce a feast at court. It stops after five bars, and from the background a delightful *volte* appears. Scarcely has it time to pass by when the overture returns, moving in dialogues between the two violins. Suddenly it stops again. Couples of dancers reappear, always in perspective, this time dancing a vigorous *bransle*. After a jump in the air, they halt abruptly on two D's heavily scanned. The two violins that had been interrupted unite and start anew, chasing one another in imitations and echoes; not for long though, because the lively dancers will not relent. Once more, and not for the last time, this double play, multiplied by other invisible couples, continues. The variety of the dances that march past—*bransles, basses-dances, gaillardes,* and *voltes*—and the constantly increasing briskness of the two soloists keep us alert and delighted. We are witnessing a most lively spectacle.

And now comes a moving surprise, a mazurka in G major enters. Loving and full of happiness, it offers itself with a soaring grace typically Sarmatic. Its aristocratic and feminine incurvation, in the midst of a whirlwind of vigorous rhythms, more and more marked, comes as a refined interlude. The motive of this mazurka of popular origin is certainly the most beautiful of all the dances Mielczewski included in his Sonata.

The spirit in which this piece is built—two solo violins alternating with a small tutti—gives us the clue to the manner of organizing the various sonorities and of setting the stage. Is it possible that this tiny instrumental ballet—exuberant, brilliant, and frolicsome—which depicts the flirtatious splendor of the court can be contained in the thin and bare score that came to us? Compared with the luscious instrumentation of modern scores, those of Mielczewski's time seem rather poor. The bass especially looks like a destitute advancing on crutches. Over this naked basso continuo, the instruments are only sketchily indicated. But we should not come to the conclusion that at that time scores were performed as written. To the harpsichords, theorbes, and lutes—all instruments capable of playing rich and full chords which go through the body of the strings, setting them ablaze— was given the role of coloring the grisaille of ancient scores.

The instrumental ballet, rather than sonata, of Marcin Mielczewski—such is the ignored marvel which was given to me to rediscover!*

Another interesting Polish composer of the seventeenth century was Adam Jarzebski, who was born around 1590 and died in 1649. Attached to the court of King Ladislas IV as musician, Jarzebski was also an architect and a poet. With a mind curious about everything, he was endowed with a natural sense of humor. Besides instrumental pieces of logical, dense, and lively writing, he left a poem entitled *Gosciniec abo Opisanie*

* ED. NOTE: Landowska gave the first performance of this work in Paris on June 28, 1932; she repeated it at a concert in St. Leu-La-Forêt in 1933 in the presence of the Polish ambassador to France and again in June 1937 at the Théâtre des Champs-Elysées in Paris as part of the official spectacles given during the International Exhibit. Unknown to Landowska, Mielczewski's Sonata has been published in Cracow in 1956 by the Editions of Polish Music. The manuscript score that Landowska had made from the Bibliothèque Nationale's original manuscript—together with many others from her library— were taken away from Landowska's School at St. Leu-La-Forêt in 1940 by the Nazis. Books sometimes travel far and wide. If this one happens to reach someone who knows of the whereabouts of any of Landowska's library, it is fervently hoped that the information will be relayed to us. It would be deeply appreciated and of great help in our efforts to reunite all that represents Landowska's lifelong work.

Warszawy, which was published in 1643. If it is not a literary masterpiece, it is, however, a most precious document because it gives details on the architecture of the time, particularly that of Warsaw, its chapel and theater. Jarzebski traveled extensively and wrote musical portraits of the cities he visited, such as *Berlinesa, Nuremberga*, etc. The manuscript of these concerts is to be found in the library of the city of Breslau under the title:

Canzoni è Concerti
a due tree quattre voci cum Basso Continuo di
Adamo Harzebskij
Anno MDCXXVII

Once more it is a misspelled name which should begin with J, not H.

Stanislaw Sylvester Szarzynski also lived in the seventeenth century. According to one tradition he was a Benedictine monk, and according to another he belonged to the Cistercian order. His Sonata for Two Violins and Harpsichord in D Major is of noble proportions and has an exquisite balance. The animated dialogue between the violins is supported by a bass that proceeds with ease and assurance. This sonata opens with a sarabande followed by vigorous *fugatti*. They alternate with *graves* of a beautiful melodic inspiration. A lively gigue crowns this superb chamber music work.

Jesus spes mea, dated 1698, is written for soprano solo, two violins, and basso continuo. Built on a theme of both popular and sacred origin, this beautiful cantata is imbued with a poetry full of melancholy. It may seem monotonous at first, but a closer approach to the work reveals the flavor and richness of its refined and slender arabesques.

The dynasty of the musicians bearing the name of Podbielski spanned three generations. J. Podbielski belongs to the oldest. Sowinski believed that he was born in Thorn. J. G. Walther, in his *Musikalisches Lexicon* of 1732, wrote that he was organist in the neighborhood of Krolewiec in 1703. A *Praeludium* by him is a short piece written in the style of organ preludes with passages and arpeggios running along the two keyboards of the harpsichord.

C. G. Podbielski, the last of the dynasty, was a remarkable organist and harpsichordist. He published in 1780 his first and in 1783 his second series of sonatas. Tender and gracious, his works are imbued with an adolescent romanticism of delicate fragrance. It makes us think of Karl Philip Emmanuel Bach and his contemporaries.

As for the Oginski princes, they were famous for their chivalry, their ardent patriotism, and their love of music and the fine arts. They represent the perfect type of eighteenth-century amateur.

Prince Michael Casimir, disappointed in his high political aspirations, retired to his estate, where he maintained an orchestra composed of the best musicians, both Polish and foreign. There were also distinguished singers. He showered them all with his generosity. He played several instruments himself, particularly the harp. The addition of pedals to this instrument is attributed to him. It was he who suggested to Haydn the subject of the Creation for oratorio. Prince Michael Casimir was also a distinguished painter.

His nephew, Prince Michael Cleophas, born in 1765 at Guzow, near Warsaw, continued the family tradition. Soldier, diplomat, writer, poet, and composer, he was above all a fervent Pole. Michael Cleophas' fame rests mainly on his polonaises. Chopin knew them from childhood, played them, loved them, and took them as models. The versatility of Michael Cleophas is very curious. Along with a polonaise pathetic and rhythmically intense as that in A minor, he gave us another, playful and gracious, in G major, in the Italian style of the end of the eighteenth century. It is said that Michael Cleophas Oginski composed his famous Polonaise in C Minor for a lady whom he loved. On the title page of the Paris edition of this work, dated 1793, one finds a lithograph of a young man, pistol in hand, with the following legend, "Oginski, in despair because his love was met with indifference, kills himself while his ungrateful mistress is dancing with a rival to the music of the Polonaise Oginski composed for her."

Influence of Polish Music on Foreign Composers

The influence of Polish music upon the music of foreign countries during the sixteenth and seventeenth centuries was both vast and profound. The extraordinary riches of Polish folklore explains this influence which extended up to the eighteenth century and even beyond.

Giovanni Picchi who was organist at the Casa Grande in Venice, about 1600, composed a *Ballo alla Polacha*. Although short in form, it is one of the most extraordinary compositions of that epoch. It abounds in harmonic and rhythmic complexities.

François Couperin in *La Princesse Marie* (*Ordre* 20), a gavotte, sketches a portrait of Marie Leszczynska, the fiancée of Louis XV. He seems to insist here upon using a French popular tune for his theme, while in the *Air Dans Le Goût Polonais* that follows he distinctly evokes the rhythm of a mazurka. The betrothal of the Polish princess and of Louis XV is thus symbolized by a French gavotte and a Polish mazurka.

In the opera *Les Indes Galantes* by Rameau, an *Air Grave Pour Deux Polonais* is part of the prologue. According to instruction at the head of the piece it has to be played *fièrement* (proudly). That was Rameau's way of depicting the lofty bearing of great Polish noblemen. It also refers to tempo and the right placement of accentuation.

Bach too composed many polonaises. One of them is part of the French Suite in E Major.

Georg Philipp Telemann tells us in his autobiography that during his sojourn in Cracow he enjoyed participating in county fairs. Thirty-six bagpipes, eight fiddles tuned a third higher, a *quint-posaune* (bass trombone) and a *regal* (portable organ)— just think of it—shrilled out Polish folk songs which Telemann exalts for their wild beauty and savage originality. He was amazed and delighted by the wealth of musical ideas displayed by the instrumentalists who improvised while the dancers rested. He said that any composer who heard them could only be enriched, and he admitted frankly that he himself did not hesitate to make use of Polish folk motives. His works, especially his Polonaise and Bourrée, attest to this in an eloquent way.

In the country where I was brought up, near Kielce, I saw, as a child, a farm girl milking the cows, in 2/4 time, while soothing them by singing a *mazur* in 3/4 time. This, which seems incredible to a stranger, is natural for a Pole because of the peculiar accentuation of the mazurka. And I am thinking of the famous dispute between Meyerbeer and Chopin. Chopin was enraged at Meyerbeer, who insisted, while hearing a mazurka played by Chopin, that it was in 2/4 time. What a pity that Meyerbeer did not see the Polish milkmaid at work and hear her singing!

The words of Polish popular songs speak of violins, flutes, bagpipes; also of the contrabass, nicknamed "big Maryna." The contrabass, especially, growls out the famous and indispensable fifth in the bass on which the *mazur*, the *obertas*, and the *kujawiak*, all in triple time, ride so lustily. The fifths of the contrabass stimulate and fan the flame of the dancers.

It is important to be aware of the character of the mazurka to avoid turning it into an elegant salon piece accented like a Viennese waltz.

Life abroad only increased Chopin's nostalgia for his country. The mazurkas tell us this eloquently. Passionate and melancholy, some are of a heartbreaking sadness. Others evoke peasant life, the inns, the harvest festivities, and the authentic *mazur*, which Chopin saw danced in his childhood and youth. "You know how anxious I was to reveal our Polish music, and I feel that I have been partially successful," wrote Chopin to his friend and schoolmate Tytus Wojciechowski. There is one of Chopin's mazurkas in particular that can be considered a prototype of this dance; it is the one in C Major, Opus 56, No. 2. We find in it the most striking features of the *mazur*—the fifths in the bass, the stamping, the solo of the male dancer (the melody in A minor in the left hand), etc.

I like to play this mazurka on the harpsichord. Chopin on the harpsichord? Yes, on the harpsichord! Do not be angry with me, my pianist friends; let me tell you why I do this. The harpsichord, reservoir of sharp colors, able to evoke flute, strings, nasal oboes, bagpipes, or contrabass, is the ideal instrument for rendering folk music.

This is also why I have transcribed some of our Polish folk songs, not solely for harpsichord, but in combinations with other instruments. I have kept in mind the fondness Polish peasants have for woodwinds. Therefore, my transcriptions are scored also for flute, oboe, and bassoon, occasionally with a string quartet, or a viola solo.

Polish Folklore

Polish folk music is extraordinary in its scope, not merely in terms of its bold harmonies, but through the exceptional vitality of its melodic lines and the utterly unexpected variety of its rhythms. Many of the songs are of ancient origin and go as far back as pagan times. Consequently we come, here and there, upon phrases reminiscent of Gregorian chants. We may also find in this music a key to the mysteries of Chopin.

A great ethnographer, Oskar Kolberg, gathered and presented in their best form the major part of Polish popular songs. Some of them have also been collected by Gloger. Although most of the songs I chose to transcribe may be found in the Kolberg Collection, I gathered them myself around the Polish countryside, at weddings, burials, harvest celebrations, and similar occasions.

One of them, *The Hop* (*Oj Chmielu, chmielu*) is a very old genuine *mazur*. It glorifies the hop, which in Poland is a symbol of marriage. Its resemblance to some of Chopin's mazurkas is very moving to the heart of a Pole.

Podolanka is a ballad of tragic though sober character. As for the second motive of the *Whitsunday Polonaise*, it was used by Oginski in one of his polonaises.

In *Kolendy*, a carol, there is a motive used by Chopin in his B Minor Scherzo.

As for *Wedrowali Krawczycy*, it is the ballad of journeymen tailors.

The whimsical curves, the verve, or melancholy of Polish popular tunes are enchanting. Usually these tunes are composed of four or eight bars. But more often than not, they contain an odd number of measures. How fortunate! Because then we can breathe freely and forget the classroom. All would be well if composers were not so eager to appropriate these popular motives and to harmonize them; but here begins the tragedy. According to epochs, schools, or esthetics, folk motives undergo the most diverse and contradictory treatments. One inflicts upon them the torture of development, which deprives them of their initial character to the point of making their true faces unrecognizable. Others submit them to an accompaniment in the manner of

Grieg or in the form of a procession of chords going up or down chromatically or with heavy harmonizations in keeping with the taste of the day.

Ever since I had the good fortune of hearing the *Orfeo Catala* of Barcelona sing popular songs in unison, in octaves, sometimes even two octaves apart, I have understood the idleness and puerility of our harmonic refinements. They add nothing to popular tunes. Harmonized in such a way, popular motives will always bear the stamp of one school or another and therefore will be dated. Moreover, a popular motive demands free motion in the open air of its native plain or mountain, or should resound in villages, inns, and farms. It will always be out of context when it is imprisoned within the form of a composition, even that by a master.

Yet how many pages by Palestrina, Schütz, Bach, or Couperin are prodigious because of the strength and flavor that emanates from their popular themes. But then it is due to the fact that the warmth of imagination of a great musician brings to fruition musical worth, the germ of which exists only in a popular motive.

In my teens I often went to the home of my piano teacher, Michalowski. In his drawing room there was a picture representing a peasant woman washing clothes in a brook. The frame of this picture was made of red plush, which was in fashion then. Although I was just a young girl, unconscious of her own thoughts and lacking judgment, I was disturbed by the proximity of this frame—although at the time it represented luxurious elegance— to the subject of the picture. That too I have kept in mind in scoring my transcriptions of Polish folksongs.

At the Time of Shakespeare

SHAKESPEARE revered music. In his works hundreds of lines reveal this passion, and it is with deep conviction that he said in *The Merchant of Venice* (Act V, Scene 1):

> The man that hath no music in himself,
> Nor is not mov'd with concord of sweet sounds,
> Is fit for treasons, stratagems, and spoils;
> The motions of his spirit are dull as night,
> And his affections dark as Erebus:
> Let no such man be trusted.

What was this harmony which enraptured the great poet? What was the timbre of those tender sounds which moved him with such intensity?

Until quite recently it was believed that England never had any original musicians except for Purcell. And while Handel— that Italianate German—was glorified as a national genius, England's music previous to Purcell's time remained forsaken, almost forgotten, until musicologists came to reveal it. And it was a surprise, a wonderment. The first reprint of *Parthenia* (originally published in 1611 as *The First Musicke That Ever Was Printed for the Virginalls*) was made by Rimbault in 1847 (although it may not have been made from the original plates). In 1899 Fuller-Maitland and Barclay-Squire published the celebrated collection known as *The Fitzwilliam Virginal Book*, the manuscript of which is in the Fitzwilliam Museum at Cambridge. And it is to Charles Van den Borren that we owe the most important work treating this subject, *Les Origines de la Musique de Clavier en Angleterre*, 1912. Admirable for its documentation and for the insight of its author, this book has yet to be surpassed.

In its primitive freshness ancient English music appears young and colorful. Whether vocal or instrumental, music was in full bloom at the time of Shakespeare. Besides the motets and madrigals of Gibbons, Morley, and Dowland, descriptive pieces, learned or for dancing, by Byrd, Bull, Farnaby, Peerson, and others, were played upon viols, theorboes, lutes, serpents, trumpets, flutes, organs, and virginals. They were heard at court and everywhere else. The Tudor family cultivated music. Catherine of Aragon played the virginal very well. Henry VIII owned a superb collection of instruments, among which were many virginals. As for Elizabeth's passion for music, it was notorious. Not only did she love to play the virginal, but she played it admirably well. Charles Burney wrote in his *General History of Music* in 1789, "If her Majesty was ever able to execute any of the pieces that are preserved in a manuscript which goes under the name of *Queen Elizabeth's Virginal Book*, she must have been a very great player, as some of these pieces are so difficult that it would be hardly possible to find a master in Europe who would undertake to play one of them at the end of a month's practice."

What was this virginal spoken of with such enthusiasm by musicians, poets, and writers of the sixteenth and early seventeenth centuries? Very simply, it was the term given in England to the earliest form of harpsichord. Much loved at the time, the virginal did not belong exclusively to aristocratic circles. Its popularity was widespread. Various musical instruments, including virginals, were often found in barber shops. While waiting for customers barbers diverted themselves by playing upon them. And during the terrible London fire of 1666, one could see a great number of virginals among the furniture saved from the fire and piled up on the boats that covered the Thames.

Shakespeare kept abreast of the musical creations of his contemporaries, many of whom were his personal friends. He even had a perfect knowledge of the virginal and of its structure; for in the exquisite Sonnet CXXVIII, *Invocation to Music*, a precise description of the mechanism of the virginal mingles with an expression of loving tenderness for the young lady playing it.

> How oft, when thou, my music, music play'st,
> Upon that blessed wood whose motion sounds
> With thy sweet fingers, when thou gently sway'st
> The wiry concord that mine ear confounds,
> Do I envy those jacks that nimble leap
> To kiss the tender inward of thy hand,
> Whilst my poor lips, which should that harvest reap,
> At the wood's boldness by thee blushing stand!
> To be so tickl'd, they would change their state
> And situation with those dancing chips,
> O'er whom thy fingers walk with gentle gait,
> Making dead wood more bless'd than living lips.
> > Since saucy jacks so happy are in this,
> > Give them thy fingers, me thy lips to kiss.

Having sprung from hearts that were worthy of ours and were nourished by folksongs, ancient English music, whether impassioned or serene, naïve or pathetic, sings of nature and love. It exalts life. When mystical, it glorifies God. Of an infallible workmanship, it is spontaneous and bold. Often it appears more modern than the most advanced music. Abandon yourself to the charm, strange as it is, of this music. Forget that it is old; and just because of that, do not think that it is devoid of warmth or human emotion. How could the music that moved Shakespeare so passionately have been only a plaything, a charming toy, and nothing more? As for the virginal, whose praises were ecstatically sung by Shakespeare, how could it have been, as we are persistently asked to believe, just like an old man always accoutered with a faded jabot and always gabbling away?

How did it happen that this music remained forgotten and unappreciated for centuries? I believe that the explanation is to be found in the perpetual fluctuation of taste. Our delight in hearing the strange, almost exotic beauty of the music of the virginalists is, therefore, comparable to the amazement felt by refined artists tired of romanticism at the beginning of the twentieth century, when they saw the paintings of Fra Angelico or the Cambodian ballets at the Paris Opera.

Because the art of the virginalists came from the motet and the madrigal, it shows an incomparable mastery of counterpoint. Harmonic successions being the result and not the determinent cause of the melodic march of the voices, it follows that contrapuntal writing is the only one that generates harmonic or melodic invention. This is why the music of the virginalists is rich and complex. The animation of the parts and the vivacity of the ripostes constantly give it plasticity and keep it in motion. Add to that the fragrance of folklore, which is the basis of all sixteenth-century music, and the almost exclusive use of ancient modes, and you will understand the attraction that this art has for us.

In *The Two Gentlemen of Verona* (Act V, Scene 4) Valentine says,

> And to the nightingale's complaining notes
> Tune my distresses, and record my woes.

Listen to the liquid sob of "The Nightingale," an anonymous piece, the autograph of which may be found in the British Museum in the Virginal Book of Elizabeth Rogers dated 1656. It bears no identifying marks. A copy of that manuscript was presented to me by the eminent English musicologist, the late John Shedlock. This exquisite composition is bathed in the crystalline freshness of C major. The whole forest sings, and the cascading trills of the nightingale mingle with the call of the cuckoo and its everrecurring interval of a third. In listening attentively to the tender motive, which toward the end emerges in the tenor voice, cannot one hear the first harbinger of romanticism? In this piece of no more than twenty-four bars impressionism and expressionism are blended with ineffable poetry. It was written one hundred fifty years before Couperin composed his langorous and consciously sensuous *Rossignol en Amour*.

An incomparable lutenist, John Dowland was one of the most

inspired English composers of the sixteenth century. Shakespeare praised him in *The Passionate Pilgrim* (No. VIII) by saying:

Dowland to thee is dear, whose heavenly touch
Upon the lute doth ravish human sense.

The friendship between these two great men is affirmed by certain historians and denied by others. Some of them even go as far as supposing that upon returning from one of his sojourns in Denmark, where he was lutenist at the court of Christian IV, Dowland saw Shakespeare and described to him the landscape of Elsinor, inspiring him in the completion of *Hamlet*.

Dowland's long sojourns abroad allowed him to get acquainted with French and Italian masters; these encounters enriched his talent in a magnificent way. His learned music, composed with a perfect knowledge of vocal and instrumental art, strikes us at first with its intensity of expression and dramatic power. Death, tears, *tenebrae*, *tombeaux*, etc., were subjects treated by all composers, great or small, during the sixteenth century and up to the end of the seventeenth. But Dowland reached the sublime in his passionate *Pavanes Lacrymae Antiquae, Gementes, Tristes*, and above all in his *In Darkness Let Me Dwell*.

The compositions of William Byrd and John Bull are the basis of the famous Fitzwilliam Collection. They are the most numerous and, above all, the most important. Byrd is the elder of the two by twenty years. What is strikingly different between them is not, however, a great divergence of workmanship because of the number of years that separate them. Both drew from the same source of folklore. Skillful plays of augmentations and diminutions were familiar to the one as much as to the other. And both were intoxicated by perpetual motion, by robust and lusty rhythms. See these bunches of sixteenth-notes which, in the music of Byrd as well as in that of Bull, roll along, overflowing and spreading over the bar-lines with such lively exuberance. But aside from that close unity of style, what dissimilarity there is between these two natures! Solid gait, straight angles, as well as rugged, sometimes cantankerous, deportment are Bull's features. He loved space and blowing wind; if he retired in solitude, it was to reflect on the text of a *Gloria tibi Trinitas* or a *Christe Redemptor*.

But secular music attracted him too; the light irony of the *Gigge Doctor Bull's my selfe* and the harsh passion of the *Duke of Brunswick's Alman* are proof that Bull did not remain indifferent to life. And what sweet melancholy there is in the *Duchesse of Brunswick's Toye!*

Bull also knew how to be forcefully picturesque. His *King's Hunt*, piaffing pantingly and trumpeting victoriously, evokes parks inhabited by roebucks and deer, with hunters riding full speed, bow in hand, shouting, and killing the animals on the run. One can understand that Bull would also choose a popular tune such as *La Bergamasca* as a theme for his *Buffons*. The straightforwardness of this rather squarely cut motive could only spur his inventive mind and his musical imagination.

As for Byrd, he was a poet. The curve of his melodic or ornamental line is sinuous and full of sweetness; its substance is fresh and flavorful. Byrd contemplated nature lovingly. There is not a path in the wild woods he could resist treading. If he used folksongs, as his contemporaries did, it was not only to ornament them with numerous variations, but to extract from them all their essence and fragrance. With a feathery touch Byrd harmonized and ornamented some popular tunes, such as *Wolsey's Wilde*, and, thanks to his genius, preserved their naïve poetry.

Like the composers of the rest of the world, English musicians followed the current of the Florentine Renaissance and applied themselves to painting with sounds. These musical images are poetical and colorful. Let us refrain from saying that they are naïve. Hundreds of years from now, will not the most fulgurant pages of Wagner or Stravinsky be considered naïve?

Byrd liked the effects of sonorous perspective very much. Listen to his *March before the Battle*. From far away we perceive the hammering of the horses' steps, the rattling of silver bits, and the clicking of spurs. A martial and magnificent parade approaches. Kettledrums, fifes, trumpets, and drums resound. Little by little the parade goes away and the sonorous whirlwind vanishes. Then comes *The Trumpets*. These instruments were always favored at the English court. Elizabeth I had sixteen trumpet players at her service under the command of a Sergeant Trumpeter. It is followed by the *Irish March*, given over to the flutes and fifes. Under the spell of an exquisite pastorale everything quiets down at the sound of the bagpipe.

Throughout its hundred bars *The Bells* of Byrd is built entirely on two notes, C and D. In spite of this simple basic pattern, Byrd succeeds in achieving incredible variety and richness. The composition runs through all imaginable rhythms and ranges from the crystalline tinkling of small bells to the calm and serene tones of those of moderate size and on to the deep and grave peals of the largest—all of them finally united in a powerful chorus. This piece with its bold and extraordinary impressionism is still another proof of the modernity of so-called "ancient music."

This composition reminds us of what Père Mersenne wrote about bells in his *Harmonie Universelle* (1636): "It is said that the sound of bells can be so violent and powerful that it will make wine ferment in cellars and that it will kill infants in their mothers' wombs, which is also true of thunder. Add to this the fact that bell sounds dissipate clouds, which is why bells are rung when there is a storm. Although many people believe that this effect is supernatural and due to the benediction bells received when they were dedicated for church service and disengaged from secular use, others think that the effect is quite natural and that it is the disturbance of air produced by their vibrations that chases thunderbolts away."

John Bull and William Byrd were both supreme masters of their craft and both lovers of nature. Around them, among a crowd of anonymous authors, were grouped composers such as Giles Farnaby, mischievous and tender; John Munday, elegant and refined; Thomas Morley, delicate and inventive; Martin Peerson, bucolic. What an immaculate freshness there is in his *Primerose!* There is also Richardson, whimsical, prodigal in harmonic discoveries. In each one of these musicians we detect some of Shakespeare's universal genius. English musicians knew how to depict; but they knew equally well how to keep within themselves the impressions received from the outside world; they let them ripen and then sang their emotions with touching simplicity. One can hear it in Martin Peerson's *Fall of the Leaves,* which expresses the feelings created by a desolate autumn landscape. This is also true of *Why Ask?*.

In *Hamlet,* Ophelia sings,

> "For bonny sweet Robin is all my joy."

It is a popular song that John Munday transcribed with much delicacy.

Dancing was an intimate part of life at that epoch. With what joyous passion, with what lustiness Shakespeare spoke of it! And certainly he did it with full knowledge because he must have been an excellent dancer. He often used the names of dances to establish beautiful images. For example, Beatrice in *Much Ado About Nothing* lengthily developed the theory that "wooing, wedding, and repenting, is as a Scotch jig, a measure, and a cinque-pace" (Act II, Scene 1).

The *Gaillard* of Richardson reminds us of the exclamation of the Duke of York in *Henry VI* (Part II, Act III, Scene 1):

> "I have seen
> Him caper upright, like a wild Morisco,
> Shaking the bloody darts, as he his bells."

This *Gaillard* has something truly wild, vindictive, and bloody. In *King Henry V* (Act III, Scene 5) the Duc de Bourbon says:

> They bid us to the English dancing-schools,
> And teach lavoltas high, and swift corantos;
> Saying our grace is only in our heels,
> And that we are most lofty runaways.

The volte, bold and lively, originated in Provence and was very much in favor during the fifteenth and sixteenth centuries, delighting the court of the Valois; it was also widespread in England. The dancer, hugging his lady with one arm, made her swirl and then tossed her up in the air, causing her skirts to billow out in the wind, to the great indignation of the Church.

Louis XIII, finding the volte much too free, banished it from the court, and thus it disappeared bit by bit from France. Ronsard, however, sang it:

> The King, dancing the Volte of Provence
> Made his sister Charity jump.
> She, very sweetly following
> With light leaps, was flying across the hall.

In *Love's Labour's Lost* (Act III, Scene 1) Moth says: "Master, will you win your love with a French brawl?" No ancient French dance is more forgotten today than the *Bransle* (*brawl* in English), and yet none was more universally known at the time of the last Valois and the first Bourbons, nor more wide-spread abroad, especially in England. Antoine Francisque, the admirable French lutenist, of whom only one thing is known with certainty—that he married in 1612—composed many *bransles*. One of them, *Le Bransle de Montirandé*, danced by the elders at kermises, reminds us of a Breughel. A very dear and moving memory is, for me, tied to this piece. Tolstoy loved it. When I was at Yasnaya Polyana, I had to play it again and again for him. He wept with joy while listening to it.

Purcell's Ground and the Portuguese Fado

The ground bass, or *basso ostinato*, is a short musical phrase usually consisting of four to eight measures. Situated in the bass, it is repeated an unlimited number of times. Over this bass one or more upper voices of contrasting character impose melodic lines which vary with each return of the *ostinato* phrase. The *ground* has become by extension the English term applied to dances based on this device. The passacaille and chaconne belong for the most part to the large family of dances constructed on the *basso ostinato*. So does the *folia*, that time-honored *Folie d' Espagne* of Portuguese origin, despite its name, and which from the earliest stages of music exerted such a prodigious influence over the imagination of composers.

One might expect that the monotony and limitations of the *ostinato* would confine the composer and prevent his giving free rein to his creative impulses. But we know that no device in art is of intrinsic value in itself. One is all the more aware of this fact when examining the innumerable grounds by mediocre composers who saw nothing more in this form than a pretext for turning out the greatest possible number of variations on the *ostinato*— a veritable deluge of banalities and commonplaces which flooded the seventeenth and eighteenth centuries.

Let us now consider the extraordinary way in which the imagination of the great musicians responded to the persistent bass motive repeated *ad infinitum*. They devoted themselves with passion to the invention of a thousand and one melodic lines, each of a different turn, enlivened by bold harmonies and complicated with subtle counterpoint. But that is not all. Byrd, Monteverd Cavalli, d'Anglebert, Buxtehude, Corelli, and Couperin, who wer poets as well as musicians, were aware of the latent and unlimited power of expression in this deceptively insignificant bass. We find the most eloquent confirmation of this in the Chaconne for solo violin, in the organ Passacaglia, and, above all, in the Crucifixus from *The B Minor Mass* by Bach.

The ground was used in many different ways by Purcell. Sometimes he entitled *Ground* a composition in triple meter, as the *Ground in Gamut,* for example, which has all the predominant characteristics of a *Folia.* On other occasions, as in *New Ground,* in quadruple meter, while preserving the fundamental character of the ground, he would proceed by omitting certain phrases, thus tightening the melodic line and bestowing upon it an exquisite asymmetry. Yet everywhere else the fundamental character of this dance remained, with its melancholy and obsessive repetitions, its strange and exotic beauty. But it is in the "Lament of Dido" from *Dido and Aeneas* (Act III, No. 37) that Purcell achieves the most sublime music on a *basso ostinato.*

In the Ground in C Minor (Volume VI of *The Complete Works of Purcell,* Novello, p. 51) Purcell combines the principle of the ground with that of the refrain and couplets in the French manner. Thus he gives us an exquisite piece of subtle construction. The refrain is a diminutive procession of broken chords in syncopation to be played on the lute stop. These broken chords cease; and while the *basso ostinato* begins again, the couplet appears— a fluted voice rising and singing a plaintive song, which in turn stops. The procession of broken chords returns. Then the fluted voice resumes the interrupted song, and so on. The recurrent movement of the refrain and couplets, evoking the chiaroscuro of a checkerboard, is symmetrical, yet deeply moving. The last couplet, in place of a single voice, brings forth a choir which rings out in a magnificent and martial mood. The diminutive procession of broken chords returns for the last time, and the piece vanishes on a chord of low notes.

One of my most colorful and revealing experiences occurred while I was on a tour in Portugal playing in Coimbra, that city of dreams picturesquely situated on a hill above the Mondego River. The ancient university with its poetic atmosphere, its students in their black capes roaming through narrow and tortuous streets, the strains of a fado accompanied by a guitar echoing constantly from the distance—all filled me with delight. That evening I played a program which included Purcell's Ground in C Minor. The reaction of the audience to this piece was strangely intense and in turn had a curious effect upon me. In response to the demands of the audience, I played the Ground once more, and I seemed to hear somewhere in the background the monotonous rhythm of muffled feet following the insistent beat of Purcell's dance. Leaving the stage and entering the wings, I witnessed a striking scene. Four men in working clothes and espadrilles, humming to themselves, were going through the motions of a dance. I had the impression that my Ground was still going on. The moment the men saw me, they stopped, obviously embarrassed. One of them came forward and spoke: "We were told to be here at eleven o'clock, but the concert was not over; so we danced a little. That tune you played was very nice. We know it very well. Can we go ahead now?" These men were the movers who had come to pack my harpsichord and take it to the station. I had to leave that night for Lisbon, where I was giving a concert the following day.

What could have led these men to break into a delicate dance by a seventeenth-century English composer in such a natural and spontaneous way? Was it the monotony of Purcell's rhythm, the strange melancholy of the melodic line, the broken syncopated chords, the lute-stop with its resemblance to the twang of the guitar—any of those characteristics equally typical of the Portuguese fado, the dance so beloved by the people of that country? Who will ever know? Perhaps it was a trace of the original *folia* brought to light in a warm and sunny climate and transmitted through the vanished centuries to these responsive and sensitive people!

The harpsichord was finally packed off to Lisbon, and I followed it, as I always do, musing over an episode which I would never forget.

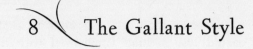

8 \ The Gallant Style

Wilhelm Friedemann and
Karl Philipp Emanuel Bach

JOHANN SEBASTIAN BACH'S sons, as well as Haydn and Mozart, lived and wrote their works during a period of transition in esthetics. Rigid counterpoint was gradually dying out and giving way to the gallant style. Melody was taking the upper hand, escorted by other parts, which were now filling in a servile fashion the role of accompaniment. According to Forkel, Johann Sebastian Bach used to say to his eldest son, "Friedemann, shall we go to Dresden to hear the pretty *Liederlein?*" This jovial epithet characterizes the gallant style very well as it was beginning to take root in the latter part of Johann Sebastian's life. But it was left to his sons to cultivate the new style and to see the blossoming of the *Blaue Blume* (forget-me-not) tinged with German sentimentality—the harbinger of romanticism.

To understand better the works of Schumann, Brahms, and Weber one should first become familiarized with the music of their predecessors who provided the seed of their inspiration— the music of Wilhelm Friedemann and Karl Philipp Emanuel Bach, the founders of the great German romantic school and the ancestors in direct lineage of Beethoven. We must not think, however, that these Bachs were merely steppingstones to the great romantics; each of them had his own distinct personality and original talent. The profusion of Johann Sebastian's genius overflowed in his sons, who were, however, very different one from the other.

Wilhelm Friedemann, his eldest and favorite son, makes us think of Brahms. The work by which he is best known is not his at all; it is an organ concerto in D minor transcribed by his father after a Vivaldi concerto (Schmieder 596) and on which Wilhelm Friedemann substituted his own name. His original compositions, however, are bold and full of ideas and harmonic riches. Unfortunately, they languish in obscurity. Among them, the twelve Polonaises are perhaps the finest works he wrote. Lyrical and tender, now candid, now filled with accents of sorrow, they are presented in the purest, most perfect form. Brahms felt such an admiration for Wilhelm Friedemann that he published one of his compositions, a *Concerto a duoi Cembali concertante*. For a time this work was erroneously attributed to Johann Sebastian.

Wilhelm Friedemann makes us think of Brahms, while Karl Philipp Emanuel strongly evokes Schumann. His excessively sorrowful and morbid character indicates degeneracy. His melancholy, well-nigh effeminate, is not that expressed by his father. Take a melodic phrase of Karl Philipp Emanuel; it meanders endlessly in the truest sense of the word. When we think it has arrived at its termination, it immediately resumes its course. Then we discover how far we were from understanding it. These lengthy sinuosities and lyrical arabesques express tenderness or become anxious question marks or sobs. An enthusiastic joy succeeds despair. The exaltation of this music infiltrates us and becomes obsessive. Whereas Johann Sebastian's music, carved out of granite, powerful and inexorable, is sensuousness itself, that of his son Karl Philipp Emanuel, the king of the gallant style, is emotive, but devoid of sensuousness. But it would be wrong to consider shapeless this accumulation of breathless, difficult to follow lines, these circles and half circles that come and go, and these embellishments which are sometimes suffocating. Karl Philipp Emanuel's music has its own construction; despite being entirely different from that of Johann Sebastian, it is no less solid and logical.

Karl Philipp Emanuel was a peerless virtuoso. Burney, who often had the good fortune of hearing him play, wrote in his memoirs that "Philipp Emanuel knew like no other how to draw the cry of pain from his instrument." In his admirable treatise *Versuch über die wahre Art das Klavier zu spielen*, Karl Philipp Emanuel solved many problems of interpretation of harpsichord, clavichord, and pianoforte music.

I had the privilege of acquiring at the sale of the celebrated collector Prieger, in Bonn, July 15, 1924, the separate parts of several of Karl Philipp Emanuel Bach's concertos copied by Ernst Ludwig Gerber, the justly famous author of the *Lexicon der Ton-kunstler* (1790). His father, Heinrich Nicolaus, was one of Johann Sebastian Bach's pupils. They were men whose knowledge had been handed down from one generation to the other. Therefore, these manuscripts are of great value, and it is from them, together with a confrontation of Karl Philipp Emanuel's original autograph, that I have reconstituted the full scores.*

The Concerto in G Minor (1754, Wotquenne No. 32) gives a splendid idea of the strange genius of Karl Philipp Emanuel Bach. The romantic character of his inspiration astonishes us, but what attracts and fascinates most is the perpetual conflict of opposing elements. Following whole pages conceived under the influence of the early eighteenth century, we come upon long passages announcing romanticism. Echoes of Lully, of the elder Bach, and even of Scarlatti mingle with passionate and pathetic accents, presaging the oncoming of Schumann. Hear, in the first part of the concerto, those phrases full of chivalrous heroism in French dotted rhythm, and then the admirable *un poco andante*, beating out the slow rhythm of a sarabande of old while dwelling voluptuously on se-

---

* ED. NOTE: These manuscripts, as well as Landowska's reconstituted scores were part of her library seized by the Nazis in 1940. See p. 285.

Early in 1943 Wanda Landowska was asked to identify manuscript copies of several of Karl Philipp Emanuel Bach's concertos, then in the possession of the late Adolf Koldofsky of Toronto, Ontario. Subsequently, she played seven of these concertos on the Canadian Broadcasting System from March 14 to April 25, 1943. See p. 423.

The Gallant Style   305

quences of purely Parsifalian flavor. Far from being uneven because of these contrasting elements, this work is marvelously coherent. In his powerful and unerring grasp, Karl Philipp Emanuel gathers all the warring influences and molds them into a whole; from them he chisels out a living work.

Wolfgang Amadeus Mozart

Today much confusion exists as to how Mozart's keyboard works should be performed. First of all comes the question of instrument. What was Mozart's instrument? And how can we play his music on our modern piano?

In the voluminous correspondence between Mozart and his father we come upon countless descriptions of harpsichords, clavichords, and pianofortes. Hence the confusion. Yet it is very simple; in his childhood Mozart chiefly played the harpsichord. Later, as a result of his encounter with Stein, that remarkable instrument maker, it was the pianoforte which became his keyboard instrument par excellence. (See p. 137) Yet the harpsichord, so rich in tone colors, could not be banished from Mozart's memory. Above all, it is in the pieces of instrumental character like the Rondo in D Major (K.485) or in the picturesque and spirited Rondo alla Turca (K.331) that he remembered the harpsichord. On the plucked-string instrument the delicacy of Mozart's melodic outline is sharpened.

But it was the pianoforte which, to Mozart's taste, best suited the most expressive resources of bel canto. Those who had the good fortune to hear Mozart play the pianoforte were ecstatic in describing his cantilena, which seemed to issue from the throat of a singer rather than from the keyboard of an instrument. His playing in the virtuoso passages was brilliant without being loud and in a moderate and human pace. In the slow movements it became sensuous, yet spiritual, lively, punctuated by question and exclamation marks and by cesuras, which set off each phrase like an aria or a recitative sung with the loving intelligence only to be found in the greatest singers. There were those who even went so far as to say that when Mozart played a simple scale, it became transformed into a cavatina. "He had small and pretty hands," said Franz

Niemetschek in his biography of Mozart, "and he knew how to use them at the keyboard in such a caressing and natural manner that the pleasure of watching him was no less great than that of listening to him."

Now, on our modern instrument, how can we give to Mozart's keyboard works all these qualities?

For a true understanding of these works and of the multiplicity of sonorous and expressive means Mozart had at his disposal, it is of prime importance for all present day pianists to study the resources and effects of eighteenth-century keyboard instruments as well as the manner of manipulating them. They should be instructed in the science and art of creating on the modern piano a special touch which can reproduce most faithfully the tonal esthetics of Mozart's time. This science of touch can only enrich the performer with multiple and varied means and enable him to transfer to the modern piano not only the sweetness of the clavichord, the sharpness of the harpsichord, but above all, the many nuances and the crystalline transparence of the pianoforte. Because of its double escapement the modern piano is conducive to veiled sonorities. But under the expert touch of a knowing performer it is possible to obtain from it the color and particularities of the pianoforte. The gray and neutral tone of the modern piano can be set ablaze and yield hitherto unsuspected colors.

At Salzburg in the house where Mozart was born there is a moving relic—a long box of dark wood which I hardly dared to open. It is Mozart's confidant, his pianoforte, admirably preserved. On it I studied some of his sonatas and concertos. With its sharp but aristocratic voice, it gave me many priceless indications and revealed to me the spirit of Mozart's keyboard works.

The special touch, indispensable to playing Mozart, takes its substance from the pulp of the finger and produces a well-defined fleshy, and firm sound, one that is independent. Its neatly defined outline precludes any agglutination with surrounding tones. In its autonomy it carries within itself its own life. When associated, such sounds, short or long according to their note values, conjunct or disjunct, tied or loose, move about and flow without ever overlapping one another or dissolving into a formless mass. Although interdependent, these tones keep their distinctive qualities in the midst of an innumerable company. Their assemblage forms an organic and inseparable chain. These grained sounds, comparable to the tappings of a fine hammer, and set against a clear background, trace melodies of the purest bel canto. As for the bass notes, they are ample without being heavy.

Out of this particular contact between the fingers and the keys the authentic qualities of the pianoforte will be reborn. Their freshness and novelty will delight us. True pianoforte color, enhanced with proper expression, will uncover and make us understand in its real meaning the plenitude and warmth of a Mozartean phrase.

But what about the pedals? Should they be used or not? We know that the pianofortes of Mozart's time had either knee levers or pedals; their effect was comparable to that of our modern piano pedals. Also the description Mozart made of the qualities of the Stein pianoforte, as well as that of his own manner of playing, are clear indications that the pedals should be used, but with discretion, so that the harmonic and melodic texture will remain unencumbered, crisp, light, and transparent.

And thus our modern piano—an admirable instrument in itself and incomparable in its versatility—will become enriched by a thousand new nuances.

Another problem which confronts the modern interpreter of Mozart is the question of ornamentation. And this, indeed, is a real problem.

What is ornamentation in Mozart's works? Karl Philipp Emanuel Bach gave us an explanation when he wrote in the heading of his *Six Sonatas for Clavier with Ornamented Repeats,* 1760, "To vary the repetitions is today indispensable. We expect it from every performer." What today would be described as the taking of "peculiar liberties" was in Mozart's time the *sine qua non* of every performer. No virtuoso would have dared play certain phrases of Mozart as Mozart wrote them. There are many places, especially in the slow movements of his sonatas and concertos, that are merely sketched; they are left to the performer to be worked out and ornamented. Those performances which we respect today for their literal devotion would have been called ignorant and barbaric by Mozart's contemporaries; for it was in his art of ornamentation that the eighteenth-century interpreter submitted himself to his audience to be judged an artist of good or poor taste.

Improvised ornamentation was not left to inspiration alone.

It was a science based on very severe laws. One had to know them before starting to embellish a masterpiece. Fortunately, Karl Philipp Emanuel Bach, Quantz, Leopold Mozart, and many others have left us detailed treatises which are our guides. They tell us that one should play the principal theme upon each of its recurrences in a slightly different way. They lead us in the art of using appropriately the *groppos*, softly rolling; the *harpègements*, or breaking of chords; the *circolos* and *semicircolos*, so luscious; the venturesome *ribattute*; and the bold *tirate*, which Leopold Mozart compared to gun shots. All these so-called "arbitrary embellishments" were not indicated with signs; they depended entirely upon the interpreter's will and his inspiration. Mozart himself did not always merely sketch out his slow movements— those which obviously call for more ornamentation than the rapid ones; he often ornamented them with subtle care and refined taste. The most striking example of his great artistry in this domain is given us in his Rondo in A Minor (K. 511). Therefore, an interpreter, who should feel free to improvise candenzas in the third movement of the B Flat Major Sonata (K. 333), must perform the Rondo in A Minor with the most fervent and obedient devotion.

Mozart wrote down cadenzas for several of his keyboard concertos (K. 624). Unfortunately they are neither very interesting nor very beautiful. They were written for his pupils or sometimes for a contemporary performer. But when Mozart himself played his concertos in public, he always improvised the cadenzas.

What is, in fact, a cadenza? It may be an improvised suggestion or a retrospective glance over that which has already taken place or perhaps a stroll through familiar places, those we liked and are happy to see again.

It was Hummel who vulgarized the role of the cadenza. It was he who started the habit of opening a cadenza with the din of a triumphant conqueror; and needless to say, this vulgarization distorted the original meaning of the cadenza. Although he had been a pupil of Mozart, Hummel became estranged from the Mozartean tradition, and he introduced wild virtuosity into the interpretation of the keyboard works of his master. In short, Hummel was responsible for a false tradition and among other things for the exaggerated length of cadenzas.

If the beauty of a certain kind of musical refinement has

been misunderstood, it is that of Mozart. It has been too lightly qualified as being *charming* and *adorable* with all the pejorative connotation of these virtues. Today Mozart is presented in two different ways. One is clean, sharp, brilliant, dry, and very strict in tempo. The piano works are played without pedal, but with a rather heavy touch in order to demonstrate Mozart's inherent grandeur. The other manner is small, dainty, very thin, and quasi-elegant in tone, to convince us of Mozart's everlasting charm. One inflates, the other deflates Mozart. One shouts; the other whispers. Does either one give us a true version of Mozart's sonority, of his mood, or of his esthetic? I do not think so.

Mozart hated all distorting exaggerations, all exertion, and all fireworks. Remarkable for its delightful simplicity, its moving and profound expression, Mozart's manner of playing even won over Clementi, his redoubtable rival. Mozart reproached him above all for his "heaviness and lack of delicate feeling in the melody." Mozart's own cantabile was a mosaic, all made of incisive, light, and fluid sounds, which, without mixing, united in a noble and soaring canto. Mozart always remained vocal, even when he wrote for instruments. On the other hand, when composing a highly ornamented passage for one of his contemporary coloraturas, the essence of his music is full and rich, infinitely varied in its illumination. It creates, one might say, a sort of chiaroscuro.

Mozart's frequent indications *Fp* brings us a first taste of the Mannheimer crescendo and diminuendo. And here we see the demarcation line between Mozart and the blocklike dynamics of Bach and Handel. Although Mozart knew how to use strict counterpoint masterfully, we distinguish immediately a Bach fugue from another fugue by a composer born in the midst of the blooming gallant style, perfect as it may be.

The works of Mozart may be easy to read, but they are very difficult to interpret. The least speck of dust spoils them. They are clear, transparent, and joyful as a spring, and not like those muddy ponds which seem deep only because the bottom cannot be seen. The mania of width and depth was not yet the fashion in Mozart's time.

On January 15, 1783, the *Wiener Zeitung* printed the following announcement, "Kapellmeister Mozart informs the inestimable public that he is publishing three new concertos for clavier."

The Concerto in F Major (K. 413), the first of the set, was composed in 1782. It belongs to the happiest period in Mozart's life; he had just married Constanze Weber. This work breathes pure joy from beginning to end and may be described as one long minuet. We know how much Mozart loved to dance and what a good dancer he was. The first and last movements of this concerto are, in fact, minuets. Between the two, Mozart introduced a sublime larghetto, truly a larghetto amoroso, full of the excitement and tenderness of his adolescent love for Constanze.

Concerning this and the two other concertos, Mozart wrote to his father on December 28, 1782: "These concertos are a happy medium between what is too easy and too difficult; they are very brilliant, pleasing to the ear, and natural, without being vapid. There are passages here and there from which connoisseurs alone can derive satisfaction; but these passages are written in such a way that the less learned cannot fail to be pleased, though without knowing why." (Translation by Emily Anderson.)

It has been concluded from this letter that Mozart attributed little importance to these concertos, and consequently they have been underestimated. The irony of Mozart's "modest" remarks is too apparent to require further explanation, although we might still ask why these concertos have been relegated to oblivion. Probably because they—and the K. 415 in particular—require more extensive extemporization on the performer's part than do any of his other concertos.

The first movement of the Concerto in C Major (K. 415), is a type of *alla marcia* which advances in canonic imitations. Tranquil at first, it augments little by little and develops into the same kind of triplet motive which marks the opening of the *Jupiter Symphony*. Thus this concerto, which has been neglected and ignored for so long, contains from its first notes elements of grandeur and dramatic power.

The Andante is a tender and lyrical dialogue between the soloist and the strings, the latter supported from time to time by

oboes, bassoons, and horns. But above all it is the Finale, a frolicsome dance in 6/8, which deserves our fullest attention.

While so much importance has been attached to the letter
quoted above, another letter of Mozart to his father from Vienna,
January 22, 1783, throws much more penetrating and informative
light on the subject: "I shall send the cadenzas and *Eingänge*
(short introductory passages announcing the approach of new
moods; they had to be extemporized like the cadenzas, although
they represented a very different aspect of improvisation), to my
dear sister at the first opportunity. I have not yet altered the
Eingänge in the rondo, for whenever I play this concerto, I always
play whatever occurs to me at the moment."

The use of cadenzas at the end of each movement is still
common today, while the small fermatas, upon which we come
unexpectedly here and there, and most significantly at the
Eingänge, which twice announce the approach of the sublime
adagio in C minor, have been virtually ignored since the performances by Mozart himself or by the musicians of his time.

At the end of the rondo, Mozart introduces a popular folksong, ingratiating and fresh in mood, against the murmuring of
the strings.

The Concerto in E Flat Major (K. 482), belongs to the
period of Mozart's great virtuosity, which extended from August
1784 to January 1786. Mozart had become the fashionable musician of the day in Vienna; he was feted by the Emperor, the
aristocracy, and even by his own colleagues. During this period
he composed a great number of works which were performed in
public and at private academies. Mozart played the E Flat Major
Concerto in Vienna on December 16, 1785.

The Allegro, with its symphonic features, is powerful, joyous,
and solidly built, with broad themes against which garlands and
light arabesques tenderly nestle. Between this movement and the
happy and spirited Finale, the admirable Andante—a sorrowful
and touching lament—gravely stands out. Ornamented throughout with infinite care by the master himself, this Andante is
perhaps one of the most beautiful in all of Mozart's works. The
sweet serenity of a little interlude by woodwind instruments
interrupts this pathetic and poignant lament so divinely simple.
Mozart had to repeat this movement after the first performance
of the concerto.

In the Finale, a marvel of grace and sprightliness, Mozart seems to have forgotten his despair and his tears. From the very first note it bounces with that waggish gaiety that is Mozart's alone. The effervescence of a Neapolitan dance mingles with the sentimental tenderness of a Viennese *ländler*. The strings set upon a mischievous chase; the whole piece rings out in exuberant joy. The bassoon suddenly takes on an unsuspected agility; it whirls about, curtsies, and touches us by its efforts at being light-footed. Over a pedal-point the flute sings away madly with the tender abandonment of a prima donna, with trills, mordents, and appoggiaturas in the purest Italian tradition.

In this Finale, all is gay, light, carefree, and diaphanous, although it is solidly built and inexorably strong. It is filled with radiance, sonorous cascades, and arabesques. Everything in it sings, laughs, and dances; it is like a small *opera buffa* with its outbursts of tender feelings and happiness. But toward the end a surprise awaits us—a strange and delicious intermezzo. There is a sudden modulation and a fermata that invites the soloist to improvise. Then a minuet, andantino cantabile, appears, stately, delicate, and somewhat precious, as if amazed at finding itself in the midst of those exuberant and tumultuous voices. Its structure is so clear that we become immediately aware of Mozart's intention. It is a dialogue; the orchestra proposes a theme of simple outlines which the soloist takes up and must embellish with ornaments according to the laws of the time.*

The Concerto in D Minor (K. 466) was composed in Vienna. Mozart finished it there on February 10, 1785, and played it for the first time the next day.

The autograph of this work is in the library of the Friends of Music in Vienna. The concerto was not engraved during Mozart's lifetime. In looking over the manuscript, which was

---

* ED. NOTE: Here may be quoted Georges de Saint-Foix, the celebrated biographer of Mozart. In volume IV of his authoritative book W. A. *Mozart*, Paris 1939, p. 123, he says:

It is undeniable that this minuet, so poetic and so unexpected, in which Mozart exposes a melody that seems intended for the violin, must be varied by the soloist according to the principles observed in Mozart's epoch. Wanda Landowska has demonstrated in an irrefutable manner the principles of the art required of the performer in this respect—principles recognized as correct usage in Mozart's time.

shown to me in 1909 by Eusebius Mandyczewski, the archivist, during the Haydn Festival in Vienna, I noticed a detail of the greatest interest. Mozart had originally written another theme for the last movement of this concerto. It is in the same hand and written with the same ink of the rest of the autograph. This former theme is also in the same tonality and same meter as the one which served as a basis for the rondo. Moreover there is a great similarity of character between those two themes. I used the first in my cadenza. (See opposite page.)

The first and third movements of this concerto are very romantic. Mozart here appears as a younger brother of Beethoven. This Mozartean romanticism, though, has an adolescent freshness. Its accents are plaintive rather than full of pathos. Its effusiveness is more tender than impassioned. Its tempests—which by the way never degrade themselves with shrieks of despair or grandiloquence—dissolve naturally into a radiant serenity in the second movement, *Romanza*, in the purest Italian taste. This movement is built in rondo form, as are most of the andantes in Mozart's concertos and sonatas. Particularly dear to him, this form was in great fashion in his time. Sketchy, it is like the webbing that stimulates the imagination of the embroiderer. The interpreter, according to prescriptions fastidiously given in the treatises of the time, had to entwine it with clusters of ornaments, light and diaphanous, which would not obliterate the purity of the melodic line.

It is interesting to notice the power certain tonalities have over the moods of great composers. Mozart, for instance, becomes dramatic and sometimes tragic when he writes in D minor. It is impossible to avoid bringing together the D Minor Concerto and the overture from *Don Giovanni* as well as the Commandore's scene, both in D minor. In the last movement of the concerto, the symphonic character of the orchestra before the first solo, its impetuosity, and also its gravity surpass in scope and vehemence the frame of a concerto, even one of vast proportions.

The Concerto in D Major (K. 537) bears the title of *Coronation Concerto* because Mozart played it during coronation festivities in Frankfurt in 1790. He had played it previously in Dresden on April 14, 1789.

Joy, humor, and loving tenderness abound in *The Marriage of Figaro* (completed April 29, 1786) and are perpetuated in the

Landowska's autograph sketch of her Cadenza for the first movement of
Mozart's Piano Concerto in D Minor (K. 466)

Coronation Concerto, composed two years later (February 24, 1783). Does not this concerto seem to be a continuation of the immortal *opera buffa?* The most diverse elements participate in this work, each of them of a prodigious vitality. They form a powerful and perfect entity.

The first and last movements especially are remarkable for their resemblance to *Figaro.* The character of the motives, the abundance of witty allusions in the dialogue between the piano and the other instruments, and the manner of treating the key of D major—which Mozart loved so much and which always put him in high spirits—and, above all, oblivion of everything, this divine carelessness are common to both works.

From the first bar of the Allegro, the impatient, though regular, beating of the D in the bass (to be played *piano* according to Mozart's indication, a fact that enhances its dynamic value) announces the approach of festive activities. Joy augments and spills over into the Allegretto. Its initial theme, seemingly naïve, surprises at first. But patience! Robust and sturdy, it expands vigorously, and after undergoing many transformations during the development it comes to a conclusion. At this moment the motive given to the altos, sustained by two horns and the strings and escorted by oboes and bassoons, has a prodigiously comical strength. The little parade dawdles along with an irresistible buffoonery. And with what grace the flute tries to bring this jesting—unseemly for a keyboard concerto—to an end! It pecks the upper G in the conclusive phrase, giving a lesson in elegance and deportment to all in this little world of instruments, so crazily joyful. Is this the culminating point of the piece? One would be tempted to believe it. What could be said, though, about the inexhaustible treasures of invention that Mozart constantly lavishes on every page of the work?*

* ED. NOTE: Wanda Landowska played and recorded this concerto in London on the occasion of the coronation of King George VI in 1937. Referring to this recording, André Gide wrote in his *Journal,* July 13, 1940:

My heart is restored and reinvigorated after having heard on the radio a recording of Mozart's D Major Concerto admirably interpreted by Wanda Landowska. Strength and kindness, grace, wit, and tenderness—nothing is lacking in this work (which I recognize note by note) nor from the perfect playing of the pianist; one of my regrets will be that I did not hear her more often.

The first movement of the G Major Sonata (K. 283) is a minuet. The ascendancy of the dance over the musicians of the past was very great indeed. Almost all music at that time was a dance in disguise. It was the reign of triple meter, 3/4 as well as 3/8 or 6/8. This triple meter was already found in the Italian *corrente*; robust or light, it dominated the entire eighteenth century. Bach and Handel used it with prodigality and passion. With Mozart we see this triple meter become a *Ländler* and then a waltz. The glory of the pompous minuet was coming to an end. Mozart, however, wrote minuets, which were chivalrous, tender, or sentimental; they suggest a ball at court during the carnival. But in Salzburg as well as in Vienna, waltzes were danced to a minuet step. In this transformation we discover affinities with Schubert and even with some of Chopin's mazurkas.

The Andante of the G Major Sonata is of an extraordinary simplicity. The same year—Mozart was eighteen—he composed *La Finta Giardiniera*. There are many similarities between the Andante of the sonata and Sandrina's aria "Geme la Tortorella." In it Sandrina compares herself to a plaintive dove. The orchestra imitates the cooing of the dove. Speaking of this aria, commentators dwell on the Italian influences it shows. There is no doubt about that, but it is also clear that it is permeated with Handelian afflatus. Could it be that Mozart heard *Acis and Galatea* when he was in London as a child?

The third movement of the sonata is in 3/8, but this time it marks a new rhythm which has nothing of a minuet or of a waltz. It is a *ronde*, like one of those danced at the end of kermises. This type of 3/8 derives from the Neapolitan *forlana*. Inspiration of the same nature can be found in the chorus from *Don Giovanni*, "Giovinetta che fate all'amore."

On his way to Paris with his mother, Mozart, then twenty-one years old, stopped at Mannheim, the seat of the famous Mannheimer Schule. The significance of that school in the development of instrumental music was great. Thus it is not surprising that Mozart remained deeply impressed by his contact with the musicians and the music of that city. In a letter to his father, Mozart dwells on the disposition of the Mannheim orchestra and its power—all new to him. At Mannheim Mozart developed a friendship with Cannabich, a pupil of Stamitz, the almighty musician of Mannheim. Mozart was received into Cannabich's home, where he spent many days feasting, playing, and dancing. Cannabich admired him, and so did his daughter Rose. Who knows? She may even have fallen in love with him. In this atmosphere of new musical impressions and familial joys Mozart composed the Sonata in D Major (K. 311). A new era had begun for him, and he tried in this work to demonstrate the results of his recently acquired experiences. Was it to please Cannabich or his daughter that Mozart elaborated this sonata with so much care? In his letters he did not hide his ambition to win the esteem of Cannabich with the instrumental character of the sonata in keeping with the spirit of the Mannheimer School. The structural extent and the symphonic nature of the first movement are, in fact, remarkable. The profusion of crescendo and diminuendo signs are a testimony to the influence of the school of Mannheim.

In many editions of this sonata (including the revised edition by Nathan Broder*) the first chord is marked with an *arpeggiando* sign. The autograph indicates, however, an oblique bar between

---

* Ed. Note: In the preface to this revised edition (1960) Nathan Broder says, "Since the first edition was published, I have been able to procure, through the kindness of the late Mme Wanda Landowska, photostats of the autograph of the Sonata in D Major, K. 311. On the basis of these, a number of corrections have been made in that work in the present edition." Yet the oblique bars are still missing.

Mozart's autograph of the opening bars of the Sonata in D Major (K. 311)

the F sharp and the A in that chord and no vertical undulated line, usually representing the *arpeggiando*. This bar is an ornament used profusely by the Italian masters of the seventeenth and eighteenth centuries and is often found in Mozart's keyboard works. It is an *acciaccatura*, from *acciaccare*, meaning *to crush in*. This piquant ornament was the favorite of Scarlatti; the romantic school, and especially Hans von Bülow, did not understand its originality. This *acciaccatura* is a side-note—in this case the G between the F sharp and the A—and should be played, or rather crushed, with the rest of the chord, only to be released immediately. The chord itself may or may not be broken (*arpeggiando*). Similar *acciaccature* appear again in the chords three bars before the end of that movement.

Because of its symphonic character this Allegro reminds us of the overture to *The Marriage of Figaro*.

In listening to the second movement, Andante, one no longer wonders who inspired this exquisite page! It certainly was the young Rose Cannabich, about whom Mozart wrote with obvious feeling: "Cannabich's daughter who is fifteen (Mozart corrected it to thirteen later in the same letter), his eldest child, is a very pretty and charming girl. She is very intelligent and steady for her age. She is serious, does not say much, but when she does speak, she is pleasant and amiable. Yesterday she again gave me indescribable pleasure; she played the whole of my sonata excellently. The Andante, which must not be taken too quickly, she plays with the utmost expression. Moreover she likes playing it. I had already finished the Allegro, as you know, on the day after my arrival, and thus had only seen Mlle Cannabich once. Young Danner asked me how I thought of composing the Andante. I said that I would make it fit closely the character of Mlle Rosa. When I played it, it was an extraordinary success. Young Danner told me so afterwards. It really is a fact. She is exactly like the Andante." (Translation by Emily Anderson.)

Was it to the memory of Rosa that we owe *Das Veilchen* (the violet) composed eight years later? There is a strange resemblance between these two pieces. Both have an incomparable candor and purity.

The last two bars are representative of the music of Mozart's time. A modern pianist would try to cover up the left hand, finding it dry, poor, and even thin. But, on the contrary, it should not be blurred with pedal, because in this resides the sonorous esthetic of Mozart and of all the pianofortists.

The title of the third movement is in French in the autograph, *Rondeau*. It is in 6/8, a meter Mozart loved. He used it in his violin sonatas, his lieder, the finale of his concertos, and in his operas. He always remained faithful to this rhythm, which is a fusion of a *sicilienne* with the *Ländler*, or Viennese waltz. It would be difficult to identify it more precisely. The last movement of the E Flat Major Concerto (K. 482) is in the same rhythm, and the first movement of the A Major Violin Sonata (K. 305), composed a year later in Paris, seemed to be the continuation of the *Rondeau*. Another A major violin sonata (K. 526), composed nine years later in Vienna, marks the same rhythm. And we find it once more in the lieder *Komm, lieber Mai* (K. 596), written January 14, 1791. This tune became popular and is sung by every child around Salzburg. It has a lightness, a candor, and a carefree spirit which is very moving when one realizes that Mozart was poor, ill, and near death when he wrote it.

The *Rondeau* of the D Major Sonata is not a page of virtuosity. It must be played in the same spirit as *Komm, lieber Mai*, with the innocence suggested by its soft and irresistible rhythm.

Biographers of Mozart place the composition of the Sonata in A minor (K. 310) between March and June 1778. Two facts, however, demand our attention—the date of the death of Mozart's mother, on July 3 of that year, and the deeply tragic character of the sonata in which, for the first time, Mozart discloses a pathetic style. Is there not a direct relation between the character of the sonata and an event that could only have torn apart so loving and tender a heart? Personally I do not doubt it, even for a moment.

In the A Minor Sonata, Mozart is not the painter who consciously and masterfully evokes a scene of dramatic tension, as he did later in *Don Giovanni*, when the Commandore's ghost appears. The pathos of this sonata is entirely subjective. From its very beginning Mozart reveals his inner life, which, we feel, has been upset by a great sorrow. Of course this sorrow alone could not have produced a grandeur unknown until then in Mozart's keyboard works. The breadth, the vehemence of the Allegro—a

majestic *alla marcia*—the ineffable and profound expressivity of
the Andante, and the uninterrupted afflatus of the Finale, deva-
stated by an inner febrility, have a power that belies Mozart's age.

Wyzewa and Saint-Foix said that Mozart was not influenced
by Karl Philipp Emanuel Bach before he was twenty-six. Karl
Philipp Emanuel was then sixty-eight. But since they also recognized the undeniable and earlier influence of Haydn upon Mozart,
why not admit that Mozart may have been moved by Karl Philipp
Emanuel's revolutionary genius through Haydn? If we bring together this A Minor Sonata, the Fantasia in C Minor (K. 475),
and that in D Minor (K. 397), and a Concerto by Karl Philipp
Emanuel, it becomes clear that Mozart must have known and
loved this tormented and celestial music before he was twenty-six.
But rejecting instinctively all exaggerations, Mozart filtered his
impressions with self-assured artistry. Mozart's pathos has a solid
frame and well-defined outlines.

The dotted rhythm of the first theme of the sonata must be
sharply dotted, since it is derived in direct line from the rhythm
à la française. And if we think of Beethoven's funeral march in his
Sonata, Opus 26, he must have known Mozart's A Minor Sonata
very well.

The second subject of Mozart's A Minor Sonata, which is
in sixteenths, has been belittled. It is very beautiful, but it must
not be played with that superficial touch called *jeu perlé*. It requires a full touch; each note must sing. In this way it becomes
clear that an exaggeratedly fast tempo may mean death to a piece
of music.

The passionate Andante *cantabile con espressione* is a marvel. Here the influence of Johann Schobert can be detected,
especially in the repetition of a single note, a procedure found in
both Schobert and Mozart. Mozart knew Schobert, a harpsichordist and pianofortist who died very young, poisoned by mushrooms.

Spiritual encounters are most interesting—for instance that
of Bach and Telemann, a minor master from whom Bach extracted what he needed. Schobert lacked only a spark of genius.
But it was left to Mozart to perpetuate Schobert's repeated-notes
motives.

Mozart's Andante may be a minuet or a sarabande step. It
begins very serenely; but soon a storm arises, and with extreme
rapidity it bursts out and calms down. And all this in one page!

The Finale, with its short, halting breath, is a rare instance in Mozart's music. It was a procedure dear to Haydn (Sonata in E Minor) and also reminds us of Beethoven's Sonata in D Minor, Opus 31, No. 2.

The A Major Sonata (K. 331) was composed in the summer of 1778 during Mozart's sojourn in Paris. It differs entirely from all other sonatas. Instead of an allegro, it begins with a theme and variations. A minuet supplants the usual slow movement, and the finale is a rondo which Mozart called *alla turca*.

In composing this rondo, Mozart was merely following the very widespread craze of the day for everything exotic. Starting in France at the end of the sixteenth century and increasing all through the seventeenth and eighteenth centuries, it extended to everything bizarre or strange, but was centered especially on *Chinoiseries* and *Turqueries*. Musicians, poets, painters, dancers, *couturiers*, and craftsmen in every art were fascinated by the opulent and rare qualities of Chinese and Turkish taste. Painters were allured by its colors and musicians by its tone shadings and rhythmic designs. The vogue of *Turqueries* and *Chinoiseries* on the stage of the official theaters and at the fairs was extraordinary. Muphti, master of the Turkish ceremony in Molière's *Bourgeois Gentilhomme*, played and danced by Lully himself at the first performance; Rameau's *Turc Généreux* in the first *Entrée* of *Les Indes Galantes*; *Les Chinois* of Couperin, as well as the *Sultanes, Pachas,* and *Osmins*—all this multicolored world sang, danced, and had an uproarious time. In composing the *Rondo alla Turca*, and later the *Janissaries* of *The Abduction from the Seraglio*, Mozart was not inspired solely by *The Mecca Pilgrims* of Gluck, as we are told. One can take it for granted that Mozart was familiar with the very long tradition of Turkish buffoonery. It is to be noted that exoticism frequently aroused the satiric, comic, or bantering vein in the artists of the period. Mozart proved it eloquently in his *Rondo alla Turca*, which is truly a Janissary orchestra in miniature. That is why, in this instance, the harpsichord, better than the modern piano, evokes the piercing cry of the piccolo flute, the truculence of the kettledrums, cymbals, triangles, and crescents. Let us not forget that the pianofortes of the eighteenth century had numerous stops producing the sounds of bells, drums, and kettledrums, forming an ensemble known as *Musique Turque.*

The autograph of the Rondo in D Major (K. 485) composed January 10, 1786, in Vienna, has passed through many hands after having belonged to Franz Niemetschek, the son of Mozart's biographer.

The form of this Rondo makes us think of a movement of a sonata with reprise, development, and coda. Perfection and balance give this piece a place by itself. And what surprises it holds for us! In the last movement of the Quartet in G Minor (K. 476) a theme in D major appears and disappears like a flash. It is playful and tender; Mozart did not forget it, and three months later took it up again to build upon it the Rondo in D Major. It is of little importance that this theme is not really Mozart's, but Johann Christian Bach's, the eleventh and youngest son of Johann Sebastian. Plagiarism? Irreverence? No! On the contrary, it is an homage to an admired master. In the first movement of Johann Christian's Quintet, Opus XI, No. 6, the pastoral and joyful oboe plays the theme. After having stated and extended Johann Christian's motive, Mozart followed it, in the Rondo, by an exquisite figure, light and vivacious, which he used again twenty months later. This time it is played by the first violin in the Allegro of the *Kleine Nachtmusik* (35th measure). We are glad to meet on various occasions themes and motives that become familiar and dear to us; and also we are able to understand better the instrumental character of the Rondo. It evokes the smooth strings, the swift and gentle flute or oboe, and the bassoon with its roguish smile. Scales rush along exuberantly. After the adventures of the development, and after many modulations, Mozart reaches the dominant, where he leaves the interpreter free to improvise a short cadenza, very short because one must not exceed the limits of the piece.

And here comes our theme again, slightly ornamented according to the fashion of the time. A brilliant passage runs from one end of the keyboard to the other and merges with a small tutti which, after a lull, suddenly stops on a deceptive cadence. But this time, Mozart decides irrevocably to come to an end, and he says farewell with a tiny coda, so graceful in its innocent simplicity.

The eminent Mozart authority, Georges de Saint-Foix, was right when he pointed out that the Minuet in D Major (K. 594 a) had been classified too early by Köchel in his catalogue, where it bore at first the number 355 (this has been rectified in later editions). The harmonic boldness and the conciseness of its form place this composition at the time of Mozart's full maturity. The instrumental character of the minuet is evident above all in the exquisite ritournelle, which suggests a violin *col arco, dolcissimo,* accompanied by strings *pizzicato piano.*

The Sonata in D Major (K. 576), the last of Mozart's keyboard sonatas, was composed in Vienna in July 1789 and was dedicated to the Princess Frederike von Preussen. The first movement begins with a hunt motive in the rhythm of a gigue. This, at once determines the tempo of the piece. The Adagio moves along with the grace of a slow minuet, disclosing an enchanting bel canto in the best Italian style. The concluding movement is an allegretto in the same spirit as the Finale of the Coronation Concerto. It is solid, precise, and full of humor. Consequently, it should not be hurried.

The direct influence of Karl Philipp Emanuel Bach on Mozart is often mentioned, especially regarding the Fantasias. I confess that these affinities appear to me hardly perceptible. That Mozart felt a desire to know the works of Karl Philipp Emanuel and that he admired them is not surprising. But one may say that the more Mozart studied the works of Karl Philipp Emanuel, the more he asserted his own personality and the more he remained himself. Some elements in Mozart's Fantasias are evidently analogous to those employed by Karl Philipp Emanuel. There are, for instance, the arpeggios, the passages, the chromaticism, the broken cadences, and the abundance of certain ornaments such as the slow appoggiaturas, a favorite of Karl Philipp Emanuel. But Mozart's nature is too lucid to abandon itself to vague improvisations. Therefore his fantasias have the logic and solid structure of a sonata movement. God knows that Mozart perceived the invisible, the intangible and that he knew how to translate them into a musical language that was transparent and light. One feeling, though, remained foreign to his nature —the rhapsodical.

In the structure of the C Minor Fantasia (K. 475) there are, of course, some reminiscences of Karl Philipp Emanuel's fantasias, although Karl Philipp Emanuel's unfold according to a completely different plan. Here, in Mozart's C Minor Fantasia, the frame is solid and logical in spite of the title and of the improvisatory elements introduced by the composer. That Mozart recalls at the end the initial motive gives to this work a perfect unity; for the interpreter it is a precise indication as to how he should coordinate the various tempi which succeed one another in the course of the piece.

The C Minor Fantasia was published during Mozart's lifetime as a preamble to the C Minor Sonata (K. 457). This in no way proves that the two works are inseparable.

Each year Mozart had to deliver a certain number of varied dances for the Redoute ball. He was not well rewarded for his work, and after signing the receipt for his meager fee, he added, "Too much for what I delivered; too little for what I could give."

In 1791, in Vienna, Mozart composed six *Ländlerische Tänze* (K. 606) for two violins and bass. I have transcribed them for piano, as I have done for those of J. F. C. Lanner.

J. F. C. Lanner

Lanner was born in Vienna, where he also died. Renovator of the German dance and creator of the Viennese waltz, he was self-taught. While still an adolescent, he formed a small orchestra, the same one in which the elder Johann Strauss later served his apprenticeship. A captivating violinist and a wild conductor, Lanner composed *Ländlers* and waltzes of incomparable verve and grace. We can visualize him at the head of his joyous band, going from one suburban café to another with his Tyrolian yodelers, entrancing the Viennese, who loved to dance all night long. This vision brings to mind the remembrance of an old engraving which hangs in the library of the Friends of Music in Vienna. It has for a title "Ball at Atzenbruug" and shows Schubert in the country, surrounded by friends, dancing and singing to the strains of a violin. It is not surprising to find echoes of Lanner in the *Ländlers* of Schubert. He knew this music well; he danced more than once to the soft, irresistible rhythm of the Lanner waltzes. Both the singer of grief as well as the bewitching violinist drew their inspiration from the same fresh and inexhaustible source of popular music. The theme of one of Lanner's waltzes has been used by Stravinsky in the first scene of *Petrouchka.**

Joseph Haydn

Whereas Haydn's cello concerto had long been part of every cellist's repertoire, his keyboard concertos had fallen into oblivion by the beginning of this century. His keyboard sonatas possess such unbelievable wealth of invention that I could hardly wait to find out what he had done in the field of the concerto. Consequently I started forthwith on a quest for material. But I could not find any autograph. Finally I came upon separate parts of the D Major Concerto (Hoboken, Gruppe XVIII, No. 11) in an eighteenth-century manuscript copy and in an edition contemporary with Haydn, that of Artaria. From them I reconstituted the full score and gave the first performance of the D Major Concerto in Paris.† Since then I have played it all over the world. In every instance, it has met with the most enthusiastic and spontaneous response. No wonder that publishers have been eager to print such a sure-fire work! (The first modern edition appeared in 1931.)

---

* ED. NOTE: Besides Mozart's *Country Dances*, published by Carl Fischer in 1945, and the *Valses Viennoises* of Lanner, published by G. Schirmer in 1926, Wanda Landowska also transcribed a chain of Schubert waltzes, which were published in 1911 by Breitkopf and Härtel in Leipzig and by A. Gutheil in Paris.
† ED. NOTE: It must have been in 1924. Wanda Landowska gave the first American performance in New York with W. Mengelberg on March 31, 1925.

Very concise and sparkling, this concerto contains within itself all the characteristics of Haydn's genius. The Larghetto is a marvel of suavity and gentleness, and at certain moments in its development we cannot help thinking of Beethoven.

Here are the last lines Wanda Landowska ever wrote. They are dated July, 1959, a month before her death. They accompany an album of Haydn's keyboard works that she had recorded a few months earlier.

As a girl of twelve or thirteen, I was given Haydn's Variations in F Minor (Hoboken, Gruppe XVII, No. 6) to study—on the piano, of course. I played them, loved them, and I have never ceased to find delight in Haydn's music.

When early this year I finally decided to record these same Variations, along with some of Haydn's sonatas, I had failed to recall that 1959 would mark the hundred and fiftieth anniversary of the composer's death. But reminiscing, I became aware of something quite amazing and, to say the least, unusual. For the third time in my life I have the privilege of participating in celebrations of Haydn's anniversaries.

Fifty years ago, in 1909, in Vienna a festival was held to commemorate the hundredth anniversary of Haydn's death. Musicians and scholars came from all over the world; it was a great event. I was invited to participate in the festivities and to play at some of the concerts.

Then in 1932, the two hundredth anniversary of Haydn's birth, commemorations were held in many cities. I took part in several of them, playing the D Major Concerto with orchestra as well as sonatas on the piano and on the harpsichord.

And now, in 1959, thanks to these recordings, I once more have the joy of paying homage to Haydn.

Today, a century and a half after his death, I am wondering

if we give Haydn the place of honor he deserves and if we really understand his music. How often we still hear people exclaim with some pity and disdain, "Good old Papa Haydn!" as if to say, "Very nice music, but so childish, so old-fashioned, so poor!" But why? Haydn, all fire, whose creative powers were inexhaustible; Haydn, who, seated at his harpsichord or pianoforte, composed marvels; Haydn, who knew how to arouse passions and transport the soul—why consider his music old-fashioned and poor? It has happened probably because it has been unjustly overlooked and scorned instead of being studied and profoundly grasped. How much better would we understand Beethoven if we knew thoroughly the symphonies and sonatas of Haydn! The joyous exuberance of his allegros, the sparkling liveliness of his prestissimos, the *amoroso* of his andantes are incomparable. The works of Haydn are great not because they are steppingstones to Beethoven, but because they contain their own resources of inspiration and originality which mark them as masterpieces.

I believe that today Edward Dent, the famous English musicologist, could be more optimistic than he was in 1932, when he wrote: "In all my experience of concert going, I cannot remember ever having heard a sonata by Haydn, except on one occasion when, if I remember aright, the Sonata in E Minor was played by Wanda Landowska. And I suspect that it was in 1909, the centenary of Haydn's death." (I once had the joy of playing this sonata for Debussy.)

During my concert tours, I often happened to be in Vienna, where I had the opportunity to visit the Museum der Gesellschaft der Musikfreunde and the Haydn Museum. There I saw Haydn's harpsichord made by Shudi and Broadwood and his pianoforte. Touching relics and to us proof, if need be, that Haydn played both instruments, just as Mozart did. Within the span of his long life Haydn—even more so than Mozart—witnessed the tremendous transition in esthetics that was then taking place.

Haydn's keyboard works of the first period bear very few signs of interpretation. Later we encounter such indication as crescendo, and in the E Minor Sonata (Hoboken, Gruppe XVI, No. 34) Haydn demands for the first time a *mezzavoce* and a *perdandosi*, refinements of touch that could be obtained on his favorite pianoforte made by Schanz, the famous instrument maker.

We do not know, except in a few instances, on which instrument specifically Haydn meant each of his sonatas to be played since almost all of the contemporary editions bear in the title "for harpsichord or pianoforte."

Some of these sonatas can actually be played on either instrument, as we know that the pianoforte of Haydn's time, with its crystalline and diaphanous sonorities, bore a closer resemblance to the harpsichord than does the modern piano. (See p. 136)

Chronology, of course, gives a clue as to the intended instrument. Haydn is supposed to have said that after 1790 he had "completely lost the habit of playing the harpsichord." But in deciding to play certain sonatas on the harpsichord and others on the piano, I have been influenced not merely by their known dates of composition, but rather, by their character and specific keyboard writing.

For instance, the first and third movements of the Sonatas in D Major (Hoboken, Gruppe XVI, No. 37) and C Major (Hoboken, Gruppe XVI, No. 35), both composed before 1780, are very instrumental; and it is on the harpsichord, with its varied registers and colors, that their sparkling and glittering qualities are best revealed.

As for the Sonata in G Major (Hoboken, Gruppe XVI, No. 40) of 1784, its first movement is of a pastoral mood. The flutelike four-foot register and soft drone of the upper keyboard of the harpsichord enhance this atmosphere.

About the E Flat Major Sonata (Hoboken, Gruppe XVI, No. 49), written in 1789 or 1790, we have an exchange of letters between Haydn and Marianne von Genzinger in which the pianoforte is mentioned exclusively. But had we not had these documents, the purely vocal character of the admirable second movement of this sonata would have been sufficient indication that Haydn wrote it for the pianoforte.

The Andante and Variations in F Minor, composed in 1793, shows unmistakable evidence of new keyboard writing effects. This is why I play those works on the piano, as well as the E Minor Sonata, although that one was composed before 1778. I feel it is on this instrument that they are revealed in their true light.

PART THREE

Foreword to Part Three

Wɪᴛʜ the exception of "Why Does Modern Music Lack Melody?" and some of the thoughts on musicology written in 1913 and 1923, respectively, none of the material presented in this third part has ever been published before. It has been culled from among Landowska's numerous notebooks.

Parts of the texts included herein were written in the 1930's, the heyday of St.Leu. Most of the others date from the late '40's and early '50's, after Landowska had found a new home in Lakeville, Connecticut.

In these notes Wanda Landowska poured out her deepest thoughts and her most intimate reflections on the various aspects of the art of interpretation. She expressed them with total candor and the wisdom of a lifetime of experience. Such was the logic of her convictions that more than once a sentence left unfinished in 1934, for instance, could be completed perfectly by another written twenty years later.

Save for bringing together in the best possible order the notes connected with a particular subject, we have not attempted to complete sentences or supply any tie-in phrases. A few explanatory remarks, clearly set apart from Landowska's own text, are, however, added.

Here, even more so than in previous writings, Wanda Landowska seems to be addressing imaginary interlocutors, or rather ideal beings, spiritually akin to her. In translating we have tried to preserve this conversational tone for its direct impact on the reader, who thus may feel that he is being spoken to in complete confidence by Landowska herself.

1 ᐰ Thoughts on Modern Music

WHAT interests me passionately is to listen to everything, to the most diverse and contradictory music. I do this in order to discern the particular language of an epoch and the style of each one of the composers who have been leaders of a school. I have lived long enough with the sole desire of listening only to what I love. If I wish now to listen to everything, it is not that I love everything, but because I must see with absolute clarity not only the obvious differences, but the most subtle nuances as well, between languages and styles. In order to make deductions one must see clearly.

Why Does Modern Music Lack Melody?

On the first page of a notebook containing the complete manuscript of the following essay, her first on modern music, Wanda Landowska wrote, "On the way from Tiflis to Moscow, February 9, 1913, Shrove Tuesday!"

During my long travels through these lovely countries, I have swallowed a whole trunkful of newspapers and musical periodicals. And do you know what subject impassions everybody today? It is *Melody*, beautiful "Me-elod-e-e"!

That is good. We are going to hear once more about this plump and charming person. One always returns to one's first love. Not only journalists, critics, and old-fashioned musicians speak about her, but Vincent d'Indy himself bestows upon her a supreme consecration. "Melody alone never grows old," he says; and this brief and lapidary sentence is repeated again and again.

Somebody unearthed a saying of Haydn which delights the champions of melody, "Melody is the main thing; harmony is useful only to charm the ear." Probably "good old Papa Haydn," with his pockets always full of sweetmeats, did not foresee that the day would come when musicians would lean upon his philosophical dogma with such confidence!

If melody is the main thing, then how shall we classify such works as *The Chromatic Fantasy*, most of the Toccatas, and certain preludes from *The Well-Tempered Clavier* of Bach which are so devoid of melody that the first prelude, for instance, excited Gounod's pity? I could enumerate hundreds of other admirable works—and not only Bach's—lacking in what one calls melody or in which this element plays only a secondary part. But is it necessary to multiply the examples? The few compositions mentioned above are worth most of the melodic beauties of Haydn. And let nobody accuse me of irreverence toward the composer of *The Creation*. I have devoted a fair portion of my life to the study of his works, and I shall continue to do so of my own volition.

Why does our modern music lack melody? Do you care to

guess? The answer is simple: because it is modern. Modern music never was melodic. In the seventeenth century the French accused Italian music of wanting melody. A century later the Italians and their supporters, the Encyclopedists, reproached the French for depriving learned music of melody. Next it was Gluck's turn to replace beautiful airs by clamors of despair and convulsive groans without calling on the charms of melody. And what shall we say about Bach, whose own sons eagerly went to seek the secret of beautiful melody from Padre Martini? Beethoven and even Chopin were similarly accused. And then came Wagner, that monster who killed melody for all time!

Obviously the good lady has a tough constitution. The more attempts made against her, the more she blooms with health and rotundity. It is interesting to note that all those accused of being her murderers are becoming, in turn, her benefactors and her saviors. In the seventeenth century Italy could claim that it had freed melody from the polyphonic bonds which gripped it too tightly. Lully is supposed to have saved us from the dragging and lugubrious singing style of the ancients; Rameau, to have freed us from the plain song that had been psalmodized for a century. The Italians of the eighteenth century released us from the dryness of Rameau with the delicacy and tenderness of their vocal art. The romanticists liberated us from the lightness of the Italians and the French as well as from the contrapuntal cuirass which armored the music of Bach.

What is melody? Recently Jean Huré gave an excellent definition. He said, in substance, that melody is a succession of notes forming a precise design which stands out against a background of harmony. Very well. But what stands out for Jean Huré will not stand out for a mediocre musician and will totally elude the layman. Take, for instance, Caucasian, Persian, Georgian, or Armenian music, in the midst of which I now am. I discover in it treasures of melodic beauty. Now read the accounts of travelers and observe that wherever exotic music is mentioned, you will run across the same phrases, "strange sonorities," "monotony," "lack of melody." Yet all such music must be melodious, since the natives of these places sing it with no less tenderness and fervor than we do our own. Only, the melodic curves and the ornaments of their songs are not familiar to European ears. And this has always been so with new music. When ears are not yet accustomed to modern combinations and when vocal chords are not used to reproducing them, people raise scandalized outcries about the disappearance of melody. Certain wines sweeten with time. Probably an accumulation of years makes music sing; it melodizes it, so to speak. Some music becomes so melodious in the process that it grows sickening! Melodious music is the music of yesterday. The music of today is not yet so, but will be later; that is why we call it the music of tomorrow. That of the day before yesterday is either too melodious or is no longer so at all.

Melody, it is said, is that which speaks most directly to the heart and to the mind. Quite true. The longest lasting melodies have been those accompanied by words and situations which have stamped them with a definitive significance. They form a highly conventionalized musical language bound to a specific era and to a certain cultural level.

All this reminds me of what Nietzsche said of a painter: "Look at this artist, he paints only what he thoroughly likes. And do you know what he likes so much? Only what he knows how to paint, what he has learned to paint."

Melody is what touches us most. And do you know what kind of melody touches us most? That which our ears can most easily grasp and that which our throat or fingers have learned to reproduce.

The melomaniac does not wish to content himself with a general impression of an opera or of a symphonic work. That is too vague, too tenuous for him. He needs more palpable memories; he needs melody—that is to say, some bits of song which he will hear droning in his ears all night and which he can hum the following days at his office, at the table, and in his bedroom, to the despair of his wife and others about him.

For the musician melody is a broader concept, but so indeterminate that after a long discussion he never fails to add, "It goes without saying that all I have said concerned only *beautiful* melody."

Then, what is beautiful melody? That which is beautiful for one person is not so for another. Berlioz was insensitive to the melodic beauties of Bach. Chopin, a lover of the songs of Poland, remained deaf to the folk music of Spain. But why go back so far? Submit a Massenet aria to Saint-Säens, Vincent d'Indy, or

Debussy; I doubt very much that their decision would be unanimous. And what would it be if various races, countries, or epochs were concerned?

Melody, beautiful melody, is a very vague concept, meaning very little. For this reason probably so much is being said about it and so much ink has been spilled; even I cannot resist adding a few more drops.

I am afraid I have attacked an age-old subject much too complicated for my poor brain. I should be terribly sorry if I were misunderstood. It was not my intention to pose as a pioneer of modern music, which already includes masterpieces that champion it far better than I can. I do not believe in the least that something new must be created at any price. I know conservatives of genius, and I also know ridiculous revolutionaries. It is much easier to smash all molds than to have a grain of talent. Beethoven, Mozart, Haydn changed relatively little. Bach was rather reactionary. Wagner owes his greatness to the immensity of his genius and not to his innovations.

Someone once said, "I like to stay at home among the objects that have accompanied me all my life; and if some of this bric-a-brac shocks you by its banality, you would look at it differently if you knew how many dear memories are attached to it." But these are very respectable feelings!

Another person cannot remain for long in the same place; he needs new impressions, new sensations. That also is a very respectable feeling. Evidently those two persons could not get along.

The traditionalist deplores the massacre of melody, the sour taste of new harmonies, and covers his face in horror, like an old man who sees young folks cracking nuts with their teeth. "When you were young, didn't you do the same thing?" With pride he replies, "Yes, but I am sorry I did." We too shall do likewise, because we shall wish for a real old age including all the feelings that go with it—wisdom and, for want of anything better, belated regrets. We want a real old age after a real youth.

Do not mention healthy art and healthy melody! The most easily digested food is not always the most palatable, and the most delectable kind loses its tang once it becomes familiar.

In the second half of the eighteenth century the *Bergères*

Légères ended up by weighing as heavily as Wagnerian mythology does today. And see with what pleasure we revert now to the shepherdings of the past! Suffocating in the heavy atmosphere of overworked romanticism, some of us strive to refresh our souls in our magnificent past; others do so in novel harmonies.

Modern music does not seem melodious to you? Well, it will become so. Just have a little patience; it is merely a question of time. "Yes, but this melody will never be the same," I am told. So much the better! We have had an entire century of broad and stout, thick and violent, burning and sticky melodies. If modern melody is short of breath, a little asthmatic, and is not meant for powerful lungs, again, so much the better!

To be sure, there is nothing like the sight of a great big curly cabbage, a superb Milanese cabbage in full bloom. But let us also plant here and there some more delicate flowers. Our garden is big enough, isn't it?

At Random from Saint-Saëns to Poulenc

In July, 1914, having returned to Paris for a brief stay, Wanda Landowska wrote:

I am happy that I made Saint-Saëns like the Chaconne of Louis Couperin. I observed him while I was playing. He was obviously thrilled by several passages of this piece. Until the last minute I doubted that he would respond to this Chaconne, because he has a sharp, clear, and logical mind; he does not like exaggeration. And Couperin's sensibility is overrefined. His inspiration often changes moods, and in pieces of grayish melancholy there is suddenly an unexpected revolt, a raging impatience. It is like a fire smothered with ashes; at first it is pink-gray; and all at once, it becomes bloody with upsurging flames.

Much later Landowska wrote:

Saint-Saëns is recognized as a master of form. Yes, the form is there, bright, like latticework. But there is nothing in it!

Reviewing Emile Vuillermoz's book The Music of Today *in 1923, Landowska said of Debussy's music:*

Silver threads subtly interwoven by inspired weavers encircle this secret, precious, and refined garden. All there is order and voluptuousness. As Rameau said, "Art is hidden by art itself."

About belief in novelty and originality, Landowska wrote in the same review:

In this obstinate race after the original—while avoiding thoroughly that which has already been said and taking refuge on an island that we thought was uninhabited—do we not risk running into a good old acquaintance who has just been dropped? If only we would gallop joyously, this chase would turn into a cheerful game, a light and foolish gambol; it would be fine. But there is nothing funny about these grasping, anxious ferreters with their preoccupied faces and greedy hands. The gracious human beast seems to lose its good humor every time it sets out to practice an art. It becomes grumpy. Is it necessary to hate music to make it? Is it really indispensable to believe with such seriousness that every little change will, at last, bring the definitive salvation? If it gives us a thrill, it is already delightful enough; and if this thrill reminds us of the dear caresses of old, it is all for the best!

Landowska added her comments on this thought of Vuillermoz about jazz:

"Jazz is not a game of chance. Its sonorous disorder is only an appearance. It is an organized force obeying obscure laws, conforming to a secret technique, codified or not, and we discover that no one can become a virtuoso on the spur of the moment in this orchestra of 'noisemakers.' Evidently, as our European ears have been impoverished by a good education, dazed by the square and symmetrical cutting of the melodic phrase, by the eternal regimen of refrains with their sharp angles, and by their rigorously balanced periods, our ears heard only, in this form of orchestration, the triumph of disorder, the glorification of tin-kettle music, and the apotheosis of racket."

Incapable of discernment, we perceive only a shapeless, inextricable mass of sounds disdainfully qualified as monotonous noises. Jazz is inextricable for you, poor ears too well-bred! To understand it listen rather to Vuillermoz's refined analysis: "Squareness, geometrical plans, and right angles have disappeared. The melody is continuously reborn from itself; its periods are interlocked. Syncopation, like a strong and autogenous welding, hides the junctions, suppresses the reliefs. There are no more symmetrical falls, no more musical rhymes. Melodic prosody has discovered the free verse which undulates ad infinitum, eternal, and always similar. No more breathing, no more stops. Syncopation is here to raise the melodic line when it feels its energy weakening. If motion would stop, the "charm" would be broken. One must ceaselessly spring anew on this elastic trampolin which allows jumping over strong beats and bar-lines. We know that the constraint of the metrical bar is becoming more and more painful to modern composers. All that tends to liberate musical discourse of its formulatory bondage and of its symmetrical cross-ruling makes them quiver with hope."

These profound thoughts carry me back to the music of sixteenth-century French lutenists, to the preludes of Gaulthier Le Vieux and of Louis Couperin. Written without bar-lines, they had to be played without observing any measure. In this music, unexpected voices arise, only to disappear mysteriously; they are born out of caprice, contrary to logic and the security of safe combinations of contrapuntal writing. In turn, does not the style of these lutenists—spirited, evanescent, rich in harmonic inventions, although usually reduced to two voices— draw us close to Ravel's Sonata for Violin and Cello? Ravel's tour de force in this two-part writing consists in keeping his harmonic system in all its complexity and refinement. As incredible as it may seem, this Sonata is in principle written harmonically. The problem is resolved by the acrobatic mobility of the two parts. They find the means of being everywhere at once, thanks to a serpentine agility and suppleness. They graze quickly and with precision the essential nerve centers of a chord at all levels of the sonorous ladder.

Oh, how exquisite is this oscillation between that which has been and that which is! It seems that the one augments and completes the beauty of the other while infusing us with a more experienced comprehension, a more indulgent love; it immerses us in the plenitude of endless bliss.

May I be forgiven for always coming back to my ancient music? But all that precedes makes me think that those well-bred ears closed to the marvels blossoming forth from our adolescents are no less shut to the new beauty of former times. For them the only beautiful music is that of yesterday. Today's has no beauty yet; it will acquire some later, and this is why we call it the music of tomorrow, while that of the day before yesterday has beauty no longer. Ancient music is forgotten and with it the way to handle it.

TCHAIKOVSKY AND COUPERIN

It is undeniable that certain phrases of Couperin's Passacaille have a striking resemblance to the *Pathétique* of Tchaikovsky, the key of B minor included. But resemblance does not mean affinity. What is it that makes these two works belong to different families?

In Couperin's work there is an immutable and restricted frame—the refrain and couplets—which does not disturb him. He moves in it with ease, as did the actresses and dancers of the past, even though they were tightly laced in their corsets. Within this frame Couperin is able to express himself freely with accents of despair and tragic chords.

Tchaikovsky would have broken this frame, not through the strength of his despair, but because of his inability to express himself within such self-imposed limitations. And it is precisely Couperin's proud and dignified reserve which moves us most. He does not dwell on his suffering. We divine all that his French modesty prevented him from saying. As for Tchaikovsky, he cries louder than any suffering could justify.

TCHAIKOVSKY AND DVOŘÁK

The typically Russian interval saves Tchaikovsky by conferring something wild on his music. But this delightful little shock loses its power. One gets used to it, and it has no more effect. Yet in listening to *The New World Symphony* of Dvořák, one misses it. Then one understands how flavorful it was.

The pathos of Dvořák is old-fashioned. That of Tchaikovsky has a military impetus. It is even one of its attractions. Tchaikovsky felt the beauty and power of military music.

As for Dvořák, one has the feeling that his music has much of Tchaikovsky without the spaciousness and desolation of the Russian steppes.

ON PROKOFIEV AND SCRIABIN

I listened on the radio to Prokofiev playing his *Suggestions Diaboliques*, Opus 4. It is ridiculously silly. This, as well as the *Poème Satanique*, Opus 36, by Scriabin, irritates and tires me. In a piece by Couperin just a few bars long, like *La Ténébreuse* or *La Mézangère*, there is more despair and pathos than in the threats of a Prokofiev or a Scriabin. Notice the brevity of these seventeenth-century pieces and the good sense of their composers, who avoided trying our patience.

STRAVINSKY

Tchaikovsky would not have cared for Stravinsky, who at first despised him and later loved him, to the amazement of the snobbish faddists who stood there, knowing no longer which way to turn.

Once, during lunch at Misia Sert's, I remember hearing Stravinsky speak disparagingly of Handel. Today he loves him.

I do not reproach Stravinsky for his change in taste. But why the haste in criticizing before knowing and understanding? It is true that because of his habit of merely sketching his music Handel left himself open to criticism. But an interpreter of the time knew that the "holes" had to be filled in and that, at places, certain ornaments were needed.

I just heard (*title missing*) by Stravinsky. All I understood was the square symmetry of the phrases and the infatuation with progressions. After all, it is not worth the effort, taking such a conquering attitude, insisting on certain dissonances, and ending with a bunch of chords in which a C and a B crush each other as they did in the good old time of *acciaccaturas!*

After Stravinsky I heard without transition a Haydn symphony. With its appearance of naïveté and helplessness it is still quite strong. It can face Igor without being intimidated.

This sudden passage from one work to the other gave me a feeling comparable to that of passing from an air-conditioned room to the normal temperature of the street.

In Stravinsky's *Nightingale* I feel that it was the exotic imagery only slightly suggested by Andersen that prompted Stravinsky to display such oriental sumptuosity in his fabulous orchestration. I say "only slightly suggested" by Andersen because Chinese or Japanese art and customs were really "Chinese" to him. In his *Nightingale*, the inspired poet that Andersen was sings a popular song of an irresistible purity and tenderness. I search in vain for tender accents in Stravinsky's *Nightingale*; but I am dazzled by an orchestration of such refined luxuriance, although any exotic subject would have inspired it just as well. I miss the naïve, shy, and tender nightingale in Stravinsky's work as I also miss Andersen's exquisite humor, fresh as spring water. After all, it is my fault if I am deceived. I love Andersen too much, and I know his *Nightingale* too well. While listening to Stravinsky's, I think of Andersen; and I realize the abyss that separates these two men.

The sumptuosity of Stravinsky dazzles me indeed, but it rarely gives me happiness.

Who is the real Stravinsky? He who wrote *Petrouchka* and *The Rite of Spring* or he who composed *The Rake's Progress?*

AFTER HEARING A SYMPHONY BY SHOSTAKOVICH

This music is of undeniable vulgarity. Therefore it is impossible for me to like it, even less to judge it.

Shostakovich certainly has the sense of rhythm. But why these unsuccessful attempts at being grotesque, at humor?

The frame is apparent and rough; it is like the wood used for crating furniture. There is no mystery in this music, but at least it is honest, and I prefer that to mystificators with empty bellies.

GERSHWIN

The music of Gershwin is always a delight. His natural, inherent richness, his ceaselessly renewed fantasy happily springing forth—all this gratifies and enchants me. With him I never have the impression of the newly rich showing off with arrogance and conceit. I feel neither the process of manufacturing nor that of orchestral ostentation, which tires me in other composers of today and makes me long for a Purcell chaconne, composed for strings and just a few woods, and for the bareness, the strict minimum of an orchestral ensemble of the seventeenth century.

MANUEL DE FALLA

Manuel de Falla was the first modern composer to write for the harpsichord. About this Landowska said:

In 1922 I spent several days in Granada with my friend Manuel de Falla. He was then working on his *Retablo de Maese Pedro*. Being on a concert tour in Spain, I had my harpsichord with me; and I was able to play for him a great deal and to tell him about the various possibilities of the instrument. He became increasingly interested. On November 26, 1922, he wrote from Granada, "Our conversation of yesterday, after reading the *Retablo* and all your precious indications on the use of the harpsichord, have awakened in me a multitude of ideas and of projects to realize." He grew so enthusiastic that he not only wrote a harpsichord part in the *Retablo*, but resolved to write a concerto for harpsichord and several instruments. It took him three years to complete it. When one becomes acquainted with this music, one understands that such a deep work had to come to life little by little.

Wanda Landowska played the harpsichord part of the Retablo *at its première, June 25, 1923, at the home of Princess Edmond de Polignac, to whom the work was dedicated. As for the Concerto for Harpsichord, Flute, Oboe, Clarinet, Violin, and Violoncello, it is dedicated to Wanda Landowska, who gave the first performance in Barcelona, November 5, 1926, with de Falla conducting. She played it subsequently in several cities, notably in Boston and in New York, under the direction of Koussevitsky, and in Philadelphia with Stokowski conducting.*

In his Entretiens *with Claude Rostand, Paris, 1954, Francis Poulenc said, "It was at the Princess Edmond de Polignac's that I met Wanda Landowska. She was playing the harpsichord in Falla's* Retablo. *It was the first time that the harpsichord had entered a modern orchestra. I was fascinated by the work and by Wanda. 'Write a concerto for me,' she said. I promised her to try. My encounter with Landowska was a capital event in my career. I have for her as much artistic respect as human tenderness. I am proud of her friendship, and I shall never be able to say how much I owe her. It was she who gave me the key to the harpsichord works of Bach. It was she who taught me all I know about our French harpsichordists. What is so prodigious about Landowska is that she makes the music of the past actual and alive."*

Francis Poulenc composed for Wanda Landowska his Concert Champêtre *for harpsichord and large orchestra. She gave the first performance, May 3, 1929, in Paris, with Pierre Monteux conducting and played it many times afterward in many countries.*

Of the role of the harpsichord in a modern work she said:

The harpsichord, the basis of the orchestra in the seventeenth and eighteenth centuries, "this column which supported the whole ensemble and whose harmonious warbling had an infinitely beautiful effect on the choir" appears today in a modern work. Without trying to imitate the effects or procedure of older composers, the king of instruments, resuscitated, will lend an attentive and benevolent ear to the nostalgic searching of modern composers, granting them the unexplored wealth of its sonorous possibilities. It will set ablaze the whole ensemble with its rhythmical flashes; it will pour out the flamboyant rustling of its radiant timbres. With its volatile double keyboards, now a mysterious organ, now a hyperbolic guitar, it will stir by its sharpness and enrapture the somewhat blasé body of the orchestra. Surrounding it with its quivering and scintillating sonorous web, and its slender although firm rays, the harpsichord will allow imagery and that which is whimsical or unexpected to escape from its swishing meshes.

In one of the notebooks of 1952, Landowska confided:

I wonder what modern music can bring me. Will it be a refuge, a diversion, joy, or consolation? I wonder. . . .

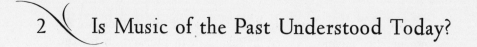

2   Is Music of the Past Understood Today?

About Music of the Past and Us

Since the beginning of the renaissance of the music of the past, little progress has been made in the knowledge of the inner meaning of this music. True, the harpsichord has become popular, and societies and baroque ensembles have multiplied. Yet real contact with the music itself has not been well established.

As it is presented today by many performers, music of the past is like frozen meat. Many of the reconstitutions seem to be made of stucco, like the buildings of world fairs meant to be destroyed after use; or they have only a front without a base or depth; one sees the papier-mâché framework and the trembling canvas.

Masterpieces are defenseless against their "executors," not to mention their transcribers.

349

Musical forms with which we have lost contact, those we do not practice anymore except in school or in preparation for the *Prix de Rome*, these forms, because of their remoteness, have ceased to provoke immediate reactions in us. They are, so to speak, veiled by an isolating screen and, according to specific cases and individual sensibilities, they extract from us only respect, veneration, and often boredom.

If polyphony—as mastered so supremely by Bach—moves us deeply, it fills us first of all with wonderment. Our emotions grow in intensity only after being clarified by the effort we must make to understand and unravel the polyphonic network of intermingled voices. These poems of Bach, bulging with life, cannot be accepted with complete joy unless they are understood. They are deeply moving, but they also demand understanding.

When listening to a complex piece of ancient music, people with lazy minds become angry if they do not find it beautiful at first hearing. They have no idea that this music is too proud to rush toward them, smiling and begging for easily won applause. To listen again and again, each time with more attention, to try to follow and understand the melodic line and the harmonies better—all that work which should be the auditor's own—never occurs to them.

G. Mourey said, "If through a slow and broad education of the senses and spirit we were prepared to feel beauty rather than to understand it, to enjoy it rather than to analyze it, we would find life truly sweeter." As if analysis were a workman's labor, while casualness would represent Sunday to him who toils six days a week! It is understandable that dismantling one by one the refined machines, plunging into the arcana of that which is mystery, and wandering into the labyrinth that is the thought of a great man means work and very great effort. But he who knows how to love beauty, will he renounce this effort? Will he prefer to submit to a work of art without trying to penetrate its meaning?

The only laudable nonchalance is that which an artist or a thinker who knows how to analyze can afford to indulge in.

The gluttony with which the public rushes to buy tickets to hear *The Goldberg Variations* saddens and discourages me. Is it through love for this music? No, they do not know it. [*This was written in May 1933.*] They are prompted simply by the base curiosity of seeing a virtuoso fight with the most difficult work ever written for keyboard. This and the snobbery of the first performance are the driving forces which inspire the crowd.

And to think that my only dream is to play beautiful and noble music!

The Art of Listening

·There is an anguishing mystery for us interpreters and also for composers. What does a listener hear? What is he able to perceive? In what way does a musical text register in the listener's ear and in his brain? I think of this even before approaching the problem of taste, of attraction or aversion, as it is experienced by every listener. We now have microphones to capture and reproduce sound, but we shall never have an exact picture of what the listener perceives, and we shall never know, even approximately, what he actually hears.

And who among us knows how to listen? This absolute sense of hearing—which without preparation can at once embrace an entity, perceive it, see through it, and at the same time divide and subdivide it in all its components—is a rare gift refined by ceaseless practice.

In my lifetime I have met very few people who could really hear. And hearing everything does not necessarily mean understanding everything. I do not ask a listener to be able to dissect all there is in my playing, for instance; it would be too much to ask. But for pity's sake, do not replace listening skill with general ideas!

When one listens to a masterpiece for the first time, one is astounded, crushed, gripped, and unable to understand or discern any detail. One submits passively and lets oneself be carried away by its beauty. But little by little, through subsequent hearings, one begins to feel, to distinguish, and to perceive isolated fragments at first and then to follow them in the ensemble. The first contact with a great work of art is a shock comparable to what we experience when we first meet the person who is going to play an important role in our life. Little by little we dare approach, look closer, and by and by we become familiarized with this person's characteristic movements, looks, and expressions. In the same way, ties—affectionate ties—are formed between us and the masterpiece. They make it become familiar to us. The richer the work, the more numerous and stronger are these ties. I believe this is the kind of rapport my audiences now have with *The Goldberg Variations*. [*This was written in 1952 or 53.*]

What is the cause of our emotive reactions to music? Is it the remote reminiscence of something we have loved in our childhood? Is it because a secret string in us is touched upon that this total delight blossoms out? Or is it, on the contrary, nostalgia?

Sometimes the discovery of a most unexpected or superficial likeness is at the basis of our reactions. A phrase of Couperin may evoke the curve of a Chopin melody; or certain progressions in Scarlatti may remind us of a Beethoven period or of a popular Spanish dance. We love to cling to these associations. They are something to lean upon or to spring from, and we feel their invaluable help when embarking upon the unknown.

Is it because previously unknown music demands a real investigation that the apprehensive listener is usually hostile to any novelty? The dauntless one, however, eager for originality at any price, undertakes this investigation at his own risk and peril according to his capacity for absorption. The snob alone, always oscillating between the most contrary esthetic movements, can put up with anything and come out safe and sound from any redoubtable expedition. Yet timorous or dauntless, only he who knows how to listen will be able to follow through. But there is more to it than mere hearing. What can be said about the innumerable impressions—so minute that they are hardly perceptible—which a sound or an ensemble of sounds generates in us? The meaning of these impressions grows as they invade us, and they dictate a specific image or a particular expression—that one and no other.

Who shall ever understand what provokes these nuances in our joys and reactions? While one of us vibrates in listening to a certain melodic line or harmonic encounter, another will remain indifferent. These reactions may correspond to those which touch us most in other human beings or in animals. For instance, the ingenuousness, or innocence, of a motive always touched my brother Paul because innocence in all its manifestations always moved him. But what seems innocent to one person will be teasing, profound, or philosophical to another. Edmond Jaloux qualified the beginning of Mozart's G Minor Symphony as "full of gladness," while Saint-Foix said it was "hasty and anxious." This does not represent solely the eternal and permanent misunderstanding between interpreter and listener. It goes much further and much deeper. It is the misunderstanding between the work itself and the interpreter.

We often hear musicians discuss in earnest the acoustics of a concert hall. Obviously it is rather important. But I confess that it never was one of my main concerns. A hall with an echo? Too bad for the listeners, who will have to hear me play a Bach fugue twice without having asked for it! If a hall has poor acoustics, amplification of the sound is not the solution. The task of an interpreter should be to open the ears of his listeners.

What interests me above all is the degree and quality of the receptivity of those for whom I am playing or to whom I am speaking. It is for the good acoustics of the souls of my listeners that I care. For him who knows how to listen music and words have a carrying power. You, my listeners, with your exceptional reactions to music, with your vivid and rich imaginations, you are like vibrating sympathetic strings; you represent the most beautiful spiritual acoustics.

Knowing how to listen is a great art. Let us not be mistaken about that! We, the interpreters, are searching for intense, pathetic, moving accents, for refined sonorities, for a pure line, and an ideal ensemble. We are searching, and sometimes it seems that we have reached our goal. Yes, but how seldom we encounter listeners ideally understanding, with keyed-up attention, cultivated taste, and refined ears! I shall never forget the days I spent at Tolstoy's home, nor the hours I played for him. He adored music, and he knew how to listen admirably. While playing I observed this luminous old man with his silver hair, his sweet and penetrating blue eyes, and I could see, as though reflected in a mirror, the agitation music provoked in him. He drank it, was steeped in it. He purred with pleasure or burst into big, rich, and sonorous laughter. He felt each piece with such intensity that it gave him a new life. Tolstoy was a creator-listener.

Fluctuations in Taste

We read a phrase, musical or literary, written several centuries ago. It strikes us and enchants us. But was it received in the same way by those who lived when it was written? Was their understanding different from ours? And if so, in what way?

How can we explain the fluctuations in taste? Berlioz, for instance, was truly revolted by Haydn's music, and the sincerity of his reaction cannot be doubted.

I have been reading Paul Valéry. During his youth it was the time of the Beethoven invasion. Baudelaire and Mallarmé were under the spell of Wagner, Valéry under that of Schumann. I wonder what these great poets would have said had they known Bach and Couperin. I think of their wonderment. But suddenly I say, "No, it could not have been. The time had not yet come. Bach was not far enough removed, and contempt for the eighteenth century weighed upon Couperin." Bach's *Well-Tempered Clavier* had been revered by all the romantics from Schumann, Chopin, and Liszt to Tausig and Bülow. But to hear it on the harpsichord would have hurt their ears and offended their taste. I never forgot the exclamation of Nikisch who said to me, "How can you play *The Chromatic Fantasy* on the harpsichord? What an aberration!" The strident, acidulous, and nasal sound of the harpsichord made people wince then. Yet this instrument is only a mirror of the sonorous color of Bach's orchestra. This color has been neither understood nor appreciated. What is more, it was despised. I remember how Urban, my composition teacher, used to hum derisively fragments from *The B Minor Mass*.

But we went through Beethoven and Wagner and finally became sated with their music. One has only to read Berlioz's writings to understand that. And now we turn to the music before Bach. We quench our thirst at the source of Monteverdi. We go back even much earlier. Josquin des Prés, Lassus, and Ockeghem delight us.

I shall never forget Brahms's numerous annotations on Scarlatti and Couperin. They are preserved at the Musikfreunde library in Vienna. In his enthusiasm for this music, Brahms went as far as to edit Couperin's harpsichord pieces for Novello. This alone should suffice to quiet those who vociferate against Brahms's heavy romanticism. Through what channel did Brahms's love for Couperin come about? I often wonder. Yet bringing together Brahms's *Saphishes Ode* and Couperin's *La Garnier* or his *Ténébreuse* and Brahms's *Auf dem Kirchof* shows their affinity, although one must not look for literal likenesses. It is rather a question of "climate" or "atmosphere." As much as I loathe to use these worn-out terms, they are apposites.

Authenticity in the Interpretation of Music of the Past

How can we men of today have the presumption to believe that we feel and play exactly like Bach, Couperin, their predecessors and contemporaries? It is altogether folly, lack of intelligence and of assimilated culture.

Can we guess what a poet, a great man of the past, would have said had he lived today? No, since we see him only in a stationary state, as death left him. But alive he would be in perpetual evolution and would surprise us all the time.

From a car or a train we look at the fleeting scenery. But just close your eyes and reopen them a few moments later. Surprise! Do we foresee what is to come? No. Our eyes keep the imprint of what they saw last.

Research goes on continuously, it is true. We follow musicological discoveries step by step with great attention. We study deeply, trying our best to understand ancient precepts to the letter. With all our heart we approach as closely as we can this remote music and these revered masters. But between them and us Beethoven, Chopin, Wagner, Debussy, Stravinsky, and so many others have existed. Can we disregard the torrent and sublime pathos of their music by which, willingly or not, we have been permeated? The romantics and the moderns are now (in the middle of the twentieth century) more or less accepted and assimilated by us. We represent an accumulation, and we are powerless against that fact. And why should we rebel? Let us submit consciously to this transformation of matter.

When we listen to Monteverdi or to the Virginalists, we feel them through the music that has settled in us, layer upon layer. Physically, humanly it could not be otherwise. We cannot escape these influences.

Anyway, would it be desirable? Must this fateful and marvelous enrichment of which we are the recipients prevent our feeling rightly the music of the past? Historical sense and awareness of perspective can be developed, cultivated, and refined if they are not inborn. They can and should be.

Oscar Bie once wrote, "Landowska plays the ancient masters as if Beethoven had never existed." I was flattered by this homage, but never took it too seriously. And I am exasperated when I am told, "If only Bach or Mozart could hear you, how happy they would be!" It reminds me of what Chopin said to Liszt, who had just played one of Chopin's Nocturnes, "Whose piece is this?"

At no time in the course of my work have I told myself, "This is the way it must have sounded at the time."

Why? Because I am sure that what I am doing in regard to sonority, registration, etc., is very far from the historical truth. To the purists who say to me, "This was done in such a manner; you should conform, etc.," I answer, "Leave me alone! Criticize as much as you please, but do not shout. I need peace and silence around me and those grains of irony and scepticism, which are as necessary to research as salt is to food."

At no time in the course of my work have I ever tried to reproduce exactly what the old masters did. Instead, I study, I scrutinize, I love, and I recreate.

The means are of no importance. With the Jesuits I say, "The result sanctifies the means." When I am working out a registration, for instance, I search for one that seems logical and beautiful to me, one that does justice to Bach's prosody by being punctuated in the right places. I am aware that the disposition of the registers in the harpsichords of Bach's time differed somewhat from those of my Pleyel. But little do I care if, to attain the proper effect, I use means that were not exactly those available to Bach.

On Musicology

The transformation of musical expression produced by romanticism brought along the glorification of subjectivity and of contempt for the history of art, a scorn which, of course, was to generate ignorance. While at the beginning of this century admirable musicologists bestowed upon us their often staggering discoveries, the virtuosos, ignoring these revelations, persisted in going about their automatic routine. Their lack of curiosity for all that touches the history of their art very often assumed an aggressive character. That is why the works of restoration, in which any refined artist should be passionately interested, inspired only a sneering hostility in the virtuoso. With a nonchalance that ignorance alone could explain, they "arranged" the masterpieces, they played harpsichord works on the piano, the clarinet, the contrabass, the harmonium; they transformed them into *Ave Marias* and *Méditations*. Everybody found that very natural. But the day someone took the liberty of playing *The Well-Tempered Clavier* on the harpsichord, they cried "Shame!"

Persevering and zealous musicologists pursued nonetheless their beautiful work. Little by little it was realized that an epoch which gave birth to works such as *The St. Matthew Passion, The B Minor Mass, Samson, Hyppolyte et Aricie*, etc., must have known conditions which were certainly not inferior to those of our time. Cultivated artists understood that in order to do justice to this music they had first to know those conditions thoroughly. And for that one could not be satisfied with a *Small Manual of the Arts through the Ages* or with a *Master Key to Ancient Music, with Directions for Its Use*. The necessity to go deep, to scrutinize, to search, and, above all, to try to understand and bring to life an inanimate score was recognized.

How long did it take to understand that in the writings of these so greatly despised *rats de bibliothèque*, the musicologists, there is often more piety, poetry, and love of music than in the most extravagant passages and ecstatic ritardandos of many a virtuoso of fashion? Musicologists were blamed because they were not musicians. This is a commonplace. A true musicologist is a musician. To occupy oneself with the history of music does not mean plodding through a dull and sterile job smelling of mildew. It is not enough to parade with dates that can easily be found in any dictionary or to dwell on the number of decorations given the relative of a famous musician. Yet daubers and dealers in trash exist almost everywhere, in musicology as well as in other domains, alas. And among the musicologists there are also those who cannot make a musical analysis that I would call "alive." Their works, often very good, do not achieve, however, that intimate contact with a musical phrase from which the spark of revelation springs forth. But when musicology is understood and treated by human, lucid, and generous minds, this beautiful and fecund science guides, enlightens, and fortifies us.

Although born late, musicology has progressed with giant strides. At first, of course, it was dogmatic. One did not venture beyond the letter of documents. We were a little rigid. It would be difficult for me to define now, step by step, each discovery which contributed to liberating me from this rigidity by illuminating the meaning of documents, revealing the life of the music of the past, and by lifting the shroud in which it was buried.

I worked alone, and I played constantly. I accompanied *The St. Matthew Passion*; I gave concerts with singers; I acquainted myself with the concertos of Karl Philipp Emanuel Bach, etc. The light came little by little, and without breaking away from the letter of documents, I began to understand the immense circuit in which music of the past revolves.

Blessings and Failures of Recordings

Blessed is he who invented recording! But what a pity that he was not born centuries earlier! Think only of all that we would be able to hear and therefore understand better. Oh, the unending research in libraries and museums, the readings and collations of texts, the maddening desire to know the truth! We have come to understand that intuition alone, so glorified by the romantics, is not sufficient and that it is necessary to sustain it with knowledge. Natural gifts have to be nourished with historical studies. Our indefatigable zeal in scrutinizing has been rewarded by a few hard-won discoveries; yet how many difficulties remain! At every step redoubtable interrogation marks spring up before us, burdening us with new anguish. Then we have to go back to reading the treatises on interpretation in former times, to reading musical scores and reports from contemporaries of our idols, those who had known them and heard them play or sing. Reading, always reading . . . but how did it sound? What were the tempi, the registration of a fugue on the harpsichord? The ornamentation of a largo? The dynamics of Mozart's and Haydn's pianoforte? Handel's manner of improvising?

Just imagine if in the midst of these tormenting thoughts we could place on our phonograph a recording of Scarlatti playing some of his sonatas or of Mozart improvising cadenzas for one of his concertos! Imagine Bach's playing captured on records, his touch, his tempi, his registration, the unexpectedness of his inspiration, the pulsation of his heart. . . . I hardly dare to think of it; I stagger at this idea. Little white dog, all ears and so attentive, if only you had been there some two hundred and fifty years ago! Bach, source of miraculous life, kept alive forever! His voice which our anxious love seeks, that our nostalgic imagination tries in vain to divine—all this transmitted faithfully. . . . Imagine hearing the multifarious voice of our master, his menacing roar at the organ, the superb duel he unleashed on the keyboards of his harpsichord. . . . But also, oh surprise, oh delight! the sweet chirping of the musettes, the joyous obstinacy of the bourrées, and those arabesques so light, and those trills, like cascading pearls. . . . The creator of the *Passions*, the builder of fugues, the architect of grandiose and learned thoughts, our god Bach, close to us, playful, mischievous, and tender . . . What joy without shadow, what security it would be to hear him!

And what a lesson for grave men! Yet a recording catches only one moment, one aspect of an interpretation when there are a thousand and one others, always different.

And here lies the tragedy of recordings!

3 \(The Making of an Interpreter

About Genius and Gifts

An interpreter must know how to arouse expectation and then satisfy it. Genius must go beyond expectation; it must exalt it. A musical form bears in itself the rigidity of a mold. Genius escapes this tyranny. Thus in exalting the fugue form, as in *The Art of Fugue*, Bach surpasses it and soars above the fugue itself. Cimarosa's overture to *Il Matrimonio Segreto* is empty; it merely tramples from tonic to dominant and vice versa. What is the difference between this procedure as used by Cimarosa, devoid of genius, and that used by Mozart or Haydn?

Mozart was of a flighty disposition, and yet what touching sincerity there is in the aria "Porgi amor," in which the Countess sings, "Give me back my spouse!" Is it because he understood through personal experience the sorrow of a forsaken lover? Or is it simply the strength of genius which does not need the actual experience of a feeling to be able to depict it truthfully, or even more, to describe divinely the opposite of his own nature?

A genius has his own ways, as genius dictates to him. And after what he does someone establishes laws and founds a school. But to understand the evolution of an art, the character of a period, or an esthetic transition, one should bear clearly in mind that creative geniuses do not spring up like supernatural phenomena in isolation and out of touch with their contemporaries. On the contrary, the whole is held together organically, and one is explained by the other.

Sometimes nature provides us lavishly with gifts. Yet we should know how to deal with them. We should be our own manager.

I often think about what one calls too casually the innate physical aptitudes of a musician, those aptitudes which usually serve him prodigiously well. It is recognized that the conformation of the palate, tongue, and lips are very important for wood players. Everyone agrees that some singers have their own peculiarities in the attack of a note, in their way of beating a trill, in *portamenti*, etc. These peculiarities, theirs alone, cannot, of course, be imitated, because they result from a physiological complex. The same individuality applies to violinists, guitarists, lute and keyboard players of any kind for which the individual make-up of the fingers and an innate rapidity of reflexes play an immense role. Chopin provides a marvelous illustration of this. As everyone knows, he was not strongly built and apparently did not possess the kind of technique others need to master his works. Yet all of his contemporaries agree in saying that no other pianist could obtain such fulgurant effects in some of his Etudes and Polonaises.

Certain physical conformations are predestined. Look at Couperin's portrait; his full lips and his fleshy hands. It is obvious that his fingers, with their sensuous padded tips, must have produced a mellow touch, his alone, which must have done marvels in *Les Langueurs Tendres,* to quote but one example. Compare this face and these hands to those of Rameau. Emaciated, Rameau had long thin fingers. The "exorbitant" intervals which abound in his harpsichord pieces are a resultant demonstration of his conformation.

These peculiarities, or inborn gifts, are more than just physical dispositions. A thorough study of these aptitudes would lead to the discovery of their mysterious source. Why do Brazil and Argentina produce born pianists, Holland flutists, Russia, Czechoslovakia, and Hungary violinists? Creative artists in their embryonic stage already bear an indescribable imprint, a kind of destiny they cannot escape.

About Teaching

What an abyss there is between the perfect happiness we experience in reading a score of ancient music and the sickly feeling which seizes us when we hear the same work performed by musicians untrained for this music. Each one of them expresses a personal opinion about dotted notes, triplets, rests, etc. Listen only to a fugue subject phrased in a certain manner and to its answer phrased in an absolutely different way. Does not that sound like the ironic raillery of a chatterbox making fun of a neighbor? And what about the trills realized sometimes on, sometimes before the beat, starting on the main note more often than not, and so forth. All of it is proof that these musicians suffer from the insecurity of those who grope their way in the darkness of ignorance. We would be wrong in blaming them. It is almost impossible for a musician busy at learning all the general repertoire to study by himself the principles of interpretation of music of the past. He lacks the musicological basis, and modern editions, often contradictory on essential matters, only increase his confusion. Thus a musician who is attracted to the music of the past is also beset by doubts because he is not armed with the knowledge indispensable to approaching this music. How can he be helped?

It is a grave error to believe that only those who wish to specialize should undertake a thorough study of the music of the past. The works of the great contrapuntists constitute substantial nourishment; in fact, it is the only one that really counts for our brains and fingers. A pianist who has assimilated a polyphonic culture will move about with much greater ease among the impetuous waves of romantic music. By developing our sense of time values and their reciprocal rapport and by giving us the notion of space, contrapuntal writing leads us to the perception of balance. The mystery of tempo, which is the life or death of a musical phrase, is revealed through this kind of music.

Bach's *Inventions* are the most expert guide for pianists as well as for harpsichordists in their studies. They should learn first how to play and register with precision a two-part piece before attempting more involved polyphonic works.

The plan of studies of every keyboardist should include the complete works of Bach in their original version. And to understand Bach better, students should study the works of the great and lesser French, German, Italian, and English masters who were Bach's predecessors, contemporaries, and successors. The characteristics of each school and their reciprocal influences should be taught to them. Only through historical studies will their sense of the style and taste of each epoch be developed. That is unfortunately neglected. Also it is essential to devote classes to the history and evolution of musical instruments with practical demonstrations. Harpsichordists should learn thoroughly the mechanism and voicing of their instrument. Proper voicing represents a large part of the art of harpsichord playing. That also is too often ignored. Reading the treatises of Quantz on the flute, of Leopold Mozart on the violin, of Tosi-Agricola on singing, of François Couperin, Rameau, Frescobaldi, Marpurg, Karl Philipp Emanuel Bach, and so many others on keyboard playing should be obligatory. At least the teacher would be assured that while busy reading these books, students would skip a few of the hours they otherwise would spend repeating endlessly, and brainlessly, Czerny's *Great Velocity* or Kalkbrenner's exercises for the independence of the fourth finger of the left hand!

Evidently the ideal would be to start every music student on this fortifying diet. Nevertheless I have observed its incredible blessings on pupils who were no longer adolescents, but who had been kept in ignorance of Bach. When these unsuspected marvels are revealed to them, such students react with the greatest enthusiasm because they become conscious of what they had been missing. And one witnesses an outburst of joy, something like the discovery of love.

When consciousness has been awakened and chastised by training in counterpoint, "note against note," and when it has been under the control of self-criticism, this inured consciousness revolts against aimless sentimentality.

It is in that wonderful atmosphere of faith and love, united with analytical and constructive criticism and animated by the fervent desire to respect the will of the Bachs and of the Couperins, that I work with my pupils. While submitting them to the most Spartan discipline, I also leave room for their individuality.

My destiny was to be an educator. I was made to initiate, to give public classes illustrated with many examples, to bring together works that nobody would have expected to see juxtaposed.

At no time in my teaching did I ever think of exposing publicly the mistakes of a pupil. Foresight, maternal solicitude, care to prevent troubles, sometimes catastrophe for a student unaccustomed to playing for an audience—such have always been my dominant thoughts. I say to them, "Do not use the fourth finger in this phrase; here, lean comfortably on the thumb, breathe at this place, and do not accentuate that beat," just as I would say, "Take a walk; breathe through your nose; do not stuff yourself with chocolate." All these manifestations of maternal love have always been the leit-motive of my teaching. The beautiful hours of work spent with my pupils are those I cherish most. I have the compelling urge to share with them what I have learned and what I think I have discovered. This is an inheritance from my mother; spontaneous, she was unable to savor fruit or anything else alone. I shall never forget her gesture when she was saying, "Taste this apple!" She gave it all. I am only a feeble echo of my mother. Is there any merit in sharing? None. When I play a sarabande of Chambonnières, I wish to call out, "Come, help me bear this burden of love, this flame!"

What kills all seeds of taste in a student is to confine him at first to technical studies only. Interpretation is reserved for later. It is like that woman of little virtue who postponed, until she had made a fortune, the luxury of having a real lover. What is of capital importance for a future musician is to be acquainted as early as possible with the ideal sonority that some day he will be able to produce himself. The teacher must emphasize this sonorous vision toward which the student has to direct all his efforts from the moment he puts his hands on the keyboard for the first time. If music were taught this way, the world would not be inhabited by so many monsters whose monstrosity is caused by their lack of consciousness.

The task of a teacher is not to work for the pupil nor to oblige him to work, but to show him how to work.

Excerpts from a letter by Landowska in 1950 to a former pupil who had come to visit her after a separation of almost ten years and who was stunned to discover the evolution of Landowska's interpretative freedom:

I told you that I feel strongly the need to share the fruits of my meditations with those who love and understand me. This is probably why my music scores are now covered with annotations and fingerings. But you were far away for so many years. How could I in a single evening make you understand my unending work made up of happiness and of struggles? How could I tell you all that my reading of musicological essays and art criticisms has taught me? Unexpected, unbelievable things, I assure you!

You said you were perturbed. Why?

Because I improvise a *double* for a Handel sarabande, inspired by Bach's and Couperin's own *doubles?* Examine them closely, see the curves and the inflections of their lines, follow the life which flows among these eighth- and sixteenth-notes, and you will understand that what I am doing is the truth.

"We came to you in search of Truth" you said.

Yes. There are axioms; we have Bach's table of ornaments and those of the French harpsichordists, realized by them. But is this all? Is it enough to realize an ornament? Is it not necessary to interpret it? And what about the arpeggios in *The Chromatic Fantasy?* They were not realized by Bach. And what about the "discretion" in Froberger's *Plainte,* which is nothing but an invitation to improvise? And Chambonnières's Sarabande in D Minor, to which I have added ornamentation? And Rameau's *Dauphine?* Rameau improvised it at the dauphin's wedding. Is that not a hint that we, too, should improvise when playing it? Truth? Even years ago I revealed a great deal to you. But now let me take off in complete freedom. Do not restrain me in my flight in the name of what I said a decade past during this or that lesson. You have not even attended all my classes. Is it worthy of a disciple to say to me with such accents of reproach and deception, "You never told us about the *doubles*"?

Did I not share everything with all of you then, as I do today? Do you really think that I ever keep secret the best of my knowledge? But I cannot help it if, having never stopped working, I have learned a great deal, especially about this divine freedom that is to music the air without which it would die. What would you say of a scientist or of a painter who, like stagnant water, would stop his experimentation and remain still?

"You will wreak havoc!" you exclaimed.

Do I have to take into consideration non-musical, clumsy people, but, worst of all, pedants who—and this is serious—number my thoughts, label, and file them, although they understand nothing of their spirit, anymore than they realize the fury of my ecstasy for music?

Was music created for musicologists? Did Bach write for teachers' meetings?

The most beautiful thing in the world is, precisely, the conjunction of learning and inspiration. Oh, the passion for research and the joy of discovery!

I followed my vocation and never ceased to work without ever compromising. That is all.

"Do you realize your responsibility?" you said.

Responsibility toward whom? Those who understand me will never trouble me. About the others—alas, they are numerous—I could not care less. Besides, I can explain every one of the "liberties" I take and prove them. And God knows how much I love to explain. I shall never tire of it.

Chef d' Ecole you called me.

I never aspired to that pompous title, which is too narrow for my nature. I beg you to relieve me of it. It would weigh upon me and encircle my head and my heart too tightly. No *chef d'école*, no vestal chaste and pure. *Bacchante* would suit me better, but one that works hard, zealous as a schoolgirl, trying to understand the letter, fustigating herself "to make it sound," and then, forgetting everything—books and laws—unleashed, intoxicated with freedom.

How to Work

If everyone knew how to work, everyone would be a genius! I hate the word *practice*. Practice breeds inurement. Instead of discovering, of distinguishing traits that are deeply hidden or merely veiled, one ends seeing nothing anymore. One ceases to be aware.

To be aware, to be conscious at all times is what appears to me the worthiest in my thoughts and in my work. While interpreting, even at the most impetuous moments when a musical phrase overflows with passion, I want to remain conscious. I may forget a liberty I took at one place or another, but this does not change in any way my state of consciousness, which is always on the alert.

Awkwardness and mistakes in playing are always due to a lack of concentration.

I attach great importance to concentration because I was born into a family of undisciplined individuals. I had to kick and scold myself. But I believe that I have acquired the faculty of concentrating, and now I can teach it to my pupils.

I work best with closed eyes. Only then I see and I hear. How should one start to play? One has to concentrate and be entirely ready so that when the first note is struck, it comes as a sort of continuation of a soliloquy already begun. Too often the value and importance of the start in playing is belittled. And yet all depends on its being carefully prepared. Before I begin a phrase, between the preparatory gesture of the hand or of the finger and the first note, there is an infinitesimal period of time, always surprising because of its unpredictable duration and because of its expressive impact. The listener can never anticipate the exact dosage I apply to this rest. This silence preceding a phrase—be it the initial one or not—acts as a background upon which the motive is sketched and set into relief. Breathings and cesuras, especially those that precede a beginning, have a positive value equal to that of the notes themselves.

Similarly, the last note is never the last. It is rather a point of departure for something to come.

Whistler went out at night trying to steep himself in the mood of a nocturnal landscape before he attempted painting one. Corot said, "After my excursions, I invite my friend Nature to spend a few days under my roof. Once she is there, I give free rein to my imagination. Brush in hand, I start out in the forest of my studio. I hear right there the songs of birds and the murmur of the branches agitated by a ghost wind. . . ."

A landscape painter should be able to paint a masterpiece representing the countryside without leaving his studio.

There is a very close rapport between the preceding examples and the way I work, or rather, let us say it is the same thing. I consult as many documents as possible. I do my best to understand and assimilate them. Digested and assimilated, they work in me, tracing their own way. I do not think of them anymore. I let them act. The more my documentation increases, the more I feel light and free. It is not that I am sure of everything—who can boast of such a thing?—but I have the feeling of being honest, of not cheating; and probably this gives me a quiet confidence.

But most of all, I absorb or rather I let myself become permeated by each musical phrase, slowly and for a long time. It is through playing it again and again that this phrase will unveil for me, a little at a time, its expression and its true character. Finally my fingers touch its core, so deeply hidden; I feel it with delight.

The more I live with a work and absorb its substance, the more I discover in it new beauties. Then I amplify, augment my interpretation. I feel submerged, carried away by irresistible waves. It is not the successful performance of a piece that counts, but it is this eager and patient struggle, this stubbornness in facing each difficulty that brings an always renewed joy.

How wrong it is to say that some pieces are simple! There is no such thing. Everything has to ripen. Some people say, "For you it is a trifle." But especially for me it is more difficult than for anyone else. The more I advance, the more I discover that I know nothing.

One must have an immense perseverance and also be philosophical to avoid despair. It is true that I am attempting the absolute, and this absolute often resists me. But I must obtain it, and then will come a divine freedom. One must play for hours and hours in a dimly lit room before one can feel "this is *it*."

I know and I hear what I want to obtain from a piece of music. As long as I cannot obtain it, I shall slave, fight, swear, and say, "Happy are those who do not know what they want!" But I well know that would be a wretched happiness.

Sometimes finding a solution for setting in relief a certain phrase demands a complete change of fingering and more work. All the better, as long as it will sound! One must never be afraid to start all over again as many times as it is necessary.

I attack even difficult pieces in their definitive tempo without transition, even if this tempo is very fast. I assimilate it, and only later do I work slowly. Is it a search for perfection? No, it is something else. I cannot stand to be disturbed by a technical imperfection or anything that blemishes the realization of my vision.

What I fear most is not the worsening of a piece, but its being in a state of stagnation, which is a kind of death. A break is necessary before resuming the course with freshness. Strength is renewed after a rest. But it is a luxury that one can afford only if there is time ahead.

To play a phrase with relief and vivacity and then to perform it nonchalantly, as if one never had to study it, is difficult. There is a great difference between something solidly sewn and something timorously adjusted.

One has to dominate matter in a regal way to allow oneself to forget and to make the listener forget the difficulty of a piece.

There is a fundamental error in the manner of practicing. It consists in always starting a phrase at its beginning and going up to its end. To know a phrase in all its detail one must be able to pick it up at any place. As a preparation for this method of practicing, it is essential to write out fingerings to serve as guide marks. The same idea can be applied to orchestral parts, in which bowings for the strings and breathings for the winds replace fingerings. Working on overlong phrases, taken always at their beginning, results in being unable to play from memory any part of these phrases.

Very often a phrase that had remained hermetic to us will reveal itself when we sing it. What is there in a human voice that makes the heartbeat of a phrase become more understandable and closer to us?

At the origin of expression there is the quality of the sound. Nuances called too lightly "minute" are truly important and can change completely the expression of a phrase. One can create miracles with a *subito piano* or a *meno mosso* at places where they are most unexpected.

When I begin to dream up a new program, a fever of happiness seizes me. I want that concert to be an extraordinary event as the result of the atmosphere I hope to create. I spin an enchanted thread, a web that must envelop us all. I forget everything, all previous pains and torments, and I start anew. All day, all night I work, and I feel—I always do—that I need many more days and nights to modify, retouch, improve, and go deeper into the meaning of the works I play. Oh! the hours of folly, of oblivion, of happiness—my hours of work in the middle of the night! What intoxication it is to play again and again what one loves—to plunge into it!

One can postpone writing a letter, but work for a concert? Never. The proper execution of a single ornament is much more important than any business or social activity. It is best to work the most difficult parts in the evening because they will ripen during the night.

Observe how much the undiscriminating audience likes the exaggerations of a performer. There are probably two reasons. First, because it facilitates for them the access, the understanding of a phrase which otherwise would have meant little to them. Exaggerated ritardandi, accentuations, etc., are, in a way, some sort of mask like those worn by Greek actors and so conceived as to be seen even by the spectators seated farthest from the stage. And yet it is in reducing and simplifying exterior gestures that one can intensify the expression. In concerts or any live performance our impressions are divided between hearing and seeing. Sight receives a part from the ensemble of our sensations. With recordings, however, hearing alone is impressed.

How often after my concerts some small professional comes to me and asks me to teach him how to play the most showy pieces of my repertoire! It reminds me of some fat and homely little bourgeoise who, after seeing a svelte and elegant aristocratic lady, runs to the same dressmaker; she thinks that in wearing the same dress she will acquire the same elegance.

It is interesting to observe the various transformations a work undergoes during the lifetime of its performer. Take, for example, *The Italian Concerto*. I learned it first with Michalowski in the Bülow transcription. Later I reworked it all by myself at the piano. Then I had to forget everything I did previously and relearn it on the harpsichord. Finally it was in my fingers and in my brain. For many years I played it all over the world. It was my war horse. It became a little worn out in the process; dust settled on it in addition to a few bad habits contracted during all these travels. We had become an old *ménage*. Its beauty, its contrasts had lost their sharpness. But I had to teach it to a student, and suddenly the work woke up and showed itself under a new and exciting light.

4 \ Reflections on
Some Problems of Interpretation

On Fingering

BETWEEN our two hands lies the fate of a masterpiece, its life
or its death. We do not play with our soul; we play with our ten
fingers, ten poor little beings, thoughtless, clumsy, and cruel. Let
us chastise them, whip them, make them conscious; let us breathe
into them our soul, and let us try to play!

Are not our ten fingers like ten instrumentalists obedient
to a single conductor, ten creatures who should answer instantly
his call? And is not the ideal of interpretation for a soloist identical to that of an a cappella choir or of an instrumental ensemble?

Fingers are inattentive and allow themselves many irrever-
ences as soon as they are not under surveillance. But a sharp
command from the brain brings them back to order. It reminds

me of my dog Othello; he turned into a docile and repentant creature at the sound of a severe voice.

The physical constitution of the hands is in close rapport with the entire being. Were not my hands predestined? I do not see myself with large and bony hands. I believe that in giving me life, God organized my being as a whole—musicality, love of polyphony, and round hands. (See p. 361)

I shall never forget the disdain with which Busoni once looked at my hands. That was before 1900. He said to me, "With such hands you will never be able to achieve anything." In saying that he was thinking of the current romantic repertoire that meant everything to him. Of course he knew Bach also, but through transcriptions from the organ to the piano with octaves in the bass and enlarged and multiplied chords. Although he edited *The Well-Tempered Clavier*, Busoni did not learn anything about Bach's own keyboard writing. Ignoring the harpsichord and its technique, how could he have guessed the predestination of my hands?

Fingering is the strategy of the hands. Its importance is fundamental. But when fingering is written out in a score, it has only a theoretical value. The "savoir-faire," the sleight of hand, or rather "sleight of fingers," is everything. Certain fingerings should be accompanied by pictures and explanations to be understood.

Evidently the authentic fingerings of Couperin or of Chopin are of the greatest interest to every keyboard player. They constitute an invaluable document from all points of view. But beware of using them to the letter. Fingering more than anything else is a question of the individual structure of the hand, of its being chubby or lean and bony; it also depends on the degree of sensitivity of the tip of the fingers and the rapport of this sensitivity with the organism as a whole. Certain principles of fingering are axiomatic. They can and must be taken into consideration by every keyboardist. But between that and a standardization for all hands and especially for all natures, there is an abyss.

To establish a fingering one has to reflect upon it and search. After deliberate thought and trials I finally decide to adopt one that seems to be good. I practice it a long time. It is a hard struggle; sometimes it does not take hold. And suddenly another fingering I never thought of before comes very naturally to my fingers. And that one takes easily. This does not mean that one should leave certain phrases unfingered on the pretext that the fingers will fall into place by themselves. No. One must write down a fingering, even if it is the wrong one. Out of revolt and need for justice the true and right one may impose itself. This reminds me of my trip to Yasnaya Polyana, Tolstoy's home. We were overtaken by a storm; terrifying snow drifts prevented the driver of the sled from recognizing where the road was. He stopped; and loosening the reins, he let the horses find the way all by themselves. I apply this same principle to certain phrases in which a planned fingering does not give satisfactory results. I wipe out the traces of that fingering, and I let the fingers find their own way. It is like an overflowing river returning to its bed.

The brain orders a fingering. Fingers accept or reject it, either because they are stubborn—then they must be cudgeled— or because they feel subconsciously that this is not what they need to produce a maximum effect. Then we have to search, sometimes for a long time, until we find the fingering that will make the phrase sing, flow, cry, laugh, rush, or slow down. Each phrase hides within itself its own fingering, the true one which will enable it to blossom out.

Very often one must invent a fingering that looks clumsy and is not smooth. It is intentional. Such fingering will break the impetus of a group of notes which otherwise would run into each other.

Chopin spoke of using the third finger over the fourth as daring and against the rules. Yet Couperin had already demonstrated that same fingering. Chopin's fingering derives from the structure of his hand. He composed at the piano. If his fingering seemed pure madness to Kalkbrenner, it is only natural. But interestingly enough, the generation of pianists who followed Chopin accepted his fingerings and found them comfortable. The break with tradition was accomplished. If some traditionalists rebelled, others, freed from the pedantic yoke imposed by schools, breathed a sigh of relief.

What an error it is to believe that a fingering should remain identical in sequences! The fact that in sequences a musical design is reproduced on different degrees is one thing. But fingering is concerned only with the topography of each phrase as it appears on the keyboard. When the disposition of the black and white keys is modified because the motive is repeated on another degree of the scale, it requires a different fingering.

Did the musicians of the past use the thumb on the black keys? When one knows that the black keys were then often white, this question is obviated!

While fingering polyphonic music, many pianists disregard the legato which should exist in the middle voices. This is a deficiency in their listening ability because they fail to be shocked by the lack of binding, as indispensable in the middle voices as it is in the upper one. Notice, though, that their fingering becomes more careful when a theme is given over to this middle voice. The carelessness regarding finger-legato in the middle voices may be due also to their vicious habit of relying on the pedal, as if it were putty, to fill up the gaps in sound. Yet only a legato obtained through good fingering can give relief to the voices we wish to set off. The need for absolute legato in all the voices, but especially the inner ones, becomes more and more imperative for me. I upset all fingerings; I expose my hands to tortures to obtain it.

On Touch

It has been said that my touch is a perpetual staccato. This is a fundamental misunderstanding. The great precision required to strike the keys at the harpsichord is sometimes misconstrued for staccato touch. This error also stems from the sharpness of tone that plucked strings produce and from the elasticity of my bouncy touch, with its precise and neat outlines. I use perfect legato, however, as harpsichord touch requires. This is a condition *sine qua non*. Even when staccato is required for certain effects, the basis of harpsichord touch remains the legato. When the touch is not hermetic enough, there is a loss, a waste of sonority.

Nothing would be more opposed to a full substantial touch like mine—at the piano as well as at the harpsichord—than the *jeu perlé* of a Raoul Pugno or of a Jean Doyen. If my playing is sharp, it is not because it is finicky, but because of the particular quality of my touch.

It is only through a certain heaviness of touch that shocks and dissonances, as well as harmonic plenitude, become apparent.

Sometimes I hold certain notes beyond their written value. This licence is justified by the harmonic background—always present in Bach's music, for instance—and by being an answer to this need for perfect legato, which is of such vital importance at the harpsichord.

When several voices move on at the same time and modulate, they require an even tighter touch. Thus the modulation will acquire all its importance—for example, bar 36 in Fugue XI from Book II of *The Well-Tempered Clavier*.

I cannot stand unevenness of touch. Do not try to convince me that it is a mark of sensibility. Impotency, yes! But not sensibility. The cause of unevenness resides in the ears, not in the fingers. If the ears heard and were more demanding, the fingers would be obliged to follow. But if ears are deaf, how do you expect the fingers to act?

Perhaps it is because of the evenness of my touch that some critics have found my playing cold; they say that it works like a perfect mechanism.

About Phrasing

Clavichord playing requires a constant legato interrupted now and then by pauses that seem like sighs. As for the harpsichord, it demands outlines of sharp precision, as well as frank and neat breathings. This explains Couperin's sign ❜ .

To cut the melodic line with cesuras required by logic, impetus, and fantasy, and to allow air to circulate is like breathing a constantly renewed life into musical phrases; it gives them a relief indispensable to their comprehension. This is why all ancient treatises compare musical interpretation to eloquence.

Nothing could be more annoying than those melodic lines that are never interrupted by the slightest breathing. They are comparable to an unpunctuated literary text or to extremely elongated spaghetti endlessly rolling with neither beginning nor end, but lasting forever! I remember my fights with oboists, flutists, and singers on that subject. Once during a rehearsal with an orchestra the oboist became offended when I asked him to breathe in a certain phrase. "They will think that I have no breath sustaining power!" he grumbled.

Air is what plays the principal role in phrasing. What would become of a phrase if it did not float and if it did not detach itself freely from an azure or gray sky?

Breathing in music is not only a cesura, a slice of air; it is also a redoubling of strength, therefore, an accentuation.

In order to give a breathing all its value, it is necessary that the note preceding it be full, never shortened. This does not mean an allargando, but it is something belonging remotely to the same family. It is rather an imperceptible rubato.

The note before a breathing must expire; then one must draw in the air.

The use of two different registers is not a sufficient means for throwing into relief the subject and the countersubject of a fugue. What is most important lies elsewhere. The character of the subject is different from that of the countersubject; that is the first law of counterpoint. What matters is to underline these respective characteristics with the particular phrasing, touch, and breathing indispensable to their liveliness. Thus they will stand out.

When a theme appears in imitation or in the course of the development, it does not always have to be phrased in the same way.

Nothing could be more presumptuous than believing it was the romantic and modern composers who invented musical prosody. There is no truer declamation than Rameau's or even Clérambault's. In what respect then did Gluck's prosody bring improvement over that of his predecessors? Assuredly one of Gluck's innovative particularities resided in stripping the drama; that led inevitably to the bareness of musical writing. This naked-ness of Gluck's musical phrases must have appeared raw and strange to his contemporaries accustomed to ornamentation and melodic lines adorned with volutes.

On Registration

The predominant ideas which guide my registration are purity in the progress of the voices and logic and taste in the choice of colors. In saying "the progress of voices" I do not think exclusively about fugues. When a certain register has been chosen because it corresponds best to the character of a phrase, one must not interrupt the course of this phrase by a change of register. This continuity is part of logic and taste.

I am fully conscious that most harpsichords of the past had hand stops, while my Pleyel is equipped with pedals which allow for a much swifter change of registers without having to lift a hand from the keyboard to move a stop. Yet it would be senseless and narrow-minded to believe that the structure and the inspiration of a piece, its breathings, fermata, changing of colors, etc., depended on whether or not it was possible to reach a hand stop. We know that organists had helpers who drew the stops while they were playing. Why not admit that harpsichordists too might have been helped? And no one takes into account the fact that musicians of the past, trained to the great mental discipline of counterpoint, had also probably developed great adroitness and rapidity of reflexes. To cite only one example, it was said that Bruhns, a pupil of Buxtehude, and one of the greatest organists of his time, improvised fugues on the violin while playing the lower voices on the pedal board of the organ. This is known, but no one deduces the consequences that this feat suggests.

No argumentation, however, can subsist before the only thing that counts—that a piece by its structure, dimensions, and character demands a certain registration. The duty of the performer is to provide this registration even at the price of great effort and difficulty.

All instruments have limitations. A harpsichord with two, even three keyboards, cannot fulfill all the exigencies or fancies of composers. And this question arises: did composers create the instruments, or were the instruments created to serve the composers? This parallel, or simultaneous, concurrence of builders and composers is interesting to study. At the time of the harpsichord the collaboration between musicians and builders was a very close one. (See Part I, Chapter 12.)

In establishing the registration of a highly contrapuntal work, avoid vain coquettishness and constant changes of color. Let a fugue unfold with simplicity in spite of its complexity. The more involved the texture of a piece, the simpler should be the registration.

About Rhythm

What is rhythmic precision?

It is the exact sense of the time value of notes and rests.

What is measure?

It is the distribution and organization of these time values among themselves.

A striking feature of my playing, I was told, is the accuracy I give to time values. It may be striking simply because one has too often to deplore its absence! The sense of time values and their reciprocal rapport is one of the most difficult things to teach.

When a tempo is erratic, when a phrase is unsteady, limping, and invertebrate, it happens first of all—I dare say solely—because the performer does not pay attention to the sharply defined space that should be observed *between* notes.

But strict accuracy of time values is not the only thing that characterizes my playing. There is more to it. Graphic signs of rhythmic notation have their individual signification, their own character. A half-note, a quarter-note, or an eighth-note are like many living organisms; each of them has a distinctive aspect. Yet if we consider them in isolation, separated one from the other, they die. They become alive only because of their mutual rapport, which in turn determines their individuality.

This reminds me of what the father of one of my pupils once asked me in confidence. "Madame, I do not know anything about music. Please tell me what is a half-note?" A half-note is . . . and I explained. Interested, he asked again, "And what is a quarter-note?" I explained that too. "What is an eighth-note?" As I went along explaining, my interlocutor became more and more pensive. He seemed to follow a train of thought. Finally after a long pause he said, "Please, Madame, play for me a thirty-second!"

Half-notes, quarter-notes, thirty-seconds, triplets, rests—all are conventional signs, pawns that we move according to rules learned in school. But it is the network of relationship and interdependence established by the composer among these signs that provides them a personality. To discover that personality and to breathe into each of these signs its proper soul, to identify its character, to underscore it, to bring it to its highest power, to make it human or superhuman, and, above all, to obtain from the various note values a to-and-fro motion, relief, and incisiveness, light and shadow—that is what constitutes a creative interpretation. It demands more of a series of thirty-seconds than being merely played scrupulously according to their precise time value in the manner of a virtuoso passage. According to the character of the piece, these notes may become a whirlwind, a passionate soliloquy, or a burst of laughter. This—and not the vague notion of genius, intuition, or inspiration—makes for a creative interpretation.

Silence is at the origin of the rest signs in musical notation. One must give rests the same care that is given to notes. A performer must make the rests resound; he must "play" the pauses. Silence is as eloquent as the sounds that surround it. Are we aware enough of its importance and positive value within the musical discourse? A silence between two phrases, one ending while the other resumes the thread of an interrupted speech, can be striking.

I am asked, "How do you produce this well-grounded solidity, this straightforwardness of movement in *The Italian Concerto*, for example?" It is very simple; I give the same importance to weak beats as to strong ones. This may surprise the average listener. Weak beats require a weight and a dynamism of their own in relation to their nature and their meaning in the musical phrase. To convince ourselves of this, let us take any musical phrase starting with an upbeat, such as the last movement of Bach's Concerto in G Minor, which is a gigue. The character of this gigue is revealed only when the weak beat is given its full weight and duration.

The importance of the weak beat leads to the problem of *anacrusis*, one that has been misunderstood and badly treated. Riemann in particular went too far and gave the order to start every phrase on an upbeat, be it real or imaginary, even in phrases that are obviously square, in blocks, and should start resolutely and undeniably on the downbeat.

The triplet is an intermediary between one note value and the next. It has its own aspect and a certain weight. Too often the tendency is to rush it. But a triplet has a certain heaviness that must be emphasized; it must give the impression of rolling with ease. Let us not forget, however, that as an intermediary value, slightly held back to prevent its running wild, it must also be kept moving along.

On Tempo

It is said, "Tempo is justice."

Is there one tempo that can be the only right one?

I believe that each work bears in itself its own tempo as well as its own ritardandi and allargandi. Discovering them has to be achieved through comparisons, research, and also intuition. When the piece is a specific dance, it is relatively easy to identify its tempo if one knows the character of that dance.

In choosing a tempo one should always remember that fastness as well as slowness have limits beyond which outlines are either altered or stilled. It is also true that in order to do justice to each note and each rest one must not exceed a certain rapidity. Therefore the tempo of a piece should be based on the speed that allows playing with ease and clarity the shortest note values to be found in that piece.

Generally pieces with many sixteenth-notes are reduced to finger exercises by being played too fast. Works that are considered "profound music"—like the Fugue in D Sharp Minor from Book I of *The Well-Tempered Clavier*, for instance—are played too slowly. Yet authentic contrapuntal writing, that of Bach, does not stand too much rigidity; that kills it.

A moderate tempo is more difficult to sustain than a very fast one. It demands complete domination of the strength and independence of the fingers.

Unity of tempo is relative. During the adventures of the development and its animation, tempo warms up and fluctuates slightly.

Between one metronome stroke and the next there is emptiness. Between one heart beat and the next in a human being there is a whole world. And this brings us to the relation between tempo and feeling.

Once when Moritz Rosenthal was speaking to me of Scarlatti with enthusiasm, he said this significant thing, "It is too often believed that Scarlatti wrote only pieces of virtuosity. Yet what really reveals Scarlatti are his second themes, the slow ones, which prove that he was able to create feeling and profundity too."

Right then I saw clearly what had always disturbed me—the connotation generally given to "feeling" in music. We hear comments such as, "He has a great technique, but no feeling whatsoever." What is this feeling? It could mean many things. But for most people feeling represents a lyricism, more or less sticky, which pours out like slightly turbid water. And this manner of understanding feeling naturally excludes fast movements. As if, to be profound, one had to maintain the tempo of *La Prière d'une Vierge!* Yet in Scarlatti's Sonata (Longo S. 20), for example, does not the apparent monotony of the quick 3/8 tempo contain a whole world of unappeased passion?

The art of performing has been simplified in a singularly summary way; it has been divided into two sections—feeling or virtuosity. There are works incarnating passion, however, which call for a fast tempo, as, for example, the scherzos of Chopin.

About Allargando

To retard the movement in the last bars of a piece is one of the commonplaces of interpretation of music of the past. Its use has become stereotyped. Interpreters offer it without even questioning if it is called for or not. Yet how many times does it happen that a piece ought to end abruptly? An allargando only stops the movement of the phrase, distorts its meaning, and congeals it. On the other hand, how often an allargando, more or less important, is required in the middle of a piece, only to be followed by a swift return to the original tempo? But whoever dares to do it is sharply criticized. This happens because the life of a phrase and, above all, its fluctuations, influenced by the harmony, are misunderstood.

It is true that Frescobaldi said, "Cadences, though written to be played fast, should be somewhat sustained; when they are found at the end of passages preparatory to a final cadence, the tempo should be retarded." But at the same time he advised us to give suppleness to the playing and to follow the flunctuations of the phrase so as to bestow upon it the pulsation necessary to its life. Let us dwell on this thought to understand better its truthfulness. One of the thousands of examples of freedom of tempo inspired by the ebb and flow of the phrase is found in Prelude VII, Book II, of *The Well-Tempered Clavier*. In it the double fugue that follows the preamble, as well as the chorale of instrumental character, would both become a mechanical *perpetuum mobile* if one did not breathe into these sixteenth-notes the beating of the heart—a regular beating to be sure—but one that has nothing of the metronomical.

One should not compress a ritardando into just the last two bars of a piece; one must feel its approach. If there is a trill, it must be spread out and given its own allargando. The amount of ritardando must be in relation to the tempo, character, and length of the piece. It is an architectural fault to give it inordinate proportions; one runs the risk of unsettling and disrupting the whole edifice. It is obvious that a concerto by Bach requires a kind of ritardando different from that needed in his Inventions.

About Rubato

Rubati must not be symmetrical. A rubato occurring in the course of a progression, for instance, should never be repeated. Otherwise it ceases to be "stolen time." Can one steal systematically?

If musicians had the slightest idea of what a ritardando or an accent out of place might reveal . . . they would blush!

What is more deplorable than the spectacle of a vulgar person trying to imitate or copy the rubato of a born artist? This is where recordings may become detrimental.

Someone said to me, "I love the way you play *The Goldberg Variations*. In one of the Variations, however, you make a rubato that I do not understand. I cannot follow you there." I answered that it did not matter, and I thought, "I am perfectly happy, alone with my rubato. Why should you follow me?"

Those who imagine that I play strictly in tempo are to be pitied because they have no ears. I remember my experience with a conductor with whom I was to play a Mozart concerto the following week. Very enthusiastically he said to me, "What I like is that you play in tempo." Evidently I have enough sense, or rather memory, of the tempo; I understand that in all pieces, whether large scaled, like the first movement in the English Suites, or very short, as some of Couperin's are, the immutability of the tempo gives them grandeur as well as scope and perspective. As far as short pieces are concerned, their proportions will stand neither too many tempo fluctuations nor too many changes of registers. Beware, however, those of you who swear by the unity of my tempi and who do not hear the thousand and one minute particles of stolen time, of inserted breathings, of phrases brought into relief, now in shadow, now in full light, that I obtain through retards or deliberate infinitesimal rushings!

The Dance in Music of the Past

Dance held a predominant place in the sixteenth and seventeenth centuries and during most of the eighteenth, not only as an art in itself—that of moving around with dignity, elegance, and nobility—but also because of its rapport with the other arts, especially music, with which it had intimate ties.

Men and women of a frivolous turn of mind were not the only ones dedicated to dancing. On the contrary, the art of *tracer l'amour avec les pieds* (tracing love with the feet) was considered a very serious art, worthy of awakening interest and passion even among philosophers and ministers. The famous Sully, counselor and friend of Henri IV, loved to study new steps, and he took pride in his achievement as a dancer. Forgetting the grandeur and pomp of the church, Cardinal de Richelieu cut capers and pirouetted before Anne d'Autriche; in the grotesque attire of a buffoon—a green velvet costume ornamented with small bells—and castanets in hands, he danced the sarabande to please the queen.

We know the passion for dancing that reigned at the time of Louis XIV. This king himself was an incomparable dancer; probably it was his love for the dance that accounted for his friendship with Lully.

The first dances of Italian origin appeared in France under François I and Henri II; and Catherine de Medici contributed to make them attractive and varied. To spread their popularity, the queen organized magnificent balls at the height of which courtiers who excelled in this art presented series of new dances. At one of these festivities she introduced a novelty which became a lasting success. Each French province was portrayed by its most popular instrument—the violin for Brittany, the tambourin for Provence, and the bagpipe for Poitou. It was then very fashionable at court to reconstruct popular dances of a robust and picturesque character. Thus besides genuine folk dances art dances, or rather stylized dances, were created.

These stylized dances were extensively discussed by all eighteenth-century musicians. But it is in France that they were cultivated the most, and it is there that they attained a marvelous development.

Now comes the most important problem, the concern of all modern musicians. How were these dances performed? What were their tempi, their character? What rapport was there between the choreography of a dance and its interpretation in purely instrumental form? How freely were these instrumental dances treated?

This problem becomes even more extensive when one realizes that the dance was so deeply anchored in the imagination of the composers of the sixteenth to the eighteenth centuries that it created a special language. This is why we encounter so many pages of music that are dances, although it is not specified at the head of the piece. To discover and establish which particular dance is meant is possible only for someone who knows perfectly the form and the cadence of all dances. This knowledge is indispensable. Reading the treatises of the time is but the first step. It is only through close examination and comparisons between a great many works of the period that one can hope to extract little by little the secret of the true cadence of the various dances.

It is interesting that although the musicians of the past differentiated between sacred and secular music, they used dances extensively in their spiritual music. Mattheson, for example, transformed certain chorales into bourrées and recast others in gavotte or polonaise forms. Bach wrote for his wife, Anna Magdalena, the aria "Bist du bei mir," a meditation on love and death, in the form of a minuet. To depict the funeral procession of the faithful

—the tragic and grandiose final chorus of *The St. Matthew Passion*—Bach used a sarabande. Christ's symbolic words, "Take, eat, this is my body," from the same *Passion* are sung also to the rhythm of a minuet. Truly enough, this minuet takes on a sublime character with prophetic accents through Bach's ecstasy.

The mystical Fugues in C Sharp Minor, G Minor, F Sharp Minor, and C Minor from *The Well-Tempered Clavier* are preceded by preludes that are dances. I believe that mysticism inhabited Bach. I also believe that from mysticism to secularism there is but a single step, perhaps not even that. Did not Bach deliberately use parts from his church cantatas in his secular pieces? Is not his "Tabakspfeife Lied" as profoundly mystical as the aria "Aus Liebe will mein Heiland"? And what a pleasure it is to discover secular aspects in a sacred cantata! That suggests angels with upturned skirts!

The tenderness and fervor that overflow from Bach's almost too human heart extend to all his music. Perhaps the only difference between his sacred and his secular music is that his church style is more rigorously contrapuntal.

How essential it is to have the key to the interpretation of certain pages of the music of the past! Otherwise, they would remain for us undecipherable enigmas.

Rhythmic Alterations

Today some musicians interested in the music of the past have come to realize that rhythmic alterations, such as notes inégales, were required in the execution of this music. Here is Landowska's warning:

To apply this style constantly and to play all the notes unevenly is evidently a barbarism. A researcher who is a true artist will avoid doing that because it would be a denial of the magnificent long and pure lines of Bach, Handel, and so many other musicians of the past.

Certain phrases within a piece demand rhythmic alterations, while others do not. To use this alteration all along would give the piece a uniformity detrimental to its flavor. Here enters what

I call discrimination—to know where, when, and how rhythmic alterations should be employed.

The French dotted style deeply influenced Bach and Handel, who created magnificent overtures. This style brought its own particular way of playing. The dotted note had to be played as if it had two dots instead of one. The length of the following note had to be shortened in such a way that it was played very close to the note coming after it. This way of playing the *stile francese* was rigorously observed at the time of Bach and Handel. It slackened off, little by little, toward the second half of the eighteenth century. Quantz, being conservative, observed it to the letter, while Karl Philipp Emanuel Bach—a budding romantic— was less rigorous. This slackening increased, and nineteenth-century romanticism went as far as to reject completely this manner of shortening the note after the dot. Busoni said in his edition of *The Well-Tempered Clavier*, apropos of the D major Fugue from Book I: "Take care not to play the dotted note too long or the sixteenth-note too short—mistakes to which teachers' ears have

long since grown accustomed; not this way

but so

It is thus that my revered master Michalowski taught it to me. According to him, the prolongation of the dot brought vulgarity to the phrase. Oh, the puerility of esthetics! That which from Lully to Bach was proud, chivalrous, and magnificent became vulgar in the nineteenth century!

Interpreting the Ornaments

Music of the past is studded with small signs fascinating to the eyes—the ornaments. Despite the various names given to them —embellishments, grace notes, etc.—ornaments are not, however, some kinds of superadded little bows or flourishes that one can take or leave according to one's fancy. The notes they are made of are music too, and these notes must be inlaid and incorporated to become one with the musical text they decorate. They are not appliquéd; therefore one cannot suppress them at will. Ornaments are organic; they spring from the depth of the musical thought of the composer and reinforce the expression of his intentions, just as they are a vital part of folk songs. An ornament has as much expressive value as the main notes in the midst of which it stands.

Ornaments have a double role—vertical in relation to the harmony and horizontal in regard to the enrichment, rhythmical and melodic, they bring to the musical line. Ornaments animate space by introducing dissonances as though hooking foreign notes to a chord; this provokes shocks and conflicts. Monotony is banished.

It is inconceivable that so many good musicians who know and understand harmony and counterpoint are so far from understanding the *raison d'être* of ornaments.

On the other hand, one hears about the importance of a scrupulous execution of the signs of ornaments. It is, of course, of great importance, but it is not everything.

Most modern musicologists who have treated the subject of ornamentation have applied themselves to collecting the tables of signs left by the composers of the past and to reconstituting their realization. This is very useful preparatory work. None of them, however, has said how this realization must be *interpreted*. Yet between realization and interpretation there is an abyss. Among these musicologists, few have considered the realization of ornaments within the musical phrase in which they occur; or if they have attempted it, they have not taken into account the rhythmic and expressive character of the piece in its entirety, although in this resides the true meaning and the role of the ornament. None of the modern studies on ornaments has revealed the fundamental secret, the essential significance, and the purpose of ornaments in conjunction with the harmonic as well as the melodic structure of the phrase.

Signs of ornaments are comparable to stenography; they also instruct us as to what species an ornament belongs. But in their tables of ornaments, Bach, Couperin, d'Anglebert, and so many others, gave us only a theoretical way of realizing them. If there is such a thing as a mathematical realization of an ornament based on a rigorous observance of the laws fixed by the theorists of the past, the result is merely notes. One can execute ornaments correctly, yet play them badly.

A table of ornaments with their realization is like a piece of canvas on which is sketched a design to be embroidered. But will the trill be long or short? How much should the first note be emphasized? Will the mordent be simple or double? Measured or glided? Will it be introduced within the harmony or just in the melodic line? What will be the distribution of the notes in space? Their duration? Should they be slow or fast?

The sign, even with its realization, indicates only the nature of the ornament. Its execution is left to the discretion of the interpreter.

The decision to make an appoggiatura long or short, to play a mordent fast or slow, etc., should be based upon the predominant traits of the work because ornaments bear the imprint of the principal motives of the piece. An ornament enlightens the phrase it graces because it enhances and fixes the particular expression of this phrase. Sometimes an ornament should have the sweetness of a caress; often it must give the sensation of a passionate bite. Why can an ornament not be a sob, more or less prolonged? Or the "Ohé!" of a peasant woman calling to supper men working in the fields? It could be the joyous cry of a dancer during a square dance.

Who will ever understand and describe the poetry of a simple ornament beaten evenly and slowly?

There is a certain common way of playing trills which reminds me of an electric doorbell. An ornament badly played is like a smile in a toothless mouth.

Ornaments can produce grotesque or comic effects, as in *La Commère* and *La Pantomime* of Couperin or in *The King's Hunt* by Byrd.

Against a background of silence an ornament must draw lines —straight, slanted, or curved; in short, one must be aware of the importance of the ornament in space because it is there to fill that space with arabesques.

Ornaments may become precious indicators of tempo, as in the second *Gigue en Rondeau* from Rameau's E Minor Suite (see the second bar of the second reprise in particular, in which a trill, an appoggiatura, a mordent, and a turn, all in the same 6/8 bar, preclude playing too fast).

What identifies the nature of an ornament is its rhythm. It reveals its life and unveils at the same time its melodic structure and its origin. Therefore the difficulty of realizing an ornament does not reside solely in a faithful translation in so many notes of its scheme as indicated by the composer. It consists in grouping and in embracing those notes in a rhythmical ensemble, the closest in nature to the cut, the expression, and the spirit of the piece.

The most cogent explanation of what an ornament can do to reveal the justness of expression is to be found in the Prelude in C Sharp Minor from Book I of *The Well-Tempered Clavier*. Play it once without ornaments. The piece becomes unintelligible. One senses that it is filled with an expression that does not come through. The emptiness and the long bare notes congeal the motion, stop life, and prevent the unfolding of the long melodic line.

Many ornaments are inspired by the harpsichord—vibrations of interlacing voices, of intercrossing overtones, and all that mysterious world of barely grazed sonorities that vibrate and fill up space. Sometimes it is possible to transpose these ornamental discoveries to the piano; but it is out of the question to think that the piano could inspire them. This is why so many pianists fail to understand the reason for the presence of a certain ornament at a specific place. And this explains the erroneous manner in which pianists frequently play ornaments.

It is too often said that no one agrees about the realization of ornaments. This happens mostly because musicians do not understand that although signs may differ from one composer to another, the ornament itself, its root, remains almost always the same.

For a musician of today, the beginning of a trill by the upper note represents a difficulty that is overcome with effort. And he really balks if the trill is placed on the first note of a motive—for example, in Prelude 16 from Book I and in Fugue 13 from Book II of *The Well-Tempered Clavier*. As if a phrase could not begin with an appoggiatura! In Prelude 16, especially, the expression is intensified by the upper note of the trill, on which one must dwell a little.

The fundamental rule of realization of the trill is that it

should be played on the beat together with the corresponding bass note. Even when the bass part has a rest on that beat, the same rule applies. Those who are unaware of this principle cannot place an ornament over a void with any kind of security.

The realization of a trill should not be vague and indefinite. A trill should sound like small kettledrum beats well distributed into the space it has to fill.

Musicians argue whether an appoggiatura should be long or short. But why not in Lombard taste, that antithesis of French rhythm? Bach liked its angular jerky motion, which refreshes and awakens long appoggiaturas from their slumber. See, for example, Prelude 4 from Book II of *The Well-Tempered Clavier*.

Certain ornaments, such as the slide, etc., are indispensable to hide skips forbidden by the rules of harmony.

As for the *acciaccatura*, it is in its interval of a second—crushed in passing—that all the flavor lies; by pinching it, this second becomes so teasing. We like to repeat it to sharpen our pleasure. After all, were ornaments created as a subject for learned dissertations or for our joy?

One ornament, the repeated note, is much neglected by today's musicians. Yet it has great importance, especially in impassioned, pathetic, or, simply, in tender and affectionate music. This ornamental repeated note was revived by Chopin, who cherished it particularly. Examples of it can be found in Bach's twenty-fifth *Goldberg Variation* and in the Andante of *The Italian Concerto*. We encounter it also in arias from his cantatas and in his flute sonatas. It occurs mostly in connection with a jump of a sixth. Vocal in origin, this ornament flourishes best in soft water, so to speak. It is at its best when the voice and human breathing impart to it that *je ne sais quoi* which is unforeseeable, that which imbues interpretation with this lovely oscillation, this hesitation, this light to-and-fro motion, and this quivering of branches stirred by a soft breeze.

Couperin avoided symmetry in the disposition of his ornaments. His progressions are rarely ornamented in a similar way. Just see the measure before last in *Les Langueurs Tendres*; study and admire how in *La Douce et Piquante*, before the end, the ornament is placed sometimes here, sometimes there, and how much this increases the expression. Couperin knew how to produce equilibrium without conforming to symmetry.

Bach was meticulous and authoritarian. We know he wrote in main notes certain ornamental phrases that Italian composers would have left to the discretion of the interpreter. He preferred to realize them himself. It is obvious that Bach took particular care to avoid misunderstanding. Let us not forget that he corrected in his own hand the *Clavierübung* engraved during his lifetime. This did not prevent his leaving alone a good number of places where ornamentation has to be introduced. Sometimes Bach even indicates an ornament without completing it. For example, in Fugue 1 of Book II of *The Well-Tempered Clavier*, bar 8, a ⌇ is obviously intended. Why then is there only a simple indication and not the complete ornament? Because Bach was certain that the musicians of his time knew what was required at such a place. He did not anticipate the ignorance of today's musicians. (I say this without rancor; it is simply an acknowledgment of fact.)

Bach wrote sarabandes and other dances which are ornamented with astonishing and almost exaggerated profusion. Others are very simple, almost bare. The first should be played as they are; the others demand ornamentation. It was certainly not a lack of imagination that made Bach leave those denuded. When he had time, he ornamented and chiseled with complacency. When he did not do so, doubtless it was because a more important or urgent task prevented him. Bach's spirit was powerfully didactic. We often are under the impression that he ornamented certain of his pieces for our education. And it is perfectly good to consider them in this light.

The more I plunge into a musical phrase, the more I am aware that if one knows the nature, the character, and the relation between ornaments and harmony in general, as well as the particular harmonic and rhythmic pattern of a phrase, it is impossible to go wrong in the choice of ornaments to be added. The musical text itself is a sufficient guide; the author's own ornamentation becomes unnecessary because one knows in advance what ornament he would have used at this or that place. For me, the need for a trill, long or short, or for a mordent, or for any other ornament does not have to be confirmed by the autograph. I often play an ornament which is not marked by the composer. Later, at a similar place, I find it indicated in the text. This confirmation does not surprise me. It happens because I practically live in this music, and I believe that I know intimately the habits of the composer whose work I play.

What does taste mean in the adjunction of an unwritten ornament? It means knowing that at a given place a certain ornament, and no other, is called for.

Because many musicians lack taste and discrimination as well as skill in improvisation, they prefer bare texts for fear of being cheated. A well-known conductor once asked me, "Can you guarantee me one hundred per cent that Bach wanted these ornaments the way you play them?"

It goes without saying that it is daring to graft ornaments on a motive of Bach or to improvise a cadenza for a Mozart concerto. But I do it, since it must be done, telling myself that one must have the courage to unveil one's ego, one's taste, good or bad, and one's skill. Not every interpreter at the time had good taste. Mattheson fulminated against the abuses of some of them in this domain. Yet it was required of all of them to ornament and improvise cadenzas. The art as well as the science of ornamentation was so widespread at that epoch that it had created listeners capable of discernment. Today very rare are those who know when ornamentation is needed and who can differentiate between a good and a bad one.

As paradoxical as it may seem, improvised ornamentation and freedom of imagination can be attained only through learning and strict discipline. While improvising, my taste for adventure sometimes carries me away. But my training in a severe discipline enables me to hold the reins. One has to watch out. The great art of the improviser consists in avoiding overburdening the melodic line. One must keep a perfect equilibrium among the parts and give to the ornaments a graceful and easy gait or, in grave passages, plaintive or pathetic accents, like the breathing of a human voice or the throbbing of the heart. One should be like that Bach interpreter mentioned by Debussy who played without assuming the appearance of an intruder.

The Role of the Accompanying Harpsichordist

The realizations of continuo parts in modern editions of works of the past are deceptive and painful to the eye even before they are heard. The bass, in eighths or sixteenths, plods along while the right hand imperturbably strikes chords, especially on the strong beats, or advances continuously in three or four parts, pedantically realized in a way that smacks of the music school. Above these two hands busy doing a contradictory and joyless job the solo instrument or voice floats separately. Progressions which demand to be ornamented and diversified pass by, dull and monotonous in their bareness. No wonder that music presented in this fashion lacks attractiveness! It should be called "old music" rather than "music of the past." Where are the unexpected chords, the joyous warbling of arpeggios with their lasting vibrations and also that neat voice which, without shouting, decides and cuts through? Alas, this manner of making music is lost, forgotten. All this music in which the most perfect science was so well controlled that one would hear only amiable or affecting dialogues, sallies, laughter, cascades, or majestic corteges—all this music was certainly not written for musicologists, schoolmasters, and critics, but for the joy of listening and for the comfort of our souls.

It is true that the difficulty of realizing a Bach continuo, for instance, is sometimes insuperable. Bach's two-part writing— or even one-part—contains within itself a harmony so complete that it is impossible to add anything without duplications. Bach's writing condenses the harmony and then scatters it.

Couperin, Rameau, and others all agree in stating that *batteries, arpeggiandi,* and syncopated lute-style, in short, anything but struck chords, are best suited to the harpsichord. This does not apply only to solo pieces. The accompanying harpsichordist more than the soloist must avoid all that hits, cuts, or is jerky, unless he wants to reserve them for a special effect or for picturesque music. But even then, stricken and dry chords must appear only exceptionally to contrast with the streaming of arpeggios.

In the seventeenth and eighteenth centuries the continuo (accompanying harpsichord) was played by cultivated musicians who knew their profession and sometimes also had imagination. The first requisite was to be able to follow either the mass of the ensemble or, in a lighter texture, the solo instruments or voices. This ability to adapt the realization of the figured bass to the style of music it had to sustain is indispensable. It represents the true role of the accompanying harpsichordist.

In Venetian operas of the seventeenth century the utterances of exalted beings were always accompanied by bowed instruments. The soft rays of violin vibrations encircled the divine pronouncements with a luminous halo. Pursuing this tradition, Bach framed the words of Jesus with the ethereal sonorities of strings and organ. Other utterances were accompanied sometimes by the organ, sometimes by the harpsichord. This diversification of sonority throws the musical drama of the *Passions* into admirable relief and invigorates the action by enhancing the power of its unfolding.

The words of the Evangelist, accompanied throughout by the harpsichord, form the background of these works. The ecstatic love of the disciples, Matthew or John, brings the sacred tragedy close to us and renders more human the mystic depths of the sufferings of Jesus.

The sullen monotony with which singers usually deliver seventeenth- and eighteenth-century recitatives proves how foreign this music is to modern interpreters. Besides, these recitatives are now generally accompanied by rigid chords placed at regular intervals. Their stiffness stops the flow; and failing to incorporate with the recitative itself, these chords do not participate in the action they are supposed to describe. Such a rendition deprives the recitative of its *raison d'être* and consequently fills the audience with deadly boredom.

The recitative is and should be a revealing vista, a glade. Over the foundation of an arpeggio softly murmured and with lasting vibrations, or of a chord attacked and held or hovering upon the sustained tones of the organ, the recitative, alternating with choruses and arias, pursues its progress with logic and continuity. It differs from the aria by its improvised, nonchalant melodic line suspended in space and framed by rests. One could even deny it a form, so elusive is this melodic thread which stops and starts again. These vistas, these glades, placed between more or less massive choruses and arias, are there to aerate and also to serve as ties in the evolution of the drama. The recitative explains what has just been and prepares us to understand what is going to unfold. This is why recitatives must be phrased so as to express the animation and the liberty of the spoken language with its fluidity, which requires that a certain word be set into relief while another is murmured. A recitative is recounting something as it is happening. The narrator takes us into his confidence and tells us, often familiarly, what he sees. Thus he is doubly interesting, not only because he is relating his own impressions, but because he is trying to convey his feelings to the listeners. This is probably why there are frequently in Bach's recitatives picturesque or descriptive allusions, such as "und krähte der Hahn" (and the cock crowed) in *The St. Matthew Passion* or "weinte bitterlich" (cried bitterly) in *The St. John Passion*, to illustrate the object of the recitative, reinforce its colors, and hold the attention of the audience. But the dramatic value of the recitative resides, first of all, in the choice of the accompanying chords and in their arrangement.

To accompany the *recitativo narrativo* chords should be in turn teeming, tumultuous, filled with agitation and ardor, or harsh and abrupt, replete with powerful descriptiveness. Sometimes they must dissolve into mysterious arpeggios full of sweetness and serenity. While listening to these recitatives, do we not suddenly have a vision of Bach's *Chromatic Fantasy?* Is not that work explained as if by magic? All that Bülow and Liszt found enigmatic vanishes. Instead it becomes clarified in structure and intent; it appears as an accompanied aggregate of lyrical recitatives confided to a single performer. Thus a secular instrumental work is made clear by comparing it to another work entirely different in character and purpose.

About Climax and Monotony

While progressing toward what is called the climax of a piece we feel its approach, and our blood pushes us to be impatient. Enthusiasm is responsible for that. But beware! It is precisely then that one should advance without haste. Along this march toward the culminating point ineffable beauties are found. To hurry is to kill them. A great interpreter, one who understands that, also knows to what extent he can stretch this progress. At such places one must slow down the tempo in order to extract all the expression it contains.

A climax is not always a sign of grandeur. There are masterpieces which are devoid of it.

Does a culminating point really exist in Bach's great works? Let us look, for example, at the first part of the English Suite in F Major. It spreads out like an immense plain. An unceasing life animates it; the dialogue between the parts digs grooves that bring undulations to this plain. Yet the ensemble retains the overall impression of an uninterrupted expanse and a feeling of grandeur. Is it what Rilke called *Flächen* (flatness) in his *Rodin?* It is like the sea in which each wave has its own life; only it emerges to become one with other waves. This multiplied life has ordonnance. Gigantic and dynamic, it is at the same time serene. It seethes, but does not explode. A sovereign hand guides and dominates. There is no crater spitting fire; the culminating point is absent. This moving expanse, liquid or not, sea or plain, reminds me also of certain Persian rugs, vast and monotonous, without any legend in the center. They are monotonous only for those who are unable to discern the infinite gradations of color, of nuances mixed with refinement, like an epic of tinted interlacings.

These kinds of pieces are very taxing for the interpreter, not because of their technical difficulties, which can always be overcome, but because this ceaseless volcanic eruption of uninterrupted sixteenth-notes runs the risk of becoming a *perpetuum mobile* in the manner of Kalkbrenner or Thalberg. What can be done to avoid it? Understand, try to understand, the life of the phrases, their breathings, without which they could not exist, their fluctuations, their rising and falling, their swellings and appeasements. Sudden stops or allargandi are imperative; all the modulations and what they entail must be underlined. Often one has to be bold and either lash, stop, or precipitate the movement.

In works which have no climax monotony is often feared. Why? Mostly because of its generally accepted connotation of wearisome sameness. It has been the chief reason, I believe, for European hostility to oriental music, as well as having been the principal cause for misunderstanding Bach's esthetic. Let us take, for instance, the Sinfonia from *The Christmas Oratorio*. The score calls for strings, *oboe da caccia*, *oboe d'amore*, and flutes. Woodwinds dominate the ensemble, which is bathed in their reedy and monotonous sonority, so imbued with sweetness. Despite the continuous dialogue between winds and strings that makes the piece throb with life, it is pervaded with an unalloyed monotony. Its voluptuous and sweet swaying casts a spell over us; but it opens also unlimited vistas from which all drama and violence are excluded. It is obvious that in interpreting this Sinfonia contrasts that are too sharp must be avoided. Its monotony must, on the contrary, be exalted by emphasizing the regular rocking motion of its *forlane* rhythm.

In works without climax the light is diffused in such a way that each part of the piece receives the amount of light it needs. And, after all, is not the idea of a culminating point, of a climax, a product of the nineteenth century corresponding to the concept of crescendo?

Encores

Why wait until the end of the concert to play a series of pieces which have no connection with the program, its idea, or its spirit?

I prefer—but this is purely personal—to play again a piece from a program when I feel that the audience liked it and reacted to it in a way that moved me.

Also one must acknowledge the fact that a fugue of Bach or a dialogue of Nicolas de Grigny contain beauties impossible to appreciate at a single hearing. And since I myself remain in the company of these pieces for months and years playing them over and over—not as finger exercises, but as a means of finding a key to their mysteries—why should not my audience do the same, at least in a small way? Yes, one should play again pieces already heard. It can only help understanding which, then, becomes joy.

5 ╲ The Mysteries of Interpretation

Criticism

MOST OF THE criticism I receive is complimentary. Yet those
who express their admiration for my playing do not necessarily
understand what I am doing. After a Town Hall recital one of
the leading critics wrote: "In the Bach Partita in C Minor the
opening Sinfonia, the Rondeau, and the Caprice were presented
with the artist's expected mastery. But peculiar liberties were
taken with the Allemande and the Sarabande of this work, for
which Madame Landowska probably has found justification, but
left unexplained in her program notes. The rhythmic alteration
in the subject of the Allemande was one of these new ideas
introduced."

In the same program I also dotted the allemandes of Rameau and Couperin as well as their sarabandes. But the critic did not notice it, because he did not know these pieces.

On what do critics base their criticisms? What are their points of comparisons? They judge from what they hear in concert halls, in public competitions, or in the studios where instrumentalists are rehearsing their pieces exactly as they have been taught by their teachers. Criticism is on a level with the virtuoso's productions. This is why critics hear only the degree of technique and the obvious features of a piece—those they can perceive. Fillings out, like those I introduce in the Sinfonia of the C Minor Partita, subtleties of ornamentation or registration, etc., escape them. Not a word about them. Read any criticism about me and substitute the name of another performer; it will fit just as well. Why? Because the critic is unable to notice what characterizes my playing. This is a professional distortion.

The Liberties I Take

Some people like to describe me as a humble and faithful servant of the old masters. Well, they do not look closely. · I am neither humble nor faithful although I love the old masters in my own way. Yet, the liberties I take—are they really liberties?

Critics attack me because I do not play the dotted note in the theme of the first fugue of The Well-Tempered Clavier, because I do not always observe a tie where it is marked, but mostly because I add ornaments and rhythmical alterations and because my registrations could not always have been done on the harpsichords of the time. But I take many other liberties that remain unnoticed by my critics, although they are numerous and flagrant. It is easy to single out the places where a dot, a tie, or an ornament are not played according to the so-called urtext edition. This is elementary. But where are the ears that can detect the hidden sustained pedal note which resounds in the Prelude in F Major, for instance, or in that in G Minor, bars 3 and 6? And what about my playing of The Bells by William Byrd on my Pleyel harpsichord? Do not expect a scrupulous reading.

Nothing in this world could prevent my interpreting the text as I see it, understand it, and feel it. No doubt I would be astounded were I to hear this piece played by an artist of the time of Shakespeare on an instrument of the period. But, believe me, I am not taking advantage of the fact that it can never happen. It is true that the virginal of William Byrd had few registers. But let us not forget that it was generally heard in concert with fifes, trumpets, lutes, etc.; that made the music extraordinarily colorful.

There is a great discrepancy between the liberties that interpreters were required to take in the seventeenth and eighteenth centuries and the modern transcriptions of pianists who are ignorant of what these liberties were supposed to be.

If on one hand exaggeration and roarings in bad taste are repulsive, on the other, false sobriety is just as exasperating. I admit a liking for the integral, naked text surging from silence and surrounded by solitude, devoid of weighty interpretative indications such as *allegro giocoso, adagio appassionato,* and the like. But the fear of adding a note which cries out to be inserted or of interpreting an ornament when its theoretical realization would be insufficient is a misconception of the spirit of the music of the past.

This sobriety has for its aim the objective presentation of the text without any personal involvement. But is not this tone of indigent indifference another roundabout way of being subjective, since it is deliberate and merely a simulation of indifference?

Apply this "objectivity" to Mozart—he who was a complete man, passionate or cold, tender or teasing, great in his simplicity. What would become of his music? As for Bach, reducing to straightforwardness his involved, ornate, and baroque lines would be like transforming a gothic cathedral into a skyscraper.

Because of the theory of sobriety launched by some ill-bred artist, the average person is suspicious when a phrase of Bach is played freely. For this reason style is rectitude. He considers any deviation from the printed text an act of dishonesty.

Rare are the interpreters who know how to take liberties. But rarer are the listeners who know that certain liberties were laws and customs at one time. Usually the ignorance of these people makes them aggressive.

Stiff-necked people are afraid to experience a thrill of pleasure or to smile amused while listening to the music termed *ancient*. Sometimes to poke fun at them I plan to give them their fill of grave and boring music so that they may experience the "Dignity of Beauty." But my love for music prevails over my mood for mystification, which I hardly possess; and I prefer to give them a kick rather than to be prankish.

Under the hands of some pianists, flashing pieces, Dionysian joy, or unquestionable dynamism are reduced to murmurs, caresses, light sweetness, or charming smiles. It often happens with Scarlatti sonatas, and they become coquettish trifles. Most violinists indulge in the exaggerated use of portamento, and because of this they deprive it of its real value. This manner of insinuating oneself in the good graces of an audience with sweetish obsequiousness—cold-blooded petting—is repulsive to me. It is like a breach of trust. Too often the perpetual pianissimo and a pink and blue murmur delight the average listeners guided by leading critics.

We are told of Mozart's purity and of the simplicity of a Haydn or of a Couperin. But simplicity does not mean poverty, indigence, and ignorance! When we say "the purity of Mozart," we are thinking of the impeccable tracing of his engraving tool, of his writing clear as crystal, but we are not then thinking of what his music expresses. Even when laden with amorous voluptuousness, Mozart's music remains pure.

Simplicity can be that of a brute who only sees and plays what is written. But there is also that of the visionary who discovers, dreams, meditates, throws himself into foolish adventures, but comes back bloody, battered, with his heart wounded, though happy and richer. Then quietness pervades him gradually; everything becomes clearer; waste falls away; simplicity appears little by little. That simplicity has resonances; through it one hears all that has been felt and experienced. Is it necessary to say everything? Is it not sufficient to be conscious and to make it felt through a light and transparent web, one that does not weigh, but only scintillates and vibrates?

The tragedy in the interpretation of music of the past lies in the fact that it is confined to concert halls, congresses of musicology, or conservatory classes. Let us bring it out of these respectable and dull places; let us air it; let us shake prejudices, and let us revive the dead letter of old treatises. Music needs air, sunlight, and liberty to be alive. It is then only that it will impart to us surprising secrets.

Being an Interpreter

Interpretation! What a marvelous and redoubtable adventure into the unknown!

Yes, the unknown; no matter how well we know the author or have memorized a piece, do we know how close to truth our rendition is? What is truth in interpretation? Is it authenticity? Literalism? Or should an interpretation be personal?

How greatly the expression "personal interpretation" has been abused! It is often employed when the more appropriate term "personal playing" is intended. Every one of us has a more or less individual way of playing. He who leans on the keyboard with all the weight of his body obviously obtains a different sonority from him who skims lightly over the keys. There are those who draw strength from the shoulder, the arm, or the forearm, while others seek it from the wrist or from independence of the fingers. Some performers cultivate a *jeu perlé* (pearled articulation); others watch only for the tour de force; a certain pianist, very nervous by nature, will have what is called a "genial style of playing," meaning erratic and studded with false notes.

There is little merit in having a personal manner of playing. As for "personal interpretation," this is something extremely rare. Give an unknown work to a good musician; perhaps he will play it after his own feeling. But if it is a work of Beethoven or Chopin, you may be sure that he will play it in the manner he learned from his master. The more skilled he is in his profession, the more he will be under the yoke of those numerous years of training. And the more sensitive his soul is, the more the impressions received in his youth will be entrenched in his imagination; and these will be the remembrance of the interpretations of the great virtuosos he heard. Enormous efforts are required to bring our fingers to produce other dynamics as well as to prompt our souls and hearts to perceive and feel differently. In the process of interpretation, we are always faced with two main issues—creation or routine. A new work has to be created by various artists as well as by the author. One of these interpretations will survive. The best? Not always; often it will be the one which was propagated by the most fashionable interpreter and transmitted to his pupils and to the pupils of his pupils. This is what has happened with Chopin. The Chopin of the young generation of pianists has no longer any freshness of appearance because they see him through the playing of all his more or less famous interpreters.

To judge impartially the interpretation of a performer the first requisite would be to avoid hearing the work played by anyone else before. But who among us knows a work in its virginity, having only read the score without any commentaries? Is there a well-known phrase to which is not attached the accelerando of a Toscanini or the rubato of another conductor? It is only after living intimately with the music of a composer that we become able to feel without hesitation that certain accessories brought to it by the interpreter are congenial or not to the work.

Today's musicians, especially interpreters, make their way in the domain of ancient music as they would on unfamiliar ground; they do not dare to venture a metaphor or an image, no matter how appropriate it seems to them. Their vague knowledge of the color and characteristics of the epoch stops them at every step and makes them timorous. Their interpretation is reduced to a congealed formula usually called "absolute music."

Interpreters are not sufficiently aware of the prime necessity of knowing the structure of a piece thoroughly in order to re-create it. Musical forms do not exist as intrinsic manifestations. Some among them which were innovations in their epoch can no longer be isolated in the purely theoretical domain, but they are, nonetheless, intimately tied to the genius who in creating them obeyed the demands of his own nature.

Nobody invents anything. Influences appear, they are amplified; a new touch is added, and we witness a renovation similar to a rebirth. Great men are not innovators occupied solely with technical discoveries. If they do bring any modifications to an established form, it is not from a desire to create novelties; but it is from an exigency of their genius. And what is a discovery if not a truth that has always existed and that someone has just seen with surprise and wonder?

When a surgeon operates, the life or death of the patient is at stake. When we play, it is the same thing. The life or death of a piece lies between our two hands, powerless most of the time.

Is a writer who interprets life or a painter who interprets nature more creative than he who interprets Bach, Couperin, or Chopin? At first this question may suggest an ambitious presumption. Yet is not that a creative process, the one which consists of grafting upon something already formed, of adhering to a fixed complex, and of creating upon a creation?

The power and the magic of music lie in its intangibility and its limitlessness. It suggests images, but leaves us free to choose them and to accommodate them to our pleasure.

I always suffer from an astonishment that grows into shock when I look at illustrations in a book. And yet I know some beautiful ones. But they are contrary to the image my fantasy had envisaged. And I think with melancholy of what I offer to my listeners. Tempi, choice of registration, phrasing, etc., are as subjective as these illustrations are. Of course it would be easy for me to justify the ones I use by making comparisons.

Isn't an interpreter a witness to the spectacle of creation? And, after all, is it not expected of a witness who has the inestimable privilege of attending a birth to be discreet and not to swoon more ecstatically than the father or suffer more than the mother? Gounod once said to his wife during the funeral of a friend, "Be careful; do not cry louder than the widow!"

Nothing is more interesting than to probe the quality of a musician's love for the work he is interpreting. Interesting, but also disquieting. Is it necessary to know this musician personally and to question him to make a diagnosis? Doesn't he reveal himself in his playing? As he goes along, doesn't he deposit the proof of his love, giving us a clue to his reasons for choosing this particular work? This proof may turn out to be a frightening confession!

I think of the poor public subjected to the most contradictory interpretations. They understand none of them, but they always applaud.

I sift out the interpretation of other performers. I would do better to listen to mine. Criticism, like charity, begins at home.

On what do I base my interpretations?

On some historical facts, on study grounded on analytical comparisons, and on experience.

By living intimately with the works of a composer I endeavor to penetrate his spirit, to move with an increasing ease in the world of his thoughts, and to know them "by heart" so that I may recognize immediately when Mozart is in good humor or when Handel wants to express triumphant joy. I want to know when Bach is raging and throwing a handful of sixteenths at the face of some imaginary adversary or a flaming spray of arpeggios, as he does in *The Chromatic Fantasy*. The goal is to attain such an identification with the composer that no more effort has to be made to understand the slightest of his intentions or to follow the subtlest fluctuations of his mind. To know what Mozart means when he writes in D major or what Bach wishes to express when he uses the key of E flat major, we have numerous points of comparisons at our disposal among various works on which we can lean and rely and from which we can draw conclusions. A text previously unintelligible becomes clear; then I am able to realize and reconstruct it. A single look at the graphic appearance of a composition often tells me the tempo and character of that piece. But it is only when "scrupulous ears"—the phrase is St. Augustine's—are in immediate contact with the center of understanding that the spark can flash.

Has anyone a right to remain ignorant when he loves something? Does not love give the incentive to search, to penetrate the secret, and to break the seal of mystery? Because there is mystery for those who do not understand; only they do not know it. The seeking lover, on the contrary, realizes after each one of his discoveries how little he knows.

To be an interpreter one must have visions. The richer the imagination of a musician, the more possibilities of sonority he hears. But it is not enough. He must search for means to incorporate and project these visions. In my playing I dramatize in the Greek meaning of the term *drama*—i.e., *action*.

There is a part that escapes reasoning in my interpretation.

Its fulgurant and picturesque side is precisely that about which the Germans, instinctively, had misgivings. They accepted it for Scarlatti or Couperin, but rejected it for Bach. This superman, according to them, had no contact with humanity. Evidently one must be well-bred to allow oneself a certain intimacy with great men without falling into an irreverent familiarity.

When I play, there is always a frame, although I do not care any longer about the rules of interpretation. What I do is comparable to the style of a dancer like the great Argentina or to the improvisations of a good jazz band.

What I seek is a seemingly improvisatory manner which does not let the listener foresee what is coming. I wish to keep surprises in reserve for him. Moreover, I want to experience them myself and not to harbor the knowing look of those who are so sure of where they are going. My approach satisfies me especially in a fugue, in spite of its strictly established form.

How many days and nights of relentless work, of hardship, and of indescribable effort are needed to succeed in playing with careless ease! But I shall obtain it. I pray my god Bach to help me.

I have arrived at a point [*this was written April 13, 1952*] at which I would tear to pieces anyone who would dare say to me, "Modify this or that in your interpretation." Nothing is left of my former moderation. If Rameau himself would rise from his grave to demand of me some changes in my interpretation of his *Dauphine,* I would answer, "You gave birth to it; it is beautiful. But now leave me alone with it. You have nothing more to say; go away!" I am like a tigress defending her cubs. I know that while playing *La Dauphine* I take incredible liberties. Rameau improvised this piece during wedding festivities. Why couldn't I do it too?

The idea of objectivity is utopian. Can the music of any composer maintain its integrity after passing through the living complex—sanguine or phlegmatic—of this or that interpreter? Can an interpreter restrict himself to remaining in the shadow of the author? What a commonplace! What a joke!

Am I right in elevating to such heights the pieces I play? I do not know. But one thing is sure; I shall not relent.

Probably I shall be criticized for playing Bach's fugues in a too picturesque manner. Should not this reproach be addressed to Bach himself? In each one of his fugues Bach depicts a scene or a mood that is obvious to me. I only execute his will.

Reading my commentary for the last movement of Bach's Concerto in D Major, one of our greatest conductors once said to me, "What nerve you must possess to state that this piece is a waltz!" Did the poor little girl who exclaimed, "But the emperor is naked!" in Andersen's *Emperor's New Clothes* have nerve?

Do I have to convince those who obstinately consider Bach's music as absolute and abstract speculations that even his most learned fugues can be poems? My efforts would be as futile as useless. Bach himself does it, and those who do not understand or feel it should refrain from listening to his music. It makes me think of young theological students who do not dare to look at an attractive woman for fear of falling under her charm. But it is most natural for these young men to be inclined toward sensual pleasures, although that is forbidden by their religion. As for the musicians described above, they experience the sensuousness of music only if the composer said so in the title. What poor natures! I would not trust them!

Ancient music! How harmful it was to name it so! Elevated upon a pompous pedestal and removed from mankind, "ancient" music has lost its own life. Why? Could it mean that it never was alive? Could we imagine Bach, whose passionate and constructive character exalts love and life in all its forms—could we imagine his composing only to show off his great knowledge of counterpoint? Did Bach, Couperin, and Scarlatti play the harpsichord to preserve historical truth or because on this instrument they were able to express passion, joy, or despair?

No, ancient music is not "ancient"; it is young; it throbs with an exuberant and warm life which in turn gives us new life. It is thus that we must hear it. Listen to this "ancient" music, young and vibrant. Listen to it, and let yourself be carried away!

Postlude

AT THE CLOSE of this book we might paraphrase Nietzsche and say:

Thus spake Wanda Landowska.

We feel privilged to have been enabled to present the words and thoughts of this unique artist. And our most grateful appreciation goes to our publishers, Sol Stein and Patricia Day, for their understanding, their helpful suggestions, their patience, and their enthusiasm, as well as to Merlyn Pitzele, who drew their attention to our project, and to all concerned with the making of this book.

On Music contains but a fraction of Landowska's notebooks and journals. Among the still unpublished writings a great number are biographical in character and will form the nucleus of our next volume. Also the notes that were too technical for the lay reader have been reserved for didactic purposes.

As seen now for the first time in a collection, the writings of Landowska on music, penned over a period of fifty years, reveal an extraordinary singleness of purpose, an unbroken continuity of thought, a faith and an enthusiasm as strong, as pure, and as unshakable in 1959 as they were the day a little Polish girl vowed to play only the music she loved. None of the bitter vicissitudes of life, which were often Landowska's share, nor the uprooting and destruction of two wars, no sky-high praise nor harsh criticism could succeed in disturbing in the slightest way the ineluctable course of her predestination.

A friend once compared Landowska's life to that of a centuries-old tree. How apt that comparison is! Firmly grounded and powerfully anchored, a tree will each year slowly and inevitably spread a little wider and soar a little higher in search of the freedom of the infinite.

Such a tree, an oak, whose first shoots probably sprang forth during Bach's lifetime, is still magnificently growing on the lawn of the Lakeville house. It is truly a symbol of Landowska's mission on this earth.

D. R.
R. H.

LANDOWSKA DISCOGRAPHY

** Indicates records currently
available in the U.S.A.*

COMPOSER	TITLE AND PARTICULARS	SPEED/LABEL/NUMBER		
ANON.	The Nightingale, 1656, from the Elizabeth Rogers Virginal Book. Recorded New York 1946 in Treasury of Harpsichord Music.	78	RCA	M-1181
		45	RCA	WDM-1181
		LP	RCA	LM-1217*
		LP	HMV	ALP 1246, FALP-218
		LP	RCA	France 630.462
		45	HMV	7 RF-216
	Two Polish Dances of the 17th Century. Recorded Lakeville, Conn. 1951 in Landowska Plays for Paderewski.	LP	RCA	LM-1186
		45	RCA	WDM-1586
J. S. BACH	Capriccio sopra la lontananza del suo fratello dilettissimo (Sch. 992). Recorded Lakeville, Conn. 1957 in The Art of The Harpsichord.	LP	RCA	LM-2194*
		LP	RCA	England RB-160-68
		LP	RCA	France 630.469
		LP	RCA	Germany LM-2194-C
	Chromatic Fantasy and Fugue (Sch. 903). Recorded St-Leu-La-Forêt, France, 1935. With three Little Preludes (Sch. 933-35).	78	HMV	DB-4993/6
		78	RCA	M-323
	—— With Italian Concerto, Toccata in D Major, Partita in B Flat Major. Collection Les Gravures Illustres.	LP	RCA	LCT-1137
		LP	HMV	COLH-71 (Angel)*
	Concerto in D Minor (Sch. 1052) for Harpsichord and Orchestra. E. Bigot, conductor. Denise Restout, continuo. Recorded Paris, 1938.	78	HMV	DB-11229/31
	—— Coupled with Handel's B Flat Major Concerto and Air and Variations in B Flat Major.	LP	HMV	FJLP-5056
	—— Coupled with 15 Two-Part Inventions.	LP	RCA	LM-1974

J. S. BACH	English Suite in A Minor (Sch. 807). Recorded Paris 1935.	78 HMV 78 RCA 78 RCA	DB-3240/1 14877/8 Part of M-447
	English Suite in E Minor (Sch. 810). Passepieds only. Recorded Europe 1905.	Piano-Roll	Welte-Mignon 955
	—— Recorded London 1928 with Fantasia in C Minor (Sch. 906).	78 HMV	DA-1129
	English Suite in G Minor (Sch. 808). Gavottes only. Recorded Camden, N.J. 1923, with Byrd's Wolsey's Wilde.	78 Victor 78 HMV	1599 DA-1014
	—— Reissued as Thirtieth Anniversary Record in 1953.	45 RCA	1424
	Fantasia in C Minor (Sch. 906). Recorded London 1928 with Passepieds from English Suite in E Minor.	78 HMV	DA-1129

	—— Recorded Lakeville, Conn. 1957 in The Art of The Harpsichord.	LP RCA
		LP RCA
		
		LP RCA
		LP RCA
			LM-2194*
			England
			   RB-160-68
			France 630.469
			Germany
			   LM-2194-C

	Fantasia in C Minor (Sch. 919). Recorded New York 1946 in Treasury of Harpsichord Music.	78 RCA 45 RCA LP RCA LP HMV LP HMV LP RCA	M-1181 WDM-1181 LM-1217* ALP-1246 FALP and QALP-218 France 630.462
	French Suite in E Major (Sch. 817). Recorded Paris 1936.	78 HMV 78 RCA	DB-5005 14384
	Fughetta in C Minor (Sch. 961). Recorded St-Leu-La-Forêt, France, 1936 with Italian Concerto.	78 HMV 78 RCA	DB-5008 14233
	Goldberg Variations (Sch. 988). —— Recorded Paris 1933.	78 HMV	DB-4908/13
	—— Recorded New York 1945	78 RCA 45 RCA LP RCA LP HMV LP HMV	M-1022 WDM-1022 LM-1080* ALP-1139 FALP and QALP-137
	Inventions, Fifteen Two-Part (Sch. 772-786). Recorded Lakeville, Conn. 1954-55. Issued with Bach Concerto in D Minor.	LP RCA	LM-1974

J. S. BACH —— With spoken Introduction in English and *Three-Part Inventions as Memorial Edition.*	LP	RCA	LM-2389*
—— Coupled with Polish Music.	LP	RCA	France 630.516˘
Inventions, Seven Three-Part (Sch. 787, 788, 791, 797, 799 800, 801). Recorded Lakeville, Conn. 1957 and 1959. Issued with *15 Two-Part Inventions* and a spoken Introduction in English as *Memorial Edition.*	LP	RCA	LM-2389*
—— Coupled with 4 Preludes and Fugues and a spoken Introduction in French as *Testament Musical.*	LP	RCA	France 630.554
Italian Concerto (Sch. 971). Recorded St-Leu-La-Foret, France 1936. With three *Little Preludes* (Sch. 924, 939, 999) and *Fughetta in C Minor* (Sch. 961).	78 78	HMV RCA	DB-5007/8 14232/3
—— With *Partita in B Flat Major, Toccata in D Major, Chromatic Fantasy and Fugue.*	LP	RCA	LCT-1137
Collection *Les Gravures Illustres.*	LP	HMV	COLH-71 (Angel)*
Little Preludes (Sch. 933-35). With *Chromatic Fantasy and Fugue.* Recorded St-Leu-La Forêt, France, 1935.	78 78	HMV RCA	DB-4994 M-323
Little Preludes (Sch. 936-38). With *Partita in B Flat Major.* Recorded St-Leu-La-Forêt, France, 1935.	78 78	HMV RCA	DB-4996 M-323
Little Preludes (Sch. 924, 939, 999). With *Italian Concerto* and *Fughetta in C Minor.* Recorded St-Leu-La-Forêt, France, 1936.	78 78	HMV RCA	DB-5008 14233
Partita in B Flat Major (Sch. 825). Recorded St-Leu-La-Forêt, France, 1935. With 3 *Little Preludes* (Sch. 936-38).	78 78	HMV RCA	DB-4993/6 M-323
—— With *Italian Concerto, Toccata in D Major, Chromatic Fantasy and Fugue.*	LP	RCA	LCT-1137
Collection *Les Gravures Illustres.*	LP	HMV	COLH-71 (Angel)*
Partita in C Minor (Sch. 826). Recorded Lakeville, Conn. 1957 in *The Art of The Harpsichord.*	LP LP	RCA RCA	LM-2194* England RB 16068
	LP LP	RCA RCA	France 630.469 Germany LM-2194-C

J. S. BACH	Prelude, Fugue, and Allegro in E Flat Major (Sch. 998). Recorded New York 1946 in Treasury of Harpsichord Music.	78	RCA	M-1181

	78	RCA	M-1181
	45	RCA	WDM-1181
	LP	RCA	LM-1217*
	LP	HMV	ALP-1246
	LP	HMV	FALP and QALP-218
	LP	RCA	France 630.462

Sonata in E Major, Harpsichord and Violin (Sch. 1016) with Yehudi Menuhin. Recorded New York 1944.

	78	RCA	M-1035
	78	HMV	DB-6681/3

—— Coupled with Bach's Double Violin Concerto.

45	RCA	WTC-1120
LP	RCA	LCT-1120
LP	RCA	LVT-1006
LP	HMV	FJLP-5018

Toccata in D Major (Sch. 912). Recorded St-Leu-La-Forêt, France, 1936. With Pachelbel's Magnificats.

78	HMV	DB-5047/8
78	RCA	15171/2

—— With Italian Concerto, Chromatic Fantasy and Fugue, Partita in B Flat Major.

LP	RCA	LCT-1137

Collection Les Gravures Illustres.

LP	HMV	COLH-71 (Angel)*

The Well-Tempered Clavier (Sch. 846-893). Recorded Lakeville, Conn. 1950-54 except for Preludes and Fugues 1-8, recorded New York 1949.

Limited Edition.

LP	RCA	LM-6800

Complete Set.

LP	RCA	LM-6801*

Book I. Preludes and Fugues 1 to 24.

LP	RCA	France 630.474/6

Preludes and Fugues 1 to 8.

LP	RCA	LM-1017*
45	RCA	WDM-1338
78	HMV	DB-21121/6
LP	HMV	ALP and FALP-141
78	RCA	DM-1338
LP	RCA	France 630.474

Preludes and Fugues 9 to 16.

LP	RCA	LM-1107
45	RCA	WDM-1439
78	RCA	DM-1439
LP	RCA	France 630.475
LP	HMV	ALP and FALP-142

Preludes and Fugues 17 to 24.

LP	RCA	LM-1136
45	RCA	WDM-1517
78	RCA	DM-1517
LP	RCA	France 630.476
LP	HMV	ALP and FALP-143

Prelude and Fugue 11, in Testament Musical.

LP	RCA	France 630.554

COMPOSER	TITLE AND PARTICULARS	SPEED	LABEL	NUMBER
J. S. BACH	Preludes 1 and 5, Fugue 7, in *The Smiling Bach*.	LP LP	RCA RCA	LM-1877 France 630.359
	Book II. Preludes and Fugues 25 to 48.	LP	RCA	France 630.270/2
	Preludes and Fugues 25 to 32.	LP 45 LP	RCA RCA RCA	LM-1152 WDM-1552 Italy A 12 R-0106
	Preludes and Fugues 33 to 40.	LP 45 LP	RCA RCA RCA	LM-1708 WDM-1708 Italy A 12 R-0108
	Preludes and Fugues 41 to 48.	LP	RCA	LM-1820
	Preludes and Fugues 27, 38, and 45. In *Testament Musical*.	LP	RCA	France 630.554
BACH- VIVALDI	*Concerto in D Major* (Sch. 972). Recorded New York 1946 in *Treasury of Harpsichord Music*.	78 45 LP LP LP 78	RCA RCA RCA HMV RCA HMV	M-1181 WDM-1181 LM-1217* ALP-1246, FALP-218 France 630.462 DB-6819
	—— Part of *Landowska Plays*.	45 45	RCA HMV	EP ERA-127 7 RF-246
BEETHOVEN	*Andante Favori in F Major*. Recorded in U.S.A., probably 1923.	Piano-Roll		Duo-Art 71350
BERLIOZ- LISZT	*Ballet des Sylphes* from *The Damnation of Faust*. Recorded Europe 1905.	Piano-Roll		Welte-Mignon 965
W. BYRD	*Wolsey's Wilde*. Recorded London 1928 with *Gavotte* from English Suite in G Minor by Bach. Harpsichord.	78 78	HMV Victor	DA-1014 1599
D. CATO	*Chorea Polonica*. Recorded Lakeville, Conn. 1951 in *Landowska Plays for Paderewski*.	LP 45 LP	RCA RCA RCA	LM-1186 WDM-1586 France 630.516
CHAMBON- NIERES	*Chaconne in F Major*, No. 116 and *Rondeau in F Major*, No. 106. Recorded Paris 1935 with Daquin, *L'Hirondelle*, and Lully, *Les Songes Agréables d'Atys*.	78 78	HMV RCA	DB-4973 15186
	Sarabande in D Minor, No. 88. Recorded New York 1946 in *Treasury of Harpsichord Music*.	78 45 LP LP LP LP 45	RCA RCA RCA HMV HMV RCA HMV	M-1181 WDM-1181 LM-1217* ALP-1246 FALP and QALP-218 France 630.462 7 RF-254

F. CHOPIN	*Mazurka No. 34 in C Major,* Op. 56 No. 2. Recorded Lakeville, Conn. 1951 in *Landowska Plays for Paderewski.*	LP RCA 45 RCA 45 RCA LP RCA	LM-1186 WDM-1586 EP ERA-128 France 630.516
	Waltz in B Minor, Op. 69 No. 2. Recorded Europe 1905.	Piano-Roll	Welte-Mignon 964
	Waltz in D Flat Major, Op. 64 No. 1. Recorded Europe 1905.	Piano-Roll	Welte-Mignon 963
F. COUPERIN	*Air dans le Goût Polonais,* Ordre 20. Recorded Lakeville, Conn. 1951 in *Landowska Plays for Paderewski.*	LP RCA 45 RCA 45 RCA LP RCA	LM-1186 WDM-1586 EP ERA-128 France 630.516
	L'Arlequine, Ordre 23, and *Les Barricades Mystérieuses,* Ordre 6. Recorded New York 1946 in *Treasury of Harpsichord Music.*	78 RCA 45 RCA LP RCA LP HMV LP RCA 45 RCA 45 HMV	M-1181 WDM-1181 LM-1217* ALP-1246, FALP-218 France 630.462 EP ERA-127 7 RF-216
	Album recorded Paris 1934: *La Favorite,* Ordre 3; *Les Moissonneurs, Les Langueurs Tendres, Le Gazouillement, La Commère, Le Moucheron, Les Bergeries,* Ordre 6; *La Passacaille,* Ordre 8; *Les Fastes de la Grande et Ancienne Ménestrandise,* (Nos. 2 and 3 only), Ordre 11; *Les Folies Françaises,* Ordre 13; *Le Dodo, La Musète de Taverni; Les Vergers Fleuris,* Ordre 15; *La Soeur Monique,* Ordre 18; *Les Calotins et Les Calotines,* Ordre 19; *Les Tambourins,* Ordre 20.	78 HMV	DB-4941/6
	Les Folies Françaises, Ordre 13; and *Les Calotins et Calotines,* Ordre 19; as part of *Trois Claviers Célèbres.*	LP HMV	France FCX-726
	Passacaille. Recorded Paris 1934 with Rameau, *Suites in E Minor and G.* Collection *Les Gravures Illustres.*	LP HMV	COLH-302
	Le Rossignol en Amour, Ordre 14. Recorded London 1928 with Scarlatti *Sonata L. 413.*	78 HMV	DA-1130
C. DAQUIN	*Le Coucou.* Harpsichord with chamber orchestra. Recorded Camden, N.J. 1926 with Rameau, *Tambourin,* and Mozart, *Minuet from Don Giovanni.*	78 Victor 78 HMV	1199 DA-977

C. DAQUIN —	Recorded London 1928 (Harpsichord alone) with Landowska, *Bourrée d'Auvergne* No. 2.	78 HMV 78 Victor	DA-964 1423
	L'Hirondelle. Recorded Europe 1905.	Piano-Roll	Welte-Mignon 960
—	Recorded Paris 1935 (Harpsichord) with Chambonnières, *Chaconne in F Major, Rondeau in F Major,* and Lully, *Les Songes d'Atys.*	78 HMV 78 RCA	DB-4973 15186
F. DURANTE	*Divertimento in G Minor.* Recorded Europe 1905.	Piano-Roll	Welte-Mignon 957

J. K. F. FISCHER	*Passacaglia in D Minor.* Recorded Lakeville, Conn. 1957 in *The Art of The Harpsichord.*	LP RCA
		LP RCA
		
		LP RCA
		LP RCA
			LM-2194*
			England
			  RB-160-68
			France 630.469
			Germany
			  LM-2194-C

G. F. HANDEL	*Air and Variations in B Flat Major.* Recorded Paris 1937 with *B Flat Major Concerto.*	78 HMV LP HMV	DB-3308 FJLP-5056
	Air and Variations "The Harmonious Blacksmith" from *Suite No. 5 in E Major.*		
—	Recorded Camden, N.J. 1923.	78 Victor	acoustic 973
—	Recorded Camden, N.J. 1926.	78 Victor 78 HMV	electrical 1193 DA-860
—	Recorded Paris 1936 as part of *Suite 5.*	78 HMV 78 RCA	DB-4978 M-592/4
—	Recorded New York 1946 in *Treasury of Harpsichord Music.*	78 RCA 45 RCA LP RCA LP HMV LP RCA 45 HMV	M-1181 WDM-1181 LM-1217* ALP-1246, FALP-218 France 630.462 7 RF-254
	Concerto in B Flat Major, Op. 6, No. 4. Harpsichord and Orchestra. E. Bigot, conductor. Cadenzas by Wanda Landowska. Recorded Paris 1937.	78 HMV LP HMV	DB-3307/8 FJLP-5056
	Harpsichord Suites: No. 2 in F Major, No. 5 in E Major, No. 7 in G, Minor, No. 10 in D Minor, No. 14 in G Major. Recorded Paris, 1936.	78 HMV 78 RCA	DB-4977/82 M-592

J. HAYDN	Andante and Variations in F Minor (Hoboken Gr. XVII, No. 6). Piano. Recorded Lakeville, Conn. 1957-58.	LP	RCA	LM-6073*

	Ballo Tedesco (Hoboken Gr. IX, No. 22). Harpsichord. Recorded Paris 1937 with D Major Concerto.	78	HMV	DB-3295
		78	RCA	M-471

	Concerto in D Major (Hoboken Gr. XVIII, No. 11). Harpsichord and Orchestra. E. Bigot, conductor. Cadenzas by Wanda Landowska. Recorded Paris 1937 with Minuet from Sonata No. 36 and Ballo Tedesco.	78	HMV	DB-3293/5
		78	RCA	M-471
		45	RCA	WCT-43
	___ Coupled with Mozart's Coronation Concerto.	LP	RCA	LCT-1029

	Minuet in C Sharp Minor from Sonata No. 36. Harpsichord. Recorded Paris 1937 with Haydn's D Major Concerto.	78	HMV	DB-3295
		78	RCA	M-471

	Sonatas Nos. 35 in C Major, 37 in D Major, and 40 in G Major. Harpsichord. Nos. 34 in E Minor and 49 in E Flat Major. Piano. Recorded Lakeville, Conn. 1957-59.	LP	RCA	LM-6073*

JACOB LE POLONAIS	Gagliarda and Courante. Recorded Lakeville, Conn. 1951 in Landowska Plays for Paderewski.	LP	RCA	LM-1186
		45	RCA	WDM-1586
		LP	RCA	France 630.516

LANDOWSKA	Bourrée d'Auvergne No. 1. Acoustic recording. Recorded Camden, N.J. 1923 with Scarlatti's Sonata L. 465.	78	Victor	1038
		78	HMV	DA-652

	Bourrée d'Auvergne No. 2. Electrical recording.	78	HMV	DA-964
	___ Recorded London 1928 with Daquin's Coucou.	78	Victor	1423
	___ Recorded Lakeville, Conn. 1951 in Landowska Plays for Paderewski.	LP	RCA	LM-1186
		45	RCA	WDM-1586
		LP	RCA	France 630.516

	The Hop. Polish folksong transcribed for harpsichord by Landowska. Recorded Lakeville, Conn. 1951 in Landowska Plays for Paderewski.	LP	RCA	LM-1186
		45	RCA	WDM-1586
		LP	RCA	France 630.516

LULLY- D'ANGLEBERT	Les Songes Agréables d'Atys. Recorded Paris 1935 with Chambonnières' Chaconne and Rondeau and Daquin's L'Hirondelle.	78	HMV	DB-4973
		78	RCA	15186

J. LANNER	Valses Viennoises. Transcribed for piano by Wanda Landowska. Recorded U.S.A. 1923.	Piano-Roll		Duo-Art 6828-3
W. A. MOZART	Coronation Concerto in D Major, K. 537. Piano and Orchestra. W. Goehr, conductor. Cadenzas by Wanda Landowska. Recorded London 1937 with Mozart's Fantasia in D Minor.	78 78 45	HMV RCA RCA	DB-3147/50 M-483 WCT-44
	—— Coupled with Haydn Concerto in D Major.	LP	RCA	LCT-1029
	—— Coupled with Mozart's Sonata in D Major K. 576. Collection Les Gravures Illustres.	LP	HMV	COLH-95*

	Country Dances, K. 606. Transcribed for piano by Wanda Landowska. Recorded Lakeville, Conn. 1956.	LP
		LP
		LP
		
		LP
		LP
			RCA
			RCA
			RCA
			
			RCA
			RCA
				LM-6044*
				LM-2205*
				England
				  RB-1617
				France 630.380
				Germany
				  LM-9820-E

	Fantasia in D Minor, K. 397. Piano. Recorded London 1937. With Mozart's Coronation Concerto.	78 78 45	HMV RCA RCA	DB-3150 M-483 WCT-44
	—— As part of Homage to Mozart	LP	RCA	LM-6130
	Minuet in D Major, K. 355. Harpsichord. Recorded New York 1946 in Treasury of Harpsichord Music.	78 45 LP LP LP LP	RCA RCA RCA HMV HMV RCA	M-1181 WDM-1181 LM-1217* ALP-1246 FALP and QALP-218 France 630.462
	Minuet from Don Giovanni. Harpsichord and chamber orchestra. Recorded Camden, N.J. 1926 with Daquin's Coucou and Rameau's Tambourin.	78 78	Victor HMV	1199 DA-977
	Rondo alla Turca from A Major Sonata, K. 331. Recorded Camden, N.J. 1923 with Handel's Harmonious Blacksmith. Harpsichord. Acoustic Recording.	78	Victor	973
	—— Recorded Camden, N.J. 1926. Harpsichord. Electrical Recording.	78 78	Victor HMV	1193 DA-860

COMPOSER	TITLE AND PARTICULARS	SPEED	LABEL	NUMBER
W. A. MOZART	— Recorded New York 1946 in *Treasury of Harpsichord Music*.	78	RCA	M-1181
		45	RCA	WDM-1181
		LP	RCA	LM-1217*
		LP	HMV	ALP-1246
		LP	HMV	FALP and QALP-218
		LP	RCA	France 630.462
		45	HMV	7 RF-184
	Rondo in A Minor, K. 511. Piano. Recorded Lakeville, Conn. 1955-56.	LP	RCA	LM-6044*
		LP	RCA	LM-2284*
		LP	RCA	France 630.381
	Rondo in D Major, K. 485. Harpsichord. Recorded New York 1946 in *Treasury of Harpsichord Music*.	78	RCA	M-1181
		45	RCA	WDM-1181
		LP	RCA	LM-1217*
		LP	HMV	ALP-1246
		LP	HMV	FALP and QALP-218
		LP	RCA	France 630.462
		45	HMV	7 RF-184
	Sonata in D Major, K. 576. — Recorded U.S.A. 1923.	Piano-Roll		Duo-Art
	Allegro			67560
	Adagio			67760
	Allegretto			67850
	also	Piano-Roll		Ampico
	Allegro			66333
	Adagio and Allegretto			66743
	— Recorded Paris 1938. Piano. Coupled with Mozart's *Coronation Concerto*. Collection *Les Gravures Illustres*.	LP	HMV	COLH-95*
	Sonatas in *E Flat Major*, K. 282, *G Major*, K. 283, *D Major*, K. 311, *B Flat Major*, K. 333, with *Rondo in A Minor* and *Country Dances*. Piano. Recorded Lakeville, Conn. 1955-56.	LP	RCA	LM-6044*
	Sonatas K. 282, 311 and *Country Dances*.	LP	RCA	LM-2205*
		LP	RCA	England RB-16017
		LP	RCA	France 630.380
		LP	RCA	Germany LM-9820-E
	Sonatas K. 283 and 333 with *Rondo A Minor*.	LP	RCA	LM-2284*
		LP	RCA	France 630.381
	Wanda Landowska's Introduction to her Mozart Album LM-6044. Recorded Lakeville, Conn. 1956. In English. Not for sale.	45	RCA	G RH-9164/5
	Sonata in F Major, K. 332. Piano. Recorded Paris, 1938.	Still to be released.		

M. C. OGINSKI	Polonaise in A Minor and Polonaise in G Major. Harpsichord. Recorded Lakeville, Conn. 1951 in Landowska Plays for Paderewski.	LP 45	RCA RCA	LM-1186 WDM-1586
	Polonaise in G Major only	45	RCA	EP ERA-128
J. PACHELBEL	Magnificats Secundi Toni No. 2 in G Minor. Octavi Toni No. 11 in G Major. Recorded St-Leu-La-Forêt, France, 1936, with Bach's Toccata in D Major.	78 78	HMV RCA	DB-5048 15172
H. PURCELL	Ground in C Minor. Recorded New York 1946 in Treasury of Harpsichord Music.	78 45 LP LP LP LP 45	RCA RCA RCA HMV HMV RCA HMV	M-1181 WDM-1181 LM-1217* ALP-1246 FALP and QALP-218 France 630.462 7 RF-216
J. P. RAMEAU	Air Grave Pour Deux Polonais from the Prologue to Les Indes Galantes. Recorded Lakeville, Conn. 1951 in Landowska Plays for Paderewski.	LP 45 LP	RCA RCA RCA	LM-1186 WDM-1586 France 630.516
	La Dauphine. Recorded New York 1946 in Treasury of Harpsichord Music.	78 45 LP LP LP LP	RCA RCA RCA HMV HMV RCA	M-1181 WDM-1181 LM-1217* ALP-1246 FALP and QALP-218 France 630.462
	La Joyeuse, Les Tricotets, La Poule, Menuets I and II, Les Sauvages. Recorded Paris 1935.	78 78	HMV RCA	DB-4990 15179
	Suite in E Minor: Allemande, Courante, Gigues en Rondeau, Le Rappel des Oiseaux, Rigaudons I and II, Musette en Rondeau, Tambourin, La Villageoise. Recorded Paris 1935.	78 78	HMV RCA	DB-5077/9 M-593
	Suite in E Minor, recorded Paris 1938, Suite in G recorded Paris 1935 with Couperin, Passacaille. Collection Les Gravures Illustres.	LP	HMV	COLH-302
	Le Tambourin. Harpsichord and Chamber Orchestra. Recorded Camden, N.J. 1926.	78 78	Victor HMV	1199 DA-977
	——— Recorded Paris 1938. Harpsichord alone. Part of Suite in E Minor.	78 78	HMV RCA	DB-5077/9 M-593

D. SCARLATTI	*Sonata in D Minor*, L. 413. Recorded London 1928 with Couperin, *Le Rossignol en Amour*.	78	HMV	DA-1130

Sonatas in D Major, L. 418, and in *D Minor*, L. 423. Recorded New York 1946 in *Treasury of Harpsichord Music*.

78	RCA	M-1181
45	RCA	WDM-1181
LP	RCA	LM-1217*
LP	HMV	ALP-1246
LP	HMV	FALP and QALP-218
LP	RCA	France 630.462

Sonata in D Major, L. 465. Acoustic Rec. Recorded Camden, N.J. 1923 with *Bourrée d'Auvergne* No. 1.

78	Victor	1038
78	HMV	DA-652

Twenty Sonatas. Recorded Paris 1935. Collection *Great Recordings of the Century*. C Major, L. 104; F Minor, L. 438; G Major, L. 232; G Minor, L. 488; A Major, L. 132; F Major, L. 384; F. Minor, L. 475; B Minor, L. 263; D Major, L. 463; F Sharp Minor, L. 294; D Major, L. 208; C Sharp Minor, L. 256; E Major, L. 257; E Major, L. 375; G Major, L. 527; G Minor, L. 338; E Flat Major, L. 142; E Major, L. 23; F Major, L. 474; F Major, L. 479.

78	HMV	DB-4960/5
LP	HMV	COLH-73* (Angel)

Twenty Sonatas. Recorded Paris 1939-40. D Major, L. 461; B Minor, L. 449; F Minor, L. 382; D Major, L. 56; D Major, L. 213; F Minor, L. 187; G Major, L. 103; C Major, L. 255; A Minor, L. 138; D Minor, L. 422; G Minor, L. 49; F Major, L. 228; D Major, L. 14; B Flat Major, L. 97; F Minor, L. 20; D Major, L. 418; D Minor, L. 423; B Flat Major, L. 497; D Major, L. 206; C Major, L. 102.

78	HMV	DB-11205/11
LP	HMV	FJLP-5055

___ *Sonatas* L. 422 and 206 only. *Christmas Greetings from RCA Victor*.

45	RCA	2 LA-2903/ 2 LA-3297

R. SCHUMANN *Waltz in A Minor*. Recorded Europe 1905.

Piano-Roll   Welte-Mignon 961

Unless otherwise indicated, all recordings are performed on a Pleyel Harpsichord. All piano recordings are played on a Steinway with the exception of Mozart's *Sonatas* K. 576 and 332, which are played on a Pleyel piano.

MISSING BROADCASTS

THANKS to the development of home recording equipment, some of Landowska's broadcast performances have been preserved on acetate records, wire, or tape. In an effort to locate such recordings, the *Saturday Review* and *Musical America* published in 1960 a complete list of Landowska's performances broadcast in this country and in Canada since 1941. Many answers were received, and the Landowska Collection was augmented by several very valuable tape copies generously contributed by the owners of those recorded broadcasts. These tapes are preserved with the rest of the Landowska Collection in Lakeville, Connecticut. They are frequently played for the benefit of the friends and admirers of Landowska and of the students who come here to work and rekindle their inspiration. In their name and in mine, grateful thanks are extended to all who responded so spontaneously to the appeal.

Many broadcast programs, however, are still missing. Any information about the possible existence of a recording of any one of them would be deeply appreciated. Dates are as follows:

February 15, 1942	WQXR	Interview in Polish
April 2, 1942	WEAF	RCA Victor Hour. Interview.
November 2, 1942	CBS	Bach, Concerto in F Minor. (B. Hermann, conductor)
November 9, 1942	CBS	Handel, Suite in E Major.
November 16, 1942	CBS	Vivaldi-Bach, Concerto in D Major.
November 23, 1942	CBS	Scarlatti, Sonatas L. 23, 255, 132 and 475.
November 30, 1942	CBS	Couperin, Passacaille.
December 7, 1942	CBS	Pachelbel, Magnificats; Bach, Fantasia in C Minor.
December 14, 1942	CBS	Rameau, La Follette, La Poule, Menuets.
December 21, 1942	CBS	Byrd, The Bells; Noëls by Dandrieu, Le Bègue and Daquin; Landowska, Kolendy (with orchestra).
December 28, 1942	CBS	Handel, Concerto in B Flat Major (B. Hermann, conductor).

Canadian Broadcasting Co. from Toronto. Seven Sunday evenings.

March 14, 1943	CBC	K. P. E. Bach, Concerto in G Minor (1754). Telemann.
March 21, 1943	CBC	K. P. E. Bach, Concerto in G Minor (1740). J. S. Bach, Italian Concerto.
March 28, 1943	CBC	K. P. E. Bach, Concerto in C Minor (1739). Couperin, Passacaille.
April 4, 1943	CBC	K. P. E. Bach, Concerto in A Major (1741). Scarlatti, Sonatas.
April 11, 1943	CBC	K. P. E. Bach, Concerto in F Major (1744). Handel, Suite in E Major.
April 18, 1943	CBC	K. P. E. Bach, Concerto in G Major (1745). Rameau, Suite in E Minor.
April 25, 1943	CBC	K. P. E. Bach, Concerto in D Major (1745). Vivaldi-Bach, Concerto in D Major.

November 17, 1943	CBS	Invitation to Music, 11:30 P.M. Handel, Concerto in B Flat Major and Air and Variations in B Flat Major.
November 28, 1943	WNYC	Frick Collection Concert.
February 22, 23, 1945	CBS	N.Y. Philharmonic (Rodzinski, conductor). Mozart, Piano Concerto K. 413.
January 6, 1946	WNYC	Frick Collection Concert.
December 8, 1946	WNYC	Frick Collection Concert.
March 9, 1947	WNYC	Frick Collection Concert.
March 7, 1948	WNYC	Frick Collection Concert.
February 11, 1951	WNYC	Frick Collection Concert.
March 2, 1952	WNYC	Frick Collection Concert.

One piano-roll is still sought:
LANNER-LANDOWSKA Valses Viennoises Duo-Art or Ampico 6828-3

MUSICAL WORKS COMPOSED BY WANDA LANDOWSKA

Hebrew Poem for Orchestra
Serenade for Strings
Liberation Fanfare for Band (played by the Goldman Band, New York)
Variations for Two Pianos
Rhapsodie Orientale for Piano
Piano Pieces (several of which won prizes in music contests in Paris)
Numerous Lieder
Choir for Female Voices and Orchestra
Polish Folksongs a cappella (composed for the *Orfeo Catala* of Barcelona)
Polish Folksongs for Solo Voice with Choir and Orchestra
Polish Folksongs for Harpsichord and Small Ensemble
The Hop, Polish Folksong for Harpsichord solo
Bourrées d'Auvergne for Harpsichord solo
Chain of Ländler by Schubert, transcribed for Piano (Breitkopf and Härtel, Leipzig; A. Gutheil, Paris)
Valses Viennoises by Lanner, transcribed for Piano (G. Schirmer, New York)
Country Dances by Mozart (K.606) transcribed for Piano (Carl Fischer, New York)
Cadenzas for Mozart Piano Concertos No. 9 in E Flat Major K.271
No. 11 in F Major K.413
No. 12 in A Major K.414
No. 13 in C Major K.415
No. 20 in D Minor K.466
No. 22 in E Flat Major K.482
No. 26 in D Major K.537
Cadenzas for Mozart Sonata in B Flat Major K.333
Cadenza for Handel Concerto in B Flat Major Opus 4, No. 6
Cadenzas for Haydn Concerto in D Major, Opus 21.
All Cadenzas are published by Broude Bros. New York.

INDEX

Abel, Christian Ferdinand, 250
Adam, Adolphe Charles (1803-1856), 35
Adlung, Jacob (1699-1762), 224
Agricola, Johann Friedrich (1720-1774), 106, 363
Albert, Eugène d' (1864-1932), 85, 86
Albinoni, Tomasso (1674?-1745?), 227
Alembert, Jean Le Rond d' (1717-1783), 60, 64
Altnikol, Johann Christoph (?-1759), 180
Amati, family of violin makers, 106
Andersen, Hans Christian (1805-1875), 345, 408
Anderson, Emily, 311
Anglebert, Jean Henri d' (1630-1691), 82, 88, 115, 116, 257, 301, 388
Anerio, Giovanni Francesco (1567-1620), 252
Anhalt-Cöthen, Prince Leopold of (1694-1728), 166
Artaria, Viennese music publisher, 326
Auber, Daniel F. E. (1782-1871), 34, 103
Augustus II, the Strong, King of Poland (1670-1733), 272, 273
Augustus III, King of Poland (1696-1763), 209, 271, 272
Azevedo (2d half of the 19th century), 51

Bach, Anna Magdalena (1701-1760), 144, 179, 214, 257, 385
Bach, Johann Bernhard (1676-1749), 167
Bach, Johann Christian (1735-1782), 78, 142, 323

Bach, Johann Christoph, (1671-1721), 227
Bach, Johann Jacob (1682-1722), 225
Bach, Johann Nikolaus (1669-1753), 224
Bach, Johann Sebastian (1685-1750), and recording, 359; and youth, 26; climax, 397; concerto grosso, 227-228; conservative, 49, 58; continuo, 394-396; dance, 385-386; doubles, 222; and Handel and Scarlatti, 253-255; his sons, 304; influence of French music, 77-83, 257, 387; influence of Italian music, 63, 226-228; in Landowska's childhood, 5, 6; keyboard instruments, 139-150; also: fortepiano, 137; harpsichord, 129-132, 356; lute-harpsichord, 128; organ, 133-134; first writings on Bach, 13; liberties, 401, 408; orchestra, 66, 69-70; ornaments, 114-122, 238, 390-393; rubato, 383; specialists, 84; style, 85-92; tempi, 106-107; tradition, 94, 95; transcriptions, 102-104, 226, 373; universality, 235; virtuoso, 154; works of, 165-235; also: Art of Fugue, 82; Christmas Oratorio, 7, 398; concertos, 9, 383; English Suites, 81, 83, 143; Fantasias, 81, 144, 336, 354, 365, 396, 406; French Suites, 83, 143; Goldberg Variations, 20, 21, 81, 82, 89, 143, 383, 391; Inventions, 81, 132, 141, 145, 363, 383; Italian Concerto, 86, 89, 143, 238, 380, 381; Mass in B Minor, 272, 301, 354; Partitas, 81, 82, 144, 270, 399; Passions, 145, 386, 395, 396; Prelude,

Bach, Johann Sabastian (cont'd)
  Fugue, and Allegro, 90; Toccatas, 90, 144, 336; *Well-Tempered Clavier,* 15, 22, 25, 81, 82, 85, 87, 103, 145-148, 150, 336, 354, 357, 376, 381, 383, 386 387, 390-392
Bach, Karl Philipp Emanuel (1714-1788), *Alla breve,* 106; bow-harpsichord, 128; *Cantable Art,* 132; characteristics of, 304; concertos, 21, 305-306, 358; continuo, 154; and Diderot, 77; dotted rhythm, 387; fastness, 107; fortepiano, 136, 142; German romantic school, 304; French music, 76-77; gallant style, 88, 304; harpsichord, clavichord, 126, 141-142; harpsichord and orchestra, 128-129; influence on Mozart, 321, 324-325; music and noise, 45; organ, 133; ornaments, 113, 308-309; rehearsals, 153; and Schumann, 304; sonata form, 57; translation of his *Essay,* 124; tuning, 129; unmeasured improvisation, 111; virtuoso, 305
Bach, Wilhelm Friedemann (1710-1784), 115, 134, 170, 186, 210, 212, 220-221, 255, 303, 304
Balbastre, Claude (1727-1799), 137
Barclay-Squire, W. (1855-1927), 293
Baron, Ernst Gottlieb (1696-1760), 208, 210
Bartók, Béla (1881-1945), 201
Beethoven, Ludwig van (1770-1827), 5, 49, 56, 57, 85, 90, 96, 101, 103, 111, 155, 184, 202, 304, 314, 321, 322, 328, 337, 354, 356, 403
Berlioz, Hector (1803-1869), 34, 36, 43, 70, 100, 157, 338, 354
Bie, Oscar, (1864-1938), 356
Berchoux, Joseph (1765-1839), 64
Benda, Franz (1709-1786), 210
Beligradsky, 210
Bigozzi, 44
Binenfeld, Elsa, 218
Bishoff, Hans, 177
Blankenburg, Quirijn, von (1654-after 1739), 125
Boileau-Despréaux, Nicolas (1636-1711), 51, 271
Bonaparte, Napoleon (1769-1821), 46, 68
Bonnet, Pierre (1638-1708), 34, 50, 73, 77, 126, 156

Bordes, Charles (1863-1909), 8, 9, 10
Borren, Charles van den (1874-   ), 293
Boucher, François (1703-1770), 138
Bourdelot, Pierre (1610-1685), 169
Brahms, Johannes (1833-1897), 41, 137, 304, 355
Brunswick-Lüneburg, Duke Georg-Wilhelm (1624-1705), 82, 209
Breitkopf and Härtel, Leipzig music publishers, 326
Brenet, Michel (1858-1918), 8, 77, 99, 106, 110
Briche, Madame de la, 155, 156
Broder, Nathan, 318
Brossard, Sébastien de (c. 1654-1730), 34, 283
Brosses, Président Charles de (1709-1777), 228, 229
Broude Bros. New York music publishers, 18, 244, 424
Bruhns, Nikolaus (1665-1697), 154, 378
Buchmayer, Richard (1856-1934), 140
Bull, John (c. 1562-1628), 293, 296, 297, 298
Bülow, Hans von (1830-1894), 6, 49, 90, 101, 102, 113, 319, 354, 371, 396
Burgaud Desmarets, 97
Burney, Charles (1726-1814), 293, 306
Busoni, Ferruccio (1866-1924), 82, 83, 104, 145, 373, 387
Buxtehude, Dietrich (1637-1707), 49, 78, 84, 129, 154, 181, 279, 301, 378
Byrd, William (1542?-1623), 62, 294, 296-298, 301, 389, 400

Cabezon, Antonio de (1510-1566), 149
Cahuzac, Louis de (1706-1759), 35, 36
Cambert, Robert (1628-1677), 68
Campra, André (1660-1744), 72, 82
Candeille, Pierre Joseph (1744-1827), 35
Cannabich, Christian (1731-1798), 318, 319
Cannabich, Rose, 318, 319
Carbasus, Abbé, 135
Carissimi, Giacomo (1604-1674), 35, 227
Carraud, Gaston, 137
Carrière, Eugène (1849-1906), 98
Catherine de Medicis (1519-1589), 384

Catherine of Aragon (1485-1536), 293
Catherine the Great (1729-1796), 44, 212, 278-279
Cavalli, Pietro Francesco (1602-1676), 206, 310
Celle, Duke of (see Braunschweig-Lüuebourg), 182, 209
Certain, Marie Françoise (c. 1660-1711), 132
Chambonnières, Jacques Champion de (1602-1672), and the Couperins, 258; and Bach's ornaments, 115, 116, 117; and Chopin, 274, 276; doubles, 222; movements opposed to Lully's, 105; virtuosity, 153; Works: Chaconne in F Major, 258; Le Moutier, 258; Sarabande in D Minor, 258, 365
Cherubini, Maria Luigi (1760-1842), 46
Chopin, Frederic (1810-1849), and Bach's Well-Tempered Clavier, 186, 206, 354; and Couperin, 259, 261, 264, 352; fingering, 373-374; folklore, 289-290, 338; French music, 20, 274-279; interpretation of, 15, 404; and Kleczynski, 6; and Liszt, 356; melodic line, 235, 337; and Michalowski, 6; and Mozart, 317; Paderewski's speech, 18; physical aptitudes, 361; repeated note, 391; romanticism, 55, 91, 217; and Scarlatti, 249, 252; tempo, 382; tempo rubato, 111; transcriptions, 103
Chybinski, Adolf (1880-   ), 283
Chylinski, Andrzej, 17th century, 252
Cimarosa, Domenico (1749-1801), 360
Clementi, Muzio (1752-1832), 106, 310
Clérambault, Louis Nicolas (1676-1749), 72, 82, 377
Colasse, Pascal (1649-1709), 82
Coleridge, Arthur Duke (1830-1913), 53
Colette, Gabrielle (1873-1954), 236
Commettant, Oscar, 156
Common, Thomas, 54
Corelli, Archangelo (1653-1713), 35, 36, 79, 227, 237, 301
Coremans, 18th-century singer, 77
Corneille, Pierre (1606-1684), 96
Corot, Jean Baptiste (1796-1875), 368
Corrette, Michel (1709-1795), 82
Costeley, Guillaume (1531-1606), 50-51, 61, 91
Couperin, Charles (1638-1679), 258

Couperin, François (1631-1701), 258
Couperin, François, le Grand (1668-1733) and Bordes, 10; and Brahms, 355; and Chopin, 274-278, 352; chromatic bass, 206; and Debussy, 48-49; dotted rhythm, 77; and Dukas, 10; fingering, 374; French and Italian taste, 79; and Handel, 239; harpsichord, 132; harpsichord writing, 394; influence on Bach, 80, 82-84, 89, 101, 141, 183, 197, 204, 219-220, 222, 262; liberties, transcriptions, 95, 99; miniaturist, 256; movement, 106-107; naïveté, 38; organ, 133; ornaments, 113, 116, 117, 389, 391; phrasing, 376; physical conformation, 361; progress, 40, 41; and Rameau, 271; review of a book on, 22; rondeau, couplets, 247; style, 86; taste, 267, 354; and Tchaikovsky, 343-344; the man, 259-260; touch, 168, 169; Works, 260-266, 288, 295, 322
Couperin, Louis (1626-1661), 88, 222, 257, 258, 275, 278, 340, 342
Cousser, Johann Sigismund (1660-1727), 76, 240
Cummings, Dr., tenor and musicologist, 241-242
Czerny, Carl (1791-1857), 171, 249, 363

Dalcroze, Emile Jaques- (1865- ?), 95, 96
Dandrieu, Jean François (1682-1738), 82, 115
Danner, Jr., 319
Dannreuther, Edward George (1844-1905), 117
Daquin, Louis Claude (1694-1772), 9
Debussy, Claude Achille (1862-1918), 7, 30, 48-49, 328, 339, 341, 355, 393
Deffand, Marie, Marquise du (1697-1780), 39
Delacroix, Eugène (1799-1863), 48
Denis, Jean (17th century), 67, 131
Dent, Edward James (1876-1957), 328
Despréaux (see Boileau), 51, 271
Destouches, André, Cardinal (1672-1749), 82
Diaghilev, Sergei (1872-1929), 7
Diderot, Denis (1713-1784), 77, 114
Diémer, Louis (1843-1919), 7, 9

Dieupart, Charles (c. 1670-c. 1740), 81, 114, 116, 117, 202, 257

Diruta, Girolamo (1554- ?), 114, 168

Doles, Johann Friedrich (1715-1797), 65

Dolmetsch, Arnold (1858-1940), 9

Dowland, John (1563-1626), 293, 295-296

Doyen, Jean (1907-), 375

Dukas, Paul (1865-1935), 10

Durand, French music publishers, 271

Dussek, Jan Ladislav (1760-1812), 155

Dvořák, Anton (1841-1904), 343-344

Ecorcheville, Jules (1872-1915), 8, 9, 13, 91

Edward IV, King of England (1442-1483), 45

Elizabeth I, Queen of England (1533-1603), 45, 293, 297

Elsner, Joseph Xaver (1769-1854), 274

Emmanuel, Maurice (1862-1938), 8, 9, 110-111

Enoch, French publishers, 8

Erard, French piano makers, 9

Estrées, Paul d', 155

Eutitio, Agostino, 250

Expert, Henry (1863-1952), 8, 9, 100

Faber, Daniel Tobias, Organist at Crailsheim in 1725, 125

Falco, M., 135

Falla, Manuel de (1876-1946), 18, 218, 346-347

Farnaby, Giles (c. 1560-c. 1600), 293, 298

Fauré, Gabriel (1845-1924), 10

Feicht, Dr. H., 283

Ferdinand III, Emperor (1608-1657), 45

Ferdinand VI, King of Spain (1713-1759), 246

Fétis, François Joseph (1784-1871), 274

Fischer, Carl, music publishers, 326

Fischer, J. K. F. (c. 1660-c. 1738), 76, 88, 140, 200, 240, 269

Fleischer, Johann Christoph (1676-after 1724), 224

Fontenelle, Bernard Le Bovier de (1657-1757), 57

Forkel, Johann Nicolaus (1749-1818) Bach's Fugue I, 180; Bach's *Chromatic Fantasy*, 220; Bach and gal-

lant style, 303; Bach and Handel, 254; Bach's ornaments, 117; Bach outmoded, 35; Bach's quodlibet, 218; Bach's tempi, 106; Bach's touch, 170; clavichord, 140, 141, 145; Couperin, 80; Goldberg, J. Th., 211-212; organ and harpsichord, 134; translation, 124

France, Anatole (1844-1924), 33, 39, 58, 213

Francisque, Antoine (1570-1605), 256, 300

Franck, César (1822-1890), 7, 91

Frederick II The Great (1712-1786), 33, 49, 91, 272

Frescobaldi, Girolamo (1583-1643), 88, 111, 129, 133, 138, 141, 154, 168, 214, 227, 363, 382

Friderici, 18th-century family of keyboard instruments makers, 138

Froberger, Johann Jacob (1620 or 1616-1667), 58, 78, 88, 111, 200, 227, 365

Fuller-Maitland, John Alexander (1856-1936), 208, 293

Furstenau, Antoine Bernard (1792-1852), 212

Ganz, Rudolf (1877-), 7

Gaultier Le Vieux (1580-1653), 256, 342

Gauthier, Théophile (1811-1872), 40

Genzinger, Marianne von, 329

George VI, King of England (1895-1952), 316

Gerber, Ernst Ludwig (1746-1819), 80, 90, 170, 210, 211, 212, 283, 305

Gerber, Heinrich Nicolaus (1702-1775), 144, 177, 305

Gershwin, George (1898-1937), 345-346

Gibbons, Orlando (1583-1625), 293

Gide, André (1869-1951), 316

Gillot, Claude (1673-1722), 263

Gleichmann, Johann Georg (1685-1770), 224

Gloger, Zygmunt, 290

Gluck, C. W. Ritter von (1714-1787), French and Italian music, 73; loudness, 42, 48, 64, 157; movement, 109; novelty, 58; ornaments, 114; sciolists, 95; Works: *Armide*, 52, 99; *J'ai perdu mon Eurydice*, 53, 94; *The Mecca Pilgrims*, 322

Goethe, Johann Wolfgang von (1749-1832), 35, 53, 56, 101, 213

Goldberg, Johann Theophilius (c. 1720- ?), 211-213
Goudimel, Claude (c. 1505-1572), 39, 256
Gounod, Charles (1818-1893), 43, 103, 160, 336, 405
Graun, Karl Heinrich (1701-1759), 65
Gray, Cecil (1895-), 200
Grenier, Félix (1844- ?), 124
Grétry, André (1742-1813), 42, 53, 65
Grieg, Edward (1843-1907), 279, 291
Grigny, Nicolas de (1671-1703), 82, 256, 257, 398
Grimm, Frederic Melchior (1723-1807), 80
Guarnerius, family of violin makers, 106
Guilmant, Félix Alexandre (1837-1911), 8
Gutheil, A., music publisher, 326

Handel, George Frederic (1685-1759), Andante-allegro, 109; and Bach and Scarlatti, 253-255; and Chopin, 274; and Couperin, 260; dotted rhythm, 387; double, 365; dynamics, 310; England, 293; genius of, 236; harpsichord, 11, 131, 140, 236; instrumentalists and singers, 66, 68-69; Landowska writings on, 21; mixed style, 78-79; range, 61; slumber arias, 213; and Stravinsky, 344; triple meter, 317; virtuoso, 153; Works: Chaconne in F Major, 86; Concerto in B Flat Major, 243-244; Messiah, 67, 129, 206; Suites for harpsichord, 185, 214, 238-243
Hasse, Johann Adolf (1699-1783), 65, 66, 246
Hauser, Joseph, 143
Haydn, Franz Joseph (1732-1809), Anniversaries, 327-328; and Berlioz, 354; conservative, 339; dynamics, 46, 359; gallant style, 303; harpsichord and pianoforte, 138, 228-229; influence on Mozart, 321; on melody, 336; orchestra, 67; range, 61; short phrases, 322; simplicity, 402; and Stravinsky, 344; virtuosity, 153; Works: Andante in F Minor, 329; Concerto in D Major, 326-327; Quartet in F Minor, 206; Sonatas, 328-329; The Creation, 287
Hebenstreit, Pantaleon (1667-1750), 77

Heine, Henri (1797-1856), 60
Henry VIII, King of England (1491-1547), 45, 293
Heyden, Hans (c. 1540-1613), 127
Heyer, Wilhelm (1849-1913), 11
Hildebrand, Zacharias (1688-1757), 224
Hiller, Johann Adam (1728-1804), 67, 129, 154, 211
Hindemith, Paul (1895-1963), 218
Hoffmeister, Franz Anton (1754-1812), 177
Hofman, Josef (1876-1957), 7
Hugo, Victor (1802-1885), 39
Hummel, Johann Nepomuk (1778-1837), 102, 309
Huré, Jean (1877-1930), 95, 337

Imbault, J. J. (1753- ?), 177
Indy, Vincent d' (1851-1931), 8, 34, 109, 336, 338

Jachimecki, Dr. (1882-), 283
Jacob Le Polonais (c. 1545-c. 1605), 282
Jaloux, Edmond (1878-), 353
Janin, Jules (1804-1874), 160
Jannequin, Clément (16th Century), 39, 100, 160, 256
Jarzebski, Adam (c. 1590-1649), 282, 285-286
Joachim, Joseph (1831-1907), 16
Josquin des Prés (c. 1445-1521), 34, 39, 50, 58, 111, 160, 256, 354

Kalkbrenner, F. W. M. (1788-1849), 4, 363, 374, 397
Kalmus, Edwin, music publisher, 145
Kayserling, Count Hermann Karl von, 211
Kayserling, Heinrich Christian, 211
Kerll, Johann Kaspar von (1627-1693), 58, 88, 227
Kerntnopf piano makers, 6
Kinsky, Georg (1882-1951), 150
Kircher, Athanasius (1602-1680), 58, 91
Kirnberger, Johann Philipp (1721-1783), 145, 177, 180, 233
Kittel, Kaspar (17th-century composer), 217
Kleczynski, Jan (1837-1895), 6
Köchel, Dr. Ludwig Ritter von (1800-1877), 324
Kolberg, Oskar (1815-1890), 290
Koldofsky, Adolf (1906?-1951), 305

Kostka, Stanislas, 282
Koussevitzky, Serge (1874-1951), 346
Kownacka, Polish pianist, 6
Krebs, Johann Ludwig (1713-1780), 65
Kretzschmar, Hermann (1848-1924), 16, 130
Kreutzer, Rodolphe (1766-1831), 129
Kuhnau, Johann (1660-1722), 40, 58, 87, 115, 128, 140, 204, 225
Kuhne, music publisher, 177

La Boissière, 66
Ladislas IV, King of Poland (1632-1648), 282, 283, 285
La Fontaine, Jean de (1621-1695), 42, 67, 132, 133
La Harpe, Jean François de (1739-1803), 52, 64, 73
Lalande, Michel Richard de (1657-1726), 72
La Laurencie, Lionel de (1861-1933), 8, 9, 66, 77
Lalou, René (1889-1960), 20
Laloy, Louis (1874-1944), 8, 13
La Motte, Antoine Houdard de (1672-1731), 268
Landowska, Eva (1859-1924), 12, 364
Landowska, Wanda (1879-1959), doubles, 222; on jazz, 341; last writing, 327; letter to a pupil, 365; notes inégales, 386; novelty and originality, 341; Taverny, Landowska's burial place, 265; the writer, 3-26; 29-31, 163-164, 333-334; transcription, 104
Landowski, Paul (1882-1937), 353
Lanner, J. F. C. (1801-1843), 325-326
Lassus, Orlando de (1530 or 32-1594), 111, 354
Laugier, Abbé, 72
Lavignac, Albert (1846-1916), 150
Lavoix, Henri (1846-1897), 44, 69, 127, 130
Le Bègue, Nicolas Antoine (1630-1702), 82, 115, 256
Le Blanc, Hubert, 135, 157
Lecerf de la Viéville, Jean Laurent Fresneuse (1674-1707), 63, 74, 76
Le Couppey, Félix (1811-1887), 112, 132
Lefèvre de Marcouville (1721- ?), 242
Legrenzi, Giovanni (1625-1690), 227
Legros, Joseph (1730-1793), 157
Leichtentritt, Hugo (1874-1951), 131

Le Nôtre, André (1613-1700), 259
Leo, Leonardo (1694-1744), 35
Le Roux, Gaspard (c. 1660-c. 1710), 81, 115, 116, 202, 256
Lespinasse, Mlle de (Julie) (1732-1776), 53
Leszcynska, Marie (1703-1768), 288
Levy, Sara, 144
Lew, Henry (1874-1919), 7, 9, 11, 12, 16
Liszt, Franz (1811-1886), 5, 6, 9, 37, 46, 91, 104, 152, 153, 165, 168, 217, 354, 356, 396
Lotti, Antonio (c. 1667-1740), 254
Louis XIII, King of France (1601-1643), 34, 299
Louis XIV, King of France (1638-1715), 34, 67, 77, 78, 82, 259, 277, 384
Louis XV, King of France (1710-1774), 135, 149, 266, 271, 272, 273, 288
Loulié Etienne, 107
Lully, Jean Baptiste (1639-1687), Armide, 73, 99; and Bach, J. S., 82; and Bach, K. P. E., 305; dance, 322, 384; expression, 50, 63; French music, 72, 75, 78; French overture, 74, 240; good execution, 153; Isis, 132; melody, 337; orchestra, 68; ornaments, 95, 114; power of sonority, 42, 50; pupils of, 76; speed, 105
Lyon, Gustave (d. 1936), 11

Maelzel, Johann Nepomuk (1772-1838), 107
Malherbe, Charles Théodore (1853-1911), 8
Mallarmé, Stéphane (1842-1898), 354
Mandyczewski, Eusebius (1857-1929), 314
Marcello, Benedetto (1686-1739), 168, 227
Marchand, Louis (1669-1732), 81, 202, 226, 256
Marenzio, Luca (1560-1599), 282
Maria Antonia of Saxony, Princess, 212
Maria Barbara, Princess, 246
Marie Anne Victoire, Infanta, 266
Marmontel, Jean François (1723-1799), 53, 112, 132
Marie Josèphe of Saxony, 271-273
Marpurg, Friedrich Wilhelm (1718-1795), 65, 75, 114, 128, 132, 136, 177, 211, 363
Martini, Giovanni Battista, Padre (1706-1784), 264, 337

Massenet, Jules (1842-1912), 338
Mattheson, Johann (1681-1764), *Cantable Art*, 167; clavichord, 140; dance, 385; French and Italian music, 74-75; harpsichord, 128, 130, 133; melody, 65; ornaments, 393
Mauclair, Camille (1872- ?), 60
Mauduit, Jacques (1557-1627), 34
Mendelsohn, Felix (1809-1847), 36
Mengelberg, Willem (1871-1938), 327
Méreaux, Jean Amédée Lefroid de (1802-1874), 112, 132
Mersenne, Marin Père (1588-1648), 67, 105, 153, 298
Meyerbeer, Giacomo (1791-1864), 36, 40, 289
Michalowski, Aleksander (1851-1938), 6, 291, 371, 387
Mielczewski, Marcin (c. 1600-1651), 283-285
Mikuli, Karl (1821-1897), 274
Mitchell, W. J., 124
Mizler, Lorenz Christoph (1711-1778), 82, 170, 212
Mondonville, J. J. Cassanea de (1711-1772), 35, 36, 79
Monteux, Pierre (1875-1964), 347
Monteverdi, Claudio (1567-1643), 301, 354, 356
Morley, Thomas (1557-1603?), 293, 298
Mourey, G., 350
Mozart, Leopold (1719-1787), 114, 309, 363
Mozart, Wolfgang Amadeus (1756-1791), cadenzas, 309, 312, 314, 393; and Clementi, 106; and Chopin, 274, 277; dynamics, 310; exaggerated expression, 48; harpsichord, 148; and Hummel, 102; Landowska interpreter of Mozart, 4; Mozart's instruments, 306, 308; objectivity, 401; ornamentation, 308, 312-314; power of sonority, 46; purity, 402; range, 61; and Rossini, 36; and Schumann, 40; Stein's pianofortes, 137-138; tempo rubato, 111; tonality, 314; touch, 306-308; transcriptions, 99; transition in esthetics, 303; Works: *Das Veilchen*, 319; *Don Giovanni*, 317, 320; Fantasia in C Minor, (K. 397), 220; Fantasia in C Minor (K.475), 321, 324-325; Fantasy in D Minor, 321; Keyboard sonatas, 317-324; *Komm,*

Lieber Mai, 320; *La Finta Giardiniera*, 317; *Landlerisches Tänze*, 325-326; *Marriage of Figaro*, 314, 319; Minuet in D Major, 324; Piano concertos, 311-316; Quartet in G Minor, 323; Rondo *alla Turca*, 306, 322; Rondo in A Minor, 277, 309; Rondo in D Major, 306, 323
Mueller, Dr. August Friedrich, 213
Muffat, Georg (1645-1704), 76, 95, 114, 240
Muffat, Gottlieb (1690-1770), 88
Müller, August Eberhardt (1767-1817), 176
Munday, John (c. 1565-c. 1630), 298

Nägeli, Hans Georg (1773-1836), 177
Naumann, Emil (1827-1888), 143
Niemetschek, Franz, 306-307, 323
Nietzsche, Friedrich (1844-1900), 43, 54, 338, 409
Nikisch, Arthur (1855-1922), 6, 354
Norlind, Tobias (1879-   ), 154
Norvins, Jacques, Baron de (1769-1854), 155
Nyert, Pierre (1597-1682), 67, 132

Ockeghem, Jean de (early 15th century-c. 1495), 354
Oginski, Michael Casimir, 287
Oginski, Michael Cleophas, 287, 290
Olbreuse, Eléonore Desmier d' (1639-1722), 209
Ottobuoni, Cardinal Pietro, 254

Pacelli, Asprillo (c. 1570-1623), 282
Pachelbel, Johann (1653-1706), 78, 84, 86, 87, 160, 196, 227
Paderewski, Jan Ignace (1860-1941), 7, 18, 22, 280
Palestrina, G. Pierluigi da (1525-1594), conformed to tradition, 57; *Goldberg Variations*, 216; *L'Homme Armé*, 58, 110; melody, 110; Michel Brenet's book, 106, 110; range, 60; Wagner, 57
Peerson, Martin (c. 1580-1650), 293, 298
Pekiel, Bartolomiej (middle 17th century), 282
Pergolesi, G. Battista (1710-1736), 35
Picchi, Giovanni, 288
Pincherle, Marc (1888-   ), 17

Pirro, André (1869-1943), 8, 9, 12, 81, 82, 92, 171, 202
Pisendel, Georg Johann (1687-1755), 210
Pitzele, Merlyn, 409
Plas, The Brothers, 254
Pleyel, French piano and harpsichord makers, 9, 10, 11, 16, 19, 356, 378, 400
Podbielski, J. 286
Podbielski, C. G., 286
Poglietti, Alessandro (d. 1683), 88, 216
Polignac, Princess Edmond de, 346, 347
Porta (1530-1601), 37
Potemkin, Gregory Alexandrovitch (1736-1791), 44
Poulenc, Francis (1899-1963), 18, 340, 347
Poussin, Nicolas (1594-1665), 263
Powell, Blacksmith, 241
Powell, harpist (1776-after 1863), 243
Praetorius, Michael (1571-1621), 68, 114
Prokofiev, Sergii (1891-   ), 344
Prout, Ebenezer (1835-1909), 208
Pugno, Raoul (1852-1914), 375
Purcell, Henry (c. 1658-1695), Chaconne, 346; chromatic bass, 206; *Dido and Aeneas*, 301; ground bass, 300-301; ground and fado, 279; Ground in C Minor, 301-302; Ground in Gamut, 301; *King Arthur*, 254; monotony, 81; *New Ground*, 301

Quantz, Johann Joachim (1697-1773), against exaggerated expression, 51; bow-harpsichord, 128; brevity, 59-60; dotted rhythm, 198, 387; flute treatise, 363; French and Italian music, 75, 79, 91; gallant style, 88; harpsichord, 128, 129; harpsichord playing, 132, 134; instrumentation, 69; movement, 105, 107; music in 17th-century Germany, 33; pianoforte, 136; power of Handel's orchestra, 68
Quinault, Philippe (1635-1688), 50
Quittard, Henri (1864-1919), 8, 9

Racine, Jean (1639-1699), 50, 96
Raguenet, Abbé François (c. 1660-c. 1722), 74
Raison, André, (late 17th century), 256

Rameau, Jean Philippe (1683-1764), *Air Pour Deux Polonais*, 288; Bach, 257; birth date, 253; comparison with Chopin, 274, 276, 277; comparison with Couperin, 41; criticism, 64; French and Italian music, 73, 257, 337; harpsichord pieces, 5, 141, 214, 216, 264, 268-273, 276, 365, 407; instrumentation, 69; large intervals, 276; movement, 105, 107, 108; on Art, 341; operas, 35, 268, 322; ornaments, 116-117, 389; physical aptitudes, 361; publication of Rameau's works, 8, 271; *roulements* and *batteries*, 146, 217, 394; theoretical and dramatic character, 267-268, 275, 377; touch, 168-169; Tribute to, 22
Raposki, 44
Rauch, 44
Ravel, Maurice (1875-1937), 18, 41, 266, 342
Reichardt, Johann Friedrich (1752-1814), 211, 212
Reincken, Johann Adam (1623-1722), 154, 184, 226
Richardson, Ferdinand (c. 1558-1618), 298, 299
Richelieu, Cardinal de (1585-1642), 384
Richter, Ferdinand Tobias (1649-1711), 88
Riemann, Hugo, (1849-1919), 145, 164, 380
Ries, Ferdinand (1784-1838), 57
Rimbault, music publisher, 293
Rodin, Auguste (1840-1917), 41, 60, 98, 99
Rolland, Romain (1866-1944), 48, 51, 63, 96
Rore, Cipriano de (c. 1516-1565), 58
Rosenthal, Moritz (1862-1946), 381
Rossi, Luigi (1598-1653), 73
Rossini, G. Antonio (1792-1868), 36
Rousseau, Jean-Jacques (1712-1778), against exaggeration, 48; against sonata, 59, 64; conducting, 128; French music, 72, 73, 75, 79, 108; German music, 78; musical notation, 60; orchestra, 66
Rubinstein, Anton (1829-1894), 131, 139-140, 148
Ruckers, family of harpsichord makers (between 1579 and 1667), 19
Rust, Friedrich Wilhelm (1739-1796), 90
Rust, Wilhelm (1822-1892), 179

Sachsen-Weimar, Wilhelm Ernest, 66
Saint-Foix, Georges de (1874-1953),
313, 321, 324, 353
Saint-Saëns, Charles Camille (1835-
1921), 8, 109, 271, 338, 340
Salieri, Antonio (1750-1825), 129
Saxe, Maurice Comte de (1696-1750),
273
Scacchi, Marco (b. late 16th century-
d. before 1687), 282
Scarlatti, Alessandro (1659-1725), 245,
253
Scarlatti, Domenico (1685-1757), Acciaccaturas, 319; Bach, Handel,
and, 253-255; Brahm's notes on,
354; Bülow, 90, 101; Chopin,
274; crossed hands, 207; Iberian
influences, 245-246; Landowska's
revelation of, 20; Landowska's
writings on, 22; misconstrued interpretation of, 402; Moritz Rosenthal on, 381; preface to sonatas,
3, 30, 247; reminiscence, 352;
Sonatas, 246-252; Sonatas and
The Well-Tempered Clavier, 199,
205; the Germans and the interpretation of, 407
Schanz, Johann, 328
Scheibe, Johann Adolph (1708-1776),
89, 117
Schiller, Friedrich von (1759-1805),
51, 52
Schirmer, G., music publisher, 326
Schobert, Johann (c. 1720-1767), 321
Schubert, Franz (1797-1828), 126,
317, 326
Schumann, Clara (1819-1896), 46,
155
Schumann, Robert (1810-1856), 9, 37,
40, 46, 170, 177, 264, 304, 305,
354
Schütz, Heinrich (1585-1672), 34, 291
Schweitzer, Albert (1875-   ), 9, 10,
12, 63, 130, 139, 171
Scoppio, G., 44
Scriabin, Alexander Nicholaevich (1872-
1915), 344
Sénart, French music publisher, 17
Serapion, Father, 44
Sert, Misia, 344
Sévigné, Madame de (1626-1696), 209
Shakespeare, William (1564-1616),
dramas, 59; Hamlet, 59, 299;
harpsichord, 133, 294; Henry V,
299; Henry VI, 299; Love's Labour Lost, 299; Merchant of Venice, 292; Much Ado About Nothing, 299; music at the time of,

292-300, 401; Sonnet CXXVIII,
294; The Passionate Pilgrim, 296;
The Two Gentlemen of Verona,
295; Troilus and Cressida, 38, 54
Shedlock, John, (1843-1919), 295
Shostakovich, Dimitri (1906-   ),
345
Shudi and Broadwood, harpsichord
makers, 328
Sigismond I, the Elder (1506-1548),
282
Silberman, Gottfried (1683-1753), 10,
137, 210
Simon, Dr. Alicja (1879-1958), 283
Simrock, German music publisher, 177
Sowinski, Wojciech (1805?-1880), 286
Spitta, Philipp (1841-1894), 128, 140,
145, 174, 177, 192, 212, 214, 217,
226
Stamitz, Johann Wenzl Anton (1717-
1757), 318
Steibelt, Daniel (1765-1823), 137, 155,
156
Stein, family of pianoforte makers, 137,
306, 308
Stokowski, Leopold (1882-   ), 347
St. Lambert, Michel de, 267
Stradivarius, Antonio (1644?-1737),
106
Strauss, Johann (1804-1849), 325
Strauss, Richard (1864-1949), 35-36
Stravinsky, Igor (1882-   ), 7, 297,
326, 344, 345, 355
Strindberg, August (1849-1912), 260
Sully, Maximilien de Béthune, Duc de
(1559-1641), 384
Sweelinck, Jan Pieterszoon (1562-
1621), 214
Szarzynski, Sylvester (second half of
17th century), 286

Taskin, Pascal (1723-1793), 137
Tausig, Carl (1841-1871), 6, 102, 104,
249, 354
Tchaikovsky, Peter Ilich (1840-1893),
343-344
Telemann, Georg Philipp (1681-1767),
78, 288, 321
Tessier, André (1886-1931), 275
Thalberg, Sigismond (1812-1871), 4,
397
Tiedge, Christoph August (1752-1841),
53
Titelouze, Jean (1563-1633), 256
Titon du Tillet, Evrard (1677-1762),
135

Tolstoy, Leo (1828-1910), 13-14, 300, 353, 374
Tolstoy, Sophie (1844-1920), 14
Toscanini, Arturo (1867-1957), 404
Tosi, Pier Francesco (c. 1650-after 1730), 363
Tovey, Donald Francis (1875-1940), 208

Udine, Jean d' (1870- ?), 59
Urban, Heinrich (1837-1901), 6, 354

Valéry, Paul (1871-1945), 354
Versepuy, Mario, 279
Viadana, Ludovico Grossi da (1564-1645), 95
Victoria, Tomas Luiz, de (c. 1535-c. 1608), 188
Vivaldi, Antonio (c. 1678-1741), 212, 227, 228, 229, 237, 304
Volkmann, R. (1815-1883), 176
Voltaire, Françoise Marie Arouet (1694-1778), 33, 34, 38, 39, 47, 59, 82, 107, 137, 157
Vuillermoz, Emile (1878-1960), 17, 341-342

Wagner, Richard (1813-1883), admiration for Palestrina, 57; Bach, 63; Beethoven, 36, 56; criticisms of, 65; different from Mozart and Couperin, 54; French and Italian music, 79; innovator, 59, 339; instrumentation, 70; loudness, 45; *Meistersinger*, 181, 187, 190; melody, 337; music of the past, 100; naïveté, 297; ornaments, 112; piano with orchestra, 115; spell of, 7, 354; strong beat, 111; *Tristan*, 217
Walsh, John (d. 1736), 237, 243
Walther, Johann Gottfried (1684-1748), 116, 166-167, 210, 224, 286
Watteau, Antoine (1684-1721), 41, 46, 54, 92, 97, 253
Weber, Carl Maria von (1786-1826), 53, 94, 156, 304
Weber, Constanze (1763-1842), 311
Weiss, Sylvius Leopold (1686-1750), 208, 211
Werkmeister, Andreas (1645-1706), 145
Westphal, 144
Widor, Charles Marie (1845-1937), 102
Wojciechowski, Tytus, 289
Wyzewa, Theodor de (1862-1917), 321

Zelter, Karl-Friedrich (1758-1832), 35, 53, 101, 102
Zielenski, Mikolaj (17-century Polish composer), 282
Zywny, Wojciech (1756-1842), 274